Albrecht Dürer, *St. Michael Fighting the Dragon* (1498)

The Grand Finale

The Grand Finale

The Apocalypse in the Tanakh, the Gospel, and the Qur'an

ANTON WESSELS

Translated by Henry Jansen and Lucy Hofland

WIPF & STOCK · Eugene, Oregon

THE GRAND FINALE
The Apocalypse in the Tanakh, the Gospel, and the Qur'an

Copyright © 2020 Anton Wessels. All rights reserved. Except for brief quotations in critical publications or reviews, no part of this book may be reproduced in any manner without prior written permission from the publisher. Write: Permissions, Wipf and Stock Publishers, 199 W. 8th Ave., Suite 3, Eugene, OR 97401.

Wipf & Stock
An Imprint of Wipf and Stock Publishers
199 W. 8th Ave., Suite 3
Eugene, OR 97401

www.wipfandstock.com

PAPERBACK ISBN: 978-1-7252-7599-7
HARDCOVER ISBN: 978-1-7252-7600-0
EBOOK ISBN: 978-1-7252-7601-7

Manufactured in the U.S.A. 06/26/20

For Saeid Edalatnejad,
Professor at the Encyclopaedia Islamica Foundation (Tehran).
Saeid has been active in the field of interreligious dialogue for many
years. He has translated Thomas à Kempis' *The Imitation of Christ*
into Persian and has won fellowships at the
Wissenschaftskolleg zu Berlin (2003-2004) and Harvard Law School,
Islamic Legal Studies Program (2014)

I am grateful to Henry Jansen and Lucy Hofland
for their translation services and to Stichting Zonneweelde
and the VanCoeverden-Adriani Stichting
for their financial support of this translation

Contents

Permissions		xi
Preface		xiii
List of Abbreviations		xv
Introduction		1
I	Muhammad Sent to the Peoples	20
II	The Apocalyptic Seventh Century	54
III	Luther's Apocalyptic Understanding	77
IV	Ezekiel: God and Man; God and Gog	107
V	The Book of Daniel: "The Flaming Scripture of the Holy God"	130
VI	Jesus and the Apocalypse	160
VII	Paul to the Ends of the Earth	192
VIII	The First and the Last Things: The End of Violence	222
Bibliography		265
Index of Names and Subjects		279
Index of Scripture Texts		301
Index of Qur'anic Texts		317

Permissions

Scripture quotations are taken from the following versions of the Bible. I am grateful to the publishers for permission to use them:

All Scripture quotations, unless otherwise indicated, are taken from the Holy Bible, New International Version®, NIV®. Copyright ©1973, 1978, 1984, 2011 by Biblica, Inc.™ Used by permission of Zondervan. All rights reserved worldwide. www.zondervan.com The "NIV" and "New International Version" are trademarks registered in the United States Patent and Trademark Office by Biblica, Inc.™

Scripture quotations marked as RSV are taken from the Revised Standard Version of the Bible, copyright © 1946, 1952, and 1971 National Council of the Churches of Christ in the United States of America. Used by permission. All rights reserved worldwide. https://nrsvbibles.org/

Scripture quotations marked as NRSVCE are taken from the New Revised Standard Version Bible: Catholic Edition, copyright © 1989, 1993 National Council of the Churches of Christ in the United States of America. Used by permission. All rights reserved worldwide. https://nrsvbibles.org/

Scripture quotations marked as CJB are taken from the Complete Jewish Bible by David H. Stern. Copyright © 1998. All rights reserved. Used by permission of Messianic Jewish Publishers, 6120 Day Long Lane, Clarksville, MD 21029. www.messianicjewish.net.

Scripture quotations marked as ISV are taken from the International Standard Version®. Copyright © 1996-forever by The ISV

Foundation. ALL RIGHTS RESERVED INTERNATIONALLY. Used by permission.

Scripture quotations marked as NJB are taken from THE NEW JERUSALEM BIBLE, copyright (c) 1985 by Darton, Longman & Todd, Ltd. and Doubleday, a division of Penguin Random House, Inc. Reprinted by Permission.

Scriptures quotations marked as KJV are taken from the King James Version.

Scripture quotations marked as ASV are taken from the American Standard Version.

The print at the beginning of this book is the woodcut Saint Michael Fighting the Dragon by Albrecht Dürer, 1498.

Preface

This book, *The Grand Finale: The Apocalypse in the Tanakh, the Gospel, and the Qur'an*, is the third book in a series that began a few years ago with my *The Torah, the Gospel and the Quran: Three Books, Two Cities, One Tale* (2013). The latter book was published in Arabic in 2014 and in Persian in 2018. In this work, my concern was to read the three Scriptures as telling one single tale, i.e., the story of God's establishment of his kingdom of justice and peace in a world full of violence and injustice. I continued that reading of all three Scriptures as incorporating one tale in a second book: *A Stranger is Calling: Jew, Christians and Muslims as Fellow Travellers* (2017). This present book follows that same path of reading the Scriptures as one tale, as one narrative, and is directed at understanding what is meant by "apocalypse" in the three Scriptures.

A common refrain that is heard today from both religious and political leaders is that the end of time is near. The last book in the Bible, the Revelation of John, which is called *Apocalypsis* (Apocalypse) in Greek, plays a major role in this view. According to many of these leaders, therefore, we are supposedly now living in "apocalyptic" times. The wars that are now being fought, especially in the Middle East, and the conflict concerning Israel are said to be nothing more than so many signs that the end times have truly arrived.

This is a fundamental misunderstanding of the real message of the Bible and the Qur'an. That is not what the word "apocalypse" means at all. The fundamental meaning of the term is disclosure, unveiling, revelation, bringing to light what is now happening and what has happened throughout the whole of history. What is disclosed? What is revealed? "Apocalypse" does not make any predictions but reveals and analyzes who and what is/are responsible for the injustice in the world. In that sense, all times—thus also the present—can be called apocalyptic, but in a totally different way than is usually thought and believed.

Since Alexander the Great's cataclysmic conquest of the known world in the fourth century BC, there have been apocalyptic interpretations—like that found in the book of Daniel (2nd century BC)—and apocalyptic (thus, disclosing) readings of the whole Tanakh (from Genesis 1 up to and including the book of Malachi) arose. The same can be said of the New Testament from the gospels to the last book of the Bible. These books were written in the first century of the Christian or Common Era when the Romans had replaced the Greeks as the world power. The same apocalyptic message was confirmed in the seventh century by the Qur'an when the Byzantines and the Persians were involved in a life-and-death struggle against each other.

This book is called "The Grand Finale?" But what does that mean? Are we talking about a final, great end to this world and creation? An end to all time? Or is the message that we find in the Bible and the Qur'an concerning the "Apocalypse" quite different from what it is often thought in our day and age to be? The apocalyptic message that the prophets "bring to light" is that God will certainly put an end to the unjust rule of violence (Moloch), money (Mammon), and lies ("fake news"), and that the Kingdom of God will certainly come. That is happening and will happen, but it will not be achieved through violence for, after all, "there is no violence in God." The voice of God is heard in every "present," and every person is called to hear God's Good News afresh and to give it concrete shape in his or her life.

List of Abbreviations

BIBLE VERSIONS

ASV	American Standard Version
CJB	The Complete Jewish Bible
ISV	International Standard Version
JSB	Jewish Study Bible
KBS	*De Bijbel uit de grondtekst vertaald: Willibrordvertaling*; Dutch Roman Catholic (Willibrord) translation of the Bible.
KJV	King James Version
NJB	New Jerusalem Bible
NRSVCE	New Revised Standard Version: Catholic Edition
RSV	Revised Standard Version

BOOKS OF THE BIBLE

[B]Old Testament

Gen	Genesis
Exod	Exodus
Lev	Leviticus
Num	Numbers

Deut	Deuteronomy
Josh	Joshua
Judg	Judges
1 Sam	1 Samuel
2 Sam	2 Samuel
1 Kgs	1 Kings
2 Kgs	2 Kings
1 Chr	1 Chronicles
2 Chr	2 Chronicles
Neh	Nehemiah
Ps	Psalm
Prov	Proverbs
Eccl	Ecclesiastes
Song	Song of Songs
Isa	Isaiah
Jer	Jeremiah
Lam	Lamentations
Ezek	Ezekiel
Dan	Daniel
Hos	Hosea
Obad	Obadiah
Mic	Micah
Nah	Nahum
Hab	Habakkuk
Zeph	Zephaniah
Hag	Haggai
Zech	Zechariah
Mal	Malachi

Deuterocanonical Books

Tob	Tobit
Jdt	Judith
1 Macc	1 Maccabees
2 Macc	2 Maccabees
Wis	Wisdom of Solomon
Sir	Sirach
Jub	Jubilees

New Testament

Matt	Matthew
Acts	Acts of the Apostles
Rom	Romans
1 Cor	1 Corinthians
2 Cor	2 Corinthians
Gal	Galatians
Eph	Ephesians
Phil	Philippians
Col	Colossians
1 Thess	1 Thessalonians
2 Thess	2 Thessalonians
1 Tim	1 Timothy
2 Tim	2 Timothy
Heb	Hebrews
Jam	James
1 Pet	1 Peter
2 Pet	2 Peter
Rev	Revelation

Other

BW	*Bijbels-historisch Woordenboek*, see bibliography
EI	*The Encylopaedia of Islam*, see bibliography
EQ	*Encylopaedia of the Qurʾan*, see bibliography
SEI	*Shorter Encyclopedia of Islam*, see bibliography

Introduction

Then war broke out in heaven. Michael and his angels fought against the dragon, and the dragon and his angels fought back. But he was not strong enough, and they lost their place in heaven. —Rev 12:7–8

On the wall of his prison cell, Dietrich Bonhoeffer hung a reproduction of Albrecht Dürer's Apocalypse: *Michael leading the angels in the battle against the seven-headed dragon, with a peaceful landscape as the background.*[1]

THE APOCALYPSE DEPICTED

In 1498, when Albrecht Dürer, the son of a goldsmith in Nuremberg, was 27 years old, he devoted his "Great Book" to the Apocalypse: *Apocalypsis cum figuris* (The Apocalypse with Pictures). It is a work containing fifteen large woodcuts, illustrations inspired by the last book of the Bible. This book immediately ensured his fame: news of him spread rapidly because of the printing press, and he became the first pan-European artist whose name became known to millions.[2] Dürer had to have been possessed by the "mysterious revelation of John." For Erasmus, Dürer painted what could not be painted. After 1500, Dürer owned the visual monopoly on the "Mysterious Revelation."[3] Examples of his interpretation of "the mysteries of the Revelation of John" included, among others, the Four Horsemen, the Whore of Babylon, the opening of the sixth seal, St. Christopher, and Michael's battle

---

1. Marsch, *Licht in het duistere*, 472–73.
2. Cahill, *Heretics and Heroes*, 194.
3. Van der Meer, *Apocalypse*, 283–84, 288.

with the dragon.[4] Dürer's contemporaries now had access to a book that was intended not for a few enthusiasts but "for the humble middle-class sections of German cities, for the work places of craftsmen and artists."[5]

In 1498, almost two decades before Martin Luther nailed his 95 theses to the door of the Wittenberg church, there was clear evidence already that many Germans (and many Europeans outside Germany) would have been "happy" if the Pope had lost his head—and many would have been equally content if the same thing had happened to the "Roman (Catholic) German emperor." Dürer's condemnation of the papacy and the church was more open than his condemnation of worldly power.[6] These bold visions must have preoccupied Dürer for a long time—they were present all the time, even in dreams:[7]

> In these marvelous faces, . . . all unrest, fear and the needs of the time are expressed, just as they are during storms. Many people at the end of the year 1500—including Luther—believed that the fulfillment of time had arrived, in the imminent destruction of the world. All former orders were collapsing, and radical spiritual and social upheavals were taking shape.[8]

A richly illustrated study, *Picturing the Apocalypse*, shows how the "Apocalypse" was depicted for two thousand years and the influence it had on artists, painters, writers, composers, and cartoonists: from Dürer to D.H. Lawrence, from Memling and William Blake to Ingmar Bergman.[9] They drew, painted, composed, and wrote visualizations of Armageddon, the Millennium, the Last Judgment, and the New Jerusalem.

Dürer had an important influence on many artists after him, including Lucas Cranach the Elder (1472–1553),[10] who became the court painter in Wittenberg for Frederick the Wise (1463–1525), Martin Luther's patron, in 1505. Cranach and Luther became friends there, and he and his wife served as witnesses to Luther's marriage to Katharina von Bora on 13 June 1525. Also a printer and publisher, Cranach was responsible for the illustrations of Luther's new German Bible translation and reprinted Dürer's *Apocalypse*.[11]

---

4. Waetzoldt, *Dürer und seine Zeit*, 47–82, 59–60; illustrations: 56, 59–60, 62, 67–70, 80.
5. Waetzoldt, *Dürer und seine Zeit*, 55, 65.
6. Cahill, *Heretics and Heroes*, 197–98.
7. Winziger, *Albrecht Dürer*, 42, 47.
8. Winziger, *Albrecht Dürer*, 39, 42.
9. O'Hear, *Picturing the Apocalypse*, 188, 193, 219.
10. Cranach also influenced William Blake.
11. De Hamel, *The Book*, 216.

One of Luther's early pamphlets, *Passional Christi und Antichristi* (1521) contains thirteen pairs of woodcuts by Cranach depicting Catholic spiritual practices. The money changers that were driven from the temple by Jesus were compared with the Pope (the Antichrist), who is signing documents on a table covered with money.[12]

In addition to Dürer and Cranach, there was also Jeroen Bosch. In 2016, the Dutch writer Cees Nooteboom published a book about him on the occasion of the large commemoration exhibits in 's-Hertogenbosch and Madrid.[13] At the end of his book, Nooteboom places two illustrations side by side. One is of St. Christopher, and the other a photo that seems to have been taken from a newspaper: a Turkish policeman with a drowned Syrian child on the coast of the Mediterranean.

According to the legend, St. Christopher was a giant who had to carry a small child one day across a river. But the child became heavier and heavier as St. Christopher crossed the river, until he almost collapsed and the water was up to his shoulders. The child *revealed* himself to be Jesus, and he baptized the giant in the river. At his baptism, he was given the name Christopher, which means "bearer of Christ." Nooteboom brings this illustration into conjunction with the photo of the Turkish policeman with the child, in the same bent position as Christopher. He then writes:

> On the very same day, you twice see a man with a child. A man on the front page of the newspaper . . . and a man in a painting from the fifteenth century. The former walks, slightly bowed, by a sea or a river. He wears a uniform and heavy army boots and has a child in his arms. All you see of the child are the short legs and the—oh so small—tiny feet. He is so small that someone else had to have put those shoes on him that day. You know immediately that the child is dead, you can see that on the man's face. He is grieving, not for himself but for the child, the bankruptcy of the world. In the painting *Christopher with the Christ Child*, the saint is in the same physical attitude as the policeman on the Turkish coast, bent slightly forward, he carries the child extremely carefully to the shore, where it will be safe. He walks as if this child is too heavy as well, and it is too heavy because of the weight of death. The child was too heavy for Europe [because Europe does not exist], Europe could not bear this child.[14]

12. https://nl.wikipedia.org/wiki/Lucas_Cranach_de_Oude.

13. Nooteboom, *Een duister voorgevoel*.

14. Nooteboom, *Een duister voorgevoel*, 72–73. Three human traffickers were recently sentenced to 125 years each in connection with this tragedy: https://www.cnn.com/2020/03/14/europe/alan-kurdi-syria-drowning-sentenced-intl/index.html.

APOCALYPSE NOW?

Are we—as is often claimed—living in apocalyptic times today? The theme and the language of apocalypse has been heard for decades and taken up in films as well. The most well-known example is, of course, the film from 1979: *Apocalypse Now*, loosely based on Joseph Conrad's *Heart of Darkness*, which takes place in Vietnam and Cambodia at the time of the Vietnam War.[15]

A much more recent example has been indicated by Dina Chapajeva, professor of Russian at Georgia Tech (USA) when she speaks of a concerning rise in apocalyptic rhetoric in Russia. In 2018, Vladimir Putin spoke of a "nuclear apocalypse" more often than any Western leader in the preceding decade. His apocalyptic rhetoric resonated among his sympathizers. An ultranationalist writer compared Putin to a messiah. Now that the possibility of a nuclear war seems to dominate the minds of the world leaders, many participants in the Valdai Discussion Club, a think tank in Moscow, reread the book of Revelation after coming home. The head of the Russian Orthodox Church, Patriarch Kirill predicted a day of judgment comparable to what the book of Revelation portrays. He stated in 2017 that one would have to be blind not to see the terrible moments in history that the apostle and evangelist John spoke of in Revelation approaching. He repeated recently that he believed that the Day of Judgment was near. In his novel, *The Apocalypse of Vladimir* (2007), a television journalist called Putin "the czar and the prophet," whose mission was to prepare Russia for the last judgment. According to the members of a certain sect, Putin is the reincarnation of an early Christian missionary, the apostle Paul. The founder of this sect holds that God appointed Putin to prepare Russia for the return of Jesus Christ because he has the spirit of a czar in him. Aleksandr Dugin of the neo-Eurasia movement and possibly the chief ideologue of the Kremlin, calls Putin an orthodox leader who fights against the "kingdom of the Antichrist."[16]

"We live in apocalyptic times," thus remarked the American President, Barack Obama after the attacks in Paris in November 2015. His successor, Donald Trump, spoke—in connection with the situation regarding North Korea—of the possibility of bringing about an Armageddon. Both were making use of a language that is often invoked in evangelical circles in the US. The year 2014 saw the publication of the book *The American Apocalypse*,[17] which gives a history of these evangelical churches in which such apocalyptic views dominate. Charismatic preachers (such as Billy

---

15. https://en.wikipedia.org/wiki/Apocalypse_Now.
16. *De Volkskrant*, Thursday, 31 January 2019, p. 22.
17. Sutton, *American Apocalypse*.

Sunday, Charles Fuller, and Billy Graham at the time) and their followers saw the United States as besieged by satanic forces. They explain how the biblical prophecy of the end times gives meaning to a world plagued by wars, genocide, and the threat of nuclear destruction. Billy Graham's *Approaching Hoofbeats: The Four Horsemen of the Apocalypse* is an example of this.[18] This way of thinking had great influence on political leaders in the United States, especially among the Republicans. Ronald Reagan expected Armageddon quite soon, probably within his generation, in a nuclear exchange with the Soviet Union—"the evil empire." His Middle East policy drew inspiration from the Bible as interpreted by his fundamentalist mother and later by friends like Jerry Falwell, the well-known teleevangelist.[19] Falwell preached that the end time was just around the corner and viewed the tense developments in and concerning the state of Israel and the rest of the Middle East from this perspective. He completely supported the state of Israel and was thus considered to be part of Christian Zionism. He held that the Antichrist that was to appear in the end times, called Dajjâl by the Muslims, would be a Jewish man.[20] Reagan once told a group of Jewish leaders: "Israel is the only stable democracy that we rely on as a spot where Armageddon can come."[21] When President George W. Bush decided in 2003 to declare war on Iraq, he told the French president Chirac that he was going there to fight Gog and Magog (Ezek 38–39; Rev 20:7–10).[22]

The question whether we are living in apocalyptic times today has been discussed in Muslim circles for decades as well. David Cook has mapped the "current Muslim apocalyptic literature." For example, according to one author, a series of catastrophes would be set in motion in the year 2000 by the destruction of the Al-Aqsa Mosque in Jerusalem and the building of the third temple there. The date for that event was the 3,000th anniversary of the building of the first temple (under King Solomon; 1 Kgs 5:6). The Jews were planning to destroy the Al-Aqsa Mosque in the year 2000, so someone else claimed in 1996, making use of calculations based on the Torah, the book of Daniel, and some texts from the Talmud. For example, the Jews would start a war in 1997 with the Islamic nations, in preparation for the revelation of the Antichrist. Other writers also began counting down from the year 1978, which gave more "meaning" in the framework of the Islamic context—one

---

18. Graham, *Approaching Hoofbeats*.
19. Jerry Falwell was also a supporter of President George W Bush.
20. https://en.wikipedia.org/wiki/Jerry_Falwell_Sr..
21. Keller, *Apocalypse Now and Then*, 5.
22. Wessels, *The Torah, the Gospel, and the Qur'an*, 190.

can think of the Iranian Revolution here—because of the beginning of the new, fifteenth, century of the Muslim *hijra* (lunar) calendar.[23]

The "Islamic State" (ISIS) proclaimed that the final battle would soon occur in northern Syria, in the city of Dâbiq to the northeast of Aleppo, not far from the Turkish border. A decisive battle had been fought there between the Ottoman Empire and the sultanate of Egypt in 1516, and the Ottoman victory paved the way for the occupation of Syria and Egypt.[24] ISIS is fascinated by the following "prophecy" by the Prophet Muhammad: "In the not too distant future," "the armies of Medina and the troops of Rome [the Eastern Roman Empire with the 'second Rome' Constantinople/Byzantium] will meet." One third of the Muslims will flee, and a second third will be killed in the battle. The last third "will be the conquerors of Constantinople." ISIS sees itself as "the armies of Medina." The troops of "Rome" [i.e., the West] are therefore the enemies of Islam. Because of this prophecy, "the Islamic State" is assured that, in the end, the sanguinary and self-styled "army of Medina" will be victorious.

Most Muslims have known and acknowledged the tradition about Dâbiq for centuries but have done (almost) nothing with it. In contrast, ISIS has made this prophecy the cornerstone of its "theology." Abû Bakr al-Baghdâdi, who claimed to be caliph, sees the struggle continuing until the victorious banner will be handed over into the hands of Jesus, the son of Mary ('Îsâ ibn Maryam). Not only Christians but Muslims as well believe in Jesus' second coming.

David Cook has written a thorough study of classical Muslim apocalypticism[25] and summarizes the sources of modern Muslim apocalyptic thinking[26] as follows. The first and strongest stimulus is, he indicates, the new exegesis of classic apocalyptic material: the assimilation of the classic European anti-Semitic conspiracy theory. The second level of that theory is represented by the state of Israel, which is where the apocalyptic future will occur: Jerusalem then becomes the apocalyptic capital of Islam. On the third level, this anti-Semitic conspiracy theory stems from the frustration that Muslims feel about their inability to deal with Israel and to convince the broader world of the justice of their case.[27]

---

23. Cook, *Contemporary Muslim Apocalyptic Literature*, 86–87.
24. *EI*, s.v., Dâbik.
25. Cook, *Studies in Muslim Apocalyptic*.
26. Cook, *Contemporary Muslim Apocalyptic Literature*.
27. Cook, *Contemporary Muslim Apocalyptic Literature*, 18, 21–23.

These theories are based primarily on *The Protocols of the Elders of Zion*[28]—King Faisal of Saudi Arabia did his best to convince Richard Nixon and Henry Kissinger of the truth of these *Protocols*.[29] Modern Muslim apocalyptic thinkers from both the radical and the conservative schools cite it as an authoritative text.[30] Its use is a dominant feature on the contemporary Arabic apocalyptic scene. It is the lens through which apocalyptic thinkers view daily events in the areas of politics, religion, economics, and culture.

Finally, we should mention the extensive use of the Evangelical-Protestant apocalyptic exegesis of the Bible.[31] Confronted with the reality of the power of the state of Israel, they began to use—on a large scale—biblical material from Protestant-Evangelical sources for developing their own apocalyptic scenarios. They were unable to find much material in the Muslim tradition, apart from the one tradition of *the rocks and the trees*: the time (of the last judgment) will not come until the Muslims fight the Jews, until the Jews hide behind the rocks and trees. These will cry out: "O Muslims, O servants of God, there's a Jew behind me, come and kill him."[32] This tradition is actually the only example of an anti-Jewish impulse in the classic apocalyptic sources. The large majority of these classic sources deal with the enemies that the Muslims had to face from the seventh to the ninth centuries: the Byzantines and the Turks.[33]

THE APOCALYPSE IN THE BIBLE AND THE QUR'AN

This present book is not intended to describe anew apocalyptic views from the present and the past. That has already been done in comprehensive studies.[34] Nor is it my intention to present an overview of how both past and present Muslim writers thought about apocalyptic times or to discuss their recent exegesis of both the Bible and the Qur'an. In the apocalyptic consciousness of the Muslims, the state of Israel has, since 1967, been in

---

28. Cook, *Contemporary Muslim Apocalyptic Literature*, 25–26, 147, n. 18.

29. Cook, *Contemporary Muslim Apocalyptic Literature*, 224.

30. Cook, *Contemporary Muslim Apocalyptic Literature*, 23.

31. Cf. Sutton, *The American Apocalypse*.

32. Cook refers (*Contemporary Muslim Apocalyptic Literature*, 36) to Nu'aym Ibn Hammad (d. 855), *Kitab al-Ta'rij* (Beirut: Dar al-Fikr, 1993), and states in footnote 27 that "This is perhaps the single most quoted tradition in modern Muslim apocalyptic literature."

33. Cook, *Contemporary Muslim Apocalyptic Literature*, 35–36. For a discussion of this evangelical Protestant material see https://www.memri.org/reports/antisemitic-hadith-prophecy-rock-and-tree-memri-clips-a. Cf. Sutton, *American Apocalypse*.

34. Wieser et al. (eds.). *Abendländische Apokalyptik*.

control of the most important areas where the apocalyptic future will take place. For Muslims, Jerusalem is the apocalyptic capital of Islam, the location from which the Mahdi, the expected messianic figure, will reign: it is the place where the Muslims seek a refuge from the Jews who are led by the Antichrist when he attacks the countries of Islam. It is the place where Jesus will return and defeat the Antichrist.[35] There is a striking emotional similarity between Jewish and Muslim messianic expectations. For many religious Jews, it is incomprehensible that the third temple cannot be built on the Temple Mount, where the Dome of the Rock and the Al-Aqsa Mosque are now found.[36]

The essential question that we will be concerned with is: What is *actually* meant in the Bible and the Qur'an by "apocalyptic times"? The *Encyclopaedia Britannica* speaks of the "little Apocalypse," which refers to passages from the first three gospels (Matt 24; Mark 13; Luke 21), in which Jesus speaks about the approaching end of the world: the destruction of the world and the Last Judgment. Figuratively, it is called the age of a series of events that call to mind the destruction of the world. An apocalyptic writer is viewed as a doomsayer. An apocalyptic number, 666 (the number of the beast, Rev 13:18), is mentioned, as well as the four apocalyptic horsemen (Rev 6:2–8).[37]

The book of Revelation is sometimes viewed as a kind of *appendix* to the Bible. Ministers do not often preach on it, and it is felt that it would be better to skip the book because it has led to such shocking interpretations, with all the attendant violent consequences. At the conclusion of a recent study, *Apocalyps in kunst: Ondergang of loutering* (The Apocalypse in Art: Destruction or Purification), Wessel Stoker states:

> The Revelation of John does indeed give hope to those who have been deprived of their rights . . . but it is arbitrarily at the same time the source of inspiration for those who live in religious dream worlds and want to convert the world by their own violence. Even if that use is abuse, that does not detract from the fact that the reception of this book of the Bible has been dubious. I therefore consider the decision of the church to include this book in the canon of the Bible questionable.[38]

---

35. Cook, *Contemporary Muslim Apocalyptic Literature*, 22.

36. Cook, *Contemporary Muslim Apocalyptic Literature*, 22.

37. *Encyclopaedia Britannica*, s.v., "Apocalyptic Literature," https://www.britannica.com/art/apocalyptic-literature#ref916986

38. Stoker, "God en Apocalyps," 155.

To the contrary, in my view, there is every reason to be happy about the inclusion of this book in the canon and especially to look for a precise exegesis to deal with the above misuse. That can best be done by better understanding what the author of the book of Revelation actually meant, as well as what Paul and the gospel writers meant whose books and letters are permeated by apocalyptic thinking. The above-mentioned doubt can be removed by learning to properly understand apocalyptic language, by learning the apocalyptic alphabet.[39] It is precisely this language that constitutes the key to unlocking the meaning of the *revelation* of God in the Three Scriptures—the Tanakh, the Gospel, and the Qur'an. For a proper understanding, an introduction to the apocalyptic language is a first requirement. The Greek verb *apokalyptô* means "reveal," "disclose," and the noun *apocalypsis* is translated as "revelation." The most well-known apocalyptic book in the Old Testament is the book of Daniel. The diaspora Jews in Alexandria saw Daniel as the greatest of all prophets,[40] and his greatness is due to the fact that his prophetic witness has an apocalyptic character.[41] But that also obtains for prophets in general: To whom has the arm of the Lord been revealed? (Isa 53:1). The Lord does nothing without revealing his council[42] to his servants, the prophets (Amos 3:7, Septuagint [LXX]).[43]

It is very telling that, in the Greek translation of the Old Testament, (the Septuagint, LXX; so called because it was translated by seventy scholars) follows a different order than the Hebrew Bible, which ends with 2 Chronicles. The last book of the Septuagint, however, is the book of Daniel, an apocalyptic book par excellence! It originated in the second century BC in one of the darkest periods in antiquity, which began with Alexander the Great's great march to the ends of the earth. The lowest point in that misery and disruption was reached during the reign of one of Alexander's successors, King Antiochus IV Epiphanes. The Maccabees rebelled against him, but the book of Daniel would respond in an entirely different, *non-violent*, way to Antiochus's rule. Placing this book at the end makes a clear statement. Not only does it say something about how the book of Daniel must be read, but it also says something about how the Tanakh must be understood as a whole. If we keep in mind that the book of Revelation, which is the last book of the New Testament, makes more than 200 references and allusions

---

39. Cf. Wessels, *A Stranger is Calling*, chapter III.
40. Aalders, *De Apocalyptische Christus*, 78.
41. Aalders, *De Apocalyptische Christus*, 88.
42. *Paidaia* in the LXX. Cf. chapter IV.
43. Aalders, *De Septuagint*, 65.

to the book of Daniel, then the Apocalypse of John is also determinative for how the New Testament as a whole is to be read.

It is the striking that the arrangement of the chapters of the Qur'an displays a similar intention. The Qur'an consists of 114 chapters, *surahs*. The first is the opening prayer, *surah al-fâtiha,* which is followed by the second and longest chapter, and the last, the 114th, is the shortest. It is usually stated that the order follows size, comparable to the division between the major and minor prophets in the Old Testament. That does not mean that Isaiah, Jeremiah, and Ezekiel were greater prophets than Zechariah and Malachi, but the terms do say something about the size of their books or scrolls. It is striking that the most eschatological passages are found in the last part of the Qur'an, so it is very appropriate to call the last 33 *surahs* in the Qur'an "A Qur'anic Apocalypse."[44] That also says a great deal about how the Qur'an as a whole should be understood.

That is why it must be stated particularly emphatically from the start that apocalypticism in the Bible is not limited to two books, Daniel and Revelation, or to the last 33 *surahs* of the Qur'an. There are other explicitly apocalyptic texts beyond the two most well-known books or the last 33 *surahs*.[45] With respect to the Old Testament, there are, among other things, the so-called "Isaiah Apocalypse," the allegedly most recent part of this book (Isa 24–27), and the "Little Apocalypse" (Isa 34–35).[46] A new world is coming, a new, different era is dawning, and the prophet Isaiah calls this historical change an "end," an "outcome" (*acharith*) using a term translated by the LXX as *eschaton*, from which the term eschatology, the doctrine of the "last things," derives. A shocking image of such an eschatological situation is sketched especially in the "Isaiah Apocalypse": here it is the Lord who devastates and destroys the earth. He knows the earth inside out and scatters its inhabitants (Isa 24:1). The familiar world collapses and is destroyed; a radical and far-reaching judgment on the world takes place. Just like Sodom and Gomorrah, God overthrows the earth because of the sins of its inhabitants. The Qur'an does not refer to these cities by name but strikingly enough calls them the *overthrown cities*; they were destroyed because of the wickedness of the inhabitants (Q 9:70; 53: 53, 54; 69:9). The prophet invokes the terrifying experience of a flood that submerges the world into the formlessness and emptiness (*tohu wabohu*) of the primal waters (Isa 24:18; cf. Gen 7:11; Isa 2:10).[47]

---

44. Cuypers, *A Qur'ânic Apocalypse*.
45. See Cuypers, *A Qur'ânic Apocalpse*, xxiii–xiv.
46. KBS on Isa 34–35.
47. Aalders, *De Apocalyptische Christus*, 75.

Like most of the other prophets, the prophet Zechariah (Zech 9-14) uses poetry to proclaim the coming of the Messianic kingdom and victory over the peoples (Zech 9:1—11:3).[48] The oracle was probably proclaimed in 332 BC in response to Alexander the Great's campaign of conquest:[49] "I will take away the chariots from Ephraim and the warhorses from Jerusalem, and the battle bow will be broken. He will proclaim peace to the nations. His rule will extend from sea to sea [from the Mediterranean to the Persian Gulf] and from the *River* to the ends of the earth" (Zech 9:10; cf. Isa 62:11). The "river" refers to the Euphrates, which flows in the region between the two seas and was thought to be the center of the inhabited world.[50]

Similar passages can be found in the New Testament in the gospels: the so-called "Synoptic Apocalypse" (Matt 24:1-52; Mark 13:1-37; Luke 21:5-36). When they were completely alone, Jesus' disciples asked him: "What will be the sign of your coming and of the end of the age?" (Matt 24:3). Jesus answers with a parable: "Now learn this lesson from the fig tree:[51] As soon as its twigs get tender and its leaves come out, you know that summer is near. Even so, when you see all these things, you know that it is near, right at the door" (Matt 24:32-33).

Many apocalyptic writings originated before and after the New Testament and were not included in the canon: 1 Enoch, 4 Ezra, 2 Baruch, Jubilees, and the texts of the Qumran community, the Dead Sea Scrolls. The Qumran community had withdrawn from the hopeless circumstances in which Jerusalem found itself in order to await God's new reign. Babylon is finally the symbol in the apocalyptic imagination for every power that resists God's reign (Rev 17 and 18; cf. Jer 51:59-64).

THE QUR'ANIC APOCALYPSE

As in the biblical apocalyptic, where the political context is determined by a series of oppressive imperialistic empires: Assur, Babel, Egypt, Medes, Persians, Greeks (Old Testament), and the Romans (New Testament), so the

48. KBS Introduction to the book Zechariah.
49. KBS on Zech 9:1-8.
50. KBS on Zech 9:10.
51. The fig tree and its fruit are often used in imagery and parable (Isa 28:4; Hos 9:10; Nah 3:12). And the stars of the heaven fell upon the earth like late figs, blown from the tree by a storm (Rev 6:13; Jer 8:13; cf. Matt 21:18-22). " All the stars in the sky will be dissolved and the heavens rolled up like a scroll; all the starry host will fall like withered leaves from the vine, like shriveled figs from the fig tree" (Isa 34:4). Cf. the Qur'an: "The Fig" (Q 95); cf. "when the sun is rolled up and the stars fall from heaven" (*surah* "The Rolling Up" (Q 81:1-2).

Qur'an has to be understood in the same context, with the addition of the unjust rulers of Mecca and the imperialist East Romans and Persian rulers. The texts have to be read from this apocalyptic perspective par excellence, namely, the expected near end of time and the announcement of the Last Judgment. As we will see, this is not something that will happen in the distant future but the judgment that will be carried out *hic et nunc*, here and now.

It is striking that an "apocalyptic" accent can be heard in the Qur'an in all kinds of contexts. A comparison between how Moses' call is narrated in the Bible and in the Qur'an can serve as an example. At one point Moses is driving the herds of his father-in-law Jethro, called Shuʻaib in the Qur'an and who was sent to the people of Midian (Madyan) (Q 7:85–93; 11:84–95; 29:36–37), far into the desert. He arrives at the mountain of God, Horeb, where the angel of the Lord appears to him, in a fire that flames up out of a thorn bush. Moses watches and sees that the bush is ablaze but is not consumed (Exod 3:1–6). In the Qur'an, it is described as follows:

> Did the story of Moses come to you, /when he sighted a fire, / and said to his family, "Wait! / Indeed I descry a fire! / Maybe I will bring you a brand from it, / or find some guidance at the fire." / So when he came to it, he was called, "O Moses! / Indeed I am your Lord! / So take off your sandals. / You are indeed in the sacred valley of Ṭuwâ [cf. Q 79:16]⁵² / I have chosen you; / so listen to what is revealed. / Indeed I am God / I—there is no god except Me. / So worship Me, / and maintain the prayer for My remembrance. / *Indeed the Hour [of judgment] is bound to come: / I will have it hidden, / so that every soul may be rewarded / for what it strives for.*" (Q 20:9–15)⁵³

The italicized section here presents, as it were, the message that Muhammad brings to the new era; it focuses on the announcement of the "last hour" and the judgment that actually occurs every hour.

THE STARTING POINT: WHICH READING GUIDE?

It is important to indicate right at the beginning which reading guide we will be using for the three Scriptures: the Torah, the Gospel, and the Qur'an. *For the Jews* the Hebrew Bible, the Tanakh is the starting point. *For Christians*, the starting point is the Bible, which consists of the Old and the New

---

52. The meaning of the word is unknown. Paret on Q 20:11. The name is derived perhaps from the verb *tawâ* ("to roll up"). That means that the valley is holiness rolled up or doubly hallowed. Cf. Nasr (ed.), *The Study Quran*, 1470.

53. Cf. Q 40:59; 22:7; 18:21, 45:32; 34:3; 15:85.

Testament. In addition, it must be stated immediately that the fact alone that the Tanakh is called the *Old* Testament meant in actuality for most Christians that the New Testament took priority over or even replaced the Old. The Old can be seen as having been antiquated. The Old Testament is seen as *fulfilled* in the life and work of Jesus Christ, the Messiah who has come. A Christian or even Christological reading of the Old Testament has been dominant throughout the centuries. On the basis of the Qur'an itself, *Muslims* recognize that Jesus has come to confirm the *Tawra*/Torah—by which the Qur'an understands not only the five books of Moses (Genesis, Leviticus, Exodus, Numbers, and Deuteronomy), but the whole Tanakh, just as the Jews do. But in actuality, for the average Muslim, all attention is focused on the Qur'an.

The title of my earlier book summarizes well how I try to read the Bible and the Qur'an: *The Torah, the Gospel, and the Qur'an: Three Books, Two Cities, One Tale*. This means that the Bible and the Qur'an present one coherent narrative. What narrative is this?[54] In the *Old Testament*, it is the story of the *Exodus* from Egypt, the redemption or liberation from the house of bondage. That is also the dominant theme in the *New Testament*: Jesus receives a visionary apocalyptic experience on the Mount of Transfiguration. In the company of his three most intimate disciples, he meets the two prophets, Moses, and Elijah, who spoke with God on Mount Sinai. And what did these three talk about on the mountain? They talked about *Jesus' Exodus in Jerusalem* (Luke 9:31)! That is, just as Moses had to liberate his people from the land of fear, Egypt, and Elijah had to lead his people away from the Pharaoh-like king Ahab and his wife Jezebel, so Jesus leads the Exodus out of the oppressive rule of the Romans (represented by Pilate and Herod) and by the spiritual leaders of the Temple state who collaborated with them.

The *Qur'an* relates how the prophet Muhammad, like a new Moses, became the leader of the Exodus from Mecca, the unjust, oppressive city, in order to go to Medina, also called "the city of light" (*Madînat al-munâwara*). The word that is used for exodus in Arabic is *hijra*. That event is seen as so decisive that it is the start of the Muslim calendar. It is striking that when Martin Buber speaks of the departure of Abraham from Ur of the Chaldees in Mesopotamia in order to go to the promised land, he uses the word *hijra* in his German text.[55]

---

54. See Wessels, *The Torah, the Gospel, and the Qur'an*, chapter IV: "Exodus from Babel to Jerusalem, Hijra from Mecca to Medina."

55. It concerns the same word in Hebrew. Cf. the name Hagar.

Jews, Christians, and Muslims are on the road together[56]—which is actually the best term to use in reference to a synagogue, church, and mosque. The English subtitle of my book *A Stranger is Calling* is: *Jews, Christians, and Muslims as Fellow Travellers*. One of the important themes in that book is the common language that Jews, Christians, and Muslims share. They are educated in the same Exodus grammar and have to learn the same biblical ABCs, the same ABCs that the theologian K.H. Miskotte taught to various generations. In 1941, during the Second World War, Miskotte published his *Bijbels ABC*.[57] (The ABCs of the Bible). With this book, Miskotte wanted to help people understand the basic lines of Holy Scripture. He took his starting point in the Tanakh in which the language of the New Testament is rooted. Learning the core terms with their unique meaning and power of expression is necessary for understanding the message of the Bible—thus, the Old and the New Testaments. Miskotte speaks in this connection also of the "grammar of Scripture."[58] He wanted to teach the "congregation" that language anew, to raise them in it and encourage them so that they could offer "better resistance" to the "foreign language," the language of the Nazis.[59] Are we not hearing the latter language everywhere in Europe again?

If one wants to learn to read the holy books of the Jews, Christians, and Muslims in their internal coherence and connectedness, it is above all necessary to learn to understand the ABCs of the "language of Canaan" in the Bible and in the Qur'an. By "language of Canaan" I do not mean the "language used by pious people," usually understood in a negative way, a kind of pompous language associated with ministers,[60] but that of the prophet Isaiah, when he says that "on that day"—in an apocalyptic sense!—the Egyptians will learn to speak the language of Canaan (Isa 19:18). Why will they do that? Because God will bring the two great powers Assur and Egypt onto the highway of his laws and divine justice.[61] It is the new language,

---

56. Translator's note. In the Dutch text, the author uses the phrase *samen op weg*. This was the term used for the relationship between the Reformed Church of the Netherlands, the Reformed Churches in the Netherlands, and the Lutheran Evangelical Church in the Netherlands that were engaging in unified activities before their formal unification as the Protestant Church in the Netherlands.

57. Miskotte, *Bijbels ABC*.

58. Miskotte, *Bijbels ABC*, 67–68.

59. http://www.hervormdnunspeet.nl/drplcm/content/verslag-bijbels-abc-2013 (course leader: R.H. Reeling Brouwer).

60. Van Daale, *s.v.*, Kanaän. For a more extensive treatment, see Wessels, *A Stranger is Calling*, chapter III.

61. This is how it is worded (in Dutch) by Joost van den Vondel in a "language of Canaan translation" of Psalm 23: 'D'Almachtige is mijn Herder en geleide': 'op de heerbaan van zijn wetten en 't goddelijke recht'. Cf. *Liedboek*, 23a, couplets 1 & 2.

the language of Canaan, that will be spoken on that highway. This is not a language of economic self-interest; it is not the language of "the ideology of national security." Nor is it the language of "How can we arrange it so that the rich get richer and the poor poorer?" No, the language of Canaan is a completely different language. It is the language of justice and peace: where goodness meets faithfulness, and justice greets peace with a kiss.[62]

In that language, the Bible and the Qur'an, all three Scriptures, proclaim "the good news," whether that be in Hebrew, Greek, or Arabic. The *foreign* language is not that of strangers or foreigners, but the language of imperialist rulers and oppressors throughout all the centuries that the whole Bible and the Qur'an cover: the Nimrods in Ashur, Babel, *and* Nineveh, the "Pharaohs" of Egypt, the "princes," the "emperors" of the Greeks and the Persians and those of Rome and Byzantium, and Persia. The latter two were the world powers in the time of the prophet Muhammad.

The starting point of my two earlier books is also the fundamental starting point of this book on apocalyptic in the Three Books. The Tanakh is and will always remain the First Testament.[63] It is and will always remain the basis not only for the Jews, and it must also remain that for Christians and Muslims as well. Abandoning that starting point can only lead to disaster, and that is putting it extremely mildly. The inconceivable, horrible event is still present as proof of how bad things can get: the destruction of six million Jews in the twentieth century, the Holocaust. That event happened in "Christian" Europe, where the Nazis were inspired by and could make use of a centuries-old anti-Judaism that was based on a completely wrong and twisted exegesis of both the Old and the New Testament.

It is usually thought that the New Testament took the place of the Old, and the names that are used for them can thus lead to the wrong conclusion that the First Testament belongs to the past. That is not what the New Testament itself says. It is the later, primarily dogmatic exegesis that led to this alienation from its Jewish roots, to hatred of the Jews, anti-Judaism, and anti-Semitism. There are also Muslims who believe that the Qur'an has taken the place of both the Old and the New Testaments. That notion is not found in the Qur'an itself—to the contrary!

To understand the New Testament properly, it would be useful to call it a *midrash*. A *midrash*, "examination" or "exegesis," is a rabbinic method of interpreting the Bible, of one verse or a complete book. The same is true of the Qur'an, in that case it is a *midrash* of both the Old Testament and the

---

62. *Liedboek*, Psalm 85, verse 2, rhymed: "waar goedheid trouw ontmoet, het recht de vrede met een kus ontmoet."

63. Zenger, *Das Erste Testament*.

New Testament. The Qur'an itself states it clearly and definitively: just as Jesus came to *confirm* the Torah, so the Qur'an was revealed to *confirm* both the Torah and the Gospel (Q 5:46; 3:50). Jesus said: "O Children of Israel! / Indeed I am the apostle of God to you, / to confirm what is before me of the Torah" (Q 61:6). The New Testament and the Qur'an can be properly read and understood only from the perspective of the continuing discovery and disclosure of the internal connectedness that both have with the Old Testament. The words of Jesus Sirach are very applicable here. Jesus Sirach was a professional scribe (cf. Sir 38:25–39:11), who attempted to connect the Torah, the Prophets, and the Writings with current events.

> Instruction in understanding and knowledge
> I have written in this book,
> Jesus son of Eleazar son of Sirach of Jerusalem,
> whose mind poured forth wisdom.
> Happy are those who concern themselves with these things,
> and those who lay them to heart will become wise.
> For if they put them into practice, they will be equal to anything,
> for the fear of the Lord is their path.
> (Sir 50:27–29)

The book of Sirach is not included in the Hebrew Bible but is found in the Septuagint.

Jesus Sirach ends with the following summons:

> Draw near to me, you who are uneducated,
> and lodge in the house of instruction
> Why do you say you are lacking in these things,
> and why do you endure such great thirst?
> I opened my mouth and said,
> Acquire wisdom for yourselves without money.
> Put your neck under her yoke,
> and let your souls receive instruction;
> it is to be found close by.
> (Sir 51:23–26)

It is not known if this chapter 51 is a later addition. A fragment of this chapter was found in the caves of Qumran in between, of all things, the scrolls of the Psalms![64] This fact is particularly striking because we will see in the following chapters how much of a central role the Psalms play in understanding the Scriptures. This can also be seen in Jesus' words: "Come to me, all you who are weary and burdened, and I will give you rest [cf. Jer 31:28].

---

64. https://en.wikipedia.org/wiki/Sirach; Vermes, *The Complete Dead Sea Scrolls in English*, 11, 15–17, 50–51.

Take my yoke upon you and learn from me, for I am gentle and humble in heart, and you will find rest for your souls. For my yoke is easy and my burden is light" (Matt 11:28–30).

We are all called to attend the school of the Torah! The Torah, the Gospel, and the Qur'an—the latter two based on what will always be the First Testament—are intended to teach Jews, Christians, and Muslims the way that all people should follow. Every person, every hearer and reader of this message, is called to comply with the call of the prophets.

THE OUTLINE OF THE BOOK

This book is structured as follows. (I) We begin with the appearance of the prophet Muhammad in the seventh century and the movement of his first followers in the Arab Peninsula and the expansion across the borders into Palestine, Syria, and Persia up to the gates of Constantinople. It is fascinating here to look at the affinity that exists between Muhammad and St. Paul, both of whom are called apostles. Both go on a heavenly journey, both are called to be messengers for the peoples of the world.

(II) In the second chapter, we remain in that same seventh century in order to gain insight into the response that came from the Jews and the Christians also outside the Arab Peninsula who came into contact with the Arab Muslims. The Christians here are the Eastern Christians such as the Syrian Orthodox in particular; others were the Nestorians, the Copts, Armenians, and the Eastern Orthodox. In connection with the latter, one should think of the "imperial" (Melkite) church of Byzantium. The Byzantine emperor was the factual head of this church since the conversion of Emperor Constantine the Great in the fourth century. Here the military clashes that occurred then are important. Attention will be paid especially to the apocalyptic responses that were invoked by Jews, Christians, and Muslims.

(III) In the third chapter, we will look at the great Reformer, Martin Luther. Luther has been the subject of great interest among Muslims in recent centuries because they saw in him a reformer who could be compared with what the Prophet Muhammad was and wanted to be.

The sixteenth century is also important for the fact that it was just before, on the eve of, this century, that Albrecht Dürer (1498) managed to portray apocalyptic in an unparalleled fashion. And he did so twenty years before Martin Luther appeared on the scene.

If the times were apocalyptic for Luther, that was also how his opponents, the Turks, experienced those times. We will look at what Luther thought of the "religion of the Turks" as well as what he thought of the Jews. We will discuss the political actors in the drama from both sides, such as the Emperor Charles V, Sülaymân, the Turkish sultan who would stand before the gates of Vienna in 1529.

(IV) After this chapter, we will turn to what the three Holy Books themselves understand by apocalyptic, beginning with who Gog and Magog are and whom they represent. There have been many candidates for that role throughout history. Two American presidents seriously believed that they had to fight against Gog and Magog in their time. For Ronald Reagan, it was the Soviet Union, and for George W. Bush, it was Saddam Hussein of Iraq. This had nothing to do with the exegesis of Scripture. The discovery of the actual meaning of "apocalyptic" will have much to say about the powerful figures who use this "jargon" to justify their own political and military agendas.

(V) Probably the most important and most influential apocalyptic book of the Bible is that ascribed to the prophet Daniel. Apocalyptic books are often attributed to an important individual, such as Daniel in this case. The book itself was written in the second century BC, whereas the historical Daniel lived in the time of the Babylonian exile. *The Apocalypse of Pseudo-Methodius* derives from the late seventh century but is attributed to a church father from the fourth century. The Greek translation of the Old Testament, the Septuagint, which was done in the same second century BC, will place the book of Daniel—and not just for arbitrary reasons, as we shall see—at the end of the First Testament.

(VI) In the New Testament, the last book of the Bible is certainly *the* Apocalypse par excellence. But the first three gospels contain the so-called "Synoptic Apocalypse." There the question is the meaning of Jesus' activity. The earliest gospel, Mark, speaks of three apocalyptic moments. The first is the voice from heaven that is heard when Jesus is baptized in the Jordan by John the Baptist, called Yahyâ in the Quran. "You are my Son, whom I love; with you I am well pleased" (Mark 1:11). The second is the voice that is heard at the transfiguration of Jesus on the mountain and his meeting with Moses and Elijah—partly the same words. "This is my Son, whom I love. Listen to him!" (Mark 9:7). The third is the moment of Jesus' death (Mark 15:37). What is the meaning of the cross before and after Constantine the Great? And what is the meaning of the way of the cross, the *via crucis* that Jesus walked, compared to the way of the cross the Romans walked, from Galilee to Jerusalem?

(VII) The Apostle Paul is explicitly also called an apocalyptic writer. Just like Muhammad, he was later "called" by God like the prophets were called. Both are messengers to the peoples; their mission extends to the ends of the earth. It is crucial to pay attention to the nature of this journey.

(VIII) Right up the present, apocalyptic times have always been associated with war and violence. The Last Judgment will then come. The answer to the question "What are apocalyptic times?" is, however, not a matter of how and when the world violently comes to its end, but how a definitive end comes to violence! Perhaps the most important apocalyptic discovery is that the "last things´ can be properly understood only if they are seen as inseparably connected with the "first things."

REMARKS ON THE TEXTS OF THE BIBLE AND THE QUR'AN

In writing the Dutch version of this work, I consulted various Dutch Bible translations, including the *Naardense Bijbel* and especially the Willibrord translation (KBS). Most of the translations from the Bible in this English version are from the New International Version, but I have also consulted various other translations (see the list of abbreviations) and adjusted the translation in accordance with my understanding of the Hebrew and Greek of the Old and New Testaments, respectively. That also applies to my quotations from the Qur'an, in which I rely on the original language of the Qur'an: Arabic. Quotations from the Old Testament apocryphal books are taken for the most part from the New Revised Standard Version, Catholic Edition, unless otherwise indicated. I have also consulted various translations of the Qur'an, especially translations by J.H. Kramers, Fred Leemhuis, Eduard Verhoef, the German translation by Rudi Paret and the English translation by Seyyed Hossein Nasr, Mohammed Marmaduke Picthall, and Tarif Khalidi, i.e., *The Study Quran*. Most of the translations of the Qur'an in this English edition are taken from the translation by ʿAlī Qulī Qarāʾī. I also regularly consulted the original Hebrew, Greek, and Arabic texts, which sometimes led to an adjustment of the translation. In presenting the Arabic text of the Qur'an in particular I take the liberty of sometimes making a simple addition for clarification to make the text more understandable. Because I always provide the text references, the reader can easily check the reference in his or her own translation(s). Of course, to play on the Latin terms for translator (*traductor*) and traitor, (*traditor*), no translator wants to be betray the text. The purpose of the many references to other similar texts is to deepen the reader's familiarity with all three Scriptures and to promote that familiarity. The Arabic names for the biblical personages I will cite in the footnotes, and they can be located via the Index.

I

Muhammad Sent to the Peoples

God has made mercy incumbent upon Himself. (Q 6:12)

We did not send you [Muhammad] except as a mercy to humankind. (Q 21:107)

Whatever is prayed is what is believed and must be done.[1]

INTRODUCTION

Two years after the death of the prophet Muhammad, Jerusalem was conquered by the Arabs, and a period of "Islamic dominion" began that would last centuries. Until 1948, the foundation of the state of Israel, this city remained—aside from a short interruption during the crusades—in Muslim hands. One could actually say that Arabs began to expand beyond the boundaries of Arabia during Muhammad's lifetime. After all, the first confrontation with the Byzantines occurred at Mu'ta southeast of the Dead Sea in September 629. According to an Arabic source, Emperor Heraclius was said to have taken part in that battle, though that is considered clearly improbable.[2]

---

1. *Lex orante; lex credendi, lex agendi.*
2. *EI, s.v., Mu'ta.*

Should those conquests be seen as the beginning of a project to expand the territory under Islam (*dâr al-islâm*) to the whole world? A view would later[3] develop that saw the world divided between the "house of peace" (*dâr al-salâm*)—the territory of the *Pax Islamica*—and the house of war (*dâr al-harb*).[4] Only later would there be a division into three territories: (1) where peace and the religion of Islam reigned, (2) the region that was under the permanent threat of war, and (3) areas with which treaties had been concluded (*dâr al-'ahd*; *dâr al-sulh*) and where tribute had to be paid to the Muslim government. In this later view, the prophet Muhammad himself was the one who tried to convert the Byzantine emperor and Khosrow II, the Persian ruler. At that time, Muslims were being called to make every effort—the actual meaning of the word *jihâd* in the Qur'an—violently if necessary, to engage in the struggle for conquest on the "path of God," to the ends of the earth. Movements like the "Islamic State" also use such language. In the Qur'an, the word *jihâd* does not, however, mean "holy war."

It should be made clear, however, that the history of these conquests was not written down until the ninth century by Muslim historians who did not have any recourse or access to contemporary sources then. Studies have appeared in recent years that do make use of such sources, although most are non-Arabic, including Armenian, which thus have a different view of what happened.

THE MOVEMENT OF THE BELIEVERS

Muhammad inaugurated a religious movement called "the movement of the believers" and not an *Islamic* movement. It was not until the century after Muhammad's death that his followers were called "Muslims." While the term "believer(s)" occurs almost a thousand times in the Qur'an, the word "Muslim" appears less than 75. The true believers are those who believe in God and his Messenger, who have no doubts, and commit themselves and their possessions without reservation to the path of God. They are those who speak the truth (Q 49:14-15; cf. 9:90, 97). A believer is not identical with being a "Muslim," certainly not in the later sense of the word. In the Qur'an, the word "muslim," which is not used there in contrast to "Christian" or "Jew," for example, refers to someone who *surrenders* in complete trust to God. It later becomes a term for someone who is viewed as belonging to the Muslim community, a label, so to say. Thus, Muhammad's early followers identified themselves in the first place as "believers" who had truly

---

3. This division does not belong to *hadith* but appeared in Islamic law (jurisprudence).
4. *EI*, s.v., Dâr al-harb.

surrendered, truly committed themselves, and in that sense were "muslim" and did not just bear the label "muslim."[5] For that matter, in the Qur'an, the term "believers" can also refer to Jews and Christians, as can the term "muslim" as well. After all, Abraham, the father of all believers, was, according to the Qur'an, a "muslim," although he was so in the sense of an example, an example for all three—Jew, Christian, and Muslim. Thus, when the Qur'an speaks of "muslim," that term must be understood in its original sense and not in its later (sociological) meaning.

It is also incorrect, then, to speak about Islam in the later sense of the term when exegeting the Qur'an. That is an anachronism, just as one cannot yet speak of Christianity when exegeting the New Testament. Nor was there any single more or less uniform type of Judaism at the time of the New Testament. No more than Jesus—and no more than Paul, by the way!—founded the "church" in the later sense of the word, not to mention Christianity did Muhammad found "Islam´ in the later sense of the word. When Muhammad says in his farewell pilgrimage, "Today I have perfected your religion [*dîn*] for you" (Q 5:3), he is not speaking of Islam in that later sense of the word.[6] With the Jews in Medina in mind, the Qur'an says: "The religion of God is *islâm*" (Q 3:19). To prevent any and all misunderstanding, what the term *islam* truly means must be translated properly here: to surrender to God, to belong to him. That is the true religion. Muhammad did not found a new religion, Islam, just as Jesus and Paul did not found Christianity. *All people, including Jews, Christians, and Muslims are called to turn to serve God, to surrender to him, and thus follow his religion.*[7]

The *content of belief* is characterized by the belief in the oneness of God and the Last Day (Q 2:8, 62, 126,128, 264; 3:114; 39, 59, 136, 162; 4:38; 5:69; 9:18, 29, 44–45, 99; 24:2; 58:22; 65:2). In the early message of the Qur'an, the preaching of judgment and the oneness of God are in the foreground. The "Last Day" is depicted in detail. The individual is warned about the nearness of that Day and urged to prepare for it by truly believing *and acting justly*! That acting justly is an expression of truly believing.[8] The righteous person is he or she who believes in God and the Last Day, the angels, the book, and the prophets, who gives of his or her wealth—despite his or her love for it—to relatives, orphans, the needy, the traveler, and the beggar; who sets slaves free, and observes religious and social obligations (Q 2:177). The two latter

---

5. According to Donner, *Muhammad and the Believers*, 57, 78.

6. Although it is disputed as to whether this verse has to do with the farewell pilgrimage (cf. Paret, *Der Koran*, 114, this has no bearing on what is asserted above.

7. Cf. *EQ*, *s.v.*, Religion.

8. Donner, *Muhammad and the Believers*, 61.

obligations are called *salât* and *zakât*, two of the later five pillars of Islam: the confession of faith, ritual prayers, giving of alms, fasting during Ramadan, and the pilgrimage to Mecca (*shahada, salât, zakât, sawm,* and *hajj*). The emphasis of the Qur'an on right conduct is so great that it is justified to characterize the "movement of the believers" as both strictly monotheistic and devout. These ideas were well known in the Near East in the seventh century, including in the Arab Peninsula, known among both the Jews and Christians Muhammad met in his surroundings. What is special here is that they are given a unique expression in the *Arabic* Qur'an for the first time. There is no reason to think that the "believers" in this early stage were already busy with setting up a *separate* religious confession, separate from the Jews, Christians, and even monotheists (*hanif*, pl. *hunafâ*). The Qur'an uses the word *hanîf* for "monotheist," which can be translated as "seeker of God." Abraham in particular is a *hanîf*, the pure worshipper of God (Q 2:135; 3:67, 95; 4:125; 6:79, 161; 16:120, 123; 22:31). In most verses, the "seeker of God" stands over against idolaters. Muhammad and his followers are recommended to worship God alone, as "seekers of God" and not as idolaters (Q 10:103; 30:30). This "monotheistic" (*hanîfiyya*) belief is contrasted with polytheism as well as with a corrupted monotheism, for which Christians in particular are reproached because they called the Messiah (Jesus) the Son of God (Q 9:30) or God himself (Q 5:37, 72), or made him Lord (Q 3:35; 4:157, 171).[9] For a long time, *hanîfiyya* was the name of the religion Muhammad followed.[10] These believers in the one God between the time of Abraham and the prophet Muhammad are viewed as the faithful representatives of the Abrahamic-Ishmaelite tradition.[11]

Muhammad's message is the same as what earlier messengers brought. That is why in the initial phase, Jews and Christians could easily participate in this "movement of believers" because they, after all, also acknowledged God's oneness. Thus, some of the early adherents of this "movement of believers" were Jews and Christians. The reason for that "confessional" openness consisted in the fact that the fundamental ideas and emphasis on following strict piety were in no way contrary to the beliefs and practices of Christians and Jews. The Qur'an sees a parallel between "believers" and the beliefs of the "people of the book" (*ahl al-kitâb*)[12] the term for both Jews as the "people of the Torah or Tawra" and Christians as the "people

---

9. For the discussion of these terms and expressions, see Wessels, *Islam in Stories*, chapter 8, especially 181–82.

10. *EI*, s.v., *hanîf*.

11. Glassé, *The Concise Encyclopaedia of Islam*, s.v., *hanîf*.

12. Donner, *Muhammad and the Believers*, 69.

of the Gospel or *Injîl*." The three together form one community (*umma*) that unwaveringly recites God's verses (*ayât*) or signs during the night. With respect to content, one can think here of verses from the Old Testament and New Testament, or also of the Psalms (*zubur*). The first psalm of the Psalter praises as happy the human being who experiences joy in the Torah of the Lord and *recites* quietly from it day and night (Ps 1:1, 2). Among the people of the book, there is a community that attentively arises for prayer[13] and recites verses of the Qur'an at night while bowing reverently. They believe in God and in the Last Day, commend what is right, forbid what is reprehensible and "compete in good deeds."[14] They are counted among the righteous (*salihîna*). Because of the good they do, they will not be passed over—God knows those who are God-fearing (Q 3:113–115).

The Qur'an recommends that its followers enter into discussion with Jews and Christians in a good way, except for the wicked among them. "Say to them: 'We believe in what has been revealed to us, and our God and your God is one. And to Him we surrender in full trust'" (*muslimûna*) (Q 29:46). The dividing line between believers and unbelievers thus explicitly does not run parallel to the boundaries of the "people of the book" but crosses these borders, depending on the connectedness with God and adherence to the Torah.[15] All three, "Jews," "Christians," and "Muslims" are subject to the same prophetic critique—that is how Muhammad's preaching should be understood. For the believer, then, it was a matter of whether she or he had entrusted her- or himself to God and obeyed the "law," the Torah. Abraham was not a Jew or a Christian but a "seeker of God who surrendered" (*hanifan musliman*) and he was not a worshipper of many gods (Q 3:67; cf. 16:120; 2:135). That is not to say that Abraham is placed here *over against* Jews and Christians and claimed, as it were, by the "Muslims" or Islam. He is for all "three," and thus for all people, *the* model to which all three groups and thus all people always have to orient themselves. To be a true "muslim" means that, whether one calls oneself a Jew, a Christian, or "Muslim," one surrenders to the one God in words and righteous deeds.[16]

---

13. Cf. Q 22:26; 25:64; 39:9; 73:2–4.
14. Cf. Q 2:148; 5:48; 21:90; 23:61; 35:32.
15. Donner, *Muhammad and the Believers*, 69–70.
16. Donner, *Muhammad and the Believers*, 71.

THE MILITANT SIDE OF THE "MOVEMENT OF THE BELIEVERS"

Was the "movement of the believers" intent on conquering—in a militant struggle—not only the Arabic Peninsula but the whole world? Did Islam spread over a large part of the world via a *jihâd* (in the later and usually also current sense of the word)? If so, then the question is whether this was inspired by the message of the Qur'an itself. In principle, the answer to that question is no.

Here a parallel with Christianity can also be seen. After all, in the European Christian "movement of the believers," so to say, in the fourth century after Constantine the Great, the proclamation of the Christian faith became paired with imperialism and colonialism. A recent study, *The Triumph of Christianity*, describes how a forbidden religion in the Roman Empire managed to spread rapidly over the world.[17] But that is not the victory of God or Jesus Christ, but of "European Christianity." The first "Christian" emperor, Constantine, was perhaps more the successor of the emperors of the Roman Empire who crucified Jesus and the apostle Peter, the first among the twelve apostles of Jesus, and beheaded the apostle Paul, than he was of Jesus. If the number of Christians at the beginning of the fourth century was seven to ten percent of the population of the Roman Empire, at the end of that century Christians accounted for half (60 million) of the population, according to Christian tradition.[18] The price for that was paid by the Jews in the Holy Land and the Christian churches in the East. That process continued dramatically in the time of the "European Christian" crusades.

The Qur'an states the following regarding the attitude that the followers of Muhammad should take in their struggle: those believers who stay passively at home instead of fighting—other than those whose injuries rendered them unable, thus giving them a good excuse—cannot be considered equal to those *who do exert themselves on the path of God (jihâd fi sabîl Allâh)* (Q 4:95). In the Qur'an, *jihâd* had not yet developed into a doctrine about "holy war."[19] This exerting oneself sometimes meant working tirelessly to acting righteously in one's own life, but it can also mean that the believer has to try to spread the knowledge of what God has revealed. "'You shall explain it for the people, and you shall not conceal it,' / they cast it behind their backs / and sold it for a paltry gain" (Q 3:187; cf. 2:101).[20] If

---

17. Ehrman, *The Triumph of Christianity*.
18. Ehrman, *The Triumph of Christianity*, 105.
19. Donner, *Muhammad and the Believers*, 85.
20. Schmitz, *Der Koran* ,147.

one believes that believers are the best community that has arisen among humankind, then one has to actively enjoin what is good and forbid what is evil and believe in God (Q 3:110).

Other verses in the Qur'an, however, speak of taking *a more aggressive attitude*: "O Prophet! / Wage *jihād* against the faithless and the hypocrites, / and be severe with them" (Q 9:73). Indeed, they are clearly called to fight (*qitâl*): "O Prophet! / Urge on the faithful to fight" (Q 8:65; cf. 4:84). "A prophet may not take captives until he has thoroughly decimated [the enemy] [and release them in exchange for ransom] / in the land" (Q 8:67). This concerns prisoners the Muslims took in the first great battle of Muhammad at Badr (March 624). The prophet and his followers are apparently being reproached for stopping fighting too soon so that they could instead demand a great deal of ransom money.[21]

This harsh accusation against unbelief is, however, paired with mitigating clauses that soften the sharp edges and offer an opening for a more flexible approach. The best-known example can be found in the ninth chapter of the Qur'an, which is generally seen precisely as one of the most militant chapters in the whole Qur'an. It contains passages that command believers to capture the unbelievers or to put them to death by all means possible. But then the text abruptly restrains itself, as it were, and commands that the unbelievers have to be allowed to go free without any injuries as soon as they show remorse or ask the believers for protection:

> Then, when the sacred months have passed, / kill the polytheists wherever you find them, / capture them and besiege them, / and lie in wait for them at every ambush. / But if they repent, / and maintain the prayer [*salât*] and give alms [*zakat*], / then let them alone. / Indeed God is all-forgiving, all-merciful. (Q 9:5; cf. 9:11)

It is good to understand, with respect to the use of the terms "believers" and "unbelievers," that it is always a matter of *practicing* belief or not practicing it. It is not a question of *doctrine*—ortho*doxy*—but the *deed*—ortho*praxis*: whether people are just or unjust. The use of such "escape clauses," according to Fred Donner, is characteristic of the Qur'an and shows how one can be flexible in practice. On the one hand, believers have to try to force unbelievers where possible, but they must, on the other hand, not be fanatical about it. In both cases, the advice to be followed is that "leniency may ... be more effective than brute force."[22]

---

21. According to Paret, *Der Koran*, 192. Donner, *Muhammad and the Believers*, 82–83. Cf. Paret on Q 8:67–71.

22. Donner, *Muhammad and the Believers*, 83–84.

Another aspect also deserves attention. It is important to note that the Qur'an speaks of combatting *unbelievers*, not fighting Christians or Jews. The latter were, after all, "people of the book" who were viewed as monotheists and some of them were regarded, as stated, as taking part in the "movement of the believers."

Although the Qur'an does not use the expression "the kingdom of God on earth," Donner states, it sounds as if it is in fact proposing precisely that: the program for the establishment of a just political order, a society permeated by the pious regulations imposed by the Qur'an, should replace the unjust political order of the Byzantines and the Sassanid Persians, as well as those of the hostile leaders of the Quraysh tribe in Mecca. The prophet Muhammad himself belonged to the Banû Hâshim clan of the Quraysh. In the first period of his activity (610–622), before the *hijra* or Exodus to Medina, those leaders in Mecca were, according to the Qur'an, like the pharaohs of Egypt. In 624, two years after this *hijra* from Mecca to Medina, they won a glorious victory over these "Pharaonic" leaders at Badr.

The battle at Badr is often said to been caused by the fact that the Muslims had to leave their wealth in Mecca and were now attempting to retrieve it by attacking Meccan caravans. Muhammad put together an army of about 300 to intercept a caravan returning from Syria but encountered a Meccan army of almost 1000. According to tradition (Q 8:9), the angel Gabriel (Jibrîl) is said to have helped the Muslims with an army of angels.[23] In the Qur'an, the story of the Battle of Badr is clearly told with the story of the Exodus in mind (Q 8:5–18).[24] The Battle of Badr occurred in the month of Ramadan in the year 624, the second year after the *hijra* from Mecca to Medina—in the spring! The battle is fought precisely when Muhammad broke with the Jewish tribes in Medina and changed the direction of prayer (*qibla*) from Jerusalem to Mecca. Initially, the ritual prayer was performed in the direction of Jerusalem, just as Jews did when they were in a foreign country (1 Kgs 8:48 Dan 6:11). Despite the Meccans' superior numbers, the Muslims were still victorious (Q 3:123; cf. 8:26; 3:13). Thanks to that victory, Muhammad and his followers saw the justice of their cause confirmed.[25] In Mecca they were only a few, and God made them many. "And observe how was the fate of the agents of corruption" (Q 7:86). God helped them when they were insignificant in Badr (Q 3:123)! But, just as with the Exodus from Egypt, it is God who was victorious in Badr.[26]

23. https://nl.wikipedia.org/wiki/Slag_bij_Badr.
24. Neuwirth, *Studie zur Komposition der Mekkanischen Spuren*, 135.
25. *EQ*, s.v., Badr.
26. "Badr and the Exodus" in: Wessels, *The Torah, the Gospel, and the Qur'an*, 96–97.

To God belongs all dominion (Ps 103:22). The Kingdom of God[27] means the kingship, or royal dominion (Ps 103:19; 1 Chr 17:14; 28:5). There are the so-called royal psalms or royal songs, which were originally written for the ancient historical kings of Israel and Judah. They were included in the Psalter after the Babylonian exile because they were applied to the expected king from the future; they were the expression of hope for a coming king or Messiah.[28]

> All the ends of the earth shall remember
> and turn to the Lord;
> and all the families of the nations
> will bow down before him,
> for dominion belongs to the Lord,
> and he rules over the nations.
> (Ps 22:27–28)

> They tell of the glory of your kingdom
> and speak of your might,
> so that all people may know of your mighty acts
> and the glorious splendor of your kingdom.
> Your kingdom is an everlasting kingdom,
> and your dominion endures through all generations.
> (Ps 145:11–13)[29]

The book of Daniel uses apocalyptic language for the royal dominion of God: in that time the God of heaven will found a kingdom that will never be destroyed. It will crush the kingdoms that are described in the great statue Nebuchadnezzar saw in a dream (gold, bronze, iron, and clay; Dan 2:31–37) and bring them to an end. But the kingdom of God itself will always exist (Dan 2:44): God's dominion is an eternal kingdom that will never disappear; God's kingdom will never be destroyed (Dan 7:14). God's reign is eternal, and his dominion will last from generation to generation (cf. Dan 4:31; 7:14; 2 Sam 7:16). Then the kingship, the dominion, and the pomp of all those kingdoms will be given to the people of the Most High. His reign is eternal, and all powers will serve and obey him (Dan 7:27). The angel Gabriel announces the birth of Jesus to Mary in similar terms; He will reign forever over the house of Jacob and his kingdom will never end (Luke 1:33).

While in exile on Patmos, an island in the Aegean Sea, close to present-day Turkey, John sees how the seventh angel blows on the trumpet: loud

---

27. Hebrew: *malkût jahweh*; Greek: *Basileia tou theou*.
28. BW, *s.v.*, koningsliederen.
29. Cf. Dan 3:10; Ps 102:13; 1 Tim 1:17; Rev 11:15.

voices are heard in heaven that call out: "The kingdom of the world has become the kingdom of our Lord and of his Messiah, and he will reign for ever and ever" (Rev 11:15). The realization of God's dominion is announced with the blowing of the seventh trumpet, the revelation of God's decree.[30]

Although the expression "kingdom of God" may not be found in the Qur'an, the content that that expression reflects is certainly present. The Qur'an speaks explicitly of God as the king (*malik*), it is one of the names of God that is used in the Qur'an: God is exalted; he is the *true king*, the Lord of the excellent throne (Q 23:116; cf. 20:114). Did they then not form any idea of the kingship (*malakût*) of God over the heavens and the earth and the earth and all things that He created? Did they then not see that their fixed term had perhaps arrived (Q 7:185)?[31] God is the One to Whom dominion over the heavens and the earth belongs (Q 7:158; cf. Q 9:116; 57:2). God showed Abraham *the kingdom of the heavens* and the earth so that he would be one of those who believed with conviction (Q 6:75). He is promised he and Sarah would be the ancestors of kings of nations (Gen 17:6). God said to Abraham: "As for Sarai your wife, you are no longer to call her Sarai; her name will be Sarah [both names mean 'princess']. I will bless her and will surely give you a son by her. I will bless her so that she will be the mother of nations; *kings of peoples will come from her*" (Gen 17:15-16). Thus, she shall be the *mother of kings*.[32] Kings will also be among Jacob's descendants (Gen 35:11). But it is God who is and remains truly king: He is exalted and holds dominion or sovereignty over everything (Q 36:83; cf. 36:83; 7:185; 23:88).[33] This expression is equivalent to the Jewish/Christian phrase "kingdom of heaven,"[34] which also has to do with dominion over the heavens (thus of God) over the whole earth (from heaven).[35]

The prophet Muhammad inaugurated a movement of the believers, which can best be characterized as a monotheistic reformation *movement*, rather than as a new religious creed. This "movement" was convinced that the Last Judgment was imminent. The prophet Muhammad urged his hearers to concentrate on that: "And be on the alert for the day / when the caller

30. KBS on Rev 11:15.
31. *Dictionnaire du Coran*, s.v., royaume céleste.
32. KBS on Gen 17:15.
33. *EQ*, s.v., Kings and Rulers.
34. It seems incorrect to say that Muhammad did not understand the meaning of that phrase. Cf. Paret on Q 6:75. pp. 144-45. He derives this view from W. Ahrens, *Muhammad als Religionsstifter* (Leipzig, 1935), 33, cited in: Speyer, Die biblischen Erzählungen, 166, n. 1. He incorrectly concludes that Muhammad would have understood it as dominion over the heavens.
35. Jeffery, *The Foreign Vocabulary of the Qur'an*, 270-71.

calls from a close quarter, / the day when they hear the Cry in all truth. / That is the day of rising [from the dead]" (Q 50:41–42). That is the day when the trumpet shall sound (Q 50:20), the day of eternity (Q 50:34; cf. 64:9; 11:103).

The Meccans are referred to what happened in earlier times when God sent messengers to the various peoples and to the judgment that was imposed on unbelievers. They are reminded of the preaching of, for example, Noah and how Sodom and Gomorrah were "overthrown," as the Qur'an refers to the event, the cities to which Lot brought God's message (Q 11:25–49; 77–83). The Meccans did ask Muhammad *when the judgment would come*, but they were given the same answer that Jesus' disciples were given: "It is not for you to know the times or dates" (Acts 1:7; cf. Matt 24: 36). Only God knows the time and the hour (Q 67:25–26). But even though Muhammad could not give any answer to the question of *when*, he announced all the more emphatically that the judgment is coming and is near: "Indeed what you are promised is true, / and indeed the judgment will surely come to pass!" (Q 51:5–6). It is presupposed that Muhammad still thought after the *hijra* in 622 that there was a possibility of judgment for Mecca: after all, "How many a town there has been / which was more powerful than your town / which expelled you, / which We have destroyed, / and they had no helper" (Q 47:13).[36] The believers do not have to be afraid of that day: God sent the emissaries only as messengers and to issue warnings; those who believe and do what is right do not have to fear the Last Judgment and they will not be sad (after the judgment on the Last Day). But those who declare God's signs to be lies will be punished for what they have done during their lives (Q 6:48–49; cf. 46:12; 10:63).[37]

This "movement of the believers" felt surrounded by corruption and sin. It strove to develop into a just community so that it would be spared on that day. The early believers would have felt that they were standing on the verge of a period of great events that would lead to the Last Day. One of these events would be their conquest and the establishment of their hegemony over political powers that surrounded them. "Thus they would inherit the Earth and establish in it a righteous, God-guided community that could lead humanity to salvation when the Judgment scenario reached its culmination."[38]

---

36. Paret assumes this; cf. Paret, *Mohammed und der Koran*, 88.
37. Attema, *De Koran*, 1962, 55–56.
38. Donner, *Muhammad and the Believers*, 88.

MUHAMMAD'S RELATIONSHIP WITH THE JEWS

What kind of relationship did Muhammad have with the Jews of his time? A few months after the *hijra* to Medina in 622, a treaty called "the Constitution of Medina" was concluded between the "Muslim" emigrants (*muhajirûn*) from Mecca and the two Arab tribes, together with three Jews from Yathrib. That city would later be called Medina, the city of the prophet Muhammad. The one Arab tribe was al-Aws and the other was al-Kharâj. Both tribes were referred to now as the so-called helpers, *ansâr*, who, together with the Muslim emigrants who accompanied Muhammad from Mecca (Q 9:100; 118), constituted the heart of the first Muslim community. Jesus' disciples and apostles are also called "helpers," *ansâr* (Q 3:52). (The term also calls to mind the word for Christians, *nasârâ*).[39] That treaty concerned mutual security,[40] but serious conflicts arose soon thereafter.

What is important now is the question of what is true and what is fantasy with respect to the relation of the "Muslims" to the "Jews" in Muhammad's lifetime, how what the Qur'an says about that must be understood. Donner asserts that later conflicts with the Jews in history that arose have been projected back into Muhammad's time as *religious* conflicts. He considers it important that these tribes are nowhere mentioned by name in the Qur'an. He wonders if they no longer existed. Or should we conclude that the stories about the clashes with the Jews of Medina were exaggerated or even completely invented by later tradition, perhaps to portray Muhammad as a prophet who had to stubbornly resist the Jews?

The later tradition does mention a number of believers from the time of Muhammad who were originally Jews, i.e., they are described as "converts'" from Judaism to "Islam." One could wonder, according to Donner, whether these so-called "converts" were simply Jews who joined the "movement of the believers" without giving up Judaism and were only later seen as "converts."[41] The "movement of the believers" was, after all, open to pious, God-fearing monotheists from other faiths, Jews or Christians. That is why we will now look at an adjustment of the classical perceptions of what happened in different periods, particularly during the life of the prophet Muhammad himself.

Three Jewish tribes lived in Medina at that time: the Banû Qaynuqa, the Banû al-Nadîr, and the Banû al-Qurayza. Despite the treaty with them, the Jews were banned from the city of Medina, and—in the case of the Banû

---

39. Paret on 3:52; cf. Q 64:14.

40. Glassé, *The Concise Encyclopaedia of Islam*, s.v., "Constitution of Medina"; cf. Wensinck, *Mohammed en de Joden in Medina*.

41. Donner, *Muhammad and the Believers*, 73-74.

Qurayza—their expulsion was dramatic. After the battle and victory by the Muslims at Badr in 624, Muhammad's relationship with the Jews in Medina encountered difficulties, and they began to take a hostile attitude toward Muhammad and to form a political danger. The Banû Qaynuqa lived in the city itself, in the southwest section. Some members of their tribe were goldsmiths. When they were expelled, they had to leave weapons and tools behind. The exile is sometimes said to have been caused by a Jewish woman mocking a Muslim; at other times it is claimed that it was because the tribe became arrogant. If treason was feared, the treaty was clearly cancelled (Q 8:58).[42]

The Banû al-Nadîr tribe had moved to Yathrib from Palestine fleeing Roman suppression of the Jewish revolts. The first failed Jewish rebellion began in the year 66, and the second took place from 132 to 136 under the leadership of Bar Kochba. The latter was seen as a Messiah, and it was expected that he would reestablish Israel as a nation state. He succeeded to some extent for a short time until the Romans put down the rebellion. The war contributed to a definitive schism between Jews and Christians because the latter saw Jesus as the Messiah. The influential rabbi Akiva declared that he believed that Bar Kochba was possibly the Messiah, basing this on the text: "A star will come out of Jacob; a scepter will rise out of Israel" (Num 24:17; cf. Rev 21:28; 12:16). The name Bar Kochba means "son of a star" (in Aramaic). When the uprising was put down mercilessly and he turned out not to be the promised Messiah, he became popularly known among Jews as "Bar Koziba"—the "son of false hope."[43]

Some members of an Arab tribe converted to Judaism and settled on the old mountain al-Nadîr, which accounts for their name. This Jewish tribe was associated with the Jews at the oasis of Khaybar. A number of them had an Arabic background, like many other Jews from Medina, and had Arabic names. They earned their living from farming, money-lending, and trade in weapons and jewels.

Before the Battle of Uhud (625), where the Muslims suffered a major defeat against the Meccans, the Banû al-Nadîr had contacts with the Meccan leader Abû Sufyân. Because of difficulties that Muhammad encountered with the tribe on the payment of blood money, he became convinced of their hostile attitude and suspected them of intending to kill him. That is why he ordered the tribe to leave the city. They were allowed to take all movable property with them and even to return to pick the products of their palm orchards. When they showed resistance, however, they were besieged

---

42. SEI, s.v., Kainukâ; Paret op Q 8:58.
43. https://en.wikipedia.org/wiki/Bar_Kokhba_revolt.

for 14 days and surrendered when the "Muslims" began to chop down their palm trees. The conditions were now harsher, and the tribe left with 600 camels. Some went to Khaybar, a famous oasis 150 km from Medina; others went to Syria.[44]

In Muhammad's time, the Khaybar population consisted of Jewish Hebraized tribes. Their departure from Palestine and emigration to Khaybar brought a large number to the more fruitful regions of North Arabia. The emigration probably began after the destruction of Jerusalem but continued because of the continued persecution of the Jews in Palestine.[45]

The Banû Qurayza suffered the most dramatic fate. It is thought that Muhammad concluded a general agreement with the Jews that they would not offer any support to the Meccan enemies. In 627 Meccans laid siege to the city of Medina. This became the "Battle of the Trench [al-Khandaq]" because of the trench that the inhabitants of Medina dug north of the city to protect themselves and fend off the attack. In contrast to all other sides, the northern side was not protected by fortifications. Although the Meccans had a much larger army, they were not able to break through the defenses (Q 33:9–32).[46]

Although it is held that the Banû Qurayza did not engage in any open hostilities, the tribe was allegedly involved in negotiations with the enemy, Mecca. Soon after the Meccan siege had been lifted, the tribe was attacked by Muhammad and his followers and besieged for 25 days in their forts. The Qur'an summarizes the events as follows:

> And He dragged down those who had backed them / from among the People of the Book / from their strongholds, / and He cast terror into their hearts, / [so that] you killed a part of them, / and took captive [another] part of them. / And He bequeathed you their land, / their houses and their possessions. (Q 33:26–27)

The prophet Muhammad put the ultimate decision about their fate in the hands of Sa'd b. Mû'âdh, one of the strongest men in the al-Aws tribe and the most important of the "helpers." He had fought on Muhammad's side at the Battle of Badr in 624 and encouraged many others to take part. During the battle, he took special measures to guarantee Muhammad's safety. When the Meccans laid siege to Medina in this Battle of the Trench three years later, the Banû Qurayza tribe was secretly involved in talks with the enemy.

---

44. *SEI*, s.v., Nadîr.
45. *EI*, s.v., Khaybar.
46. https://en.wikipedia.org/wiki/Battle_of_the_Trench.

When the Meccans raised the siege, Muhammad immediately attacked the Jewish tribe, and it was forced to surrender unconditionally.

Sa'd ibn Mu'âdh had been fatally wounded by an arrow during the battle, however, and would die soon after. Nonetheless, the decision about the fate of the Banû Qurayza was left to him because he was the leader of the al-Aws tribe and various sections of that tribe were associated precisely with the Banû Qurayza. Sa'd decided that all men would be killed, 800 in all (!), and the women and children sold as slaves. Muhammad was given one of the women, Rayhana, and married her as a concubine.[47] Sa'd obviously understood that his decision entailed that the connection with the "Islamic" communities was more important than tribal or clan alliances. Shortly after his decision, the severely wounded Sa'd died. It seemed that Muhammad felt this loss deeply, given that he had done more than the other "helpers" to safeguard the growth of the community.[48]

Muhammad's appointment of Sa'd as arbitrator is often considered debatable, precisely because he had been fatally wounded. To make this decision understandable and to "assess" it, it would be well to realize that Muhammad was very seriously threatened by the breach of contract committed by the Banû Qurayza. If the Meccan hostilities had grown into a direct attack on Medina, that would have meant the coup de grace for Muhammad. Together with the Banû Nadîr in Khaybar, where this tribe had earlier found refuge, they would have formed a constant danger for him if the male members of the tribe had not been killed. That is the reasoning here.[49] Muhammad had to be wary of them. "All of that has to be noted if one does merely want to judge and condemn Muhammad's acts but also be attentive to the context in which they occurred," Arent Jan Wensinck says.[50]

Regarding the fate that fell to the Banû Qurayza, it has indeed been argued that comparable examples can be found in the Bible in which "the Jewish law" prescribes such actions, such as after the conquest of a city, even if treason is not at issue. A modern Islamic commentary on the Qur'an connects this with the presupposition that the judgment by Sa'd b. Mu'âdh on the Qurayza is expressed in this way because the tribe was condemned by their own (Jewish) law with a reference to Deuteronomy:

> If they refuse to make peace and they engage you in battle, lay siege to that city. When the Lord your God delivers it into your hand,

---

47. *EI*, s.v., Kurayza; cf. Guillaume, *The Life of Muhammad*: 461–469.
48. *EI*, s.v., 'Sa'd b. Mu'âdh.'
49. Watt, "The Condemnation of the Jews of the Banû Qurayzah."
50. Wensinck, "Mohammed und das Judentum," 289; Wessels, *A Modern Arabic Biography of Muhammad*, 184–85.

put to the sword all the men in it. As for the women, the children, the livestock and everything else in the city, you may take these as plunder for yourselves. And you may use the plunder the Lord your God gives you from your enemies. (Deut 20:12–14)[51]

This explanation or assumption reports no single source, however, and thus it seems very improbable that it can be found in any older "Muslim" source. The question is then if this explains the citation from the book of Deuteronomy. Israelite men would make women taken prisoner from a far distant city their wives (Deut 21:10–14). The killing of adult men is an extreme measure, and we do not know to what extent this mandate was carried out, a contemporary commentator says.[52] But, to put it mildly, these interpretations—however they are framed—still leave one feeling uncomfortable. Muslim exegetes are also uncomfortable with what happened to the Qurayza tribe. It is still a shocking liquidation.

One can still ask, in my view, if Donner is completely right when he claims that later conflicts with the Jews have been read back into the Qur'an. His conclusion, however, that these Qur'anic texts that are critical of the Jews should not be seen as a condemnation of all Jews or Judaism as such is important and correct. It is important to note that this judgment is nevertheless made on a large scale by "radical" Muslims!

Given that some Jews participated in the "movement of the believers," one can conclude, according to Donner, that the clashes with other Jews or groups of Jews were the result of attitudes or political actions on their part, such as refusing Muhammad's leadership or the denial that he was a prophet. But they cannot, in Donner's view, be taken as evidence of a general hostility towards Judaism in the "movement of the believers."[53]

The criteria that are the basis for making judgments in the Qur'an are clear and plain: belief in one God and *acting justly*. These criteria are directed at all three—Jew, Christian, and Muslim—in fact, to all people. These groups are constantly reminded of that when they all take their holy Scriptures seriously.

---

51. Glassé, *The Concise Encyclopaedia of Islam*, s.v., Qurayza.
52. Lundbom, *Deuteronomy*, 587, on Deut 20:13–14.
53. Donner, *Muhammad and the Believers*, 74.

THE MUSLIM VIEW OF THE JEWS' "PROMISED LAND"

The modern classical Arabic biography of the prophet Muhammad was written by the Egyptian writer, Muhammad Husayn Haykal.[54] In his *The Life of Muhammad* he writes in various contexts about the Jews and their desire for a national home. He relates how the Jews welcomed Muhammad warmly in Medina in the hope that the he would help unite the peninsula against Christianity, which was the reason for their banishment from Palestine, the land of promise, their national fatherland.[55] Speaking of the Banû Qaynuqâ, one of the three Jewish tribes that were banished from Medina and then settled on the Syrian border, Haykal comments that perhaps only the promised land, which attracted and still attracts the hearts of the Jews, drew them northward.[56] With respect to the other Jewish tribe, the Banû al-Nadîr, he wonders: "Would they then leave him [Muhammad] alone and return to their previous abodes in al-Sham (Syria) and in the promised land of Jerusalem?"[57] Haykal notes that Jesus was a Jew and that the Jews initially thought that he was the expected prophet who would "return to the Jews their lost kingdom in the promised land."[58]

What this important "modern" biographer thinks of the Jewish desire becomes clear when he discusses the occupation of Jerusalem by General Edmund Allenby of the British army in 1917, during the First World War. On 11 December, Allenby entered the Old City through the Jaffa Gate on foot, instead of by horse or motorized vehicle, to show respect for the holy city. He was the first Christian in many centuries to control Jerusalem, a city deemed holy by three great religions. The Prime Minister of the United Kingdom, David Lloyd George, described the capture as "a Christmas present for the British people." The battle was a great morale boost for the British Empire.[59] Haykal comments. "And it may even be true to say that the capture of Jerusalem was not a purely Christian effort, but that it was equally the effort of the Jews, who used the Christians so that they could realize the old diaspora dream of making the Land of Promise a national home for the Jews."[60]

Haykal's reflections—first as a feuilleton in 1920 and then in 1935 as a book—make it clear that he had an eye for and expresses no objection at all

---

54. Haykal, *Life of Muhammad*.
55. Haykal, *Life of Muhammad*, 234–35.
56. Haykal, *Life of Muhammad*, 298.
57. Haykal, *Life of Muhammad*, 342.
58. Haykal, *Life of Muhammad*, 589.
59. https://en.wikipedia.org/wiki/Battle_of_Jerusalem.
60. Haykal, *Life of Muhammad*, 596.

to the desire of the Jews for Palestine.⁶¹ He does object elsewhere, however, to the *political* realization of that dream as the foundation of the state of Israel and the proposed plan of partition: he felt that it was a regression on the part of humankind to the centuries of religious fanaticism and the crusades.⁶² It should be noted that Western colonialism was still in its heyday at this time.

MUHAMMAD SENT TO THE PEOPLES

Just as Paul is called the apostle of the Gentiles, so Muhammad is called the apostle for all peoples: *the illiterate prophet (al-nabi al ummî)* (Q 7:158). The Arabic expression *al-nabî al-ummî* is usually translated in such a way as to say that Muhammad could not read and write. This "fact" is then cited as evidence for the "miracle of the Qur'an," which was sent to a prophet who was illiterate! It is considered improbable, however, that Muhammad was indeed illiterate. In fact, the expression is intended to say something entirely different, namely, that he was the prophet for the "unlettered," those who had not yet received a book, a revelation. God sent to the peoples a messenger from among themselves to recite his (God's) revelation. Thus, the word *ummî* does not refer to his lack of ability to read or write but to those with a fragmentary or a complete lack knowledge of holy scriptures (cf. Q 2:78).⁶³ The expression probably goes back to the Hebrew *ummôt hâ-'ôlâm*, which means the "peoples of the world."⁶⁴ In contrast to Jews and Christians, the "people of the book," i.e., the *Tawra* and the *Injîl* respectively, these "peoples" did not have any book. Muhammad appeared now as a prophet for those who had not yet received any book of revelation. Thus, he is the prophet for the "unlettered."

Muhammad is the messenger, the "unlettered" prophet, who is described in the Torah and the Gospel in the Old and New Testaments (Q 7:157). Moses said: "I [Yahweh] will raise up for them a prophet like you [Moses] [cf. Num 12:6–8; Deut 34:10–12] from among their fellow Israelites, and I will put my words in his mouth" (Deut 18:15, 18).⁶⁵ This was applied earlier to Jesus—who also needs to be listened to (Mark 9:7; cf. 1:17, 21; 12:49–50; John 16:14, 26)— and here it is applied to the prophet Muhammed. This prophet Muhammad enjoins what is right and forbids what is wrong. He will make all good things

---

61. Wessels, *A Modern Arabic Biography of Muhammad*, 185–86.

62. Johansen and Haikal, *Europa und der Orient im Weltbild eines Ägyptischen Liberalen*, 223–24.

63. *SEI*, *s.v.*, *ummî*.

64. Paret on Q 2:78.p. 22; Watt, *Bell's Introduction*, 34.

65. KBS on Deut 18:15.

lawful for them and prohibit what is reprehensible. *He will relieve them of the burden and the fetters they used to wear*. Those who believe in him, and honor him, and give him help and *follow the light* that is sent down with him will prosper (Q 7:157). The Torah is called right guidance and *light* (Q 5:44; cf. 64:8; 4:174; 5:15; 42:52): "Your word is a lamp for my feet, a light on my path" (Ps 119:105; cf. Ps. 18:29; Job 29:3; Prov 6:23).[66] The Gospel, *Injîl*, is also called light (Q 5:46), and so is the Qur'an (Q 5:15; 42:52). God revealed the Qur'an to Muhammad as a confirmation of the Torah and the Gospel, as a guide for people (Q 3:3-4). The psalmist prays:

> Send me your light and your faithful care,
> let them lead me;
> let them bring me to your holy mountain,
> to the place where you dwell.
> (Ps 43:3)

Muhammad received "the *complete Scripture*" (*al-kitâba tamâman*). The significance of this agrees closely with what is said in Psalm 19:

> The law of the Lord is perfect,
> refreshing the soul.[67]
> The statutes of the Lord are trustworthy,
> making wise the simple.
> The precepts of the Lord are right,
> giving joy to the heart.
> The commands of the Lord are radiant,
> giving light to the eyes
> (Ps 19:7-8)[68]

In connection with the *burdens and fetters* the Qur'an talks about (Q 7:176), we should think of what Jesus says about the scribes and the Pharisees who put together impossibly heavy burdens and laid them on people's shoulders, while they themselves could not be bothered to lift a finger (Matt 23:4; cf. Luke 11:46).

At the assembly in Jerusalem, the so-called Council of Jerusalem, where the most prominent apostles, Peter and Paul, were present, the relation between the followers of Jesus among the Jews and those among the Gentiles was discussed. Peter declared: "[God] did not discriminate between

---

66. This comparison of the Torah with light has become so usual in the Jewish traditional literature that wherever it appears in the Old Testament, Jewish teaching can be understood by it. Speyer, *Die biblischen Erzählungen*, 297.

67. The whole human person; KBS on Ps 19:8.

68. Speyer, *Die biblischen Erzählungen*, 297.

us and them, for he purified their hearts by faith. Now then, why do you try to test God by putting on the necks of Gentiles a *yoke* that neither we nor our ancestors have been able to bear?" (Acts 15:10). Paul tells the church in Galatia in Asia Minor not to burden themselves with a *yoke of slavery* again (Gal 5:1; cf. John 8:36). The message that Jesus brought obtains equally for Jews and the peoples: "Come to me, all you who are weary and burdened, and I will give you rest. Take my yoke upon you and learn from me, for I am gentle and humble in heart, and you will find rest for your souls. For my yoke is easy and my burden is light" (Matt 11:28–30). This call is again a confirmation of the Tanakh: "[A]sk where the good way is, and walk in it, and you will find rest for your souls" (Jer 6:16). The Lord of hosts says: "I will refresh the weary and satisfy the faint" (Jer 31:25).

THE HEAVENLY JOURNEYS OF THE MESSENGERS PAUL AND MUHAMMAD

A parallel can be drawn between Paul and Muhammad. Both are called apostles,[69] and both undergo a heavenly journey. Muhammad is explicitly also called an apostle, messenger, or emissary of God (Q 7:158; 48:29). The term is usually used for Jesus' twelve disciples and for Paul because they were personally called by Jesus and given the commission to be witnesses to Jesus' life and work (Acts 1:21–22). Paul puts a great deal of importance on proving that he was called by Jesus himself (1 Cor 9).[70]

The Qur'anic word *rasûl* means apostle, emissary, or messenger. Examples of emissaries are Noah (Q 7:59), Ishmael (Q 19:54), Moses (Q 37:114), Elijah (Q 37:123), and Jonah (Q 37:139). Shu'aib is sent to Madyan, Hûd to the people of 'Ad, Salîh to the Thamûd. Jesus is also a messenger (Q 61:6; 4:171). He has the help of his disciples, his apostles (Q 3: 52,53; 61:14). The close relation the emissary has to a people is often compared to the twelve apostles, who divided the whole world among themselves so that each had the task of preaching the Gospel to a certain people.[71] God has sent an emissary, a messenger to *each* human community (*umma*) (Q 10:47; 16:36; cf. 23:44; 40:5). Muhammad was sent to a people—the Meccans—where no messenger had been sent before (Q 28:46; 32:3; 34:44). The task of the messengers is both to proclaim the good news and to warn (Q

---

69. Rom 1:1. Cf. 1 Cor 1:1; 9:1–6; 15:9–11; Gal 1:1,11–19; 2:6–9; Acts 9:1–19; 22:3–21; 26:9–20.

70. *Bijbelse Encyclopaedie*, s.v., apostel.

71. *Acta apostolorum apocrypha*. EI, s.v., rasûl.

18:56; cf. 4:65).⁷² Muhammad's mission also extends to all inhabitants of the world: God has sent him as a sign of mercy for the whole of humanity (Q 21:107). Does this not make him an expression of the God who *has made mercy incumbent upon himself*? (Q 6:12; cf. Q 6:54).

After many years of preaching, Paul himself referred to an experience that happened to him when he was on the road to Damascus in the year 42, before his great missionary journeys:⁷³ "[L]ast of all he [Jesus] appeared to me also . . .. For I am the least of the apostles and do not even deserve to be called an apostle [as the least of all the Lord's people" (Eph 3:8)]; the worst of all sinners [1 Tim 1:15], ". . . for I persecuted the congregation of God [1 Cor 15:9]." Paul saw this experience as the last of the appearances of the risen Lord to the early disciples of Jesus (1 Cor 15:5–17).⁷⁴

Paul himself exercises great restraint when writing about his own visionary experience in the third person as if it concerned someone else. He writes as follows about the ecstatic visions or revelations that he received:

> I know a man in Christ who fourteen years ago was caught up to the third heaven. Whether it was in the body or out of the body I do not know—God knows. And I know that this man—whether in the body or apart from the body I do not know, but God knows—was caught up to paradise and heard inexpressible things, things that no one is permitted to tell.⁷⁵ I will boast about a man like that, but I will not *boast* about myself, except about my *weaknesses*. Even if I should choose to boast, I would not be a fool, because I would be speaking the truth. But I refrain, so no one will think more of me than is warranted by what I do or say, or because of these surpassingly great revelations. Therefore, in order to keep me from becoming conceited, I was given a thorn in my flesh, a messenger of Satan, to torment me. Three times I pleaded with the Lord to take it away from me. But he said to me, "My grace is sufficient for you, *for my power is made perfect in weakness.*" Therefore I will boast all the more gladly about my weaknesses, so that Christ's power may rest on me. (2 Cor 12:2–10)⁷⁶

---

72. *EQ, s.v.,* Messenger.
73. We will come back to this in chapter VII.
74. Terrien, *The Elusive Presence.* 434.
75. KBS on 1 Cor 12:2–4. Augustine and Thomas Aquinas thought that he had been temporarily and in passing granted the vision of God. Cf. Moses (Exod 33:11, 18–23), Elijah (1 Kgs 19), and Isaiah (Isa 6:5).
76. Cf. "Now I rejoice in what I am suffering for you, and I fill up in my flesh what is still lacking in regard to Christ's afflictions, for the sake of his body, which is the church" (Col. 1:24; cf. 2 Cor 2:10). Any italics found in the biblical texts are my own.

Paul is speaking here in the spirit of the prophet Jeremiah whom he often cites.[77] Various parallels between Jeremiah, Paul, and Muhammad can be discovered.

> "Let not the wise boast of their wisdom,
>   or the strong boast of their strength
>   or the rich boast of their riches,
> but let the one who boasts boast about this:
>   that they have the understanding to know me,
>   that I am the Lord, who exercises kindness,
>   justice and righteousness on earth,
>   for in these I delight,"
>   declares the Lord.
> (Jer 9:23–24)

These two key words, *justice and righteousness*, contain everything that the just world order requires.[78]

Muhammad's night journey and heavenly journey occurred in 621, one year before the emigration from Mecca to Medina. The *surah* called "Night Journey" begins as follows: "Praised be God who had His Servant [Muhammad] journey at night from the sacred place of prayer [the Ka'ba in Mecca] to the most distant place of prayer—in Jerusalem—whose precincts We have blessed" (Q 17:1; cf. Q 18:80; 48:27). The original Arabic speaks, respectively, of *al-masajid al-harâm* and *masajid al-Aqsâ*. *Masajid*, which is now translated as mosque, did not yet have that meaning in the Qur'an. A mosque was later built on the Temple Mount that came to be called the "farthest mosque," the *Al Aqsâ* Mosque.

Later accounts of the heavenly journey, which do not appear in the Qur'an, speak of a dialogue that occurs between Muhammad and God on the high point of the journey. Having arrived at that "station," Muhammad pleads for God's forgiveness and mercy for the Muslim community, an act that receives a special significance. Muhammad is able to act as mediator (*shafaʿa*). The content of the conversation, which occurs at the end of the second *surah* is said to have already been given in heaven by God before it was revealed on earth, in Mecca. This dialogue is seen as part of a divine conversation in the stories of the heavenly journey.[79]

> Our Lord, do not punish us if we are forgetful or fall into error.
> Our Lord, do not lay upon us a heavy burden,

77. Cf. 1 Cor 1:31; 2 Cor 10:17; Gal 6:14.

78. KBS on Jer 9:23.

79. Colby, *Narrating Muhammad's Night Journey*, 24, n. 34. These verses are thought to be additions, Meccan verses, to a *surah* that was revealed in Medina.

> as You laid upon those who became before us.
> Our Lord, do not lay upon us what we have no power to bear.
> Pardon us, forgive us, be merciful towards us.
> You are our Patron, so grant us Your support against the impious.
> (Q 2:286; cf. Q 23:62; 2:233, 236)

Are there connections between the heavenly signs and the prophetic or visionary revelations, and can that be the reason that the Muslim stories use these images for their heavenly journey? Frederik S. Colby considers that an intriguing question in particular in light of the *surah* of the Star (Q 53:1–18):[80]

> By the star when it sets:
> your companion has neither gone astray,
> nor gone amiss.
> Nor does he speak out of [his own] desire:
> it is just a revelation that is revealed [to him],
> taught him by One of great powers,[81]
> possessed of sound judgement.
> He settled,
> while he was on the highest horizon.
> Then he drew nearer and nearer[82]
> until he was within two bows' length or even nearer,
> whereat He revealed to His servant
> whatever He revealed.
> The heart did not deny what it saw.
> Will you then dispute with him about what he saw?
> (Q 53:1–12)

This is followed immediately by a story about a second revelation:

> Certainly he saw it yet another time,
> by the Lote Tree of the Ultimate Boundary,
> near which is the Garden of the Abode,
> when there covered the Lote Tree what covered it.
> The gaze did not swerve,
> nor did it overstep the bounds.
> Certainly he saw
> some of the greatest signs of his Lord.

---

80. Colby, *Narrating Muhammad's Night Journey*, 17.
81. Cf. Q 81:19–20.
82. "And indeed, he [Muhammad] saw him [Gabriel] on the clear horizon. And he [Muhammad] does not keep anything back about what was revealed" (Q 81:23–24); cf. Wessels, *A Stranger is Calling*, index "hidden," "hiddenness."

(Q 53:13–18)[83]

One tradition speaks in detail about the heavenly journey. After Muhammad met Abraham in the seventh heaven in the company of Gabriel, he went as far as the lotus tree at the furthest border. No one could go further, and there he saw God's Glory, one of the greatest signs of his Lord.[84] There is an intriguing parallel on the one hand between the idea of God's *descent* onto the lotus tree, where he addresses Muhammad and, on the other, the scene of God's revelation to Moses in the burning bush (Exod 3).[85]

MUHAMMAD'S VISIT TO THE TWO CITIES

In some accounts of the night journey of the prophet, it is said that Muhammad visited the two cities at the end of the earth, which are called Jabalqa and Jabarsa.[86] The name Jabalqa can be read as the "mountain" (*Jabal*) Qâf. Sometimes, Qâf refers to the northern limits, especially the Caucasus and the mountains of northern Persia.[87] Qâf also emphasizes the close connection between the mountain and the Garden of Eden (Q 9:72; 13:23; 16:31; 19:61; 20:76; 35:33; 38:50; 40:8; 61:12; 98:8). It symbolizes not only paradise on earth but also the physical relation between earth and heaven.[88] Jabalq lies in the extreme West at the outermost end of the earth.[89] The Arab geographer Yâqut describes Qâf as the mountain *that encompasses and surrounds the earth*. All the mountains in the world owe their existence to Qâf.[90]

Jabal Qâf is mentioned in the Qur'an, or at least indicated by the letter Q at the beginning of the fiftieth *surah* (Q 50). *Surahs* sometimes begin with individual Arabic letters, for which there is no clear explanation: "Only God knows what the letters mean."[91] This mountain is called the world mountain, which is identified with world mountains in other traditions.[92] According to

---

83. Colby, *Narrating Muhammad's Night Journey*, 19.

84. *EI*, s.v., Sidrat al-Muntahâ; Colby, *Narrating Muhammad's Night Journey*, 21.

85. Colby, *Narrating Muhammad's Night Journey*, 244, n. 24.

86. Noegel and Wheeler, *The A to Z of Prophets in Islam and Judaism*, s.v., Jabal Sin, Jabal Qaf.

87. Qâf also plays a role in *A Thousand and One Nights*; *EI*, s.v., Kâf.

88. Wheeler, *Moses in the Qur'an and Islamic Exegesis*, 97.

89. Noegel and Wheeler, *The A to Z of Prophets in Islam and Judaism*, s.v., Jabal Sin.

90. Noegel and Wheeler, *The A to Z of Prophets in Islam and Judaism*, s.v., Jabal Qaf.

91. Jalâlayn; cf. Kramer's translation.

92. In the ancient world as a whole, mountains were associated with "God." In Ugarit, the god Baal lived on Mt. Zaphon, and for the Greeks Zeus lived on Mt. Olympus. Cf. Noegel and Wheeler, *The A to Z of Prophets in Islam and Judaism*, s.v., Mountains.

many creation myths, God created the "mountain" of the Ka'ba out of five mountains: each of which is associated with a prophetic figure:

- *Sinai,* where God revealed himself to Moses (Exod 31:1; 33:18–23; Q 95:4; cf. Q 23:20) and Elijah (1 Kgs 19:8);
- *Mount Lebanon* from which King Solomon got the cedar wood for building the temple (1 Kgs 5:16–20; 7:2–12; cf. Ezra 3:7).
- *Mount Judi* as the place where Noah's ark came to rest after the Flood; paradise is located at the foot of the mountain![93] According to the Bible, Noah's ark came to rest on Mount Ararat in Armenia after the flood (Gen 8:4; cf. 2 Kgs 19:37). Then it was said: "O earth, swallow your water! / O sky, leave off!' / The waters receded; / the edict was carried out, / and it settled on [Mount] Judi" (Q 11:44).[94]
- There are numerous connections made between the *Mount of Olives* and Jesus, such as the eschatological discourse he held there about the end times (Mark 13:3; Matt 24:3).
- *Mount Hira* near Mecca, also called "the mountain of light" (*Jabal al-Nûr*). Muhammad withdrew to the top of this mountain to meditate, where there was just room enough to perform the ritual prayer. One of his daughters brought him food so that he could stay for a month in the cave without interruption (cf. Elijah on Horeb; 1 Kgs 19: 9, 13). There Muhammad received the first revelation (Q 97) on one of the last odd days of the month of Ramadan, during the night of destiny or decision (*laylat al-Qadr*) (Q 97).[95]

These mountains are not mentioned so much to provide geographical indicators as they are used as places for *revelation* and *instruction*. The place of the so-called "Sermon on the Mount" is a typical example of this:[96] when the disciples saw Jesus ascend the mountain and sit down, they came to him, and he began to *teach* them (Matt 5:1–2; cf. Matt 15:29; 17:1; 24:3; 28:16). Jesus' teaching consisted largely of giving a new, contemporary meaning to the tradition, similar to what was done in Jewish *study houses* at the time.[97]

---

93. Korpel and de Moor, *Adam, Eva en de duivel*.
94. *EI*, s.v., Djûdï.
95. Glassé, *The Concise Encyclopaedia of Islam*, s.v., Hira; KBS on 1 Kgs 19:8; Noegel and Wheeler, *The A to Z of Prophets in Islam and Judaism*, s.v., mountain; Wheeler, *Moses in the Qur'an and Islamic Exegesis*, 110. Mount Tabor, the mountain of the transfiguration, is also mentioned (Matt 17:1–8; Mark 9:2–9; Luke 9:28–36).
96. Just as in the New Testament; cf. KBS on Matt 4:1; cf. Isa 2:2–3; Matt 14:23.
97. KBS on Matt 5:1.

Jesus' teaching is an *aggiornamento*, bringing the meaning of the Torah up to date; he himself was the *fulfilment* (Matt 5:17) or *confirmation* of that Torah, as the Qur'an also attests (Q 3:50; 5:46; 61:6).

According to the tradition, the prophet Muhammad reaches the throne of God during his night journey and heavenly journey to the highest heavenly sphere and is shown paradise and hell. He is then transported by the angel Gabriel to the edge of the world in order to visit the Jews who live in the mythical cities of Jâbalqa and Jâbars on Mount Qâf.[98] These cities, which lie respectively on the eastern and northern sides of the mountain, are described as being of monumental proportions with a thousand gates each and each gate separated by a mile. The houses of the Jews are all described as being equally high and located far from their houses of prayer, while their cemeteries are close by. When Muhammad asks about the identity of these people, the angel Gabriel informs him that they are "of the people of Moses." They are also called "the righteous people" (*qawm-i.sâlih*) or the Jewish proto-Muslims.[99]

THE PEOPLE OF MOSES

During his night journey, Muhammad visited those who were left of *the people of Moses* (*qawm Mûsâ*).[100] After he has been introduced to them, he asks them a series of questions. In answer to the question why their houses were all on the same level, they answer that it was because there was neither envy nor pride among them.[101] To the question why the places of prayer were *far away* and the cemeteries *close by*, they answered: because the reward was greater for their work in getting to the houses of prayer and because they were always reminded of their mortality through the closeness of the graves. After they had assured Muhammad that they performed the prayers and honored their parents, the Jews asked him for advice. Muhammad urged them to fear God and not be proud, to obey the commandments. The Jews accepted Muhammad's words. It then ends as follows: "They all accepted [me]. They *expressed* their *faith*."[102]

Another version of the story describes it in this way. Muhammad visits a righteous people in these two cities: "Among *the people of Moses* is a nation

---

98. Noegel and Wheeler, *The A to Z of Prophets in Islam and Judaism*, s.v, Jabal Q.

99. Colby, *The Prophet's Ascension*, 59–60.

100. Noegel and Wheeler, *The A to Z of Prophets in Islam and Judaism*, s.v., Jabal Sin.

101. Colby, *The Prophet's Ascension*, 59.

102. Colby, *The Prophet's Ascension*, 59–60. In my view, Colby's addition of "in Islam" in brackets after "faith" is not correct. It is a question of faith per se.

/ who guide [the people] by the truth / and do justice thereby" (Q 7:159). Arab biographers also report that the inhabitants of Jâbarsa are the people of Moses who were removed from the sinful Israelites during their wanderings in the desert.[103] The "people of Moses" could be a reference to the tribe of Levi, to which Moses and Aaron both belonged, with reference to "the people of Moses." The Levites were the only ones who stayed faithful to God when the other Israelites worshipped the golden calf (Exod 32:25–35). When Moses received the tables of the law, the Qur'an relates, the people on the plain resisted and fashioned the golden calf when Moses was on the mountain (Q 2:93, 51; cf. Exod 32).[104] Only the Levites rallied behind Moses, while the majority of the Israelites worshipped the calf as God. The tribe of Levi, however, did not serve the idol.[105]

The Jews from Jâbarsa tell Muhammad that they pray and fast, fulfil their religious obligations, do not visit prostitutes, do not charge any interest on loans, and have no need of *kings* because they are all *just*. Muhammad recognizes them as the community of Jews who are mentioned in the Qur'an, and they recognize Muhammad as the prophet promised by Moses (cf. Deut 18:15).[106]

Peter asserts in his address shortly after Pentecost that this above-mentioned promise was fulfilled through the coming of Jesus:

> For Moses said, "The Lord your God will raise up for you a prophet like me from among your own people; you must listen to everything he tells you. Anyone who does not listen to him will be completely cut off from their people." Indeed, beginning with Samuel, all the prophets who have spoken have foretold these days. (Acts 3:22–24; cf. 7:37)

In the Qur'an, the same prophecy is seen as being fulfilled in Muhammad: God has sent down the message to Muhammad's heart as a confirmation[107] of the revelations (Torah and Gospel) that were given before him and as right guidance and good news (*bushrâ*) (Q 2:97). It is emphasized that this revelation is confirmed now *in the Arabic language* (Q 46:12).

But did not some of the people—as already in the case of Moses, other prophets, and Jesus as well—reject that covenant (Q 2:100; cf. 8:56)? "Who has believed our message?" the prophet Isaiah asks (Isa 53:1). His message was denied, and the same thing would happen to Jesus (John 12:38). After

---

103. Noegel and Wheeler, *The A to Z of Prophets in Islam and Judaism*, s.v., Jabal Sin.
104. Cf. Schmitz, *Der Koran*, 140–41.
105. Paret on Q 7:159, p. 176; Speyer, *Die biblischen Erzählungen*, 274.
106. Colby, *Narrating Muhammad's Night Journey*, 59–60.
107. Cf. Q 2:89, 91, 97; 3:3, 81; 4:47; 46:30; 5:48; 6:92; 10:37; 12:111.

all, not everyone accepted the good news (Rom 10:16).[108] Just as Paul speaks of Israel's unbelief with respect to the Gospel that he brings (Rom 10:14–21), so Muhammad wrestles with the unbelief of the Jews he meets concerning his good news (Q 2:97): some of those who were given the book throw it behind them and act as if they know nothing (Q 2:101; cf. 12:111; cf. 3:187).[109]

Nevertheless, there are Jews and Christians who believe in God and in what was revealed to Muhammad in the same way they believe in what was revealed to them earlier. In doing so, they are humble towards God and do not sell the words of God for a paltry price (Q 3:199). There is a faithful group of people who recite during the night, just as Jews and Christians do with the Psalms (Ps 1:2), and prostate themselves. They believe in God and the Last Day, they enjoin what is right and forbid what is reprehensible and compete in doing good deeds. They are included among the righteous (Q 3:113–114).[110]

THE REMNANT RETURNS

With the identification of the inhabitants of the two cities, who are what is left of the people of Moses, it is important to reflect on what is said in the Old and New Testaments about the "remnant." The most dramatic example of the salvation of the remnant is that of Noah and his family from the flood (Gen 8:15–18; 9:8–17). The poet-prophet Isaiah compares this with the exile of the sixth century: only a remnant would be saved from the exile, just as Noah and his family were saved from the flood:

> To me this is like the days of Noah,
> when I swore that the waters of Noah would never again cover
> the earth.
> So now I have sworn not to be angry with you,
> never to rebuke you again.
> Though the mountains be shaken
> and the hills be removed,
> yet my unfailing love for you will not be shaken
> nor my covenant of peace be removed,"
> says the Lord, who has compassion on you.
> (Isa 54:9–10)[111]

---

108. Schmitz, *Der Koran*, 147.
109. Schmitz, *Der Koran*, 148.
110. *EQ*, s.v., Children Israel, 305–306.
111. Brueggemann, *Reverberations of Faith*, s.v., remnant, 169.

God sent Noah to his people, urging him to warn them before they were struck by a painful punishment (Q 71:1). God made a covenant with the prophets, and then Noah, Abraham, Moses and Jesus, the son of Mary are mentioned in one breath (Q 33:7). Muhammad sees himself mirrored in the activity of the earlier prophets, also in Noah. He hears the same things from those who oppose him as Noah did in his time from those who opposed him. Noah heard that he was just a human being like them, possessed (Q 23:24; 11:27), and a liar (Q 7:64; 10:73; 54:9).[112]

The political, "aristocratic" leaders or ministers (*al-mala'*) in various cities and countries, who exalted themselves and were proud represented, in the stories of the earlier emissaries of God, the stereotype of the unbelieving leaders like those Muhammad had to endure in Mecca (Q 7:60: 66, 75, 88, 109). Muhammad thus recognizes in his confrontation with the leaders in Mecca the "leaders" of the people of Noah (Q 7:60, 66, 75–77, 109); the people of 'Ad to whom the Arab prophet Hûd was sent (Q 7:66); the people of Thamûd, to whom Sâlih was sent (Q 87:75, 88), and the people of Madyan to whom Shu'aib or Jethro was sent (Q 7:90). Moses had to deal with such "leaders" among the people of Pharaoh (Q 7:109–110, 127). Thus, Noah is seen as a model for Muhammad who had to suffer similar hate and physical threats from his Meccan fellow citizens like the prophets before him (Q 14:9; 22:42; 51:41–46; 54:18, 23).[113]

The prophet Isaiah speaks of the *remnant* in a very special way. He was once commanded by God to go to the king of Judah together with his son, who had the very suggestive name of "A remnant will return" (*Shear-jashub*; Isa 7:3). This name is ambiguous and can have both a threatening tone or a hopeful one; "only a remnant" or "nevertheless a remnant" will return. Returning can mean "escaping a catastrophe" or "repenting."[114] Isaiah himself gives an explanation for the name:

> A remnant will return, a remnant of Jacob
> will return to the Mighty God.
> Though your people be like the sand by the sea, Israel,
> only a remnant will return.
> (Isa 10:21–22; cf. Rom 9:27)[115]

In this context, the name is ominous. It alludes to the belief that Jerusalem will be destroyed and its inhabitants carried away into exile, which for them

---

112. *EI, s.v.*, Nûh.
113. Paret on Q 11:27; *EQ, s.v.*, Noah, 540.
114. KBS on Isa 7:3.
115. KBS on Isa 10:20–23, a text that Paul cited (Rom 9:27).

is the same as dying. And from that death of exile, only a small number of the population will return to Jerusalem to take up their lives there again. Understood in this way, it is bad news: the exile is certain. Only a small number will survive. But in a later context of the exiles, this "remnant" can be viewed as insurance that *at least* a remnant will return.[116]

The "remnant" is that portion of the people who have survived a political catastrophe and thus make the future possible. Since the latter period of the exile, "remnant" was used as a term for those who could escape the catastrophe in Judah. Whoever belonged to the "remnant of Sion," whoever was spared in Jerusalem, was then called *holy*. With this, the prophets are saying that only a small number of people will be saved from the coming disasters (Amos 3:12; cf. 5:15; Isa 6:13; 10:19-22; Jer 3:14; 5:18). Thus, here the remnant is the *holy community* after the exile.[117] That remnant refers to the survivors of the Babylonian conquest of Judah and Jerusalem. They consider themselves the bearers of the promises that were made to the people (Isa 4:1; 11:11-12; Isa 46:3; Hag 1:14; Zech 8:6, 11;[118] Neh 1:1-3; Ezra 9:8, 13-14):

> As a shepherd rescues from the lion's mouth
> only two leg bones or a piece of an ear,
> so will the Israelites living in Samaria be rescued,
> with only the head of a bed
> and a piece of fabric from a couch.
> (Amos 3:12)

This is called the oldest allusion to the notion of the *remnant* who survived the national destruction and, purified through suffering, can become a new people of God: "a burning stick snatched from the fire" (Amos 4:11; cf. 5:1). God will not completely destroy the house of Jacob, "For I will give the command, and I will shake the people of Israel among all the nations as grain is shaken in a sieve, and not a pebble will reach the ground" (Amos 9:8-9). The *pebble* is something valuable, the remnant, whatever remains after the whole has been sifted.[119] "But I will leave within you the meek and humble. The remnant of Israel will trust in the name of the Lord. They will do no wrong; they

---

116. Brueggemann, *Isaiah 1-39*, 65.

117. KBS on Isa 4:3-6.

118. "This is what the Lord Almighty says: 'It may seem marvelous to *the remnant of this people* at that time, but will it seem marvelous to me?' declares the Lord Almighty" (Zech 8:6); "'But now I will not deal with *the remnant of this people* as I did in the past,' declares the Lord Almighty" (Zech 8:11).

119. KBS on Amos 9:9.

will tell no lies. A deceitful tongue will not be found in their mouths. They will eat and lie down and no one will make them afraid" (Zeph 3:12–13).[120]

The notion of *remnant* became a fixed concept that was increasingly given eschatological content: "I will make the lame my remnant, those driven away a strong nation. The Lord will rule over them in Mount Zion from that day and forever" (Mic 4:7). While "remnant" originally meant *paltry leftovers* (Isa 37:4), it is now means *mighty people*.[121]

Paul also speaks about the remnant, here citing the prophet Isaiah: "Isaiah cries out concerning Israel: 'Though the number of the Israelites be like the sand by the sea, only the remnant will be saved'" (Rom 9:27; cf. Isa 10:22–23; Hos 2:1).[122] The rejection of the chosen people seems to be the inevitable consequence of Israel's recalcitrance (Rom 10:18–21). But Paul refuses to draw that conclusion. *First*, even though it is a minority, a "remnant," a "chosen part" of this people, to which he himself belongs, has already believed in the Messiah (Rom 11:1–10). *Second*, the wrong step made by the majority serves the conversion of the nations, and this in turn serves the salvation of the Jewish people (Rom 11:11–24). Finally, all of Israel will be saved, for God is faithful to his first love (Rom 11:25–32).[123] Paul is convinced that the message of salvation will not fail in the end, but the remnant will accept the Gospel of salvation.[124]

In his letter to the church in Rome Paul uses the famous chain of "call upon-believe-hear-proclaim-sent":[125]
How, then, can they call on the one they have not believed in? And how can they believe in the one of whom they have not heard? And how can they hear without someone preaching to them? And how can anyone preach unless they are sent? As it is written: "How beautiful are the feet of those who bring good news!" (Rom 10:14–15; cf. Isa 52:7)
But the prophet Isaiah already said: "Lord, who has believed our message?" (Rom 10:16). Paul suggests that Isaiah also experienced such a failure to hear the Gospel. He mentions Isaiah explicitly no less than three times. Isaiah declares: "Though the number of the Israelites be like the sand by the sea, only the remnant will be saved" (Rom 9:27; cf. Isa 10:22–23). He had already stated earlier: "Unless the Lord Almighty had left us descendants, we would have become like Sodom, we would have been like Gomorrah"

---

120. KBS on Amos 3:12.
121. KBS on Mic 4:7.
122. *BW*, s.v., rest.
123. KBS on Rom 11:1–36.
124. Jewett, *Romans*, 603.
125. KBS on Rom 10:14–15.

(Rom 9:29; cf. Isa 1:9). Paul's citation of Isaiah's exclamation, "Who has believed our message?" (Rom 10:16; cf. Isa 53:1)[126] expresses Paul's agonizing disappointment[127] about the refusal of his fellow Jews to accept the good news. The quote corresponds fundamentally with Paul's proclamation and Isaiah's message. The quote from Isaiah also confirms where the problem lay: not in the good news itself or in the preaching but in the reception of the good news.[128] And he speaks to Israel: "All day long I have held out my hands to an obstinate people" (Isa 65:2), "to a disobedient and obstinate people" (Rom 10:21).

Paul wonders if they did not *hear* the message, for not all believed the message, as Isaiah already said: "Who has believed our message?" (Rom 10:16; cf. Isa 53:1). Nevertheless, he answers with a quote from Psalm 19: "Their voice has gone out into all the earth, their words *to the ends of the world*" (Rom 10:18; cf. Ps 19:5). These words are taken from the song Psalm 19, about God as creator (Ps 19:2–7) and *giver of the Torah* (Ps 19:8–15).[129] Paul explicitly denies that God has rejected his people, referring here to the story of Elijah who complains about Israel to God: "Lord, they have killed your prophets and torn down your altars; I am the only one left, and they are trying to kill me" (Rom 11:1–3; cf. 1 Kgs 19:10,14). The answer God gave him was precisely about the "remnant": "I have reserved for myself *seven thousand* who have not bowed the knee to Baal." And that is also how it is at the present time, Paul says, "there is a remnant" (Rom 11:4, 5; cf. 1 Kgs 19:18).

There is a formal typology between "the 7000" who did not, according to the Elijah story, bow the knee to Baal and the "remnant" of Israel. That is also true in *this eschatological time*. "The basic idea is that the salvation of the remnant consists in their having survived while the rest of the population was killed in battle or disappeared in exile (e.g., Isa 37:4; Jer 8:3; Mic 2:12)."[130] "The Lord will scatter you among the peoples, and only a few of you will survive among the nations to which the Lord will drive you" (Deut 4:27). One of the curses was that Israel's population would dramatically decrease during the diaspora until only a small number remained.[131] "It was a vital Jewish belief that, when the end of the world comes and the kingdom

---

126. Taken word for word from the Septuagint.
127. Cf. Rom 9:1–3.
128. Jewett, *Romans*, 640–41.
129. KBS Ps 19:2–15.
130. Jewett, *Romans*, 659.
131. Lundbom, *Deuteronomy*, 249.

of God is fully established, a faithful Remnant, a purified elect core of the chosen people of Israel, will survive and emerge triumphant."[132]

The exact same point is made in the preaching of Muhammad, the good news in the Qur'an that confirms the earlier messages. Was it not the case that every time the children of Israel made a covenant, there were always *some* who rejected it (Q 2:100).[133] This preaching or call is not a call to convert from Judaism to "Islam" in the sense in which the term would later be used. It is a call—just as in Moses' time—to listen to God's word. Thus, Jesus' preaching is not a call to the children of Israel to become "Christians" in the later sense of the word but to listen to this prophet whom God raised up again (cf. Deut 18:14, 18).

It is of major importance to emphasize that the good news is expressed not only in the New Testament but is also found in the Old Testament and explicitly in the Qur'an. The good news of the First Testament, which then is heard in the New, is confirmed in the good news that the prophet Muhammad brings. The Arabic term that is used for that in the Qur'an is very close to the Hebrew word (*bashâra; bushrâ*). Like all prophets he sent, God also sent Muhammad as both: one who warns (*nadhîr*) and a proclaimer of good news (*bashîr*) (Q 2:119; 5:19; 7:188; 10:2: 11:2; 17:105; 19:97; 25:56; 33:45; 34:28; 35:24; 48:8).[134]

> Humankind was a single community;
> then God sent the prophets
> as bearers of good news and as warners,
> and He sent down with them the Book with the truth,
> that it may judge between the people
> concerning that about which they differed,
> and none differed in it
> except those who had been given it,
> after the manifest proofs had come to them,
> out of envy among themselves.
> Then God guided those who had faith
> to the truth [the Qur'an] of what they [the Jews and the Christians] differed in, by His will,
> and God guides whomever He wishes
> to a straight path.
> (Q 2:213)

---

132. Michael Grant, *Jesus* (London: Wiedenfeld and Nicholson, 1977), 20; cited in: Jewett, *Romans*, 659, n. 79.

133. Schmitz, *Der Koran*, 146–47.

134. *EQ, s.v.*, Good News.

This good news will sound once again, now from the mouth of the prophet, who confirms these earlier messages.

After the death of their father Jacob, Joseph's brothers were afraid he would take vengeance on them for what they did wrong. He then says. "You intended to harm me, but God intended it for good to accomplish what is now being done, the saving of many lives" (Gen 50:20). That is the decisive climax of that story. And at the same time it is a programmatic confirmation of the good news, one can justifiably say, of the whole Bible *and the Qur'an*. "The evil plans of human folks do not defeat God's purpose. Instead, they unwittingly become ways in which God's plan is furthered"[135]—his plan for the world, for the good, for life, *l'chayim*.

---

135. Brueggemann, *Genesis*, 376.

II

The Apocalyptic Seventh Century

In the seventh century, the Apocalypse of Pseudo-Methodius was revealed on the Sinjâr Mountains.

In the twenty-first century, on 14 August 2007, suicide terrorists launched a bloody attack on the Yazidi community in Sinjar, and 454 people died. In the months of July and August 2014, thousands of Yazidis living in Sinjar fled before the Sunni warriors of the Islamic State. They fled, and most sought refuge in the nearby Sinjar Mountains, while others went to Turkey and the Iraqi Autonomous Kurdish zone.[1]

INTRODUCTION

During the prophet Muhammad's life, two major world powers were at war with one another in the Middle East: the Byzantines and the Persians. Shortly after the Byzantines had succeeded in conquering the Persians, the Arabs began their conquests of precisely those areas over which those two powers had fought. In the year 610, the Byzantine emperor Flavius Heraclius (575–641) began his reign—the same year that Muhammad first appeared

---

1. http://nl.wikipedia.org/wiki/Sinjar.

as a prophet in Mecca! When the emperor assumed the throne, his kingdom was threatened from many sides, and for most of the three decades of his reign, he was at war with the Persians and later also with the raiding Arabs as well, although it seems that he was not personally involved in any battles with the latter.[2] For the generations that followed, however, he embodied the source of inspiration for the Byzantine military resistance. It was partly because of him that Byzantium was able to withstand the Muslims for another 800 years![3]

Before, during, and after these conquests, Christians both in the Middle East and North Africa gave voice to eschatological fears.[4] But "apocalyptic" was also a vital element in many of the earliest "Muslim" communities that had sprung up in these areas,[5] and in the Jewish communities as well. Heraclius began his first offensive against the Persians in 622, the same year that Muhammad would go on the *hijra* from Mecca to Medina. The emperor penetrated to the heart of the Persian kingdom, which was the beginning of the end of the Sassanid dynasty that had existed for four centuries.[6]

HERACLIUS'S RECONQUEST OF JERUSALEM

As the last great king of the Persian kingdom, the Sassanid shah Khosrow II, (Kisrâ in Arabic), who ruled from 590–628, expanded his sphere of power far to the West—far enough to lay siege to Constantinople. That was why he was called Parvîz, i.e., "the Victorious." But the shah was unable to capture Constantinople, so Heraclius began a counterattack to regain the Eastern provinces lost to the Persians.

The most dramatic moment in the internal power struggles took place in 614 when the Persians captured Jerusalem. It was the most destructive event to happen to the holy city since the Romans had put an end to the Bar Kochba revolt and drove the Jewish population out of the city in the year 135.[7] It is understandable that the Jews now did everything they could to support the Persians, which temporarily allowed them some control of Jerusalem.[8] *Messianic expectations* arose among the Jews, and texts were

2. Kaegi, *Heraclius*, 311.
3. Kaegi, *Heraclius*, 312.
4. Kaegi, *Muslim Expansion and Byzantine Collapse in North Africa*, 267.
5. https://en.wikipedia.org/wiki/Sebeos; according to F. M. Donner and David Cook, see Kaegi, *Heraclius*, 314, n. 12.
6. Bowersock, *The Crucible of Islam*, 109.
7. Bowersock, *The Crucible of Islam*, 81.
8. Bowersock, *The Crucible of Islam*, 85–86.

written that explained the Persian conquest as a *sign of the end time* and the impending restoration of Israel. The Church of the Holy Sepulcher was heavily damaged in the conquest, and the Persian sovereign took that opportunity to take the relic of the "true cross" with him to Persia.[9]

The thirtieth chapter of the Qur'an, called Rûm, alludes to that Persian conquest of Jerusalem. Rûm refers to Constantinople, the second Rome; it is what the Arabs called the Romans from both the East (Byzantines) and the West: "The Romans have been conquered in the neighboring land" (Syria, Palestine), says the Qur'an, "Byzantium has been vanquished / in a nearby territory, / but following their defeat they will be victors / in a few years. / All command belongs to God, before and after, / and on that day the faithful [including the followers of the prophet Muhammad] will rejoice" (Q 30:2-4). This text, revealed in the year of the Persian conquest, clearly conveys the sympathy that Muhammad's followers had for the Christian Byzantines in the early period of Muhammad's prophetic activity. When Muhammad encountered great resistance in Mecca, Muhammad advised a number of his followers to seek refuge in Ethiopia because Syria and Palestine were occupied by the Persians.[10]

Around 630, Emperor Heraclius was able to recapture the city of Jerusalem, an event the Qur'an alludes to as a kind of prediction. But the "believers" (Muslims) did not sympathize with the Byzantines any longer. This is apparent from the fact that, in September 629, while Muhammad was still alive, the first military confrontation between Muhammad's Arab followers and the Byzantines took place. This was the battle near the village Mu'ta, located to the east of the southern end of the Dead Sea. Muhammad's followers were totally defeated by the Byzantines.[11] An Arab report has Emperor Heraclius himself present at this battle, but this, incidentally, is considered very unlikely.[12] A mosque, which later fell into ruin, was built in honor of those who died in that battle and was called "the mosque of the martyrs." Zayd ibn Hâritha, the adopted son of Muhammad, died in that battle; he is mentioned by name in the Qur'an (Q 33:37) and was known to be a good archer.[13]

The battle at Mu'ta took place a few months after the Persians were forced to withdraw from that location and just before Emperor Heraclius recaptured Jerusalem. On 21 March 629 or 630, Heraclius personally returned

---

9. Kaegi, *Heraclius*, 78.
10. Buhl, *Das Leben Muhammeds*, 172–73.
11. Kaegi, *North Africa*, 93.
12. *EI*, *s.v.*, Mu'ta.
13. *EI*, *s.v.*, Zayd b. Häritha.

the fragments of *the true cross* to Jerusalem in triumph. According to the "Golden Legend," he insisted on going by horse, contrary to the patriarch's advice. But, after dismounting and removing his crown, he was surrounded by a miraculous light, and the barred city gate opened of its own accord. It has been said that that gate had been sealed until the arrival of the Messiah.[14] Only a few years later, during the rule of 'Umar ibn al-Khattâb, the second caliph or successor of Muhammad, the Arabs captured the city of Jerusalem from the Byzantines. Sophronius, the patriarch of Jerusalem, struck an alliance with 'Umar in which he surrendered the city to the Arabs.[15]

"THE PLATES OF DAVID": THE NEW DAVID

Heraclius's reputation underwent many changes. A Spanish chronicle from the Middle Ages ascribes the ominous blows the Byzantine Empire had to endure from the Arabs to his great arrogance, haughty pride, and religious lapses. Seduced by his people's praise after his conquest of "the fire-worshipping Persians," he attributed the victory not to God but to himself.[16]

Iconographic scenes depict Heraclius together with the mother of Constantine the Great, Helena, who is said to have discovered the "true cross" in the fourth century. Archbishop William of Tyre, who was born and died in Jerusalem (d. 1185), later viewed Heraclius as the initiator of the crusades.[17] But this is an anachronism, and it is incorrect to view him as the "first crusader."[18] It is therefore misleading to attribute a crusade mentality to him,[19] and the idea of a Byzantine holy war or crusade is incorrect.[20] Neither Heraclius nor the patriarch of Jerusalem, Sophronius—as is apparent from his Christmas sermon of 634,[21] issued a call for a crusade. In this sermon, he expressed more concern about whether his clergy subscribed to the views of the Council of Chalcedon (see below) and only issued the most conventional of warnings about the advance of the Saracens on Palestine, who already controlled Bethlehem.[22]

---

14. Kaegi, *Heraclius*, 206, 300.
15. Bowersock, *The Crucible of Islam*, 90.
16. Kaegi, *North Africa*, 92.
17. Kaegi, *Heraclius*, 3.
18. Kaegi, *Heraclius*, 206.
19. Kaegi, *North Africa*, 267.
20. Kaegi, *Heraclius*, 256.
21. Kaegi, *Heraclius*, 256, n. 57.
22. https://en.wikipedia.org/wiki/Sophronius_of_Jerusalem.

According to a Muslim report, 'Umar ibn al-Khattâb came to Jerusalem in 637 and was shown around by Sophronius. The latter is said to have invited him to pray in the Church of the Holy Sepulchre at the times Muslims were accustomed to praying. The caliph declined the invitation so that Muslims would not be able to claim in the future that the church should be a mosque since "'Umar had prayed there." To show his appreciation, Sophronius gave the caliph the keys to the church, which are still in the hands of a Muslim family who open and close the church every day.[23]

In contrast, there are famous frescos from the fifteenth-century Italian Renaissance with the theme of Heraclius's victory over the Persian shah and his return of the cross to Jerusalem. Both subjects were very important then in connection with the rising power of the Ottoman Turks.[24] Historically, Heraclius was viewed in contradictory ways: as a *new* David, Moses, Constantine the Great, or Scipio,[25] but also as himself, i.e., deceptive and arrogant.[26] Scipio Africanus (236–183 BC), the Roman general and later consul, became famous for defeating Hannibal in the Second Punic War. It is doubtful whether Heraclius himself was even aware of that history of North Africa when he was conducting his campaigns there.

When he went to war, Heraclius invoked Davidic language when addressing his troops. Both the Bible—the Old and the New Testaments (Mark 12:35–37; Matt 22:41–46; Luke 20:41–44; cf. Ps 101:1)—and the Qur'an (cf. Q 4:163; 17:55; 21:105) attribute the psalms to King David. One of the most striking lines from the psalms quoted in the Qur'an is taken from Psalm 37:9, 29, 34: "Certainly We wrote in the Psalms, / after the Torah: 'Indeed My righteous servants shall inherit the earth'" (Q 21:105). Those same words are quoted by Jesus in the Sermon on the Mount: "Blessed are the meek, for they will inherit the earth" (Matt 5:5; cf. Ps 37:11; Isa 60:21). It is remarkable that this text appears in all three books.

But how different these psalms sound when placed in the mouth of this "Christian" emperor, Heraclius. The reference to any meekness seems to disappear: "They—the enemies—are those about whom David, inspired by God, said: Happy is the one who seizes the infants of the Persians and dashes them against the rocks."[27] This is taken from Psalm 137: "Daughter Babylon, doomed to destruction, happy is the one who repays you according

---

23. https://en.wikipedia.org/wiki/Sophronius_of_Jerusalem.
24. Kaegi, *Heraclius*, 4.
25. Kaegi, *Heraclius*, 29, 12, 301.
26. Kaegi, *Heraclius*, 5.
27. Kaegi, *Heraclius*, 114.

to what you have done to us. Happy is the one who seizes your infants and dashes them against the rocks" (Ps 137:8-9; Hos 14:1).

The intention behind this psalm is not at all what it appears to be and goes contrary to Heraclius's use of it. The psalm depicts the city of Babylon as a woman, with its inhabitants as her children.[28] An appeal is made to the God of justice to restore the just order that had been destroyed by Edom and Babylon. The defeat of Zion by Babylon was seen as an act of violence against God's plan for history, which therefore called for retribution (cf. Jer 51:20-26). We will discuss in more detail below what is actually meant by the word "retribution" in the three books—God's plan to turn what is bad back into good again.[29]

In 1902, *silver plates* were discovered in northern Cyprus that had been made during Heraclius's reign.[30] This set of plates is possibly the earliest to show biblical themes. The kings Saul and David are depicted in the attire of the Byzantine court. Obviously, this suggests that the Byzantine emperor was also a sovereign chosen by God, just like David. The "David plates" were made between 628 and 630 (!) in Constantinople after the final victory over the Persians and before the time of the first Byzantine iconoclasm (between 726-787), each with a scene from the life of King David. The largest plate depicts David's battle with Goliath (1 Sam 17:41-51; Q 2:251). Four medium-sized plates show the following scenes: Samuel (Samwîl) anointing David in the presence of his father and brothers; David being introduced to King Saul, Saul putting on David's armor, and the marriage of David to Michal, Saul's daughter. Other scenes include David fighting a lion and a bear, David playing on the harp for Saul, and speaking with his oldest brother Eliab (1 Sam 16:6-7; 17:13, 28-29).

King Saul, called Tâlût, the "Tall," in the Qur'an (he stood head and shoulders above most people (1 Sam 10:23), went into battle against Goliath (Jalût) (Q 2:249-250), but it is David who kills him (Q 2:251). The name Jalût given to Goliath in the Qur'an may have been derived from the Hebrew word *gâlât* (exile) and must have been used often by the Jews in Arabia and elsewhere. Jalut became a collective name for the oppressors of the Israelites. The giant Goliath is also associated with the people of Amalek, 'Âd, or Thamûd. The Muslim tradition also sees this story as a foreshadowing of the

---

28. KBS on Ps 137:8-9.

29. Hossfeld and Zenger, *Psalms 3*, 520; cf. chapter VIII of this book.

30. They are now part of the collection of the Metropolitan Museum of Arts; cf. Steven H. Wander, "The Cyprus Plates: The Story of David and Goliath." *Metropolitan Museum Journal* 8 (1973) 89-104. Cited in: Kaegi, *Heraclius*, 114, n. 39; https://en.wikipedia.org/wiki/David_Plates.

Battle of Badr,[31] which took place between Muhammad's followers and their Meccan adversaries in the second year of the *hijra*, the journey or Exodus from Mecca to the promised city of Medina, where Muhammad's followers achieved a great victory. According to tradition (Q 8:9), they were aided by Gabriel with an army of angels. This victory is compared with Israel's victory over the Egyptian pharaoh.[32]

These themes on the *David Plates* turn Heraclius into a symbol. Perhaps they were used to celebrate his victory over the Persians, which led to the recapture of Jerusalem. It is also believed that the nine plates together *form a cross.*[33]

THE DIVIDED CHRISTIANS IN THE EAST

Constantine the Great founded the city named after him, Constantinople, and was also the first Roman emperor to become "Christian" and attempted to maintain unity among the Christians. He presided over the First Council of Nicaea in 325, the first of the seven ecumenical councils. The oldest churches in the Middle East, however—the Syrian Orthodox, the Nestorians, the Armenians, and the Copts (in Egypt) in particular—did not agree with the decisions taken by this council that dealt with the significance of Jesus Christ, so-called Christology. The latter churches did not join the Council of Chalcedon, the later fourth ecumenical council in the year 451 named after the place where it was held, an old Byzantine harbor town on the Bosporus across from Byzantium. The as yet undivided churches in Europe did accept the conclusions of this Council on the question: "Was Jesus Christ God or man or both and, if the latter: how were the two natures related to each other?" This council rejected Monophysitism, the belief that Christ had one inseparable divine-human nature. On the one hand (over against the Syrian Orthodox), it rejected the notion of the *confusion* of the two natures and, on the other (over against the Nestorians), the *separation* between the two. The "imperial church" of Byzantium directed itself against the so-called Oriental churches (not to be confused with the Eastern Orthodox), who did not follow the Council of Chalcedon.

Since the time of Constantine the Great, the Byzantine emperors attempted to maintain or bring about unity among Christians. In his time, Heraclius advocated finding a compromise concerning the *one* divine-human

---

31. *EI, s.v.*, Djâlût; cf. also chapter VIII.

32. https://en.wikipedia.org/wiki/Battle_of_Badr; cf. Wessels, *The Torah, the Gospel, and the Qur'an*, 96–97.

33. Alexander. "Heraclius, Byzantine Imperial Ideology, and the David Plates."

nature in Christ. The word "nature" (*physis*) was replaced by "will" or "energy." Rather than the *one* divine-human *nature* in Christ, the issue now concerned the one divine-human *will* in Christ. Christ had two natures, but only *one* will or *one* energy. Thus, one could speak of one energy, one will, without being forced to acknowledge the singular nature of Monophysitism. But Heraclius's attempt at reconciliation failed. His doctrine was viewed as heretical,[34] and the Maronite church, the most important church community in Lebanon, is the only one that is said to have accepted this view. Incidentally, the Maronites themselves deny the latter. They have been fully united with the Roman Catholic Church since the time of the Crusades.[35]

The Ecumenical Council of 680–681 condemned Monothelitism and argued the opposite: the human nature in Jesus Christ had its *own will*, which is free and subject to the *divine will* in everything. Christ therefore has two wills. It was concluded that Christ is truly God and truly human. Heraclius's attempts to unite divided Christianity turned out to be his biggest failure.[36] This internal dissension led to serious damage to his empire and expedited the Muslim victories in the years immediately following his death.[37]

Religious fragmentation was also a fact in North Africa in the late seventh century. The Christians there did not welcome the Muslims, but many were opposed to the imperial ecclesiastical politics of Byzantium. Various Monophysites viewed the Muslim successes as divine punishment for the sins of the emperor and his dynasty—the preaching of anti-Monophysitic doctrines. These internal Christian antitheses weakened the Byzantines. Muhammad must have been aware of the differences among the Christians at a very early stage. In the Qur'an, the Christians are accused of having divided themselves into groups and sects: "Indeed this community of yours is one community, / and I am your Lord. / So worship Me./ *They have fragmented their religion among themselves.*" (Q 21:92–93. Cf. 23:52–53; 2:213).[38] The mutual hostility between the "imperial" church and the churches of the East facilitated first the Persian and later the Muslim conquests.

MUHAMMAD AND THE BYZANTINES

It is said that Muhammad's great-grandfather received a letter from the Byzantine emperor, the *kaysar*, that granted safe conduct for merchants from

34. Kaegi, *Heraclius*, 305.
35. Cf. Wessels, *Arab and Christian*, 104.
36. Keagi, *Heraclius*, 305–306.
37. Kaegi, *Heraclius*, 307.
38. Paret, *Der Koran*, on 21:92, 345–346; cf. Q 19:37; 43:65.

Mecca who wanted to visit Syria. *Kaysar* was the common Arabic term for the Byzantine emperor. For the Ghassanids and the inhabitants of northern Arabia, the Byzantine emperor was the supreme ruler, just as Kisrâ, the king of the Persians, was for the Lakhmids and all the inhabitants of the area that extended to the Persian Gulf. For later Arab poets, the *Kaysar* and Kisrâ were still common "negative" symbols for power and wealth.[39] When Muhammad attempted to conclude an agreement with the then "unbelieving" Meccan leaders so that he could go on a pilgrimage to Mecca a year later, 'Urwa ibn Mas'ûd[40] visited him in his camp. When he returned, Ibn Mas'ûd told the Meccan townspeople: "I have been to see Kisrâ in his kingdom (Persia) and Kaysar in his (Byzantium) and also the Negus (Ethiopia), but I have never seen a king among his people like Muhammad among his companions." For the Arabs, Kisrâ personified the Sassanid kingship, which evoked a combination of envy, awe, and fear. The capital was called Ctesiphon (*Madâ'in Kisrâ*). Kisrâ tore up the letter from Muhammad that invited him to convert to Islam.[41]

Although the word *kaysar* does not appear in the Qur'an, it is mentioned in the biography of the prophet Muhammad, the traditions, and in the Qur'an commentaries. In Muhammad's time, Heraclius was called the "great emperor" or "king of the second Rome." That was also the case in the time of Muhammad's first two successors, Caliphs Abû Bakr and 'Umar.[42]

In August 636, four years after Muhammad's death, there was a battle between the Arabs and the Byzantines near Yarmouk. Anyone familiar with the history of the rise and expansion of Islam will be struck by the fact that the locations where historic battles occurred are appearing again and again in current news reports. During the Syrian civil war, in December 2012, there was heavy fighting near Yarmouk between the Free Syrian Army and the Popular Front for the Liberation of Palestine (which had its power base here). In 2014, there was a humanitarian disaster, and people became so hungry they even started eating cats. Militants entered the camp in April 2015, and although they were forced to retreat again a few days later, their places were filled by militants from their ally *Al-Nusra*. The humanitarian

---

39. *EI*, *s.v.*, Kisrâ.

40. As an ally of the Quraysh tribe in Mecca, 'Urwa participated in the negotiations for the Treaty of Hudaybiyyah in 628. Later tradition made him a martyr for the faith, and Muhammad is said to have compared him to 'Îsâ b. Maryam. *EI*, *s.v.*, 'Urwa b. Mas'ûd.

41. *EI*, *s.v.*, Kisrâ. The "secularity" of Kisrâ was contrasted with Muslim spirituality. *EI*, *s.v.*, Qaysar.

42. *EI*, *s.v.*, Qaysar.

circumstances in the camp caused by the war between the rivaling factions were reported to be very bad.[43]

The original battle near Yarmouk was waged by Khâlid ibn Walîd (d. 642) under the authority of 'Umar ibn al-Khattâb.[44] He had become the leading general under the first caliph, Abû Bakr. In the campaign for the conquest of Syria, he defeated the Byzantines near Damascus. The prophet Muhammad called him "the sword of God" (*sayf-l-slâm*).[45]

It is said that, in the year 628 after Muhammad's return from Mecca to Medina, he wrote letters to the leaders of the world to encourage them to accept Islam and his role as messenger. It is claimed that he wrote to Emperor Heraclius in Constantinople, and to Shah Khosrow II (Kisrâ), to Muqawqis, probably to the patriarch in Alexandria in Egypt, to al-Hârith ibn 'Abd Kulâl in Himyarite Arabia, and possibly to the Negus of Ethiopia.[46] Such stories have not been historically established, but they do reflect how those original relationships with Christians were viewed at a *later* date. It is said that Heraclius questioned Abû Sufyân, the leader of Mecca, about the new prophet. In contrast to Kisrâ, the Persian king, the Byzantine emperor was inclined to convert to Islam. It was only the fear of his subjects that held him back from confessing the new religion *publicly*.[47]

"Constantinople" (Rûm) would come to play a major role in the Muslim *apocalyptic* traditions. In a classical collection of traditions, it is said or stated that Umm Haram heard the prophet say: "The first of my people to attack Caesar's city will have their sins forgiven."[48] "The Antichrist (Dajjâl) will not appear until the Byzantines have been defeated."[49] There were attempts to conquer Constantinople already at the time of the first Arab Muslim state, the Umayyad Caliphate, under the leadership of Mu'âwiyya, who had moved the caliphate from Medina to Damascus. It is claimed that he said the creed "There is no god but God" and "God is great" (*takbîr*) several times near the walls. One tradition has the omens begin with Muhammad's death and end with a violent struggle between the Byzantines and

---

43. https://brabosh.com/2012/12/17/pqpct-m3v/; ISIS beheaded dozens of Syrian pro-Hamas Palestinians in Yarmouk, and the UN sounded the alarm: https://brabosh.com/2015/04/05/pqpct-amt-2/.

44. Keagi, *North Africa*, 92; Keagi, *Muslim Expansion*, 11; Battle of Yarmouk: https://en.wikipedia.org/wiki/Battle_of_Yarmouk.

45. Glacé, *s.v.*, Khalid ibn al-Walîd.

46. Bowersock, *The Crucible of Islam*, 75.

47. *EI*, *s.v.*, Qaysar.

48. *Sahîh*, 56, chapter 93, also found in Ibn Hanbal.

49. *Musnad*, 178.

the Muslims.[50] Other traditions declare that victory will come only when *the final hour* has begun, not by force of arms but by uttering the creed several times and the phrase "God is the greatest of all" (*takbîr*), after which the walls of Constantinople will fall,[51] just as the walls of Jericho did (Josh 6:20). "By faith the walls of Jericho fell, after the army had marched around them for seven days" (Heb 11:30; cf. Josh 2:1f.; 6:17, 22–25). That was, so to speak, a liturgical capture.[52]

The Arab Muslims carried out two attacks on Constantinople. One of the prophet Muhammad's companions, Abû Ayyûb al-Ansâri, his "helper" and the bearer of his standard, took part in the first siege of Constantinople (674–678) under Yazîd ibn Mu'âwiyya, who would later become the second Umayyad caliph. He died during the first siege of Constantinople and, at his own request, was buried under the walls of Constantinople. In later times, many Ottoman officers requested to be buried in that area.[53] In 674, the Umayyad caliph Mu'âwiyya launched an attack on Constantinople by land and by sea. Although he was defeated, Constantinople was reduced to an "enclave in an ocean of Islam."[54] Only centuries later, in 1453, would the Ottoman Turks, not the Arabs, succeed in truly conquering the city.

JEWISH AND CHRISTIAN VIEWS OF ARAB CONQUESTS

As Islam began to expand, how did Jews and Christians in the Middle East, particularly Syria, Palestine and Constantinople, the center of the Byzantine kingdom that reached to North Africa, feel about the invading Arabs? We should not think that they immediately understood that this invasion meant the arrival of a new religion. Apocalyptic views were prevalent among the Byzantine Christians; they saw their kingdom as the last empire before the second coming of Jesus Christ. The end of that empire would also usher in the end of the world. Universal chaos, murder, and famine would be followed by the arrival of the Antichrist, who would rule the world, after which Jesus would appear for the *final judgement*.

---

50. Attema, *De Mohammedaansche opvattingen*, 88.

51. Attema, *De Mohammedaansche opvattingen*, 92.

52. That was the prelude to the conquest of the holy land or the earth. This word has a double meaning in Hebrew (*eretz*) and Arabic (*ard*).

53. https://en.wikipedia.org/wiki/Abu_Ayyub_al-Ansari.

54. Martin Ballard, "End-timers: Three-thousand Years of Waiting for Judgment Day," (Santa Barbara: Praeger, 2011); cited in: https://en.wikipedia.org/wiki/Apocalypse_of_Pseudo-Methodius.

The Jews were also driven by eschatological expectations and, in turn, longed for the collapse of the Byzantine Empire. For the Jews, the fall of the empire did not mean the arrival of the Antichrist but rather the arrival of the Messiah, who would restore the Israelite empire.

To understand the early Jewish and Christian responses, it is important to remember the fact that the Persian conquest of "Byzantine Jerusalem" preceded the Arabic conquest of Jerusalem (614). The relic of the "true cross" had fallen into Persian hands at that time. For a while, the Jews had a certain amount of control over the city and had *Messianic expectations*. Texts were written that explained the Persian conquest as a *sign of the end times* and the impending restoration of Israel! But with the recapture of Jerusalem by Emperor Heraclius, history took another turn. The Jewish collaboration with the Persians led to a number of Byzantine measures against the Jews, including forced baptism and expulsion from Jerusalem. Once again, Messianic expectations were awakened among the Jews. There were indications of the impending fall of the Byzantine Empire, and there was hope that the restoration of Israel from exile would follow. Jewish apocalyptic texts and an apocalyptic poem declared that the Roman Empire would give way to the establishment of the *Messianic age*. With this explanation, the leader of the conquerors—the prophet Muhammad—was seen as a predecessor of the Messiah. This role was not ascribed to Muhammad on the basis of his teachings but because of the eschatological and apocalyptic explanations of contemporary events. What Muhammad himself preached or taught was viewed as irrelevant by the Jews.

The *Byzantine Christians* had a different explanation of what was going on. The invading Arabs were seen as an instrument of God to *punish* them for their sins. These sins were viewed differently: some saw them as moral offenses and others as erroneous religious views. Because they saw the Arabs as a scourge from God, they believed that the conquests would be short-lived. That view was clearly aimed against the Jewish "claims" that the end of the Roman Empire had dawned. For Christians, as for the Jews, the religion of the Arab invaders was initially of no importance.[55]

THE DOCTRINE OF JACOBI

In the last phase of Heraclius's reign, he was confronted with conquests by the Arab "Muslims." For Jews, Christians, and Muslims, it was a very religious century. Muslim apocalyptic expectations were very strong in the late seventh century and in the first decades of the eighth. Some of these

55. Cf. Suermann, "Early Islam in the Light of Christian and Jewish Sources."

expectations were linked with the expectation that the end times would occur at the end of the first century of the Islamic Era, which had begun in the year 622. Most of the Muslim apocalyptic expectations concentrated on the conquest of Constantinople. Heraclius had had a prophetic dream about the triumph of the "kingdom of a circumcised man."[56] He died at a time in which apocalyptic thinking had become more intense in the Near East and North Africa. Fear of the end times held sway in both these regions during and after the Muslim conquests.[57]

A History of Heraclius, written by Sebêos, an Armenian bishop and historian, examines the expectations about the end times. As one of the few sources recording the history of Armenia and the surrounding areas, his writings are valuable. His history contains a detailed description of the period of the Persian (Sassanid) rule over Armenia up until the Muslim conquest in 661,[58] drawing from various sources with a prophetic and apocalyptic perspective. He manages to establish a link between biblical prophecy and his own time[59] and gives his own explanation of the four kingdoms Daniel speaks about (Dan 2 and 7), linking them with the *four corners of the earth*: The kingdom of the Greeks in the *West*; that of the Sassanids in the *East*, Gog and Magog in the *North*, and, finally, the kingdom of Ishmael in the *South*. Sebêos is the first author to clearly place the Arabs as a world empire on a par with the Greeks (Byzantines) and the Persians within Daniel's framework of the four world empires in history.[60]

At that time, apocalyptic texts appeared that spoke of the approaching end of the world, such as the *Doctrine of Jacobi super Baptizati*.[61] In the decades that followed, even more texts were circulated, such as the *Apocalypse of Pseudo-Methodius*. The news of the appearance of the prophet Muhammad and the bewildering defeat that the Byzantines suffered in Palestine soon reached "Byzantine North Africa." *The Doctrine of Jacobi*, a contemporary anti-Jewish dialogue, bears witness to this. Apparently, the Jews in Carthage, the administrative seat of Byzantine rule over Africa, had discussed these shocking events in the Near East as well as their possible eschatological meaning already before the middle of the summer of 634.[62] On 13 July 634, there was a discussion on the condition of the Byzantine

56. Glassé, *The Concise Encyclopaedia of Islam*, s.v., Heraclius.
57. Kaegi, *North Africa*, 267.
58. https://en.wikipedia.org/wiki/Sebeos.
59. Kaegi, *Heraclius*, 8.
60. Reinink, "Ps.-Methodius," 157–58.
61. *Didaskalia Iakobou* or *Doctrina Jacobi super baptizati*.
62. Kaegi, *North Africa*, 292–93.

Empire in the light of recent Arab conquests between the Jew Jacob, who had been forced to convert to Christianity, and several Jews. The discussion revolved around a Byzantine Orthodox anti-Jew polemic. Jacob compares the Byzantine Empire with the fourth beast in the book of Daniel ("terrifying and frightening and very powerful. It had large iron teeth; it crushed and devoured its victims and trampled underfoot whatever was left" [Dan 7:7]). Daniel was actually describing Alexander the Great and his successors.[63] The text contains one of the earliest external reports about "Islam." It is part of the Byzantine literature that attempts to reconcile Islam with the apocalyptic vision. There is a report about a prophet in Arabia who announces the coming of a *Jewish* Messiah: "We Jews were more than delighted. They said that the prophet had appeared who announced the coming of the 'Anointed One' (the 'Messiah'). When asked about the prophet who had appeared among the Saracens, however, an old man who was well acquainted with the Scriptures said: "He is false, because (true) prophets do not come with a sword."[64]

The *Doctrine of Jacobi* states that the emperor ordered all Jews to be baptized. The proclamation of Heraclius's decree involved the Jews in Carthage (North Africa) in the consequences of the tension in Palestine between Jews and Christians during the lengthy Byzantine Persian wars (603–628). It is also a reflection of the enmity against the Jews because of their attitude in the Holy Land during the Persian occupation.[65]

THE APOCALYPSE OF PSEUDO-METHODIUS

The Apocalypse of Pseudo-Methodius is a text that deals specifically with the Muslim conquests.[66] It is attributed to the bishop and martyr Methodius (d. 312) and is generally assumed that the revelation took place in the Sinjar Mountains, located in northwest Iraq, approximately 100 kilometers southeast of Nisibis, the center of Monophysite Christianity.[67] The *Apocalypse* is said to have been written by a person who saw the Arab conquests as an answer to the deprivations imposed by the Christians and widespread apostasy in order to avoid paying the tax that Christians had to pay under Muslim rule (*jizya*). The original Syrian manuscript was only discovered in

63. Cf. also chapter V.
64. Crone and Cook; Hoyland, *In God's Path*, 126–28; Kaegi Jr., "Initial Byzantine Reactions."
65. Kaegi, *North Africa*, 84.
66. Kaegi, *North Africa*, 91.
67. Reinink, "Ps.-Methodius," 160.

1931. The author, an unknown monk, presents himself as the church father Methodius of the fourth century, thus the pseudonym "Pseudo."

This *Apocalypse* was actually written in Syriac in the late seventh century. Syrian authors in particular viewed the situation of the world in apocalyptic terms.[68] This work must have originated between 686 and 692, around the time of the tax reforms of the Umayyad Caliph 'Abd al-Malik (683–705) in Mesopotamia.[69] 'Abd al-Malik introduced more reforms. Most important was that Arabic replaced Greek and Persian in the financial offices. This was the first step of the reorganization and integration of the various tax systems in the provinces and also a step towards a more definitive Muslim government. He minted gold coins, replacing the Byzantine dinar depicting the *likeness of the emperor* with a Muslim dinar with *Qur'anic texts*. A far-reaching reform was a republication of the text of the Qur'an from the time of the third caliph 'Uthmân with vowels and diacritical points, usually attributed to someone else.[70] It is very likely that *Pseudo-Methodius* feared a voluntary renunciation of Christianity by his fellow believers because of 'Abd al Malik's census and wanted to express the hope that Muslim rule would end.[71]

Pseudo-Methodius divides world history into seven millennia. The time of the Muslim rule is restricted to ten weeks of "years" or 70 years. The beginning of these 70 years most likely coincides with the year 622. At the end of these ten weeks of rule, the Byzantine emperor would suddenly, unexpectedly, by means of a large-scale military campaign, put an end to the role of "the sons of Ishmael" on the stage of world history. Pseudo-Methodius cites a Psalm: "Then the Lord awoke as from sleep, as a warrior wakes from the stupor of wine" (Ps 78:65).[72] The appearance of the Byzantine emperor would occur at the very moment that the Arabs feel safe and think they are strong.[73] The direct reason for the emperor's sudden intervention is the blasphemy uttered by the Muslims, who said the Christians had no savior.[74]

---

68. Reinink, "Ps.- Methodius," 155.

69. According to Ibn Khaldûn, he was one of the greatest Arab and Muslim caliphs: He followed in the footsteps of 'Umar ibn al-Khattâb when regulating state matters. https://en.wikipedia.org/wiki/Abd_al_Malik_ibn_Marwan.

70. *EI*, s.v., 'Abd al-Malik.

71. Reinink, "Ps.-Methodius," 149.

72. Elijah's ridicule of the sleeping God (Baal) (1 Kgs 18:27) and the anxious wake-up call to the sleeping God (Ps 7:7; 35:23; 44:24; 59:5; cf. 83:2) became a bitter reality with God allowing the fall of the Northern Kingdom (namely, Israel; the Southern Kingdom is Judah). According to Hossfeld and Zenger, *Psalmen 51–100*, 439. the following verses add to the importance of the acts God carries out after awakening and becoming fully conscious.

73. Reinink, "Ps.-Methodius," 152.

74. Reinink, "Ps.-Methodius," 154.

Pseudo-Methodius sees the rise of Islam in a fashion similar to Saint John of Damascus (676–749), who prayed for liberation at the hands of the Byzantine emperor from the enemies of Christ: the Ishmaelites. Saint John of Damascus wrote one of the first Christian polemics against Islam. Writing in a time when the great church of Damascus was being turned into the Great Mosque of Damascus, he saw Islam as a Christian heresy.[75] After the Arab conquest of Damascus in 634, the mosque was built by Caliph al-Walid I on the location of the Christian basilica dedicated to John the Baptist, whose head was buried there as a relic.[76] *Pseudo-Methodius* never uses the term kingdom (*malkûta*) in connection with the Arab reign. Rather, he uses the traditional pattern of the four kingdoms—the Babylonians, the Medes, the Persians and the Greeks/Romans—and simply denies the existence of anything such as an Arab kingdom. In fact, his "revelation" about the succession of kingdoms can be regarded as a plea for the view that the Greek/Roman/Byzantine kingdom, founded on the conquests of Alexander the Great, is the *fourth kingdom* in Daniel and the last empire in the history of humankind (cf. Dan 2 and 7). The role of the sons of Ishmael is restricted to that of a temporary chastisement, a scourge in the hand of God to destroy the fattened Greek beasts, to punish the Christians for their sins (especially sexual ones), and to separate the true believers from unbelievers, apostates. As usual, the Arabs are portrayed as barbaric tyrants, the uncivilized descendants of Ishmael, the wild donkey of the desert(Gen 16:12), who destroyed the civilized world and desecrated the holy places of Christianity. Ishmael's descendants are nomads who can be compared to wild donkeys because of their independence and nomadic existence (cf. Job 39:5–8).[77]

The text of *Pseudo-Methodius*, which begins with the history of Adam and Eve in the Garden of Eden and goes up to the Muslim conquests in the end time, speaks of the "sons of Ishmael" who appear out of the desert to impose God's punishment on Christians because of the evil they had done. These disasters serve not as a call to repent but as a sign that the end of the world is near. Despite the facts contradicting this, the author nevertheless stresses that the "sons of Ishmael" would reign only a short time and would not form a world kingdom. Soon after the conquests, God would allow the final king of the Greeks to arise. This would unleash a war against the blasphemous sons of Ishmael, and they would soon be defeated. The king would punish the Christians who renounced their faith and rule from Jerusalem for a period of ten years in peace and prosperity. Then he would transfer the

---

75. Reinink, "Ps.-Methodius," 156; https://en.wikipedia.org/wiki/John_of_Damascus.
76. https://en.wikipedia.org/wiki/Umayyad_Mosque.
77. KBS: Gen 25:12–18 lists Ishmael's descendants; cf. 1 Chr 1:29–31.

earthly reign to Christ by placing his crown on the true cross. This would mark the second coming of Jesus and his defeat of the Antichrist.[78]

The text of *Pseudo-Methodius* was quickly translated from Syriac to Greek and then to Latin and thus became one of the most influential apocalyptic texts in both the East and the West.[79] It became the most widely read early Christian text that dealt with the beginning of Islam and thus influenced later Christian eschatological thought in the Middle Ages. In the thirteenth century, the Russian Christians used *Pseudo-Methodius* to explain the Mongolian invasion. They believed that it predicted the arrival of the Mongols. Again, in 1453, when Constantinople fell, this very *Apocalypse* was used to help explain it.[80] Excerpts from the prophecies concerning the "sons of Ishmael" and their "imminent death" were even printed in Vienna during the Turkish siege in 1683![81]

It is possible that the author of *Pseudo-Methodius* knew of the exegetical tradition concerning Cush of Ethiopia. David, to whom Psalm 68 is attributed, says: "Envoys will come from Egypt; Cush will submit herself to God" (Ps 68:31; cf. Isa 18:7; Isa 45:1, 4; Zeph 3:10; Acts 8:27–28).[82] Tradition has it that Cush was linked with the queen of Ethiopia and with the legendary traditions in which the queen of Sheba was related to Alexander the Great. According to the author, Kûshat, the mother of Alexander the Great, who married Byzas after Alexander's death was the legendary founder of Byzantium. Out of that marriage was born a daughter Byzantia, who married Romulus, the founder of Rome. They had three children: Romulus, who ruled in Rome, Urbanus in Byzantium, and Claudius in Alexandria. The genealogy illustrates the unity of the *fourth kingdom* from the book of Daniel: Macedonians, Greeks, Romans, Byzantines and the Christian kingdom of Ethiopia are linked to the Byzantine Empire. This exegetical tradition expected one world dominion of the Christian empire, under the rule of the last world emperor who would protect all churches after his victory over the Arabs.[83]

According to *Pseudo-Methodius*, David spoke in a psalm (68:32) of the kingdom of the Greeks, who were descended from the descendants of

---

78. Penn, *Envisioning Islam*, 29–30.

79. Reinink, "Ps.-Methodius," 155.

80. https://en.wikipedia.org/wiki/Apocalypse_of_Pseudo-Methodius: The Apocalypse is noted for incorporating numerous aspects of Christian eschatology such as the invasion of Gog and Magog, the rise of the Antichrist, and the tribulations that precede the end of the world.

81. Penn, *When Christians First Met Muslims*, 108.

82. Peshittâ Ps 68:31.

83. Reinink, "Ps.-Methodius," 161, n. 57.

Kûshat, daughter of Pîl, king of the Ethiopians. David's prophecy would be fulfilled when the last emperor of the Greeks goes to Golgotha after the appearance of the Antichrist and, as stated earlier, places his crown on the top of the cross and transfers his kingdom to God the Father.[84] The last kingdom is the Greek/Christian kingdom. The author of *Pseudo-Methodius* was convinced that Islam formed a serious threat to Christianity and that the only one who was able to and also had the sacred duty to resist this threat was the emperor of Byzantium.[85] He reinforces this typological description of history by mixing the events from the recent past and his time with themes and motifs borrowed from biblical history and vice versa. He tries to lend force to his opinion that there was no *lasting* Arab kingdom, in light of the biblical history that shows that, in the past, God saved the Israelites and the entire civilized world from these sons of Ishmael. Thus, the Arabs from Yathrib, Medina, which was the center of the kingdom up to and including the fourth caliph (632–661), are only a repetition of earlier attempts at conquest and that would end in their destruction, this time at the initiative of the Byzantine emperor.[86]

Pseudo-Methodius's first objective was to establish a typological relationship between Alexander the Great, the first king of the Greeks, and the last one, the Byzantine emperor. In the genealogy in this work, the kingdoms of Macedonia, Greece, and Rome are united through a common ancestor, Kûshat, an Ethiopian princess.[87] This strengthens the above-mentioned unity of Daniel's fourth empire and creates the possibility of a typological pattern in which the first ruler can be compared with the last one. Alexander the Great, the "pious king," son of Kûshat, founded the Greek empire, marched to the East, defeated the Persians, conquered large areas of the world and locked the unclean, eschatological peoples of Ezekiel (Gog and Magog) behind the gates of the North. *Pseudo-Methodius* relies heavily on the Syriac *Alexander legend* here.[88] How is it possible for the royal house of Alexander to conquer the world at the end of time and transfer the kingdom of the earth to Jesus when Alexander had no descendants? In the Syriac *Alexander legend*, Pseudo-Methodius read the prophecy that the kingdom of the Romans would rule until the end of time and transfer the kingdom of Christ in an eschatological context; he also saw a prophecy in

84. Reinink, "Ps.-Methodius," 161–62.

85. Reinink, "Ps.-Methodius," 164.

86. Reinink, "Ps.-Methodius," 165.

87. Reinink, "Ps.-Methodius," 165; Penn, *When Christians First Met Muslims*, 109–10.

88. Neshâna d-'Alexandrôs; the Alexander legend is one of Pseudo-Methodius's main sources; cf. Wessels, *The Torah, the Gospel, and the Qur'an*, 192, 209–13.

Psalm 68:31, which spoke of Cush who would submit to God. Using biblical material, *Pseudo-Methodius* built up a brilliant structure. By creating a Cushite mother for Alexander on the basis of Ps 68:31, *Pseudo-Methodius* could establish a genealogical relationship between Macedonia, Greece, and Rome, allowing the kingdom of the house of Alexander to be seen as a historical unity that includes even the Christian kingdom of Ethiopia. This fit an eschatological pattern: the last world emperor as the last emperor, Alexander *"redivisus."*[89] The idea of restoration acquires a new function by the connection of Alexander's empire with eschatological world dominion. It is the last period of peace before the coming of the Son of Man (Matt 24:38–39) and the day of the Lord (1 Thess 5:2–3), which will last until the wicked eschatological people of the North have been destroyed.

The suggestion that *Pseudo-Methodius*'s last world ruler is modelled on the idea of the Roman emperor as an idealized protector of Christianity is reinforced by the Syriac *Julian Romance* (331–363). Julian was emperor from 361 to 363. The author compares Jovian (emperor from 363 to 364) with Constantine the Great (d. 337) and the peace that reigned in the churches under his rule. After the paganism of the tyrant Julian the Apostate, the "true Christian king" Jovian restored the Christian Roman and Byzantine kingship. He fulfilled the sacred duty of the Christian emperor to protect Christianity throughout the world and to combat paganism.[90]

The episode of Jovian's acceptance of the crown after Julian's death is striking. When the armies wanted to make him emperor, he finally gave in to their wishes on the condition that they provide proof of their conversion "by worshipping the cross, which is a sign of salvation to all who believe in Him." Witnessing their readiness to do so, Jovian took the cross, the symbol of victory, went before the army, and erected it in a high place in front of the troops. Then he gave the order to place the crown on top of the cross, with the cross as the symbol of victory of the Christian Empire.[91] As the emperor knelt in prayer before the cross, the crown miraculously moved from the cross and placed itself on his head. All the people were surprised and amazed. "Henceforth, Christ is king over us in heaven and Jovian is king over us on earth." Jovian's crown was consecrated by the cross and received directly from the hands of the Lord; the crown is the symbol of the Christian emperorship on earth, representing the heavenly kingship of Christ. The final world emperor will hand over his crown to God at the end of time.[92]

---

89. Reinink, "Ps.-Methodius," 166–67, n. 72.
90. Reinink, "Ps.-Methodius," 170–71.
91. Reinink, "Ps.-Methodius," 171–72.
92. Reinink, "Ps.-Methodius," 173.

Pseudo-Methodius stamps the figure of the idealized Christian emperor with the image of Constantine, Constantius II (the Byzantine emperor from 337 to 361),[93] and especially Jovian. It is the *eschatological role* of the idealized emperor that is emphasized here. The work was intended to convince fellow believers that they must place their trust in this emperor since he would establish a Christian world dominion that would protect all churches within the empire. This emperor, like Jovian, is the representative of Christ on earth and, by combatting the heathen Arabs and those who have renounced their faith, he is merely acting in accordance with his holy task.[94] The importance that *Pseudo-Methodius* attributes to Jerusalem and the Holy Land not only has an anti-Jewish bent but is also an essential component in his polemic against the idea of an Arab empire that has a permanent political-religious place in world history.[95]

THE END OF THE SECOND CIVIL WAR (FITNA)

The first *fitna* or war of succession took place from 656 to 661. It was caused by the murder of the third caliph 'Uthmân and the subsequent controversial election of 'Ali ibn Abû Tâlib, the nephew and son-in-law of Muhammad, as the fourth caliph. The vice-regent, Mu'âwiya of Damascus (Syria), did not recognize him. The confrontation with the latter remained undecided in the Battle at Siffîn (657). 'Alî was murdered in 661, after which Mû'âwiyya established the caliphate of Umayyad. The Shi'ites continue to follow this caliph and are of his "party," *shia-t* 'Alî—hence their name.[96]

The second civil war took place after the death of the first Umayyad caliph when his son Yazîd I (d. 683) became his successor. The most dramatic event is the unequal fight in which Husayn, the son of 'Alî and therefore grandson of the prophet Muhammad through Yazîd, who had succeeded his father Mu'âwiyya, was killed at the Battle of Kerbala in 680. Husayn's head was brought to Yazîd in Damascus in triumph (*sic!*).[97] The expectation that the Byzantine emperor would quickly rise up to defeat the Muslims was not that strange because there were many signs in 691 that pointed to a speedy conclusion of the peace treaty between the Byzantine emperor Justin II (685–695) and the fifth Umayyad caliph 'Abd al Malik (685–705).

93. Cf. chapter V.
94. Reinink, "Ps.-Methodius," 175–76.
95. Reinink, "Ps.-Methodius," 177–78.
96. https://en.wikipedia.org/wiki/First_Fitna.
97. During the caliphate of his father, Yazîd I took part in an attack on Constantinople (669 or 670).

A civil war in the Arab Kingdom meant that the situation was rather peaceful for the Byzantines in the East. The new caliph, 'Abd al-Malik, who came into power almost simultaneously with Justin, attempted to fortify his wobbly throne by making peace with Byzantium. For the Byzantine emperor Justin, this was particularly beneficial. Cyprus, Armenia, and Iberia were placed under one government so that the tax revenue was divided between them. For Cyprus, this exceptional status would last for several centuries. In 692, however, the Arab civil wars came to an end, and 'Abd al-Malik resumed the Byzantine-Arab wars.[98]

Pseudo-Methodius's view should be seen against this historical background. His problem was not the idea of a Jewish Messiah or that of an Ethiopian king-savior but how the expectation of the *immanent ending of world history* could be reconciled with the changing political circumstances: the restoration of the unity of the Arab Empire under the Umayyads. 'Abd al Malik regained control over Mesopotamia in 691, which allowed taxes to be increased significantly. As a result, an entirely different future appeared to be immanent. The unity of the Christian empire was linked to the restoration of the unity of the Arab Empire.[99] It raised the question whether this "temporary" chastisement would cease if there were no longer any expectations that the internal Arab fighting in the second civil war, the second *fitna*, would result in the collapse of the Muslim empire.[100]

THE BUILDING OF THE DOME OF THE ROCK IN JERUSALEM

In that same year 691, the Umayyad caliph of Damascus, 'Abd al Malik, had the Dome of the Rock[101] built in Jerusalem on the location where the first and second temples had stood. The Qur'an alludes to the two conquests of Jerusalem and the destruction of the temple: the first in 586 BC under Nebuchadnezzar and the second in 70 AD under the Romans. These events are placed in a "salvation history" context. At both times, the destruction was the result of the fact that the children of Israel had "brought about havoc on earth." Finally, a prediction is given with both possibilities: divine compassion or renewed punishment if the people sin again (Q 17:4–8).[102]

98. https://en.wikipedia.org/wiki/Justinian_II.
99. Reinink, "Ps.-Methodius," 180, n. 135.
100 .https://en.wikipedia.org/wiki/First_Fitna.
101. Qubbat al-Sakhra.
102. Paret on Q 17:4–8.

The Dome of the Rock was the first monumental Islamic structure erected in the heart of the *Christian* city, modelled after Christian churches and intended to surpass them in splendor. Its physical appearance must have been impressive for possible converts with regard to the power of the new faith; it could serve as an "missionary victory monument" to propagate the superiority of Islam over Christianity. That would have led the author of the *Pseudo-Methodius* to demonstrate the unity of the Greek, Roman, and Byzantine empires: "as long as [that empire] seeks refuge in the life-giving cross that has been placed in the center of the earth" (in Jerusalem!), the only heir of the offices of priesthood and kingship until the second coming of Christ."[103] *Pseudo-Methodius* focused on demonstrating that the heathen tyrants (Arabs) would never be *able* to acquire a place in the Greek empire as long as this empire clung to the symbol of the cross of victory that had been erected in the holy city. After all, the Jews lost the excellent gifts of Judaism—priesthood, prophecy and kingship—when the holy city was destroyed (*sic!*). After that, priesthood, kingship and *the holy cross* stood "in the center." Only the Christian Empire would be victorious and exist until the appearance of the Antichrist.[104] The fact that *Pseudo-Methodius* had the last Greek emperor reside in Jerusalem and allowed him to abdicate on Golgotha after the appearance of the Antichrist was meant to demonstrate that Jerusalem had become *the city of Christianity* and would always remain so.

In 363, Julian the Apostate (331–363) attempted to rebuild the temple, a plan that was considered to be anti-Christian. But a "miraculous intervention" prevented this from happening. In his *Hymns against Julian*, Ephrem the Syrian (ca 306–373) draws a parallel between the attempt to rebuild the temple and the introduction of paganism into Jerusalem.[105]

Reinink states that the hypothesis that the *Apocalypse of Pseudo-Methodius* was composed in response to 'Abd al Malik's founding of the Dome of the Rock on the seat of the Jewish temple is very attractive. Emperor Justin II was the first Byzantine emperor to issue a coin bearing the image of Christ with the cross behind his head on one side and the emperor with a crown bearing a cross and a cross in his hand on the other. It is very tempting to assume that *Pseudo-Methodius*, who links the figure of the last world emperor closely to Christ, was aware of the implication of this iconography that presents the emperor as the *servus Christi*. If this is so, then one must assume that this *Apocalypse* was composed in 692 at its earliest.

103. Reinink, "Ps.-Methodius," 181–82.
104. Reinink, "Ps.-Methodius," 183–84.
105. Reinink., "Ps.-Methodius," 184–85.

Pseudo-Methodius's apocalyptic view of history appears to be mainly a response to the rise of Islam that became manifest as a *permanent* political religious power during the caliphate of 'Abd al Malik. The caliphate claimed to be not only a *political* successor of Christianity in the Byzantine Empire but also the *religious* successor of Christianity in the Near East. Thus, the real problem for *Pseudo-Methodius* was the fear that the rapidly changing political and social circumstances would encourage his fellow believers to convert to Islam.[106] He wanted to demonstrate that conversion meant nothing less than defecting to paganism, comparable to the situation of the pagan tyrant Julian the Apostate, who, just like the Muslims, denied faith in the redeeming power of the cross, the sign of the victory of the *Christian world* and of the *Christian empire*. Firmly adhering to his opinion that he lived in the *last days of world history*, the author of *Pseudo-Methodius* declared that such *defection* was part of the *eschatological tribulations* that would separate true believers from unbelievers. But this was a temporary chastisement that would be terminated by the Christian emperor who would unite all Christians under the reign of the Christian empire and, ultimately, hand the kingship over to God the Father.[107]

---

106. Reinink, "Ps.-Methodius," 183–86.
107. Reinink, "Ps.-Methodius," 186–87.

III

Luther's Apocalyptic Understanding

Luther saw himself as "the apocalyptic prophet at the end of time." "If we sweep away his apocalypticism, his theology will make no sense to us."[1]

INTRODUCTION

Martin Luther (1483–1546) was an Augustinian monk who was ordained as a priest in 1507 and later became a professor of theology at the University of Wittenberg. His first lectures—1513–1515—were on the Psalms. For years, he attempted to read the course of the church in the past *and* in the present into the text of the Psalms. "Exegesis becomes a diagnosis of the times." "Psalm after psalm, observations are strung together, textual exegesis becomes a diagnosis of his times, the eyes are directed to the Jews then and 'our Jews' now." That he placed Muhammad with the Jews as threatening the church from outside is not surprising. "But the cusp of the threat comes from within: the church has already been damaged right down to its very structures by false teachers." "The Jews today are primarily we miserable Christians ourselves."[2] In his *Table Talk*, Luther expressed himself bluntly: The Turks were the lesser evil. The soul and spirit of the Antichrist was the

---

1. According to Heiko A. Oberman, cited in: Francisco, *Martin Luther and Islam*, 79.
2. According to Oberman, *Wortels van het antisemitisme*, 105.

pope, and the Turk his body and flesh. Just as the church defied the spiritual power of the Jews and the sword of Romans in the days of the apostles—the first century—so now it would be victorious over the *superstition* and the *idolatry* of Rome and the *tyranny* of the Turks. "Cursed be the Pope who has done more evil to the kingdom of God than Muhammad." The Turk killed the body, destroyed and stole the goods of the Christian, but the Pope was more cruel than the Turk with his Qur'an, for the Pope forced Christians to deny "Christ." Both were enemies of the church and servants of Satan. This kind of language became widespread. Luther was called the "Beer Pope," about which he commented *soberly*: "My vain conversation in the tavern shocked the papacy in a more focused way than the princes and the emperor with their knights armed with iron could do."[3]

Luther's texts were written with eschatological verve and, from the very beginning to the end of his career, were peppered with a dominant apocalyptic tone. His central assumption, which was his lens for viewing the world, was that "ultimately, history is the arena in which God and Satan wage war." The title of Heiko Oberman's biography is *Luther: Mensch zwischen Gott und Teufel* (Luther: A Man between God and the Devil). Luther called the devil "God's ape." He was convinced that the end of the world was near in his time. The most important indication for him was the end of the age-old battle between God and Satan, the restoration of the Gospel in the church, as well as the continued resistance to the Gospel by the papacy and the Jews (sic!). In this context, the Turkish expansion into Central Europe was a sign that Satan had been permitted to carry out a final attack on the elect. Thus, the Turkish threat was apocalyptic in nature.[4]

This threat was very real. Luther was quite concerned about the expansion of the power of the Turks into Europe and the consequences this had for Christians: apostasy from the Christian faith or conversion to Islam, although the term "Islam" was not yet used at that time. He spoke of "the religion of the Turks." Another Reformer, Ulrich Zwingli, spoke of the Qur'an as the "Turkish Bible."[5] Even before the Siege of Vienna in 1529, Luther had received reports about Hungarians and Germans offering their services to the Turks and, at times, being prepared to submit to Ottoman rule. He considered this an act of treason and saw it as opening the way for the spread of Islam in Europe.

The idea that the world was becoming "Mohammedan" did not simply arise out of fear. It was rather a reflection on the geopolitical context.

---

3. Reston, *Defenders of the Faith*, 259–60; cf. Francisco, *Martin Luther and Islam*, 83.
4. Francisco, *Martin Luther and Islam*, 79–80.
5. Bobzin, "Early printed Korans," 264.

According to Marshall G.S. Hodgson (d. 1968), a renowned American authority on the history of Islam, in the sixteenth century a visitor from Mars is said to have indicated that the human world was on the point of becoming Muslim.[6]

When Luther died in 1546, he was compared at his funeral with the second angel (from the book of Revelation) who came down from heaven and shouted with a mighty voice: "Fallen! Fallen is Babylon the Great!" (Rev 18:2). On that same occasion, Luther's "prophecy" with respect to the Pope was recalled: "In life I was your plague; dying I shall be your death, O pope."[7]

In that same sixteenth century, Muslims gave expression to apocalyptic ideas as well. In 1520 the son of Selim I, Sultan Suleiman, came into power (1520–1566). The name Suleiman derives of course from the biblical King Solomon, Sulaymân in Arabic. Solomon's kingship over Israel was completely unique. He was penitent and said: "My Lord! Forgive me, / and grant me a kingdom / that does not befit anyone except me" (Q 38:35). Here, Solomon's request for wisdom (1 Kgs 3:5–15) is a prayer for an everlasting kingdom. Once the temple was completed, God assured Solomon: "As for you, if you walk before me faithfully with integrity of heart and uprightness, as David your father did, and do all I command and observe my decrees and laws, I will establish your royal throne over Israel forever, as I promised David your father when I said, 'You shall never fail to have a successor on the throne of Israel'" (1 Kgs 9:4–5). That idea is also confirmed in the Gospel. With Jesus' entry into Jerusalem on a donkey, the people shout:

> Hosanna! Blessed is he who comes
> in the name of the Lord.
> Blessed is the coming kingdom
> of our father David!
> Hosanna in the highest heaven!
> (Mark 11:10; cf. 2 Sam 12–16).[8]

In the Qur'an, Solomon is the perfect sovereign who embodies the idea of justice, but he is also a great warrior.[9] The latter appears to be somewhat apocryphal, but Solomon is judged in the Bible because he has become a "pharaoh" (1 Kgs 11:1–14). He accumulated chariots and horses, armed himself excessively (1 Kgs 10:16, 26). How dangerous it was to have and keep horses becomes clear from the following story in the Qur'an. One

---

6. Cited by Francisco, *Martin Luther and Islam*, 85, n. 65.
7. Reston, *Defenders of the Faith*. 384.
8. Speyer, *Die biblischen Erzählungen*, 383–384.
9. Reston, *Defenders of the Faith*, 9.

evening at sunset, Solomon has (race) horses paraded before him and loses himself in his admiration for them. He strokes their legs and necks and becomes so involved in this that he forgets to pray at sunset and thus neglects to remember God. He loves his horses, his possession of the goods of the world (cf. Q 100:8; 89:20; 9:24), more than the remembrance of God until the time that the sun disappeared behind the veil of the night (Q 38:32).

It is quite conceivable that the text of the Qur'an reflects what a later good king of Israel did. This king, Josiah, rediscovered the book of the Torah, took the appropriate action, and read aloud all the words from the scroll of the Scriptures of the covenant in front of the entire community (2 Kgs 22:8; 23:2). One of the many consequences that Josiah carries out is removing the horses from the temple that were dedicated to the sun and having the chariots that were dedicated to the sun burned (2 Kgs 23:11). After all, God's pleasure is not in the strength of the horse nor in the legs of the soldier (Ps 147:10). The *law for kings* prohibits keeping horses, a practice that was viewed as a return to "Egypt." Solomon, however, imported horses from Egypt and many other countries—he had those weapons imported from Egypt, the country that was symbolic of slavery and oppression! In that respect, therefore, he behaved like a Pharaoh (Deut 17:16; cf. 1 Chr 9:28), a ruler who commits injustice and brings corruption on the earth!

Suleiman I was the tenth sultan of the Ottoman Turkish Empire and had the longest reign of all the sultans. At his father's funeral, Suleiman took up the sword of Osman I (Gazi), the founder of the Ottoman Empire (1258–1326). "With that act, he committed his reign, as nine sultans had done before him, to *gaza*, or holy war against the infidels."[10] Gazi originally referred to someone who had participated in a raid or military expedition. In early Islamic literature, the term *ghazwa* is the name of the expedition that was led by the prophet Muhammad.[11] The term was Later, used by Turkish military leaders to describe their wars of conquest, it became a title for Turkish champions like Osman and Mustafa Kemal Ataturk.[12] Osman Gazi was the founder of the dynasty of the Ottoman Empire around 1300. Suleiman himself led sixteen expeditions, and his conquests were directed towards Europe, primarily the Balkans and Hungary, until he advanced toward Vienna on 1 May 1529![13]

---

10. Reston, *Defenders of the Faith*, 17.
11. https://en.wiktionary.org/wiki/ghazwa.
12. https://en.wikipedia.org/wiki/Ghazi_(warrior).
13. Finkel, *De droom van Osman*, 115.

THE TURKISH CONQUEST OF CONSTANTINOPLE (1453)

To properly understand the relationship between the Christians and the Muslims in Europe in the sixteenth century, we must first look at the fall of Constantinople half a century earlier. On 18 February 1451, the future conqueror Mehmed II was inaugurated as the new sultan of the Ottoman Empire one month before his nineteenth birthday. He ruled from 1451–1481, and was called *Fatih*. "the Conqueror," The term was originally from Arabic. The *Fatih* mosque in Istanbul, which was named after him, was built by Mehmed II on the ruins of the Church of the Holy Apostles in Constantinople, one of the most important churches of the new Roman capital since its foundation by Constantine I.[14] Mehmed II was given the sword of his forefather Osman Gazi, an act that was the Ottoman equivalent of a crown with a coronation.[15]

From his youth onwards, he himself said, he had been obsessed with the desire to conquer Constantinople. He was consumed by the memory of Alexander the Great and had the history of Alexander's wars and conquests, based on stories by Arrian of Nicomedia, read aloud daily, especially his conquest of Persia (336–333 BC).[16] The conquest of West and Central Asia by Alexander the Great was the greatest military achievement of Greek antiquity. Alexander himself may have seen that differently. He took with him the inspiring stories of two other military expeditions: the *Illiad* by Homer and the *Anabasis* by Xenophon. Achilles's heroic deeds at Troy and the journey of ten thousand Greeks, who traveled from Mesopotamia, straight through the least accessible part of the Persian kingdom to the coast of the Black Sea, were the examples he followed. Mehmed's identification with Alexander went so far that he ordered an account of his own deeds to be written in Greek on the same type of paper and in the same format as his copy of Arrian's biography that could be placed in the library.[17]

The ambitious young sultan decided that the "apple," i.e., "Constantinople," was finally ripe enough to be plucked. "Golden Apple" was the name given by the Turks to each of the four Christian capitals crowned by a golden globe: Constantinople, Buda, Vienna, and Rome. The conquest of the first "Golden Apple" in the year 1453 was the Christian Constantinople

---

14. https://en.wikipedia.org/wiki/Church_of_the_Holy_Apostles.
15. Freely, *The Grand Turk*, 20; https://en.wikipedia.org/wiki/Fatih.
16. https://en.wikipedia.org/wiki/The_Anabasis_of_Alexander.
17. Fletcher, *The Cross and the Crescent*, 136.

(as 28 March 1930: Istanbul). And thus the Ottomans put an end to the thousand-year-old East Roman or Byzantine Empire.[18]

When he was 21, Mehmed II conquered the largest city of Christianity that contained the most important Christian church: the Church of Holy Wisdom, the Hagia Sophia. Constantine XI (1405–1453), who would be the last Byzantine ruler, had sent a desperate letter to Pope Nicholas V (1447–1455),[19] asking him to send reinforcements as quickly as possible and promising to reunite the Eastern Orthodox Church with the Western Roman Catholic Church[20] that had been divided by a schism since 1054. The fourth crusade (1002–1004) had actually been directed against Byzantium and had caused immense damage to this center of the Eastern Orthodox Church. Many of the art treasures are still in Venice (San Marco).

In 1453, during the siege of Constantinople, the Christians maintained their belief that, despite the devastating attacks, God would not allow the city to fall to the "evil pagans"—at least not until a prophecy attributed to Constantine the Great was fulfilled. He had prophesied that the city would not fall until the moon was pink when it rose. Because this had not (yet) occurred, the people within the walls kept hoping until there was a lunar eclipse on a stormy night on 24 May that caused a strange light to hover above the Hagia Sophia. The rumor spread among the frightened citizens that "the time of the Antichrist" had come and that the end of the world was nigh: a major battle would take place and the Antichrist would be defeated; Christ would return to judge the living and the dead. For the people of Constantinople, it was easy to imagine that Mehmed was the Antichrist and that the end of time had come. On 29 May 1453, the city fell. The sultan went to the Hagia Sophia immediately, and his own imam climbed the pulpit and recited the Muslim creed, thereby transforming the church into a mosque. The frescos of Jesus and the saints were soon disfigured or covered.[21]

The last Byzantine ruler died in that battle, one who bore the same name as the first "Christian" emperor, Constantine. In Greek folklore, he became a legendary figure, called the Marble Emperor, who would awaken someday and recapture Constantinople from the Ottomans.[22] Enea Silvio

---

18. https://ejbron.wordpress.com/2011/10/06/328-jaar-geleden-werd-wenen-bevrijd-van-de-turkse-bedreiging/.

19. In the year 1452 Pope Nicholas V issued the bull *Dum Diversas* ("Doctrine of Discovery"), with which the king of Portugal, Henry the Navigator, was given the right to enslave the Saracens, pagans and other unbelievers, including their descendants. This bull justified the colonial slave trade; https://en.wikipedia.org/wiki/Pope_Nicholas_V.

20. Delaney, *Columbus and the Quest for Jerusalem*, 3.

21. Delaney, *Columbus and the Quest for Jerusalem*, 7.

22. https://en.wikipedia.org/wiki/Constantine_XI_Palaiologos.

Piccolini, later Pope Pius II, wrote to Cardinal Nicholas of Cusa (d. 1464): "So much blood was shed that rivers of blood flowed through the city. And thus the noble city founded by Constantine has fallen into the hands of the unbelievers."[23]

With the conquest of Constantinople, an ancient desire of the first followers of the prophet Muhammad was fulfilled. According to a Greek historian, the fall of Constantinople was viewed in Rome as revenge for the fall of Troy. In any case, this was the opinion expressed by Sultan Mehmed II in 1462 when he visited Troy.[24] When he arrived, he admired the ruins and the remains of the old city, explored the graves of the heroes there, particularly those of Achilles and Ajax, and stated that they "were blessed both for their immortality and their deeds as well as for the fact that they had Homer as their eulogist." He commented:

> After so many years, God has appointed me as avenger of this city and its inhabitants. I have defeated their enemies; I have destroyed their cities and taken their possessions as spoils. Because it was the Greeks, Macedonians, Thessalians and Peloponnesians who had pillaged Troy. Now, after a very long time, I have punished their descendants for their arrogance towards us Asians at that time and often thereafter.[25]

Mehmed's visit to Troy is linked to his identification with Alexander the Great, who slept with Homer's *Illiad* under his pillow. Mehmed wanted to be regarded as his reincarnation—he was fixated on the life of Alexander the Great, whose empire stretched to India and the heart of Europe. An account of the life of this Great Conqueror written by a Persian lay next to his bed, and this appears to have lent more credence to Suleiman's ambition that he would one day expand the reign of Islam to the Rhine and the Indus River.[26]

Mehmed had obtained an expensive edition of Homer that can still be admired in the library of Topkapı Palace. Mehmed II's notion that he had avenged the West's arrogance towards "us Asians" (Trojans) concurs with the classic idea of the contrast between East and West, between Asia and Europe. Herodotus (1, 1–4) had already placed the Trojan War in the context of mutual retaliatory actions between the East and the West.[27] Of

23. Hagemann, *Martin Luther und der Islam*, 8.

24. Freely, *The Grand Turk*, 100.

25. According to the Greek chronicler, Michael Kritoboulos, who worked for the Ottomans, in his *Historiae*; Freely, *The Grand Turk*, 73.

26. Reston, *Defenders of the Faith*, 324.

27. Rijser, "De tweede ronde," and Uslu, "Mehmet II en Troje."

his own accord, Mehmed II continued to cherish the idea of being the legal heir of the Byzantine Empire. This was apparent from the ceremony at his funeral; it was borrowed from that of the founder of Constantinople, Emperor Constantine the Great in 337.[28]

The capture of Granada in 1492, the end of the "reconquest," *Reconquista*, of the Iberian peninsula from the Muslims, had an extraordinary effect on the entire Christian world and is viewed as revenge for Constantinople falling into the hands of the Turks in 1453![29]

EUROPE AND THE OTTOMAN EMPIRE

It is important now to first consider the importance of two sultans in the time of Luther: Selim I (1470–1520) and his son Suleiman (1494–1566). Under the rule of the first, the territory of the Ottoman Empire at least doubled in size.[30] First, there was an expansion to the *east*: in 1514, Selim declared war on the Persians under the Safawid Shah Ismaïl I, conquering and seizing their capital Tabriz. He then turned to the *south*. Between 1516 and 1517, he conquered Syria, Lebanon, Palestine, and Egypt. For three centuries, from 1250–1517, the dynasty of the Mamluks, originally slaves of mainly Turkish origin, had ruled over Egypt and a major part of the Middle East. Their last caliph in Egypt was a descendent of the Abbasids, a dynasty that had taken over the Umayyad caliphate. They reigned from 750 until the Mongolians destroyed Baghdad in 1258. Selim I transferred the caliph from Egypt to Constantinople, including the symbols of the caliphate: the mantle and sword of the prophet Muhammad, and from 1517 on the Turkish sultan bore the title of caliph.[31] The caliphate continued until the beginning of the twentieth century when Mustafa Kemal Ataturk, the "father of the fatherland" of Turkey, deposed the last caliph at the beginning of the twentieth century and subsequently disposed of the caliphate itself.

But in 1517 the major cultural centers of the Muslim world, such as Cairo, Jerusalem, and Damascus, had fallen into Turkish hands, including the three most important holy places Mecca, Medina, and Jerusalem. The Ottoman "emperor" became the "protector of the faith."[32] It was at this time that a fundamental change occurred in Ottoman war policy: the principle direction now shifted from the east and the south to the *west*: southeastern

---

28. Finkel, *De droom van Osman*, 115.
29. Cardini, *Europe and Islam*, 178, 182.
30. Reston, *Defenders of the Faith*, 12.
31. https://en.wikipedia.org/wiki/Selim_I; Reston, *Defenders of the Faith*, 43–44.
32. Reston, *Defenders of the Faith*, 12.

Europe and the heart of Europe itself.[33] In the autumn of 1528, preparations began for the Siege of Vienna.

In that same year, Luther was traveling from Wittenberg to Marburg. It is well known that the Turkish threat to the "Holy Roman Empire" was an important topic between Luther and his friend and collaborator Philip Melanchthon. In that year, prior to the Siege of Vienna, Luther published two small treatises: *Vom Kriege widder die Türcken* and *Eine Heerpredigt widder den Türcken*.

The Europeans called Suleiman "the Magnificent" or "the Great Turk,"[34] while the Muslims preferred to characterise him as "Suleiman the Lawgiver" because he harmonized the religious laws of the *shâri'a* with those of the sultan.[35] According to a *Tischrede* in Wittenberg, Luther had learned that Suleiman was interested in him and had inquired about his age. When the sultan had been informed of this, he is reported to have said: "'Pity. I wish he were even younger. He would find in me a gracious protector.' Luther sighed were when he heard this and made the sign of the cross. 'May God protect me from such a generous benefactor', he quipped."[36]

THE SIEGE OF VIENNA

European Christianity was extremely divided internally and therefore could not form a united front against the Turks. Venice was friendly toward the Turks, and the French arranged diplomatic alliances with Suleiman against the Habsburgs, which is exemplary of the internal division in Europe. The "success" of the Reformation was in no small part due to that division within European Christianity toward the Turks. There are rumors that when Suleiman heard of the threat that Luther formed for his greatest enemy Charles V, he urged his imams in the Constantinople mosques to pray for Luther's success![37] The Ottoman sultan could exploit this division to attack Europe. Belgrade fell in 1521, and Louis II, King of Hungary and Bohemia, was defeated on 24 July 1526; it was at that Battle of Mohács that he fled and was killed.[38] In August 1526, Hungary became a vassal state, thus opening up

---

33. Bobzin, *Von Luther zu Rückert*, 261–62.
34. Finkel, *De droom van Osman*, 152.
35. Reston, *Defenders of the Faith*, 387.
36. Reston, *Defenders of the Faith*, 268.
37. Brotton, *This Orient Isle*, 31.

38. His widow, Maria von Habsburg, would later be appointed governess of the Netherlands by Charles V; https://en.wikipedia.org/wiki/Louis_II_of_Hungary.

the road to Vienna, which was barely 100 kilometers away,[39] and *fear* of the further advance of the Turks increased in Germany.[40]

The question why both Luther, and Melanchthon were interested in the "religion of the Turks" is not difficult to answer. It is directly linked to the Turkish advance and the related political and religious dangers.[41] Luther expresses the fear of the Turkish threat in his work *Vom Kriege widder die Türcken*.[42] On 1 May 1529 Sultan Suleiman and an army of 75,000 marched from Constantinople to Vienna.[43] As was always the case with their wars, that expedition was preceded by ceremonies, first by reciting the following text from the Qur'an:

> Fight in the way of God
> those who fight you,
> but do not transgress.
> Indeed God does not like transgressors.
> And kill them wherever you confront them,
> and expel them from where they expelled you,
> for faithlessness is graver than killing.
> But do not fight them near the Holy Mosque
> unless they fight you therein;
> but if they fight you, kill them;
> such is the requital of the faithless.
> But if they relinquish,
> then God is indeed all-forgiving, all-merciful.
> (Q 2:190–192)[44]

It is clear that such Qur'anic texts, used at the beginning of the journey to Vienna, had to serve to legitimize the coming conflict. This text, however, concerns the defense of Mecca. This misuse of the text is comparable to the "Christian" use of the Psalms for justifying the crusades: "O God, the nations [pagans] have invaded your inheritance; they have defiled your holy temple, they have reduced Jerusalem to rubble" (Ps 79:1). This text was applied to the Muslims centuries later. Both instances are illustrations of how texts from the Bible and the Qur'an lent themselves to political and military

---

39. Luther wrote a comforting letter to the widow of the Hungarian king; Hagemann, *Christentum contra Islam*, 82.

40. Wagemann, *Martin Luther und der Islam*, 8, 10.

41. https://en.wikipedia.org/wiki/Giles_of_Viterbo.

42. Hagemann, *Christentum contra Islam*, 81.

43. Reston, *Defenders of the Faith*, 276.

44. The next step for the campaign was the appointment of a commander. Reston, *Defenders of the Faith*, 274–75.

purposes. On both sides there is the—erroneous—conviction that those violent plans could be justified by the word of God.

On 28 September, two days before Luther arrived in Marburg for a colloquium with Protestant leaders, the Turks reached the gates of Vienna in a heavy downpour. Because of the rain, they had to leave their heavy artillery in Hungary. Suleiman *jeered* at the besieged Christian forces by parading outside the walls, wearing an extravagant, bejeweled helmet made for him by *Venetian* (!) goldsmiths, imitating Habsburg and papal imperial crowns. After four vain attempts to capture the city, the Turks were forced to pack up their tents and leave the field.[45] Ferdinand's armies succeeded in resisting the attack by the Ottomans. King Ferdinand I (1503–1564) was the younger brother of Charles V. With the appointment of Charles V as king of Castile and Aragon and as the Holy Roman Emperor, he left the administration of Austria and Slovenia to Ferdinand.[46] Suleiman's failed attempt to capture Vienna was his only major setback during his four decades of waging war in Europe.[47] He did return to the Donau area four times, but he never threatened Vienna again.[48]

The following inscription above the main entrance of the great mosque that Suleiman built in 1560 in Istanbul reads:

> [Sultan Suleiman] has come close to [God], the Exalted Lord and the Almighty, the Creator of the World of the Earth and Supremacy. His servant (Sultan Suleiman) is, gifted with Divine Power, the Caliph, dazzling with Divine Glory, follows the commands of the Hidden Book and executes his Commands in [all] regions of the inhabited Quarter: Conqueror of the lands of the East and the West with the aid of the Almighty God and His Blessed Army, Possessor of the World's Kingdoms, Shadow of God over all Peoples, the Sultan of Sultans of the Arabs and the Persians, Announcer of the Sultanic *Qanuns* of the Sultan . . .. May the line of his Sultanate endure until the End of the Line of Time![49]

---

45. Hendrix, *Martin Luther*, 209.
46. https://en.wikipedia.org/wiki/Ferdinand_I,_Holy_Roman_Emperor.
47. Freely, *The Grand Turk*, 204.
48. Reston, *Defenders of the Faith*, 382–383.
49. Finkel, *De droom van Osman*, 152.

CHARLES V AFTER THE END OF THE RECONQUISTA (1492)

Just as Suleiman was a classic hero for Muslims, so Charles V (1500–1558) was for Christians.[50] The emperor was viewed in Christian thought as a worldly counterpart of the Pope. When he abdicated the throne in 1556, his inheritance included extended areas in the West, Central and Southern Europe as well as the Spanish colonies in "America" and Asia. He was the last emperor to receive the imperial crown from the hands of the Pope.[51] War and conflicts with France in particular characterized his reign. Francis I (1494–1547) was *the* rival of the Habsburgs. During the "Italian War" (1521–1526) the French king lost the Battle of Pavia and was captured by Charles V. During his imprisonment, he secretly wrote to Suleiman to attack Hungary![52]

In 1492, eight years before Charles's birth, the fall of Granada signaled an end to the reconquest (*reconquista*) of the Iberian peninsula from the Moors. On 2 January 1492, the last sovereign of Granada, Boabdil—nicknamed "the Unlucky"[53]—handed over the keys of the Alhambra to the Spanish sovereigns (Ferdinand and Isabella). Ferdinand II (1452–1516) was king of Aragon, together with his wife, Isabella, who ruled over Castile. From the top of a hill, now known as "the Moor's Last Sigh," Boabdil's mother, after taking one last look at the Alhambra, told her son: "Do not weep like a woman about what you could not keep as a man."[54] Church bells were rung throughout all Europe to celebrate this event. "The door through which Islam had entered Europe in the West has been closed after more than 700 years."[55] Here Muslims speak of the first of Europe's attempts at a final solution for the "ethnic cleansing" of the Iberian peninsula of Muslims *and Jews*![56] This reconquest included expelling the Jews from the Iberian peninsula. Columbus "discovered" "America" in that same year of 1492. One reason for that journey was also to be able to contribute to retaking Jerusalem from the Muslims![57]

---

50. Reston, *Defenders of the Faith*, 387.
51. Clement VII in Bologna in 1530.
52. Freely, *The Grand Turk*, 204.
53. Cf. Couperus, *De Ongelukkige*.
54. Akbar, *The Shade of Swords*, 84; cf. Wessels, *Islam in Stories*, 225–26.
55. Akbar, *The Shade of Swords*, 85.
56. Akbar, *The Shade of Swords*, 37.
57. Delaney, *Columbus and the Quest for Jerusalem*, VII, IX, XVI, 48, etc.

Charles V attempted to stop the advance of the Ottoman Turks. He himself fought in the Mediterranean region,[58] while his brother Ferdinand confronted them in eastern Europe. Encouraged by the fact that Suleiman had given up his wish for expansion toward the West, Charles V mobilized a sea "crusade" to challenge the Muslims on the Barbary coast of Africa, and succeeded in conquering Tunis in June 1535.[59] This conquest of Tunis may be the most detailed feat in Charles V's imperial propaganda.[60] Charles was compared to Scipio Africanus, the Roman general who had at one time destroyed Carthage. The Conquest of Tunis was celebrated as a triumph over the unbelievers by the undisputed leader of Christianity.[61] Even though Charles V was successful in Tunis, the city returned to Muslim rule when he failed miserably to capture Algiers in 1541 because his fleet was destroyed by a storm.

Charles V's tutor was the "Dutchman" Adrian of Utrecht. As Pope Adrian VI, he succeeded Pope Leo X, who had banned Luther. During his brief papacy (1522-1523), he attempted to restore peace among the European rulers, urging Francis I and Charles V to set aside their enmity and to unite against the Turkish threat and oppose the scourge of Lutheranism. In his view, Luther was worse than Muhammad, Although he condemned Luther, he did want to do justice to the "heretic." He was the first pope to acknowledge the abuse and corruption of the church. The three major objectives of his papacy were to unite Christianity against the threat of Islam, to resist the scourge of Luther, and to reform the corrupt church.[62]

But the threat from the Turks gave the Protestants more elbowroom. The Reformation led to a conflict between Charles V and German princes who supported Martin Luther. He had hoped to unite the Catholics and the Protestants and convened a diet in Augsburg in 1530 to counteract the two largest threats to Christianity: Lutheranism and Islam. His advisors encouraged him to use the gathering to follow the policy his grandparents Ferdinand II of Aragon and Isabella of Castile had already accepted with respect to the Muslims in Spain: forced conversion or expulsion.[63] Ultimately, however, with the Peace of Augsburg in 1555, Charles V was unable to

---

58. Koldeweij (ed.), *Maria van Hongarije*, 261.
59. Hendrix, *Marin Luther*, 242.
60. Koldeweij, *Maria van Hongarije*, 262.
61. Koldeweij, *Maria van Hongarije*, 232-33.
62. Reston, *Defenders of the Faith*. 92-95.
63. Brotton, *This Orient Isle*, 30.

prevent Germany from becoming divided along confessional lines (Catholic/Lutheran).[64]

Charles V spent his final years in a monastery. Among the costly objects he took with him was Titian's *La Gloria*, in which the painter depicted Charles and his beloved Queen Isabella and their children, including Philip II, on their way to their just rewards. He himself called the painting *The Last Judgment*, which hung above the altar in the monastery chapel. He was buried in the church of that monastery, although his remains would later be transferred to El Escorial.[65]

Charles had added a codicil to his will with the instructions that 30,000 masses be held for his soul, that the Moorish prisoners be released, and that his son and successor Philip II reinstate the inquisition so that every heretic would be tried—"a request that Philip II would be happy to grant!" The most amazing addition to his will was that he regretted fulfilling his promise to Luther to issue a letter of safe conduct so that Luther could attend the Diet of Worms, which he convened in 1521, without any personal risks.[66]

LUTHER, THE POPES, AND "THE RELIGION OF THE TURKS"

Pope Leo X issued a papal bull against Martin Luther on 15 June 1520 called *Exsurge Domine* ("Rise, o Lord"), in which he called upon Luther to reject his heretical views. Forty-one of Luther's 95 theses concerning the faith were marked as "errors." "Error 34" was Luther's comment that "waging war against the Turks meant resisting God, who was punishing our [Christians'] iniquities."[67] Luther's Catholic opponents continued to hammer on the fact that simply his unwillingness to support a crusade against the Turks was proof of his heresy. But Luther felt that Christianity should first combat its own inner demons before it took on the Turks.[68] (Islam also presents the idea that one needs to fight the great *jihâd* first—one's own wrong desires—before one is able to fight the "small *jihâd*," i.e., *armed battle*.) Luther saw the Turks as a scourge sent by God. He called Muhammad a heretic, a devil and the "firstborn of Satan."[69] Because Luther opposed the Pope, he was,

64. Reston, *Defenders of the Faith*, 58, 265, 383.
65. Reston, *Defenders of the Faith*, 385.
66. Reston, *Defenders of the Faith*, 387.
67. Reston, *Defenders of the Faith*, 19.
68. Brotton, *This Orient Isle*, 28.
69. Ehmann, *Luther, Türken und Islam*, 111; cf. https://en.wikipedia.org/wiki/Martin_Luther.

in the eyes of his contemporaries who remained faithful to the Pope, "not only a veiled friend of the Jews and Turks but an open one: *Judenvater* and *Türkenfreund*."[70] This reproach of being a friend of the Turks is understandable, given that in his critique of the politics and ecclesial conditions of the "Holy Catholic kingdom" he sometimes made comparisons with the Turks. Among the Turks "who possessed neither spiritual nor worldly rights, but only their Alcoran," he saw political and social relationships that were much better organized. Luther dared to claim that the sultan of Constantinople was "ten times more pious and wise than our rulers." He praised the external devotion of the Muslims, who adhered more strictly to the obligations of religion (prayer, fasting, and alms) than Christians did.[71] Moreover, Luther rejected any idea of a crusade or holy war carried out in the name of Christ against the Muslims as unbiblical.[72] But Luther did believe that a war could be carried out in the name of the emperor and in self-defense for the protection of the country and its inhabitants. The emperor had to be obeyed, for whoever disobeyed the emperor disobeyed God. He therefore did not exclude military action. Thus, Luther did not reject the war against the Turks as such but a war "in the name of Christianity." In his eyes, the political responsibility for war lay with the government.[73]

LUTHER AND THE JEWS

When Pope Urban II summoned the first crusade against the Muslims in Clermont-Ferrant, France, in 1095, he also unleashed a wave of Christian hostility against the Jews. On the way to the Holy land, Jews in the Rhine area were killed as the *other* "enemies of the cross." This hostility reached its peak on the eve of the Reformation. The Jews were expelled from the main places where they lived in Europe: in 1290 from England; in 1394 from France; in 1492 from Spain; and in 1496 from Portugal. Because most of the Swiss districts had already expelled the Jews, other Reformers like Zwingli and Calvin encountered few Jews in the areas in which they worked. The situation was very different for Luther in the German Empire. There were still many large Jewish communities, such as those in Frankfurt am Main and

---

70. Johannes Wallmann, "Luthers Stellung zur Judentum und Islam," 52–53.
71. Three of the five pillars of Islam: *salât*, *sawm*, and *zakât* (prayer, fasting, and almsgiving).
72. Hagemann, *Martin Luther und der Islam*, 14, n. 30, 15.
73. Hagemann, *Christentum contra Islam*, 84.

Worms, but there was also a considerable Jewish diaspora, well-organized communities,[74] in the smaller German towns and villages.[75]

In Luther's time and during the rule of emperors Maximilian I and Charles V, *the* advocate for the German and Polish Jews was Josel von Rosheim (1478–1554). He even became the *Befehlshaber* (commander) of all Jews in the German Empire. Maximilian called him the patron of the Jews and his grandson, Charles V, confirmed him in this position. He acquired his status partly from his skill as a lawyer and partly from the role that the Jews played in financing the expenditures of the emperor.[76] Three years after he succeeded in preventing the expulsion of the Jews from Alsace (1507), he was chosen as their head and commander as well. Upon the coronation of Charles V (1520), he had the privileges of the Jews in the empire confirmed.[77]

In his book, *Luther's Jews* (2017), published in the year of the 500th anniversary of the Reformation, Thomas Kaufmann writes that since 1492, the year of the Spanish expulsion of the Jews, the threat to the Jews had spread across Europe. They had been expelled from various German cities, and an apocalyptic and Messianic zeal arose within Judaism. This was the result of the pressure of increasing tribulations, unrest within Christianity, the Reformation, and the new enthusiasm on the part of Christian scholars for the Hebrew language. A Jewish physician at the court of the Turkish Suleiman the Magnificent is reported to have said that the Reformation was a sign of the weakening of Christianity. Such opinions were widespread in Jewish circles.[78] Jews from Regensburg sent a German translation of Psalm 130, the *De Profundis* ("Out of the depths I cry to you"), written in Hebrew letters to Luther in Wittenberg. On 21 February 1519 the city council of Regensburg decided to destroy its synagogue and to banish the Jewish community. The Jews attempted to make Luther aware of their lot by sending him this penitential Psalm. Apparently, they hoped for a great deal from this learned scholar from Wittenberg, who had become famous and influential since 1518/1519. "Does the fact that they wrote to him in Hebrew script suggest that they hoped to find a mutual basis with this Christian heretic condemned by the pope?"[79]

---

74. Oberman, *Wortels van het antisemitisme*, 13.
75. Wallmann, "Luthers Stellung zur Judentum und Islam," 51.
76. https://en.wikipedia.org/wiki/Josel_of_Rosheim.
77. Oberman, *Wortels van het antisemitisme*, 25
78. Kaufmann, *Luther's Jews*, 25–26.
79. Kaufmann, *Luther's Jews*, 27.

In the first period of his public activities, Luther opposed the church's attitude towards the Jews: "We should not be so unfriendly to the Jews," he wrote from the Wartburg in 1521 in his exegesis of the Song of Mary (*Magnificat*; Luke 1:46–55).[80] Two years later, in his *That Jesus Christ was Born a Jew* (1523), the first of his writings about the Jews, Luther rejects the poor treatment of the Jews. "The popes, bishops, sophists and monks . . . have treated the Jews . . . as if they were dogs and not human beings."[81] Luther argues that Christians should treat them in a "brotherly manner," because "they are brothers of our Lord." Slandering the Jews, isolating them socially (putting them in ghettos), had to stop; they had to be allowed to with and among the rest of the population, to be allowed to do any type of work they wished. What moved Luther was the hope that the Jews would be brought to faith in Jesus Christ through brotherly love, even though he did not draw up a program for Jewish missions.

This work by Luther, *That Jesus Christ was Born a Jew*, was greeted by the Jews as the sign of a fundamental change in the relationship between Jews and Christians. This volume was reprinted in numerous locations and sent by Jews themselves to their fellow Jews living in secrecy in Spain and even to Jerusalem; in many places it led to a new attitude with respect to the Jews. The rediscovery of the Gospel by Martin Luther thus led to a unique breakthrough in a Christian hatred of Jews that had been building up for centuries and also led to a new attitude towards Islam.[82] At the same time, however, in contrast to this first volume, he also wrote *On the Jews and their Lies* (1543). The harshness in this latter work arises from the supposed falsity of Judaism as a threat to Christians. This is why Luther advised the government to "burn down the synagogue as a school of lies, to confiscate the rabbinical books or, if no other means helped, to even expel the Jews who refused to be converted."[83]

Three days before his death (15 February 1546), Luther appended the following lines to his final sermon "An Admonition against the Jews": "Jews are our open enemies. They do not desist from blaspheming our Lord Christ. They call the Virgin Mary a whore, and Christ a whoreson." "And if they could kill us all, they would fain do it, and often do so too." "And yet, 'we ought to practice Christian love toward them and beg them

---

80. Cf. 1 Sam 2:1–10: The Song of Hannah, mother of Samuel.

81. According to Wallmann, "Luthers Stellung zur Judentum und Islam," 53; https://www.uni-due.de/collcart/es/sem/s6/txt09_1.htm.

82. Wallmann, "Luthers Stellung zur Judentum und Islam," 54.

83. Oberman, *Wortels van het antisemitisme*, 121.

to convert,"[84] and if not, they should not be tolerated or endured. Right up until the time of his death, he maintained that tolerance towards Jews was possible only in the sense of coexistence with the objective of conversion.[85] Thus, at the end of the fifteenth century and at the beginning of the sixteenth, there was "no place in the dream of tolerance for unbaptized Jews," according to Heiko Oberman.[86] For Luther, the Christological confession contained the actual criterion for distinguishing between Christians and all other religious people on earth. "For the Jews do not have it, the Turks and the Saracens also do not."[87]

Luther's views must be seen *in an apocalyptic connection.* The church father Jerome (d. 420) had linked the history of the Jews with the raging of primal evil in the end time and with the Antichrist. According to Luther, the destructive forces of the end times, Gog and Magog (Ezek 38–39), refer to the Jews.[88] The end times, which were rapidly approaching, demanded reformation: "Prepare the way for the Lord, make straight paths for him" (Matt 3:3; cf. Isa 40:3). Just as John the Baptist once called people to prepare the way for the *first coming of the Lord,* so the church also had to focus on *the final coming of Christ.* Luther saw the wrongs of the church as the result of growth in legalism, which he qualified as Judaism. The errors of the church in the Middle Ages originated from the Jewish mind and the Jewish nature. "The new rise of social fermentation and apocalyptic tension pour oil on those flames of the medieval hatred of the Jews.[89] Only conversion and baptism led to the Messianic kingdom. In his eyes, the Jews had to stop desiring an end to their dispersion throughout the entire earth. The basis of Luther's anti-Judaism is the conviction that, since the coming of Christ on earth, the Jews no longer have a future as Jews. "It was not only the middle-aged or late Luther but already the younger Luther to whom we have access that represented this view that the Jews had no future as Jews."[90] Luther's diagnosis remained the same as it was in the beginning: "The Jews are being punished for their blasphemy with blindness and dispersion. They will never have their own country (*sic!*)."[91]

---

84. Oberman, *Wortels van het antisemitisme*, 120.
85. Oberman, *Wortels van het antisemitisme*, 120.
86. Oberman, *Wortels van het antisemitisme*, 13.
87. Hagemann, *Martin Luther und der Islam*, 26.
88. Oberman, *Wortels van het antisemitisme*, 59.
89. Oberman, *Wortels van het antisemitisme*, 60.
90. Oberman, *Wortels van het antisemitisme*, 63.
91. Oberman, *Wortels van het antisemitisme*, 64–65.

Luther's reference point was scarcely the Judaism that actually existed in his time. He assumed that a Jew would feel addressed by the word of the Scriptures in the same way that people in the Reformation movement had felt addressed. His Jews were "*Luther's Jews*," primarily his own creation derived from Paul's letters. The point *that Jesus Christ was born a Jew* was not based primarily on the empirical situation of the contemporary Judaism but rather on the original situation at the time of the apostles that, in his view, was once again relevant now and *for the last time before the end of the world*.[92] Just as the church of Rome was called to repent, for the last time before the end of days, so the Jews were called.[93] Luther's objective was to warn Christians about the Jews, to provide them with arguments supporting Jesus as the Messiah and, on the basis of the Old Testament, to "prove" that the 1500-year history of Jewish suffering was the result of divine punishment for their stubbornness. God's assurance to David that his throne would endure forever was, Luther believed, fulfilled in Christ. Otherwise God would be a liar.[94]

At the end of his life and with the last judgment looming, the time had come to issue a final statement in his last writing *On the Jews and their Lies*. The "other path" that he had first followed had failed because the Reformation had not helped the church convert a meaningful number of Jewish converts. In Luther's view, there was no longer any reason to delay the definitive truths about the Jews. "The man (Luther) who had 'died' because of the recent death of his daughter (13 years of age) 'resigned himself to die' by throwing himself into the battle against the Jews: the greatest enemies of his Lord," this was Kaufman's shocking conclusion.[95]

LUTHER AND THE QUR'AN

Luther was the first German to translate any part of the Qur'an into German—not from Arabic but from Latin. It is striking that the general of the Augustinian order to which Martin Luther belonged as a monk knew Arabic. Not only did he have an outstanding knowledge of the Qur'an, but he also wrote his own Latin translation. It is very likely that Luther met him in Rome in 1511/1512: Giles Antonini, O.E.S.A., usually referred to as Giles of Viterbo. Pope Leo X made him a cardinal in 1517 and sent him on important missions, one of which was to Charles V in Spain. In 1523 he

92. Kaufmann, *Luther's Jews*, 61.
93. Kaufmann, *Luther's Jews*, 55.
94. Kaufmann, *Luther's Jews*, 89–91.
95. Kaufmann, *Luther's Jews*, 98.

was given the title of Latin Patriarch of Constantinople.[96] When Charles V's army plundered the city of Rome in 1527, his extensive library was destroyed. This shows that there was most likely a clear interest in Islam and its doctrine in Rome in the sixteenth century.[97]

Luther had wanted to read and study the Qur'an for a long time. In 1530 he reports that he had been unable to acquire a copy of it. He continued to try to do so in the following decade, but it was not until Shrove Tuesday on 21 February 1542 that he acquired a copy of a Latin translation.[98] "This Shrove Tuesday I have seen the Qur'an in Latin, but it is a very poor translation. If I have the time, I shall have to 'Germanize' it"—a plan that he never realized.[99] Luther did translate a passage about Muhammad and the Qur'an as follows:

> At the time of the (Byzantine) emperor Heraclius a man appeared, indeed a devil, and a first-born child of Satan, against the truth and against the Christian church . . . called Mahmet. Because he is a liar and the father of all lies, he had pronounced a law full of lies and injustice as if it had come from the mouth of God, which he called the Qur'an.[100]

Why did he not feel any real need to read the Qur'an before 1542? The apparent reason was that the "danger of the Turks" became very acute at the beginning of the 1540s. Budapest was invaded on 2 September 1541, and on 11 October his *Vermanungen zum Gebet widder den Türcken* appeared. His reading of the Qur'an, which began on Shrove Tuesday in 1542, hardened his polemics.[101]

Luther became involved in a controversy about the publication of the Qur'an in Basel. In 1542 a Swiss publisher was thrown into jail for printing a Latin version of the Qur'an by Robert Ketton (1110–ca. 1160 AD), an English theologian and Arabist.[102] At the behest of the French Benedictine monk, the last great abbot of Cluny, Peter the Venerable,[103] Ketton had

---

96. Cf. the fourth crusade, when Constantinople was invaded and a Latin patriarchate, associated with Rome, was established at that time.

97. https://en.wikipedia.org/wiki/Giles_of_Viterbo.

98. Francisco, *Martin Luther and Islam*, 97–98.

99. Hagemann, *Martin Luther und der Islam*, 29.

100. Hagemann, *Martin Luther und der Islam*, 22. Cf. Riccoldo da Monte di Croce in Luther's translation: "Mahmet's law is murderous, tyrannical, and incensed"; Hageman, *Martin Luther und der Islam*, 23, n. 57.

101. Hagemann, *Martin Luther und der Islam*, 22.

102. Francisco, *Martin Luther and Islam*, 211.

103. Peter the Venerable wrote some works against Islam (some of which have been

translated the Qur'an into Latin around 1143 with the title: *Lex Mahumet pseudoprophete* (*The Law of Mohammed, the False Prophet*), the first translation of the Qur'an into a European language.[104]

Luther intervened and asked the authorities of Basel to release the publisher and offered to write a "Preface"[105] to this new edition, arguing that it was necessary to understand Islamic theology in order to counter it. Luther dearly wanted to have the complete text of the Qur'an because he was certain that the more these writings were read, the better Muhammad's errors could be countered.[106] Luther attached high priority to reading and studying the Qur'an as *the* way to understanding Islam properly. But when he states that "it is valuable for scholars to read the writings of the enemy," it appears that Luther's interest was motivated by apologetic and polemical purposes. If people are informed about the religion of the Turks, especially by reading the Qur'an, he wrote to Basel, their apostasy could be prevented. Only a thorough knowledge of the Qur'an could help in strengthening the Christian faith.[107] With the availability of the translation, the time had come for the church to confront the religion of the Turks, not in the form of a military crusade as the Pope wanted, but theologically.[108] After studying the Qur'an, Luther was convinced that Islam not only had a different belief concerning God but that it also displayed a fundamental antithesis toward Christianity.[109]

THE REFUTATION OF THE QUR'AN

In his *Refutation of the Qur'an*,[110] Luther published a German translation of Riccoldo da Monte di Croce's (ca. 1243–1320) attack on the Qur'an in 1542.[111] Riccoldo was an Italian Dominican, who was part of a papal mission to Acre, had gone on a pilgrimage to the Holy Land, and served as

---

translated into German). The most well-known texts are *Summa totius haeresis Saracenorum* and *Liber contra sectam sive haeresim Sarracenorum*.

104. Francisco, *Martin Luther and Islam*, 103.
105. *In Alcoranum Praefatio*.
106. Brotton, *This Orient Isle*, 28.
107. Francisco, *Martin Luther and Islam*, 106–7.
108. Francisco, *Martin Luther and Islam*, 213.
109. Francisco, *Martin Luther and Islam*, 214.
110. *Contra legum Saracenorum*. Verlegung des Alcoran Bruder Richardi, Prediger Ordens (Refutation of the Alcoran of Brother Richard, Preaching Order, 1542), a translation into German of a Medieval Tract Against Islam (WA 53:272–396).
111. https://en.wikipedia.org/wiki/Riccoldo_da_Monte_di_Croce.

a missionary in the Middle East for many years. He arrived in Mosul in 1289, where he vainly attempted to convert the Nestorian mayor to Roman Catholicism. While in Baghdad, he studied the Qur'an with polemical intentions and engaged in debate there with Nestorian Christians. He preached to them—in their own cathedral in Baghdad. Riccoldo wrote his most well-known work, *Contra legem Sarracenorum*, around 1300, a work that would become very popular among Christians in the West and be reprinted many times.

With his translation, Luther wished to promote mission work among Turkish Muslims. He had hoped to become a missionary once himself and was optimistic about the possibility of converting Muslims to Christianity, even though he had heard from Riccoldo that this would be difficult. He hoped that this missionary work could be done by Christian prisoners and Ottoman slaves.[112] Regarding the chances of success in such work, he referred to Daniel and his fellow prisoners who had nevertheless introduced the king of Babel and many others to the true knowledge of God. Had the Goths, the Huns, and the Franks—who had previously been conquerors, not been converted by their prisoners as well? "So now, too, God will perhaps call some of the Turks from their darkness through their Christian captives who haven been instructed"[113]

Most of all, Luther wanted to encourage Christians, especially those who lived in a "Muslim occupied area" and felt the pressure to become Muslim. It was to enable these people to defend themselves against Muhammad's faith that Luther translated this apologetic into German. Ludwig Hagemann wonders why Luther chose to translate this work by Riccoldo and not *De pace fidei* by Cardinal Nicholas of Cusa (1401–1464) into German. The latter was much more recent work and had been written in response to the fall of Constantinople half a century earlier! But Luther chose instead to translate a work that was two and a half centuries old. He said he found it useful and that "there was nothing better." Hagemann—and rightly so—did not feel this motivation was justified. In his book *De pace fidei*, which appeared in 1453 after reports about the fall of Constantinople, Nicholas of Cusa describes a peace dialogue between the various religions and nations. He developed the concept of *una religio in rituum varietate* (one religion in the diversity of customs and rituals).[114] His *Cribatio Alkorani* was the result of an intense and detailed study of the Qur'an and at the same time an attempt to cultivate understanding between Christianity and Islam.

---

112. Francisco, *Martin Luther and Islam*, 91–93.
113. Francisco, *Martin Luther and Islam*, 214.
114. https://en.wikipedia.org/wiki/Nicholas_of_Cusa.

Taking into account the tense situation after the fall of Constantinople in 1453, which is when this work appeared, Hagemann considers this work moderate in its polemics and in "the apologetics intended to be maieutic or obstetric" as exemplary against the background of the anti-Islamic literature of that time. He believed that this writing would have been much more helpful for Luther in determining his attitude toward Islam.[115] Nicholas of Cusa was also convinced of the superiority of Christianity, although he does give Judaism and Islam credit for *partially* sharing in the truth. His attitude with respect to the Jews was not always mild. On 21 September 1451 he ordered the Jews in Arnhem (Germany) to wear badges.[116]

Nicholas of Cusa wanted to "gain insight into the Qur'an," to "*sift* it for its Christian contents" separate the wheat from the chaff. He took the trouble to analyze the Qur'an for heterodox elements of Jewish and heretical Christian origin and to question its biblical content. His leitmotif in his interpretation is to understand it on the basis of the Gospel. His work can be viewed as a defense of the Christian faith; he wanted to take Muslims by the hand, as it were, to lead them to understand the Christian faith.[117]

He dedicated this work to Pope Pius II and pointed out that it concerned a "Mohammedan sect" that had emerged from the Nestorian heresy. That belonged to the general Christian thought of the Christian polemic against Islam. Muhammad is said to have been influenced by the hermit Bahîrâ, whom he met in Syria and viewed as a Nestorian. The twelve-year-old Muhammad, travelling with his uncle Abû Tâlib, is said to have met Bahîrâ in the desert city of Bosra. Bahîrâ saw in Muhammad the features of a prophet. This recalls the twelve-year-old Jesus' meeting with the rabbis in the temple where he listened to them and asked them questions. "Everyone who heard him was amazed at his understanding and his answers" (Luke 2:42–49)[118] The Qur'an speaks about such a meeting: "We certainly know that they say, 'It is only a human that instructs him. The language of him to whom they refer is non-Arabic, while this is a clear Arabic language" (Q 16:103). Nestorianism was the recognized form of Christianity under the Sassanids in Persia. The conquest of South Arabia by the Persians in 597 made Nestorianism the favored form. It was that branch of Christianity that the prophet Muhammad had contact with.[119]

---

115. Hagemann, *Martin Luther und der Islam*, 31-32.

116. Thomas M. Izbicki, "Nicholas of Cusa and the Jews," in *Conflict and Reconciliation: Perspectives on Nicholas of Cusa*, ed. Inigo Bocken, Leiden: Brill, 2004, 119-30, cited in: https://en.wikipedia.org/wiki/Nicholas_of_Cusa.

117. Hagemann, *Christentum contra Islam*, 68-69.

118. *EI*, s.v., Bahîrâ.

119. Hagemannm, *Christentum contra Islam*, 70-71.

LUTHER'S EXEGESIS OF THE BOOK OF DANIEL

Luther's criticism of the "religion of the Turks" was therefore not based on his own independent research. He attempted to interpret this religion as a power in the "end time" on the basis of apocalyptic *predictions*. That was nothing new in itself because that had already been done in Muslim-occupied Spain in the ninth century. Eulogius, the bishop of Toledo, who died as a martyr (d. 857) and Paulus Alvarus (ca 800–861), a Mozarabic scholar,[120] poet, and theologian from Cordoba, saw the rule of Islam as a preparation for the coming of the Antichrist. Through appealing to Daniel, Alvarus wanted to show that Muhammad was the forerunner of the Antichrist.[121] Joachim of Fiore (ca 1135–1202), an Italian mystic and theologian, who was well known for his apocalypticism, believed that the events happening around him, in particular the persecution of Christians, were the fulfilment of the signs of the end time predicted in the book of Revelation. An example of Joachim's reading of the signs of the times can be found in his emphasis on the figure of Saladin and the latter's capture of the city of Jerusalem in the year 1187. In his exegesis of the twelfth chapter of Revelation, Joachim saw the seven-headed dragon as seven heads of concrete historical persecutions throughout history. He identified the sixth head with that of Saladin who recaptured Jerusalem from the Crusaders. He saw him as preceding the seventh head, who would be the Antichrist, the final and great persecution of the church. Joachim served between 1180 and 1200 as an apocalyptic advisor for various popes. When Richard Lionheart (1157–1199) was leading the Third Crusade (1189–1192) and spent the winter in Messina on Sicily, he asked Joachim for some prophetic advice on what would happen. Joachim traveled to Messina in the winter of 1190–1191 and predicted a victory for Richard. The crusade, however, ended in failure.[122] Joachim contemporized Daniel's apocalyptic vision in his own way. For him, Islam and its power in Spain under the Almohads and in Palestine under Saladin were also the tool of Satan.[123]

The fact that the papal authorities rejected God's word was, for Luther, already enough to see that as a sign of the end time. But the presence of the advancing Turks in the Balkans had a direct connection for him with the *Apocalypse*. Luther saw the Turks as the contemporary manifestation of the "little horn" in the book of Daniel (Dan 7:8–10; cf. Rev 13:5) that had come

---

120. Mozarabs: Christians under Arabic rulers
121. https://en.wikipedia.org/wiki/Álvaro_of_Córdoba_(Mozarab).
122. https://nl.wikipedia.org/wiki/Joachim_van_Fiore.
123. Hagemann, *Martin Luther und der Islam*, 16, 27.

to engage in war and to defeat the saints of God and as Gog and Magog (Ezek 38–39; Rev 20:7–10). Luther viewed the invading army of the Turks under Suleiman both as God's punishment of the faithless Christians and as "the servant of Satan" who came to bring devastation.[124] Along with the rest of the Muslim world, the Turks were followers of the beast (Rev 20:10; cf. 9:20) that was Muhammad.

The archetypal "beast," *dabba*, also appears in the Qur'an: "And when the word [of judgement] falls upon them, We shall bring out for them an Animal from the earth" (Q 27:82). The coming of the "beast" is a sign that precedes the last judgment (Q 27:82).[125] In the Muslim tradition, the beast is also called al-Dajjâl, al-Masîh al-Dajjâl, the deceitful Messiah, which is called the Antichrist (1 John 2:18, 22; 4:3; 2 John 7), one of the evil figures who will lead people astray in the last days and whose coming is one of the signs of the approach of the "Last Hour."

Luther's exegesis of the book of Revelation was as follows: Muhammad's kingdom (the beast) reigns in the East and the papacy (the false prophet or the Antichrist) reigns in the West. Both wait for orders to start the final assault on the church. Luther almost always saw the papacy as a greater threat than Muhammad and the Turks. He often remarked that: compared to the Pope, "Muhammad appears before the world as a pure saint."[126] Although his reading of Daniel taught him that the days of the Turks were numbered and he had been convinced for some time that they would never make it into Germany, he sometimes began to wonder what would happen if his predictions proved to be wrong and the Turks advanced toward the West. After all, when the Turks annexed Hungary in 1524, he thought they were intending to rule Europe.[127] He had heard that there were Christians who admired the *Pax Ottomanica*, and he had heard and seen how the people in the Balkans and even Hungary converted to Islam. Thus, when he witnessed the apparently endless conquests of Suleiman's army and constantly heard about the Islamization of Eastern Europe, he became increasingly worried about Christian apostasy, not only in the Balkans but also in Germany itself. He therefore gave the highest priority to equipping ministers and laypeople by giving them enough thorough knowledge of the faith and enabling them to confront Islam by the use of apologetics, which was perhaps also useful for prosyletising Muslims.[128]

124. Jones, "The Apocalyptic Luther."
125. *Dabba*; cf. Wessels, *The Torah, the Gospel, and the Qur'an*, 197, 264.
126. Francisco, *Martin Luther and Islam*, 84.
127. Francisco, *Martin Luther and Islam*, 87.
128. Francisco, *Martin Luther and Islam*, 95.

Because of Luther's view of the "Turkish danger" as a punishment by God, he wrote, at the behest of Elector John Frederick of Saxony, *An Admonition to Prayer and Penance* in 1541. Already in his earlier "Turkish works" of 1529, both before and after the Siege of Vienna,[129] he had repeatedly called the German people to prayer and penance.[130]

According to Luther, the Antichrist of the end time was already living in Rome (!) and would soon ascend the papal throne as the fruit of the womb of the church. Islam was his harbinger.[131] Because Luther viewed the pope as the worst enemy of Christianity, he did not see the Antichrist in the founder of Islam: "I don't see Muhammad as the 'Antichrist' . . . . But the Pope here with us is the true Antichrist .. who is within Christianity."[132] The two empires of the Pope and of the Turk were the last two abominations with which "God's wrath was completed" (Rev 15:1): "the false prophet" and "the beast" are captured together and thrown into the fiery oven (Rev 19:20).[133]

Although he did not see Muhammad as the expected Antichrist (*Endechrist*), he did nevertheless see in him and his religion a decisive power in the end times, and Luther had no doubt that the end time had arrived. Finally, given that the Christian faith would win in the end, he counted on an end coming to the political—and religious—power of Islam.[134] If the apocalyptic age had already dawned and death at the hands of the enemy was certain, so Christ's promised victory was even more certain. He knew that God's apocalyptic war with evil was being fought not only on the front lines between Suleiman and the armies of Emperor Ferdinand. It was on the battlefield of the human will, and Luther concentrated on sharpening the weapons of the Spirit by introducing a revolution in the proclamation of the Gospel for sinners.[135]

As Heiko Oberman has shown, Luther's mental world was more and more dominated by an apocalyptic understanding. He sought to perceive a *divine plan* behind the chaotic events of his day. That led him to reach for parts of the Bible, such as Daniel, Ezekiel, and the Revelation of John, that appeared to describe the tumultuous events that were happening in his day, especially the rise of the Ottoman Empire. Although what the Scriptures

---

129. *Vom Kriege widder die Türcken* and *Heerpredigt widder den Türcken*.
130. Hagemann, *Martin Luther und der Islam*, 12.
131. Hagemann, *Martin Luther und der Islam*, 16, 27.
132. Hagemann, *Martin Luther und der Islam*, 19, 20.
133. Hagemann, *Martin Luther und der Islam*, 20.
134. Hagemann, *Martin Luther und der Islam*, 21.
135. Jones, "The Apocalyptic Luther."

described was terrible, they also offered hope for the foretold collapse of the *external* enemy of Christianity—the Turks—as well as its *internal* enemy—the papacy.[136]

> If we are successful against Mahmet, the external enemy of Christianity, so we must renounce the internal enemy, the Antichrist with his devil by righteous penance and turn to our Lord and Saviour in true earnestness and simplicity of heart. For the Scripture predicts that two abominable tyrants will devastate and disrupt the Christian faith before the last day. The one tyrant spiritually with deceptions and false religion and a doctrine against the true Christian faith and the Gospel. Daniel writes about that. The tyrant will exult himself above all gods and religion: "The king will do as he pleases. He will exalt and magnify himself above every god and will say unheard-of things against the God of gods. He will be successful until the time of wrath is completed, for what has been determined must take place." (Dan 11:36)[137]

Luther then also refers to Paul's *Endechrist*: "Do not be deceived by anyone! There will first be a great falling away, and the man of lawlessness with be revealed, the son of perdition, who will oppose and will raise himself about all that is called God or is worshipped, so that he sits in God's temple as if he were God himself" (2 Thess 2:3–4). Luther identifies this figure as the pope.

Daniel also predicted *the other tyrant* with the sword physically and externally at his most horrible: he will set himself against the Most High, mistreat the saints of the Most High, and plan to change times and laws. They will be given into his power for a time, times, and half a time (Dan 7:25).[138] Luther applies what is said in Jesus' discourse about the coming of the Son of Man at the end of time to the Turks in his time: for that time will be so terrible, such as has not been seen since the beginning of time nor ever will be (Matt 24:21). The papacy and Islam are, as far as Luther is concerned, cut from the same antichristian cloth.[139]

Thus, he saw two threats in his time: the Pope and the religion of the Turks. The Roman Catholic Church and Islam were both, in his view, demonic manifestations of the same enemy, Satan. Islam was the *external enemy*, whereas the papacy was the *internal enemy*; Muhammad was the

136. Francisco, *Martin Luther and Islam*, 95.

137. Hagemann, *Martin Luther und der Islam*, 18, n. 41.

138. KBS. Three and a half years, which is how long the persecution under Antiochus IV lasted. See chapter IV.

139. Hagemann, *Christentum contra Islam*, 18–19.

beast from the East and the Pope the false prophet from the West. Both were sent to mislead the world and to devastate it. He expressed this twofold threat in a hymn (1542) that would find its way into one of Bach's cantatas, J.S BWV126:

> Preserve us, Lord, with your word,
> and control the murderous rage of the Pope and the Turks,
> who would want to cast down Jesus Christ your son
> from his throne.[140]

The text in particular on which Luther based his view was Daniel's vision of the four beasts (Dan 7:2–14). According to Luther, each of the four beasts represents four different successive empires (*Keiserthum*) that he identified as the Assyrians and Babylonians, Persians and Medes, the Greeks under Alexander the Great, and finally the fourth and last, "certainly" and "without any doubt" the Holy Roman Empire. The ten horns that protrude from the head of the fourth beast were, according to him, the kingdoms of Spain, France, Italy, North Africa, Egypt, Syria, Asia Minor, Greece, Germany, and England.[141] The small horn was nothing else than the kingdom of Muhammad (*Mahometh's reich*), which had long ago uprooted the two horns or kingdoms of Asia and Egypt among the Arabs and recently, in Turkish form, conquered the third horn, Greece.[142]

This interpretation of the fourth beast and the eleven horns was not an idea unique to Luther.[143] Luther's thinking about the religion of the Turks appears, namely, to be directly influenced by the German Franciscan Johannes Hilten (1425–1500). In conversations with Melanchthon, among others, he speaks "of the rare *predictions* of the Franciscan monk Hilten," who had already years before discovered the *predictions* of the "Turkish affliction" in the dark prophecies.[144] Hilten lived in the time of Mehmed II and was very hostile towards the Turks. He was perhaps most remembered for his prediction, already in his time, of the decline of the papacy in 1516 and the appearance of a great reformer, who would of course later be identified

---

140. "Erhalt uns, Herr, bey deinem Wort / und steur des Bapts und Turcken Mord / die Jhesum Christum deinen Son / Wolten stürzen von deinem Thron." For the English translation, see https://bach-cantatas.com/Texts/BWV126-Eng3.htm. Wallmann, "Luthers Stellung zur Judentum und Islam," 55–56. The sentence (unde stürze des Papst und Türcken mordt) "and control the murderous rage of the Pope and the Turks" was modified after Luther's death. https://nl.wikipedia.org/wiki/Maarten_Luther.

141. Cf. his *Vorrede über den Propheten Daniël*; Francisco, *Martin Luther and Islam*, 81, n. 45.

142. Francisco, *Martin Luther and Islam*, 81–82.

143. Francisco, *Martin Luther and Islam*, 82, n. 48.

144. Hagemann, *Martin Luther und der Islam*, 17.

with Martin Luther. Hilten sought keys in Scripture. On the basis of Daniel 7 and the Revelation of John, he *predicted* that the Turks would finally invade Europe and become established, around 1600, in Germany and Italy, as Gog and Magog. But after a time, there would be a mass conversion to Christianity, and the destruction of Islam would quickly follow. Islam was not the Antichrist, but the Antichrist would appear shortly after the fall of the Turkish empire, before the year 1651. Then, he was convinced, the end of the world would come.[145] The chapters about Gog and Magog point, according to Luther, to the tribulation that Christians (= Israel) would experience because of the Turks (= Gog and Magog) as well as to the destruction of the Turks by divine punishment.[146]

Luther did not question his exegesis of Daniel 7. He ascribed the following significance to the small horn that, in his human eyes, symbolized the Qur'an, *the law of Muhammad*. In his view, the Qur'an "lacked the divine eye." Instead, "it taught nothing else than human wisdom and what reason can accept." The blasphemous mouth of the small horn was synonymous with the false teachings of Islam, especially the claim that Muhammad had made an end of the teachings of Christianity. Daniel's view of the battles that took place in his time was of course a prophecy of the conflict that was taking place in Luther's time with the Turks, most recently at the gates of Vienna. Given that the small horn was the last to appear before the "Ancient of Days" would destroy it, before the establishment of his own eternal kingdom (Dan 7:21–22), Luther was convinced that the last days were at hand in his time: "The world was going faster and faster, hastening to the end, so that I have the strong impression that *the last days* will dawn before I have translated the Holy Scriptures into German." "According to the Scriptures, everything has happened, everything has been fulfilled, the "Roman Empire" is finished, the Turk is at the height of his power, the power of the pope is on the point of collapse." "If the world would continue as it has then certainly the whole world would be Mohammedan, or Epicurean, and no Christians would be left." "We have," he added, "nothing more to expect than the last day, for the Turk will cut off no more than these three horns."[147] The only thing to do now is to wait for the last day. Luther found other prophecies as well that, according to him, describe the Ottoman Empire and play a key role in the events of the end time. The most pronounced chapters were those of the thousand-year reign (the Millennium) (Rev 20) and on Gog and Magog

---

145. Francisco, *Martin Luther and Islam*, 22–23.
146. Hagemann, *Martin Luther und der Islam*, 17, n. 39.
147. Francisco, *Martin Luther and Islam*, 81–83.

(Ezek 38–39), who were none other than the Turks.[148] While he was certain that the events described in the books of Daniel, Ezekiel, and the Revelation of John were occurring now, he hoped that the battle would be short, for all three prophecies predicted the imminent destruction of the Turks.[149]

Luther viewed Islam as a power of the end times. In his view, the devil intends not only to rule the world through Islam but also to use it to cause Christians to fall away from the faith, as Daniel says in chapter 7. It is thus no longer a matter of Islam as a military-political power but also of Islam as a religious and spiritual power.[150]

---

148. Francisco, *Martin Luther and Islam*, 83.
149. Francisco, *Martin Luther and Islam*, 83.
150. Hagemann, *Christentum contra Islam*. 86.

IV

Ezekiel: God and Man; God and Gog

An old Jewish tradition includes the following descents of God to earth: his descent to punish Adam after Eve and Adam both ate from the forbidden tree (Gen 2:16,17; 3:8; cf. Q 2:35; 7:19–22; 20:120–121), then he comes down to earth to look at the Tower of Babel, which people had built for their own glorification and so that they would not be scattered across the earth (Gen 11:4, 9; cf. Q 28:38; 40:36).[1] *He also descended to ascertain for himself the evil of the sinful cities Sodom and Gomorrah (the "overthrown" cities) (Gen 18:21; Q 9:70; 53:53–54; 69:9) and then to liberate Israel from the power of Egypt (Exod 3:8) and to drown the Egyptians in the Red Sea (Exod 15:10; 2 Sam 22:10; cf. Q 7:136; 43:55–56; 8:54; 17:103; 26:66–67; 44:24; 28:40; 51:40; 20:78; 2:50; 10:90), to reveal the Torah on the top of Mount Sinai (Exod 19:20; Q 7:145, 154), to send his Spirit upon the elders (Num 11:17), and to have his Shekinah (Q 2:248)*[2] *dwell in the temple (Ezek 44:2). (9) He will also come down in the future, when he will appear to pronounce judgment over Gog.*[3]

 1. In the Qur'an, Haman is a servant of Pharaoh who is commanded by Pharaoh to build a tower (Q 28:6, 8; 29:39; 40:24; cf. Speyer, *Die biblischen Erzählungen*, 383–384; Paret, *Der Koran* on Q 29:39; cf. Speyer, *Die biblischen Erzählungen*, 268–72.
 2. *Sakîna*: "Rest of God"; this is the ark (Q 2:248) in the hearts of the believers (Q 48:4); sent down upon Muhammad (Q 48:26).
 3. The last reference is to *Mekilta Bahodesh* 6, 64a; Ginzberg, *Legends of the Jews*,

INTRODUCTION

Gog and Magog play an important role in the course of history in the expectations of the end times of the Jews, Christians, and Muslims. While it is initially Gog and the country of Magog that are mentioned (Ezek 38:2), the terms later refer to two individuals (Rev 20:8). In the Qur'an they are called Yajūj and Majūj. For a proper understanding of their significance, it will not suffice to look simply at the two chapters in Ezekiel (Ezek 38–39; cf. also Rev 20:7–10; 19:17–18) that mention these figures; we also need to show the context in which they have to be placed in the book of this prophet as a whole.

Ezekiel was a young man training to be a priest—he was 25 years old when he was sent into exile in Babylon. His name means "May God give him strength." He was born precisely in the same year (622 BC) that the book of the law, the Torah, "suddenly" surfaced in the temple in Jerusalem with the ten commandments or guidelines for every person—personally, socially, and politically—that could be summarized in two concepts: to do justice and to show love. This discovery of the guide for the journey of life gave an impulse to the reforms of one of the few just kings Judah ever had: Josiah. Important religious reforms were implemented during his reign.[4] His son and successor, Jehoiakim, was the complete opposite of his father again. The rabbinic literature describes him as a godless tyrant who committed terrible sins and crimes.[5] The prophet Jeremiah, an older contemporary of Ezekiel, says about him:

> Woe to him who builds his palace by unrighteousness,
> his upper rooms by injustice,
> making his own people work for nothing,
> not paying them for their labor.
> He says, "I will build myself a great palace
> with spacious upper rooms."
> So he makes large windows in it,
> panels it with cedar
> and decorates it in red
> Does it make you a king
> to have more and more cedar?
> Did not your father have food and drink?
> He did what was right and just,
> so all went well with him.

---

vol. two, 824, n. 919.

4. He was the king of Judah from 641/640 to 609 BC; cf. 2 Kgs 22–23; 2 Chr 34–35.
5. https://en.wikipedia.org/wiki/Jehoiakim.

> He defended the cause of the poor and needy,
> and so all went.
> Is that not what it means to know me?"
> declares the Lord.
> (Jer 22:15–16)

Josiah's son was, politically speaking, so shortsighted as to rebel against the almighty King Nebuchadnezzar of Babylon. The latter besieged Jerusalem immediately, and after three months the city was forced to surrender. To prevent further rebellions, Nebuchadnezzar exiled the king of Judah, along with all his high officials and military men, and all the smiths and locksmiths—a convoy of 10,000 men. He left only the poorest behind (2 Kgs 24:13–15; Jer 52:15) to take care of the vineyards and fields (Jer 52: 6). This exile has been called the *first deportation* (597 BC). Ezekiel was among those who were deported, and, five years after he arrived in Babylon, he would be called to be a prophet. In the year 592 BC he received a vision (Ezek 1:1) to admonish and to comfort his fellow exiles. That happened five years before the destruction of Jerusalem in 587 BC (Ezek 1).[6]

Although Ezekiel, Hizkîl, is not mentioned by name in the Qur'an, traditional Muslim exegesis considers him the prophet of those who were removed from their homes by the thousands in fear of their lives. Then God spoke to them: "Die," and then revived them again (Q 2:243; cf. Ezek 37:1–10).[7] Some exegetes also identify Ezekiel with Dhû al-Kifl, a mysterious prophet who is mentioned in the Qur'an without any other details, along with Ishmael, Enoch, and Elisha, included among those who showed patience (Q 21:85; 38:48).[8]

Over the course of the centuries, Gog and Magog have been identified with different figures. These figures are just so many examples of how these apocalyptic texts were also read, understood, and used in questionable ways. But both the Bible and the Qur'an use the language of parable. That is the key for understanding the meaning of Gog and Magog and comprehending the character of these texts.

---

6. Terrien, *The Elusive Presence*; cf. Peter Schäfer, *Die Ursprünge der jüdischen Mystik*, 59–82.

7. *EI*, s.v., Hizkîl.

8. *Dictionnaire du Coran*, s.v., Ézéchiel. Muslim exegesis says that Ezekiel is called Ibn al-Azûj or "son of the old (man)" because his mother had asked for a son even though she was very old and barren. Speyer, *Biblische Erzählungen*, 412–413. That these exegetes, including Wahb ibn Munabbîh, mention this in their exegesis (and thus are allegedly thinking of Ezek 37) does not mean anything, according to Paret; cf. Paret on Q 2:243.

IDENTIFYING GOG AND MAGOG

Throughout the centuries Jews, Christians, and Muslims have read and applied the texts about Gog and Magog to their own time and used them *against* each other, the other community! When the American president, George W. Bush wanted to start the war in Iraq in 2003, he attempted to recruit allies for the battle. When he wanted to convince the French president Jacques Chirac to join the "coalition of the willing," he told him that he was going to fight Gog and Magog. Chirac did not know what to do with that announcement and even consulted a theologian in Lausanne about it.[9]

Identifications of this kind have been made throughout history. The Jewish historian Flavius Josephus identified Gog and Magog as the Scythians, nomads from the Central Asian steppes, who established a kingdom north of the Black Sea that lasted from the eighth century BC to the second century AD. He discusses the story of Alexander the Great in *The Jewish War*, who built an iron gate between two mountains to keep Gog and Magog away from the civilized world, though he did not make the eschatological connection that it was a sign of the last days. For him, it was simply a military structure to keep an enemy under control. He was the first author to tell this story about the iron gate.[10]

Gog and Magog were popular themes in the sermons of the Syrian Orthodox priests. The *Hymns* of Ephraim the Syrian also connect details about Gog and Magog with Alexander the Great.[11] In the *Sibylline Oracles* (3:394),[12] Gog and Magog are connected with the people "who live in the midst of the rivers of Ethiopia," probably Ethiopians, who were associated with Antiochus IV Epiphanes and his oppression of Jews in Judea. The *Sibylline Oracles* are a collection of Jewish and Christian texts that were composed between the second and fourth century AD. The name was derived from the sibyls, female prophets in the Greco-Roman world. In the works of Virgil, a sibyl, for example, proclaims the golden period of Augustus's rule and a sibyl accompanies the hero Aeneas to the underworld. The *Oracles* originated probably in Western Anatolia and was later associated with the Delphic Oracle.[13] In Book 3 of the *Sibylline Oracles* there are two

---

9. Fundamentalism—George Bush—Iraq—The Middle East—psychology—psychopathology—religion—USA. Bush, God, Iraq, Gog, the world—The "War on Terror." Cf. Wessels, *The Torah, the Gospel, and the Qur'an*, 193–94, n. 6 and 7, but see also https://foreignpolicy.com/2016/11/15/bush-chirac-and-the-war-in-iraq/.

10. https://nl.wikipedia.org/wiki/Gog_en_Magog.

11. *Hymns III*, 194–213; *EI, s.v.,* Yâdjûdj wa- Mâdjûdj.

12. See https://www.sacred-texts.com/cla/sib/sib05.htm.

13. https://nl.wikipedia.org/wiki/Sibillijne_orakelen.

references to Gog and Magog, even though the verses have no apocalyptic or eschatological significance.[14] Gog is then identified with Edom, which represents the city of Rome.[15] For Ambrose, the bishop of Milan (d. 397), and the church father Augustine (d. 430), the *Goths* (Germanic tribes) were *the* "candidates" for Gog and Magog. For Augustine, their appearance was a sign of the end of the then known "Christian civilization" in the West. For Procopius of Caesarea (d. 562), in his *De bello Persico*, it was the *Huns*, the people who were locked out behind the gate Alexander built.

It is via Syrian literature that the Alexander story of the iron gate and the locking out of Gog and Magog found its way into the Qur'an.[16] In the *seventh century*, when Islam began to expand in the Middle East, a Syrian Apocalypse on the latter days was composed that spoke of the rise and rule of the Antichrist, the invasion of Gog and Magog, and the calamities that would precede the end of the world. The *Saracens*, as the Muslims were then called, were marching toward the Byzantine Empire and Jerusalem as Gog and Magog.[17]

In the twelfth century, Joachim of Fiore used the dragon as the image for the eschatological enemy (Rev 12); the *seven* heads indicated the Antichrist, while the tail of the dragon was Gog, who would appear at the end of the world.[18] But for the Muslims in the twelfth and thirteenth centuries, just like European Christians, the *invading Mongol hordes* came to be linked to Gog and Magog (before, of course, they converted to Islam!).[19] The Mongols who devastated the Abbasid Empire and Baghdad in 1258 were the armies of Gog and Magog. Willem van Ruysbroeck (ca 1210–ca 1270), a Flemish Franciscan monk, wrote one of the earliest Western reports about the Mongols. He took part in the crusade led by King Louis IX (St Louis; 1214–1270), to Palestine to recapture Jerusalem from the Saracens and linked Gog and Magog with the Tatars, the collective term for a number

---

14. https://nl.wikipedia.org/wiki/Gog_en_Magog.

15. Beale, *The Book of Revelation*, 1024.

16. Van Donzel and Schmidt, *Gog and Magog in Early Eastern Christian and Islamic Sources*.

17. The term was already used by classical writers in the first century for a northern Arabic people who had resisted the Eastern Roman emperors for a long time and had converted to Islam early on (eighth century). In the course of the Middle Ages, the term was expanded to include almost all Muslims and later all those who opposed Christianity, whether Arabic, Persian, or Turkish; cf. https://en.m.wikipedia.org/wiki/Saracen.

18. Wannenmacher (ed.), *Joachim of Fiore and the Influence of Inspiration*, 247.

19. Attema, *De Mohammedaansche opvattingen*, 135.

of—particularly Turkish—peoples who lived spread out over a large part of Eurasia.[20] For Martin Luther, the *Turks* were Gog and Magog.

In the nineteenth century, the Hassidic Jews connected Gog and Magog to *Napoleon*'s campaigns against Russia. The coming of the Messiah would follow the Napoleonic wars. Other "righteous people" warned against such exegesis: the dawning of redemption would occur not through such actions but only through the conversion of the whole person.[21] Some Russian Christians also saw Napoleon as Gog, and, in the twentieth century, Hitler was an "ideal" candidate and later in the same century Ronald Reagan viewed the Soviet Union as Gog and Magog.

For radical Muslims in our time, Western nations are Gog and Magog.[22] In both the classical and contemporary Muslim apocalyptic literature, they are linked to Russia because of the repeated Russian attacks on Muslims in Afghanistan and Chechnya.[23] An Egyptian apocalyptic writer proclaims in his exegesis of Ezekiel 38 that the state of *Israel* itself is Gog and Magog.[24] The immigration of Russian Jews to Israel that took place at that time (1989–1992) points to the imminent invasion of the Muslim world.[25] The contemporary Muslim apocalyptic literature that makes much use of evangelical apocalyptic material has been extensively analyzed.[26]

EZEKIEL'S CALL VISION

During his stay with the exiles at the Kebar river, a tributary of the Euphrates, Ezekiel sees the heavens open, and he is given one of the most impressive and significant visions in the whole Bible (Ezek 1; cf. Ezek 10:10–22). It has even been called one of the most influential visions in the whole history of humankind.[27] Ezekiel was in exile at the time, in a strange land over which the god Marduk ruled. To go by the occupation of Jerusalem, it seemed that Marduk was stronger than the God of Israel and had defeated him. It was up to Ezekiel to reveal to his people that God still reigned and could still intervene in a strange land. It was precisely when his faith was failing that

---

20. https://en.m.wikipedia.org/wiki/Tatars; Whalen, *Dominion of God*, 298, n. 50.
21. Buber, *Werke*, vol. III, 1257.
22. https://nl.wikipedia.org/wiki/Gog_en_Magog.
23. Cook, *Contemporary, Muslim Apocalyptic Literature*, 151.
24. Cook, *Contemporary, Muslim Apocalyptic Literature*, 46–47, 122.
25. Cook, *Contemporary Muslim Apocalyptic Literature*, 207.
26. Cook, *Contemporary Muslim Apocalyptic Literature*.
27. Wink, *The Human Being*, 23.

Ezekiel received this vision.[28] God appears in all his glory, in a very peculiar chariot, surrounded by four living beings, cherubs, winged guards.[29] *Glory* is what makes someone weighty, "of weight." God's glory is the radiation of his presence, his being and holiness becoming visible.[30] A voice speaks from above a vault, and there Ezekiel sees what seems to be a throne made of sapphire or lapis lazuli—from time immemorial, sapphires have been gems loved for their great beauty—and saw a human form sitting on it (Ezek 1:26; cf. Rev 4:2–3).[31] That means that God turns to Ezekiel with *a human face*. As soon as the glory of the Lord is revealed to him, he falls prostrate and hears a voice (Ezek 1:28; cf. Dan 8:17; Rev 1:17) that says: "Son of man, stand up on your feet and I will speak to you" (Ezek 2:1). Thus, "God" with a human appearance, a human face, speaks to Ezekiel: *ben 'adam, son of man*. Idiomatically, *ben 'adam* (Hebr.; in Aramaic: *bar enash*) means "son of man": a human person, a human being. Modern translations see this as a purely human or mortal human being.[32] The prophet is addressed as "son of man" 93 times in the book of Ezekiel. This title is specific for this book. Over against God, the prophet is a human being like all others.[33] "He said to me: 'Son of man, I am sending you to the Israelites, to a rebellious nation that has rebelled against me; they and their ancestors have been in revolt against me to this very day'" (Ezek 2:1, 3).

Ezekiel is given the task of performing a kind of street theater[34] and is involved in a number of prophetic dramas such as lying on his side for 390 days to symbolize the exile of the Northern Kingdom (Ezek 4:4–6). He has to eat a scroll (Ezek 3:1) and must not, as a symbol of God's attitude towards Jerusalem, mourn the death of his wife (Ezek 24:15–27).

About ten years after this vision, Nebuchadnezzar laid Jerusalem and the temple to waste. A refugee reports to Ezekiel in Babylon the fall of the city (Ezek 33:21). This is not a historical report of how terrible King Nebuchadnezzar wreaked havoc; rather, Ezekiel is given a *vision* regarding the event: God can be said to be, as it were, the one who takes initiative:

---

28. Wink, *The Human Being*, 25.
29. KBS on Ezek 1:4; Wink, *The Human Being*, 24.
30. KBS on Exod 24:16. "And the glory of the Lord settled on Mount Sinai. For six days the cloud covered the mountain and on the seventh day the Lord called to Moses from within the cloud."
31. Wink, *The Human Being*, 25.
32. Wink, *The Human Being*, 22.
33. KBS on Ezek 2:1.
34. KBS on Ezek 4:1.

And you, son of man, on the day I take away their stronghold, their joy and glory, the delight of their eyes, their heart's desire, and their sons and daughters as well—on that day a fugitive will come to tell you the news. At that time your mouth will be opened; you will speak with him and will no longer be silent. So you will be a sign to them, and they will know that I am the Lord. (Ezek 24:25–27; cf. Mark 13:1–2)[35]

Ezekiel himself had come to Babylon as part of the first deportation; now a second deportation of the Jews from Jerusalem to Babylon takes place.

EZEKIEL'S VISIONARY JOURNEY TO THE TEMPLE IN JERUSALEM

A parallel can be drawn between the visionary journey of the prophet Ezekiel from Babylon to Jerusalem and the night journey and heavenly journey that the prophet Muhammad makes from Mecca to the same city (Q 17:1); Muhammad went to Jerusalem a year before the Exodus or *hijra* in the year 622![36] The story of Ezekiel's visionary journey is about the still *future* devastation of Jerusalem and the temple. Both stories are concerned with the reasons for the destruction. "Temple" is not translated in the Qur'an as *masjid*, "a place where one bows down," but by *mihrâb*, which can be translated as "place of prayer." It appears in passages that are about David: "Has there not come to you the account of the contenders, when they scaled the wall into the sanctuary?" (Q 38:21). This is explained as an allusion to the parable that the prophet Nathan told David,[37] when the latter had Uriah, the captain of his army, killed so that he could marry his wife Bathsheba with whom he had committed adultery. The prophet Nathan reproachfully held a mirror up to David in the form of a story about a rich man who had stolen and slaughtered the only lamb of a poor man. David found this a great scandal: "This man deserves to die." Nathan then looked straight at the king and said: "You are the man!" (2 Sam 12:7).[38]

The *place of prayer* also appears in the Qur'an when Mary is entrusted to Zechariah, the father of John the Baptist (Yahyâ). "Whenever Zechariah visited her in the sanctuary, he found provisions with her. He said, "O Mary,

---

35. Cf. Jesus' words about the destruction of the temple in his apocalyptic discourse (Mark 13).

36. Neuwirth, *Die Koranische*, 184–90.

37. Paret on Q 38:20.

38. *Alle Bijbelse personen*, s.v., Natan. For a different reading cf. Speyer, *Die biblische Erzählungen*, 378–380.

from where does this come for you?" She said, "It comes from God. God provides whomever He wishes without any reckoning" (Q 3:37). When Zechariah prayed in the *sanctuary*, the good news of the advent of John the Baptist who *confirmed* the Word of God, was announced (Q 3:38-39; cf.19:11).[39]

Several well-known stories from the New Testament and from the apocryphal books took place in the temple of Jerusalem. When thinking of that place of worship, people often imagine a palace-like building with arches found in the mosaic images of the Byzantines.[40]

Ezekiel was a priest (1 Chr 24:16) and therefore his place was in the temple. The last part of his book culminates in an expansive vision of the new temple in an ideal end time (40-48)[41] with the new law and the new Canaan (Ezek 43-46). The Jews, however, remain oriented to Jerusalem while in exile in Babylon. When they prayed, they did so in the direction (*qibla*) of Jerusalem. The Muslims in Mecca followed the same practice initially and also for the first few years in Medina until the *qibla* was changed to Mecca (Q 2:142). "To God belong the east and the west: so whichever way you turn, there is the face of God!" (Q 2:115). King Solomon already spoke about the direction of prayer in his prayer of dedication for the temple: "When your people go to war against their enemies, wherever you send them, and when they pray to the Lord toward the city you have chosen and the temple I have built for your Name, then hear from heaven their prayer and their plea, and uphold their cause" (1 Kgs 8:44-45, 48). The believer prays: "Hear my cry for mercy as I call to you for help, *as I lift up my hands toward your Most Holy Place*" (Ps 28:2; cf. Pss 5:8; 138:2). The prayer direction is oriented to the presence of the ark and the throne of the cherubs (cf. 1 Kgs 6).

The prophet Daniel is a striking example of a Jew who, while in a strange land, prays in the direction of Jerusalem. In Babylon, Daniel learned that a law of the "Medes and Persians" had been issued that stipulated that, for a period of 30 days, whoever prayed to a god or a human being other than the king, i.e., Darius the Mede,[42] would be thrown into the lion's den. Daniel thereupon went home, where the upstairs windows were open in the direction of Jerusalem, a custom dating back at least to the time of the

---

39. *EQ*, s.v., Sacred Precincts, 516.
40. Neuwirth, *Die Koranische Verzauberung*, 195.
41. KBS (Willibrord translation), introduction to the book Ezekiel.
42. KBS on Dan 6:1. He had the person of Darius (522-486) in mind but describes him as a king of the old Mede empire.

exile.⁴³ There he knelt three times a day to worship and to praise his God, just as he always did (Dan 6:11). After all, Jews were called to do so: "Remember the Lord in a distant land, / and call to mind Jerusalem" (Jer 51:50). And Psalm 137 declares:

> If I forget you, Jerusalem,
> may my right hand forget its skill.
> May my tongue cling to the roof of my mouth
> if I do not remember you,
> if I do not consider Jerusalem
> my highest joy.
> (Ps 137: 5–6)

It is not, therefore, just a question of following the "custom" of observing the direction of prayer right up to the present time. It is also a question of continuing to orient oneself to the Torah that continues to emanate from Sion: "The law will go out from Zion, / the word of the Lord from Jerusalem" (Isa 2:3; cf. John 4:22; Rom 9:4)

The book of Ezekiel contains a series of prophecies about the temple in Jerusalem (Ezek 8–11). In one of those visions, the prophet Ezekiel is brought from Babylon to Jerusalem to witness the idolatry⁴⁴ that takes place there and the punishments that that came as a result.⁴⁵ Those visions follow those that announce the end: "Son of man, this is what the Sovereign Lord says to the land of Israel: 'The end! The end has come upon the four *corners* of the land!'" (Ezek 7:2; cf. Amos 5:18; Zeph 1:14; Joel 1:15). The book will culminate in the temple vision (Ezek 40–48).⁴⁶ Ezekiel who saw the Lord leave his sanctuary (10:19; 11:23; cf. 1:24) was now the witness to how God takes possession of his property again:

> Then the man brought me to the gate facing east, and I saw the glory of the God of Israel coming from the east. His voice was like the roar of rushing waters, and the land was radiant with his glory. The vision I saw was like the vision I had seen when he came to destroy the city and like the visions I had seen by the Kebar River [cf. Ezek 1], and I fell facedown. The glory of the Lord entered the temple through the gate facing east. (Ezek 43:1–4)⁴⁷

---

43. KBS on Dan 6:11. Cf. Tob 3:11: "With hands outstretched toward the window, she prayed . . . ."
44. The Qur'an uses the word *shirk* for this.
45. KBS on Ezek 8:1.
46. KBS on Ezek 8:1; 7:2.
47. KBS on Ezek 43:2.

This concerns the prophecy of God's return to Jerusalem through the gate of the temple facing east, the gate that, according to Ezekiel was closed because God left Jerusalem through this gate with the exiles for Babylon (Ezek 10:8, 19). The cherubs, with the wheels next to them, spread their wings, while the glory of the God of Israel hovered above them. The glory of the Lord rose up from the city and settled on the mountain east of the city. "The Spirit lifted me [Ezekiel] up and brought me to the exiles in Babylonia in the vision given by the Spirit of God" (Ezek 11:22–24). According to Jewish and Christian tradition, the closed gate will be opened once again when the Messiah comes.[48]

The Qur'an also relates that Mary withdrew from her family and went to a *place in the east*, cutting herself off from them (*hijâb*): "whereupon We sent to her Our Spirit and he became incarnate for her as a well-proportioned human [Gabriel]." "And mention in the Book of Mary, when she secluded herself" from her family to an easterly place for the announcement of the birth of Jesus (Q 19:16–19). This "place" is connected with a text from Ezekiel: "Then the man brought me back to the *outer gate* of the sanctuary, the one *facing east*, and it was shut. The Lord said to me, 'This gate is to remain shut. It must not be opened; no one may enter through it. It is to remain shut because the Lord, the God of Israel, has entered through it'" (Ezek 44:1–2).

Coptic texts, which borrow from the apocryphal gospels, also talk about Mary withdrawing to an eastern place. Mary sits with her face to the east because she prays without ceasing.[49] On the basis of this passage from Ezekiel, according to the ancient church, the eastern gate of the temple would be opened by God: *solus Christus clausas portas vulvae virginalis aperuit*.[50] Only the Messiah can open the closed doors of the uterus of the virgin.

When Ezekiel sat in his house in Babylon and the elders of Judah sat before him, the hand of the Lord God came over him (Ezek 8:1). He was obviously housebound, but the elders from Judah were sitting in front of him and treated him with some deference, even though his message was not taken seriously (Ezek 14:1–3; 20:1–3; 33:30–32). From his home, he was able to make a "visionary" visit to Jerusalem so that he, with a guide, could inspect the city in order to witness the worst excesses of idolatry. The date of this prophetic vision is known precisely: 17 September 592 BC, about fourteen months after his call vision. The most significant thing about that

---

48. Neuwirth, *Die Koranische Verzauberung*, 197.

49. O'Shaughnessy, *The Development of the Meaning of Spirit in the Koran*, 54.

50. Paret on Q 19:16; p. 323. Ambrosius: "Solus Christus clausas portas vulvae virginalis aperuit. Haec est porta orientalis clausa." https://corpuscoranicum.de/kommentar/index/sure/19/vers/1.

is that the final destruction of Jerusalem confirms that Ezekiel was truly speaking for God. It cannot be disputed that he predicted these events in advance. Ezekiel gives prophetic information about the beginning of the siege of Jerusalem (cf. Ezek 24:2; 33:33), which the exiles could only observe a few months later: "I looked, and I saw a figure *like that of a man*. From what appeared to be his waist down he was like fire, and from there up his appearance was as bright as glowing metal. He stretched out what looked like a hand and took me by the hair of my head" (Ezek 8:2–3).[51]

This stretched-out hand recalls the hand that fed him the scroll to eat (Ezek 2:9). The spirit lifted him up between heaven and earth and brought him to Jerusalem in a heavenly vision,[52] to the entrance of the north gate of the inner court, the place where the idol[53] that aroused the jealousy of the Lord stood. And there he saw the glory of the God of Israel, just as he had seen in the plain of Kedar (Ezek 8:3–4; cf. 1:26–28). The spirit was the same Spirit of God who had raised him to his feet earlier (Ezek 2:2; 3:12, 24). It is the Lord who transports Ezekiel, and it is he who stands at his side during the whole visionary experience.[54] Ezekiel has to leave his home and his guests for some time, although it is also conceivable that his experiences could have taken place in their presence. When the vision left him, he did in any case share with the exiles what the Lord had shown him (Ezek 11:24b, 25).

What was the purpose of this detailed report of what was happening in Jerusalem? Perhaps God wanted to show him in this way that the destruction was justified because of the evil that held sway in Jerusalem. The question "Have you seen . . . ?" that is repeatedly asked of him suggests that he witnessed things that he found shocking. It seems that his fellow exiles were constantly telling him that the punishment was too severe, that they did not actually deserve it. Ezekiel knew better. The judgment of God was completely deserved, and Ezekiel could now give detailed reasons why.[55]

---

51. Cf. Dan 14:36: (NRSVCE): "Then the angel of the Lord took him by the crown of his head and carried him by his hair; with the speed of the wind he set him down in Babylon, right over the [lions'] den."

52. The activity of God's Spirit is often cited in connection with Ezekiel's vision. Cf. Ezek 3:12, 14; 8:3; 11:1, 5, 24; 37:1; 43:5; KBS on Ezek 2:2.

53. Allegedly, an allusion is made here to the image of Asherah, which was placed in the temple by King Manasseh (2 Kgs 21:7; 2 Chr 33:7–15).

54. Other prophets, such as Elisha, Al-Yasa', also had the experience that they saw events from a distance, (2 Kgs 5:26; 6:32). Al-Yasa' is mentioned in Q 6:86; 38:48.

55. Wright, *The Message of Ezekiel*, 97–99.

GOG, THE PRINCE OF MAGOG

Who was this mysterious figure who was called an "enemy from the north" and "the prince of Magog" (Ezek 38:2–39:15)? Ezekiel sees in his vision a storm coming out of the north, a large mass of clouds filled with flashing lightning and surrounded by a brilliant light (Ezek 1:4). The term "enemy from the north" recalled, in particular, empires like Assyria (Zeph 2:13) and Babylon (Zech 2:10; 6:6, 8).[56]

In the Ancient Near East, it was thought that the gods lived in the north. In a passage on the fall of the last king of Babylon it is said: How you have fallen from heaven! (Isa 14:12):

> You said in your heart,
> "I will ascend to the heavens;
> I will raise my throne
> above the stars of God;
> I will sit enthroned on the mount of assembly,
> on the utmost heights of Mount Zaphon.
> (Isa 14:13)

Zaphon is the mountain where the gods gather (cf. Olympus).[57] The Hebrew word Zaphon can also coincide with a Canaanite mountain of the gods in northern Palestine.

For eschatology, the north is the place where the judgment of Israel begins. It is from the north that the catastrophes burst over all the inhabitants of the land (Jer 1:14; cf. Isa 14:31; 4:6; 13:20). If the north is thus principally the land of *judgment and doom*, there is also nonetheless a message of *salvation* in connection with the mountain of the gods in the far north: "Mount Zion, in the far north, / the city of the great King" (Ps 48:2, RSV).[58]

What connects the Canaanite tradition with the mountain in the north (cf. Isa 14:13; Ezek 38:6, 15) is that everything "in fact" happens on Mount Zion. The Lord is not only active on this mountain as the giver of rain and fertility, but he also reigns as the great King who robs the small kings with their chaos[59]-causing plans of their power. Given that this Psalm 48 was written in the period before the exile, this "political" title is transferred to God who robs the Assyrian great king, who threatens Zion of the people of

---

56. Enemies from the west (Philistines), the east (Moab), the south (Ethiopians) (Zeph 2:4–12).
57. KBS on Isa 14:13.
58. Cf. Isa 14:14; Ezek 28:14. *BW*, *s.v.*, noorden.
59. *tohu wabohu*; see chapter VIII of this book.

God, of his power,[60] just as he did to Pharaoh and all his successors right up to the present.

In Ezekiel's text, Magog is a mythological country,[61] but the term is used elsewhere as the name of an individual. He appears in the genealogy of Japhet as the grandson of Noah (Gen 10:2; cf. 1 Chr 1:5). Jewish tradition made Magog a second apocalyptic king alongside Gog. Thus, both are mentioned in the New Testament (Rev 20:8) and in the Qur'an (Q 18:94-97; 21:96) as persons. The name Gog brings to mind King Gyges (716-678 BC) of the kingdom of Lydia in Asia Minor, with Sardis as its capital.[62] In Sumerian, the name Gug means darkness. Apparently, God takes a "darkling" into his service.

The Babylonians are usually thought of as the enemies from the north since they usually attacked Israel from the north. The Scythians, who rode on horses and could shoot arrows while riding, are sometimes mentioned. They could shoot backwards at full gallop. The same is said, for that matter, of the Parthians. But God disarms the archers on horses, the terrifying warriors. They are no match for him: "Then I will strike your bow from your left hand and make your arrows drop from your right hand" (Ezek 39:3; cf. 38:3-4). The prophet Jeremiah talks about a people from the north: a great nation is being stirred up from the ends of the earth for battle (Jer 6:22-23).[63] Gog is presented as follows: "You will come from your place in the far north, you and many nations with you, all of them riding on horses, a great horde, a mighty army" (Ezek 38:15). "The enemy from the north," Gog, is a *symbolic name* for Babylon, who is an enemy from the north but is also itself attacked in turn by another enemy from the north: a great nation and powerful kings are coming from the ends of the earth (Jer 50:41). A nation is being stirred up from the north that will lay waste to Babylon (Jer 50:3). Catastrophes will break out from the north over all the inhabitants of the land (Jer 1:14; cf. Jer 3:18; 4:6; 6:1, 22; 10:22; 13:20; 46:24; 50:3, 9:41, 48. Isa 10:28-31).

The army that carries out God's judgment usually comes from the north (Jer 1:14,15; 4:6; Ezek 38:6).[64] Because of its apocalyptic nature, the

---

60. Hossfeld and Zenger, *Die Psalmen*, 297.
61. Zimmerli, *Ezechiel*, 973-975.
62. KBS on Ezek 39:1; see also Herodotus.
63. Cf. Jer 50:41-43; Babylon itself will fall; Jer 3:18; 4:6; 6:1, 22; 10:22; 13:20; 46:24; 50:3, 9-41; 51:46.
64. KBS on Joel 2:20; that is an allusion to the apocalyptic army (Joel 2:1-11).

army is described by expressions such as "looked like," as in, for example, the visions of Ezekiel and Daniel (cf. Ezek 8:2; 10:1; 40:3; Dan 8:15; 10:6,18).[65]

> [B]ehind them, a desert waste—
> nothing escapes them.
> They have the appearance of *horses*;
> they gallop along like *cavalry*.[66]
> With a noise like that of chariots
> they leap over the mountaintops,
> like a crackling fire consuming stubble,
> like a mighty army drawn up for battle.
> (Joel 2:3–5)
>
> They charge like warriors;
> they scale walls like soldiers.
> They all march in line,
> not swerving from their course.
> (Joel 2:7)
>
> The Lord thunders
> at the head of his army;
> his forces are beyond number,
> and mighty is the army that obeys his command.
> The day of the Lord is great;
> it is dreadful.
> Who can endure it?
> (Joel 2:11)

Similar comparisons are made in the book of Revelation:

> The locusts looked like *horses* prepared for battle. On their heads they wore something like crowns of gold, and their faces resembled human faces. Their hair was like women's hair, and their teeth were like lions' teeth. They had breastplates like breastplates of iron, and the sound of their wings was like *the thundering of many horses and chariots rushing into battle*. (Rev 9:7–9)

The symbolic names Gog and Magog represent the archetypal enemy, a mythical anti-divine power who rebels against God and his people, his community.

---

65. KBS on Joel 2:4.
66. Cf. Nah 2:4–7, 11; 3:2–3, 15–17; Rev 9:7, 9.

GOD'S BATTLE AGAINST GOG

The book of Ezekiel (especially chapters 38–39) revolves around the battle between God and absolute evil, between the Eternally Merciful, who represents justice and peace on the one hand and who or what represents injustice, robbery, and violence on the other. In the Bible there are many hostile peoples that listed by name, but Gog and Magog are an example of enemies who are indicated by symbolic names. Amalek is an archetypal enemy as well. There is no mention of them in any sources from that time other than in the Bible, and there is also no single archaeological indication for their existence.[67] One could ask if that is also primarily or exclusively intended in a symbolic way. The name "Gog" could also be derived from Agag, the name of the king of the Amalekites (1 Sam 15:18–33), who were the archenemies of the children of Israel. Balaam, the pagan prophet, who was hired to curse the children of Israel, understood, however, that the Lord wanted to bless the children of Israel (Num 24:1).[68] He then pronounces an oracle: "Their king will be greater than Agag; their kingdom will be exalted" (Num 24: 7).[69] The Septuagint translates this in a way that it appears that the Messiah is intended here. A man will be born from his race, and he will reign over many peoples and his government shall be exalted above God, and his government will increase. The LXX, the Greek translation, uses the name "Gog" instead of Agag![70] Apparently, Balaam knew that Moses had marched from Egypt to the Transjordan under the guidance of the God of Israel (Num 24:8). Moses had already defeated Amalek (Num 24:7, 20). It was not unusual in the Ancient Near East to ascribe the same victory to someone else, in this case to King Saul (1 Sam 15:4–9).[71] It was the Amalekites who attacked the children of Israel during their Exodus from Egypt in a very cowardly way: "When you were weary and worn out, they met you on your journey and cut off all who were lagging behind; they had no fear of God" (Deut 25:18).

---

67. David William Cohen and Michael D. Kennedy, *Responsibility in Crisis* (Ann Arbor: Scholarly Publishing Office, 2005), p. 186; cited in: https://nl.wikipedia.org/wiki/Amalekieten.

68. Cf. Q 7:175, 176. In the mystical tradition, he is known as the prototype of the spiritual man who loses his way through lust and pride. *EI*, s.v., Bal'am.

69. The king intended here is Saul, the one who defeated Agag (1 Sam 15:8) or David (1 Sam 30).

70. KBS on Num 24:7.

71. Korpel and de Moor, *Adam, Eva en de duivel*, 247, n. 173.

In the Talmudic tradition, the war between Gog and Magog was brought into connection with the end times,[72] and Psalm 2 was seen as a reference to a rebellion by Gog and Magog against God and his Messiah. "The kings of the earth take their stand and the rulers gather together against the Lord and against his Anointed" (Ps 2:2). The New Testament mentions Gog and Magog, also in connection with the eschatological struggle. After the fall of Babylon, which actually refers to Rome, Satan, the beast, and the false prophet with their followers, "the kings of the earth" (Rev 19:19) are the only remaining enemies of God. Satan is bound for a thousand years and when the thousand years are over, he will be released from the dungeon. He will mislead the peoples living in the four corners of the earth. Gog and Magog, as numerous as the sands of the sea, will gather them for the battle (Rev 20:7–8). At that time, the earth was viewed as a rectangular flat surface (cf. Rev 7:1, 20:7. 8; Matt 24:31).[73] "They marched across the breadth of the earth and surrounded the camp of God's people, the city he loves. But fire came down from heaven and devoured them" (Rev 20:9). The city God loves is Jerusalem as the center of the earth, where God's people live in peace. The camp recalls Israel's sojourn in the desert (cf. Exod 16:13, etc.).[74] The Qur'an speaks of the cavalry of Iblîs, the devil (Q 17:64). One of the *surahs* in the "Qur'anic Apocalypse" is called "The Runners," the charging horses that people swear by (Q 100:1; cf. 51:1–4; 77:1–6; 79:105) and they could represent the apocalyptic riders (cf. Rev 6:1–11).[75]

Gog and Magog are reported in connection with the history of the "man with the two horns" (*Dhû-al-Qarnayn*), who represents Alexander the Great. On one of his journeys, Alexander came to a place between two mountains and there encountered a people that hardly understood a word he said. This people said to him, "O man with the two horns! Gog and Magog are indeed *sowing destruction* on the earth. Shall we pay you tribute so that you will build a wall between them and us?" The man with the two horns said, "The power God has given me is better than what you are offering. Bring me pieces of iron." When he had filled in the valley between the two mountains, he said "Blow on the fire!" When this was glowing hot, he said, "Bring me molten metal to pour over it. This is proof of God's mercifulness. But when the promise of my Lord has been fulfilled, he will destroy this wall. And the promise of my Lord is true" (Q 18:93–99; cf. Ezek 38:14–16).

---

72. *Eschaton*, TB Shabbat 118a.
73. KBS on Rev 7:1; 20:8.
74. KBS on Rev 20:9.
75. Cuypers, *A Quranic Apocalypse*, 226–30.

How are these stories about Gog and Magog—in the three books—to be explained? What is being "revealed" here? This story (Ezek 38–39) brings the reader or hearer to the situation after the return of the exiles from Babylon and their resettlement in the land. It is then that Gog comes to attack Israel. In this story that unfolds here there are two actors: God and Gog. An alliance of nations attacks Israel unexpectedly. But what kind of war breaks out? A destructive attack is carried out on a people who live in peace, unsuspecting of any evil, since they think that they can precisely now, finally, enjoy some safety after the exile in Babylon. Physically and militarily, Israel is not able to defend itself, for Israel is not a militarized state with strong cities and a standing army. Gog lays an ambush for Israel and thinks that he is the only actor and initiator in this business: "*I* will invade a land of unwalled villages; *I* will attack a peaceful and unsuspecting people—all of them living without walls and without gates and bars" (Ezek 38:11). But the reality is different. Behind the scenes, it is God who has control over events (Ezek 38:3–9): I will come for you (Gog), "I will put hooks in your jaws and bring you out with your whole army—your horses, your horsemen fully armed, and a great horde with large and small shields, all of them brandishing their swords" (Ezek 38:4). Ezekiel had already applied the same image to Egypt earlier: "But I will put hooks in your jaws and make the fish of your streams stick to your scales. I will pull you out from among your streams with all the fish sticking to your scales" (Ezek 29:4).

If the troops from Gog come marching, the nations around Israel do not want to be left out, however. They follow in Gog's wake and join Gog's armies. Obviously, they expect—all too eagerly—that they will be able to come away with a great deal of plunder. Merchants from far and near ask Gog: "Have you come to plunder? Have you gathered your hordes to loot, to carry off silver and gold, to take away livestock and goods and to seize much plunder?" (Ezek 38:13). They themselves are merchants who do business via the overland routes, namely, the Arab desert (for example, Sheba[76] and Dedan[77])—places that refer to the end of the earth in the East—and they sail the sea routes via the Mediterranean to the West (Tarshish in Spain), viewed as the furthest point of the world in the West. These trading nations look jealously at Gog's exploits against the safe inhabitants—"safe" is of course intended ironically, for they are simply "easy" targets.[78]

---

76. Probably an area in North Africa. Some think here of the Sabeans, a merchant people in southern Arabia; cf. KBS on 1 Kgs 10:1.

77. Cf. Ezek 25:13: "Therefore, this is what the Sovereign Lord says, I will stretch out my hand against Edom and kill its men and their animals. I will lay it waste, and from Teman to Dedan they will fall by the sword."

78. Cf. Milgrom and Block, *Ezekiel's Hope*, 13–14, 21.

On the day that Gog enters Israel's territory, God's wrath is poured out. "On that day, a severe earthquake will occur in Israel. Mountains crash down, cliffs will crumble, and every wall will collapse: I will summon all possible horrors against him; I will turn sword against sword, I will punish Gog with plagues and bloodshed; I will let rain and hail, fire and sulfur fall upon him, on his troops, and on his allies (Ezek 38:18–23). The international military coalition of nations from all corners of the world—north, south, and east—are an indication that Israel will be invaded by all the nations surrounding it. These nations will, however, be destroyed on Israel's mountains.

How are we to understand that? Will God, the Lord of hosts, the Lord of armies, himself now draw a bloody trail through history? What is he doing and what is his motivation? God now acts because he no longer accepts *his people* Israel and *his land* being attacked (Ezek 38:14, 16). He goes into action to show his greatness and that he is the Holy One: "I will make myself known in the sight of many nations. Then they will know that I am the Lord" (Ezek 38:23), just as God displayed his glory during the exodus from Egypt at the expense of Pharaoh and his whole army (Exod 14:4).[79] Gog's attack on God's people and the invasion of God's country are the same as war against God himself. That is why the real enemies facing each other in this oracle are not Israel and Gog, but God and Gog. Here Gog has become God's puppet, a mere tool in his hand, someone who will taste retribution.

But how does God put an end to this? Does he do so by organizing an apocalyptic destruction? By combatting Gog and Magog in the spirit of the "Shock and Awe doctrine" that was applied in 2003 in Iraq? That doctrine reflected a tactic that was based on the use of overwhelming power and spectacular violence in order to paralyze the enemy and destroy the enemy's will to fight. Up until now, the nuclear bombs on Hiroshima and Nagasaki are the most dramatic examples of this policy. But this is not the tactic being used here. What happens in reality is that the armies of Gog turn their weapons *against each other*. Every man's *sword will be against his brother* (Ezek 38:21). They finish each other off. That is how these apocalyptic chapters should be read and understood. It is not a literal description but a figurative story in pictures, a comic strip about the definitive defeat of evil. Some people are wary about reading these texts in a non-literal way, as if that would mean that one is thereby saying that the text is not true, that the event did not really happen or never will actually happen. But that is exactly the point. This "picture story" is intended precisely to make clear what the

---

79. Ps 148:2: "Praise him, all his angels, praise him, all his heavenly hosts." This is a reference to the angels. One can think here of Michael in this context who is a dominant form of expressing this in the apocalyptic time (cf. Dan 10:13; Rev 12:7).

true view is regarding what is going to happen and to create confidence that it will end well: there will be a definitive end to evil.

One could also speak of a *cartoon*. All that macho thinking is mocked; the powerbrokers who think they have the world in their power are mocked. The scorn and mockery can be clearly heard if one observes the energy that goes into the task of cleaning up after the war against Gog is done: the inhabitants of Israel come from their cities and burn the weapons, the large and small shields, the bows and arrows, maces and spears. They have enough fuel to feed their fires for *seven* years! They do not need to gather wood from the fields or to cut it from the woods—they will be using the weapons for fuel all that time. They plunder the plunderers and rob their robbers (Ezek 39:9–10). Israel will have enough firewood for *seven* years!

For *seven* months, the Israelites dig graves and cleanse the land. The whole population helps in this. And when the *seven* months are over, people will be hired to travel throughout the land and to bury all corpses they come across. In that way, they will cleanse the whole land (Ezek 39:12–14). John the seer on Patmos speaks about this: "And I saw an angel standing in the sun, who cried in a loud voice to all the birds flying in midair, 'Come, gather together for the great supper of God, so that you may eat the flesh of kings, generals, and mighty men, of horses and their riders, and the flesh of all people, free and slave, small and great'" (Rev 19:17–18).

The defeated armies are buried in a city that is called Hamonah, a symbolic name for Jerusalem (Ezek 5:7; 7:12–14; 23:40–42).[80] The name refers to the valley of Hinnom outside Jerusalem, where child sacrifice was practiced (Jer 2:23). Israel was guilty of such acts—which had been occurring, it should be noted, since the time of King Solomon. Solomon was the first to build an altar to Moloch, to whom sons and daughters were sacrificed: "something I [Yahweh] did not command, nor did it enter my mind" (Jer 7:31; cf. 19:5–6). Later, King Joram of Israel even offered his own son on the city wall (2 Kgs 3:27) and King Ahaz of Judah followed that example with his own son (2 Kgs 16:3), as did King Manasseh of Judah with his (2 Kgs 21:6). In the time of King Josiah, whom we discussed above, the Torah had been rediscovered and began to function again, and this just king desecrated the oven so that no one could sacrifice his son or daughter to Moloch in the fire (2 Kgs 23:10). The Torah had clearly forbidden this. "Do not give any of your children to be sacrificed to Moloch, for you must not profane the name of the Lord your God. I am the Lord" (Lev 18:21).[81] The prophet

---

80. Milgrom and Block, *Ezekiel's Hope*, 25.

81. Parts of this description can be also be found in the following texts: Deut 12:31b; 13:1; 18:10.

Ezekiel reproaches Jerusalem for such horrible deeds: "And you took your sons and daughters whom you bore to me and sacrificed them as food to the idols. Was your prostitution not enough? You slaughtered my children and sacrificed them to the idols" (Ezek 16:20–21).

The number *seven*, which is deliberately italicized above, dominates the Apocalypse of John: *seven* letters to churches, *seven* seals, *seven* trumpets, *seven* visions of the lack of power, *seven* bowls, *seven* visions of the end, and *seven* visions of a new beginning.[82]

GOD AND ALL PEOPLES

The crucial point, as always in the Scriptures, is how *God's plan* is not limited to the people of Israel but includes all people—indeed, the whole world—right from the beginning. That is why God did not think it sufficient that only Israel would learn the lesson of complete restoration, salvation, and healing when it was redeemed from exile and could return. But the peoples also had to understand and comprehend what happened and thus make the same apocalyptic, revelatory discovery! Instead of that, however, the nations laid Jerusalem to waste, and the children of Israel were carried away into exile, mocked, and God himself was mocked because, apparently, he did not have the power to protect his people and his land. That is the reason for God's intervention via Gog and Magog: "It is not for your sake that I am going to do these things, but for the sake of my holy name, which you have profaned among the nations where you have gone. I will show the holiness of my great name, which has been profaned among the nations, the name you have profaned among them. Then the nations will know that I am the Lord, declares the Sovereign Lord" (Ezek 36:22–23). The emphasis after Gog has been destroyed is on God's glory that he shows through the justice that he exercises *for his people* by his punishment of his enemies and also *against his people*. Gog's invasion occurs, according to God's schedule, his timetable, the calculated plan *for his people*.

What does God have in mind once the covenant relation between God and the people is restored completely and the people can return from exile? They can once again live in complete peace, in their own country. Living in safety is based on due observance of God's commandments and the keeping of his laws: "Follow my decrees and be careful to obey my laws, and you will live safely in the land" (Lev 25:18). After their return from exile, God now mobilizes Gog against his own people because the important point in the divine agenda is universal acknowledgement of him as God.

82. Nico ter Linden, *Het verhaal gaat door*, 285.

Gog and his troops have been brought to the mountains of Israel so that the *holiness of God* can be revealed to all peoples (Ezek 38:16, 23; 39:6–7, 22, 28). That is not an abstract theological announcement about the holiness of God. It is intended to make clear in concrete ways that if God comes into action, he does so to defend and protect his people, his community, against the universal conspiracy of evil. God comes into action to judge, to set things right. The primary goal of the whole story is the complete and final revelation of the Lord as God and the recognition, by Israel and *all peoples*, of God's true identity and the righteousness of his ways. The greed Gog shows for the innocent and unsuspecting Israel is contrasted with God's righteousness (Ezek 38:10–13). The nations will experience God's power. God's glory will be manifested among the nations through his exercise of justice and power. The primary goal, the point of the whole narrative is the complete and final revelation of the Lord as God so that Israel and the nations will finally recognize who he is.

The role of Gog and Magog in the Qur'an is, so to say, universalized when an allusion is made to *every* city being laid waste, being made *unsafe* by Gog and Magog who forbid the inhabitants from returning. It is forbidden for the inhabitants of a city that God (because of their unbelief) has destroyed to return. They remain in their graves until, at the end of days, the dam of Gog and Magog is opened and the dead will come running from each hill to the judgment (Q 21: 95–96).[83] Then the trumpet will sound, and they shall rush out of their graves to their Lord (Q 36:51; cf. 1 Thess 4:16).

Gog and Magog are not figures who will appear someday, at the end of time. They appear constantly throughout history because God executes his judgment over all who do not live according to the Torah. Those who are the recipients of his judgment can be those who belong nominally to the three communities and who should follow the path pointed out to them. But it is also always directed at all the nations of the world. Previously and just as much now: it is the prophetic vision, and the prophetic vision of history in the apocalyptic sense of the word: it reveals history to us, what happens again and again and again throughout history, right up until the present.

The Apocalypse of John speaks of a beast that plays such a crucial role in the imagery of the four beasts in the apocalyptic book of Daniel (Dan 7), the last book of the Septuagint, the Greek translation of the Hebrew Bible.[84] There it represents the Roman Empire: "And I saw a beast

---

83. *Dictionnaire du Coran*, s.v., Gog et Magog; cf. Yücesoy, *Messianic Beliefs & Imperial Politics in Medieval Islam*, 37.

84. See chapter V.

coming out of the sea" (Rev 13:1), followed by another beast (Rev 13:11). Together with the first beast, it embodies the political and religious power of the Roman Empire.

One beast especially attracts attention, which is designated by a number: 666. In line with apocalyptic outlook, a key is provided in the form of a kind of cryptogram for identifying the beast that is embodied in a specific person: it designates a specific individual (Rev 13:18). That number possibly originated by adding up the numerical values of the letters that make up the intended name. The most probable candidate is Nero (written in Hebrew letters) of Rome,[85] which is also called the whore of Babylon. The "*seven heads*" are the seven hills on which the woman sits (Rev 17:9). Three times six is absolute evil, the evil that rules brutally everywhere—"but only briefly so, six is followed by seven."[86]

---

85. KBS on Rev 13:18.

86. Numbers are also used symbolically in the Qur'an. Six, the number of the days of creation, is symbolically "incomplete," one less than the heavenly number seven. Seven refers to cosmography: the seven heavens (Q 17:44); oceans (Q 31:27), and the motif of the number seven in the story of Joseph is also telling (Q 12:43–48). *EQ, s.v.*, Numbers and Numeration; cf. Schimmel et al., *The Mystery of Numbers*. Ter Linden, 316.

V

The Book of Daniel: "The Flaming Scripture of the Holy God"

Apocalyptic always presents an interpretation of history—past, present, future—and sees the present as the beginning period just before the end time.[1]

"Where there is no revelation, the people cast off restraint" (Proverbs 29:18a)

Speaking Truth to Power.[2]

The author of Daniel presented to the world a new mutation in God-consciousness.[3]

"When tyrants suffer from bad dreams, God is at work" (Walter Lüthi).

---

1. Schillebeeckx, *Gerechtigheid en liefde*, 407.

2. The commonly acknowledged flashpoint for the spread of the phrase "speak truth to power" is the 1955 book, *Speak Truth to Power: A Quaker Search for an Alternative to Violence*, published by the American Friends Service Committee. As noted in *Hot Pacifism and Cold War*, this book received significant media attention during the first year of its publication; https://classroom.synonym.com/origin-phrase-speaking-truth-power-11676.html.

3. Wink, *The Human Being*, 51.

INTRODUCTION

In this chapter we will look at the apocalyptic book of Daniel. The name "Daniel" can be translated as "God is judge" or "God will judge"; both express the desire for justice.[4] The book of Daniel developed an "imagistic language" in order to undermine the imperialistic, ideological story of the Hellenistic regime. In the visions Daniel received, this language presents a different view of or revision of history. This apocalyptic figure unfolds a complete panorama of history in which God figures as the primary guide in the plot, the key to world history. In light of the expected "end times," the seer discovers a different perspective on history.[5] God does not overlook events in history; rather, he *oversees* them. We should look at the historical context of the book of Daniel before exploring the content of the dreams or visions Daniel has. This will allow us to get at the heart of understanding this book for his time and ours.

Although the prophet Daniel is not mentioned by name in the Qur'an, as is more often the case with other prophets, that does not mean that he does not appear in the Qur'an directly or indirectly. It is said of Abraham that his fellow countrymen said: "Build a structure for him and cast him into a huge fire" (Q 37:97; cf. Q 29: 24). But God said: "O fire! Be cool and safe for Abraham!" (Q 21:68, 69). That can be read as an echo of the story of Daniel's three friends in the fiery furnace (Dan 3:19–24). Sadrach, Meshach, and Abednego were educated together with Daniel, at the order of the Babylonian king Nebuchadnezzar in the philosophy, religion, and language of the Chaldeans (Dan 1). The three refused, however, to worship the golden image that the king had erected. He gave them another chance to worship it, but when they persisted in their refusal, they were thrown into the fiery furnace, where certain death awaited them. They were then saved from the fire by a "son of the gods" (Dan 3:25) or an angel (Dan 3:28). That is also confirmed by some Muslim exegetes.[6] The text "perish the Men of the Ditch! The fire, abounding in fuel" (Q 85:4–5) is seen as an allusion to this.[7] On the other hand, an eschatological explanation is also given of this text, namely, that it concerns the fires of hell, *Jahanna*, for the unbelievers. The text could allow both interpretations.[8]

---

4. Han, *Daniel's Spiel*, 74.

5. Han, *Daniel's Spiel*, 23.

6. Speyer, *Die biblische Erzählungen*, 424. Blachère, *Le Coran*, II, 120.

7. Al-Burudj; in: Watt. *Companion to the Qur'ân*, 302; Cuypers, *A Quranic Apocalypse*, 73.

8. According to Cuypers, *A Quranic Apocalypse*, 73–74. Rudi Paret, *Der Koran*, 505–6.

The prophet Daniel or Dâniyâl is known in Muslim tradition as the revealer of the future and mysteries about the "last days." It is said that soldiers "accidentally" stumbled on the book of Daniel, during the reign of Caliph 'Umar when they conquered Tustar in southwest Persia, finding it in the coffin that also contained his remains. At the caliph's order, the book was reburied with Daniel's body.[9] There are other places, however, such as Shush in Iran, where Daniel is said to buried.[10] The latter grave is an Islamic shrine where Shi'ite Muslims come to pray, and the Jewish traveler Benjamin of Tudela was the first Westerner to visit and describe this grave in 1167. Tarsus in Turkey has also been mentioned. It is said that the site of his grave had been forgotten for a long time but was discovered by one of the commanders of Caliph 'Umar in year 17 of the Muslim calendar.[11]

It can of course be argued that both cannot be historically true, but the point is that the prophet Daniel plays a role in Muslim tradition as well. In the first century of the Islamic calendar, the book Daniel was very popular because many Muslims wanted to know the precise date of the last judgment, although both the Bible (Mark 13:32; Matt 24:36; Acts 1:7) and the Qur'an are clear about the fact that that no one knows that day or hour. That knowledge belongs to God alone (Q 31:34; 33:63; 41:47; 43:85; 67:26; 79:44).[12]

ALEXANDER THE GREAT: THE MAN WITH TWO HORNS

In the fourth century BC, Alexander the Great (336–323 BC) started out on the Greek "exodus" from Macedonia. The purpose of this "exodus" was to establish a daughter city that was independent of the mother city in Macedonia itself.[13] This has been called an "earthquake" caused by one man in the human world.[14]

To understand the book of Daniel, it is important to be aware of the great significance of Alexander the Great both for the Jews in Palestine as in the diaspora. Alexander is not mentioned anywhere in the Bible, except

9. *EI*, s.v., Dâniyâl.

10. www.tripadvisor.com/Attraction_Review-g946400-d8317506-Reviews-Tomb_of_Daniel-Sh.

11. https://forums.hababam.nl/archive/t-52915-graf-van-profeet-danyal-daniel-in-turkije.html; Source: *Zaman Gazetesi* (Turkish newspaper).

12. *EQ*, s.v., Last Judgment, 143–44.

13. *Der Kleine Pauly*, s.v , apoikia.

14. Albrecht Altdorfer depicts this in an impressive way in his painting *The Battle of Alexander at Issus*; cf. Aalders, *De Septuagint*, 31; https://en.wikipedia.org/wiki/The_Battle_of_Alexander_at_Issus.

THE BOOK OF DANIEL: "THE FLAMING SCRIPTURE OF THE HOLY GOD" 133

in the "apocryphal" book of the Maccabees, where his story is concisely summarized. At that time, the Macedonian King Alexander undertook a campaign against Darius III (336–331 BC), the king of the Persians and Medes. His base for this campaign was the country of the people of Chittim. The Kittites were possibly the original inhabitants of Cyprus (where the city of Kition was located). In the Old Testament, the term was used for seafaring peoples (Gen 10:4; Isa 23:1; Jer 2:10; Ezek 27:6; 1 Chr 1:7). In 1 Maccabees 1:1, 8, the term refers to the Macedonian empire and in Dan 11:30 to the Roman Empire.[15] In 168 BC, the Roman consul forced Antiochus IV to leave Egypt.[16]

Alexander defeated Darius and became king in his place after having first reigned only over Greece. He conducted a number of wars, captured strongholds and killed the kings of the earth, he pressed on *to the ends of the earth* and plundered many peoples: the world no longer dared oppose him. Alexander became overconfident and, *in his pride*, mobilized an extremely powerful army; he made himself master of lands, peoples, and princes, and they owed him tribute. When he felt his death approaching, he summoned his generals, his companions who had been raised with him, and divided his kingdom among them while he was still alive. He died after reigning for twelve years. After his death, these patricians took over the administration of the area that had been allotted to them and assumed the diadems[17] for themselves. They were succeeded by their sons, and these dynasties were the source of a great deal of misery on earth during the many years they reigned. Out of these dynasties emerged a particularly evil man who became king in the 137th year of the Syrian kingdom (175 BC) (1 Macc 1:1–10): Antiochus IV Epiphanes.

Coming from the West, Alexander managed to expand his dominion in a short time over a large part of the then known world, right into India! Slaughtering peoples as he went, he sought a passage from Granicus, where the first of the major battles between Alexander and the Persian empire took place, to the Indus.[18] This had radical ramifications for world history.

In a vision that Daniel had about a ram and a goat (Dan 8), the ram represents the power of the Medes and Persians and the goat the power of Alexander. While Daniel watches closely, a *goat* comes *from the West*, crossing the whole earth without touching the ground. (Dan 8:5). The latter

15. *BW*, s.v., Kittiërs, Kittieten, Kittim.
16. KBS on Dan 11:30.
17. A sign of the dignity and enthronement of the king (2 Kgs 11:12; Ps 21:4). Cf. Rev 12:3: "Then another sign appeared in heaven: an enormous red dragon with seven heads and ten horns and seven crowns on its heads." *BW*, s.v., krans, kroon.
18. Crossan and Reed, *In Search of Paul*, 127.

detail refers to the incredible speed at which the conquests of Alexander took place. The Battle of Issus (northwest Syria) took place in 333 BC, where he defeated the Persians and ten years later marched through Mesopotamia, Persia, and Afghanistan up to the valley near the Indus River and then back again to Babylon, where he died.[19] It is said of this "goat," alias Alexander, who defeated the Persian emperor Darius III in 330 BC that he had a conspicuous *horn* above his eyes (Dan 8:5; Isa 14:9; Ezek 34:17; Zech 10:3). Horns constitute part of the headdress of eastern gods who were depicted in human form, thereby indicating their divine status. In ancient Egypt, the goddess of the heavens, Hathor "House of Horus," had a sun disk between her horns. After a visit to Hathor's shrine, Alexander had himself depicted as Ammon, the son of Zeus with ram's horns. The horns, like those of the very destructive fourth animal that represented Alexander (Dan 7) are symbolic of imperial power and violence. His first successors show the royal heads that bear horned helmets. The two-horned ram refers to the Medes and Persians, with the one horn larger than the other. The growth of the horns reminds the reader that first the Medes ruled and then the Persians (Dan 8:3–4).[20] The goat from the West with the one horn—Alexander—met the ram that defeated and replaced the Persian empire.[21]

The fast and complete conquest of the kingdoms and peoples in the Near East by the Greeks was an event of enormous proportions and left a permanent mark on the cultures of the subjected peoples, including the Judeans. These peoples wrestled with the question of how and when the Hellenistic empire would end.[22]

In the previous chapter we described how Alexander was not mentioned by name in the Qur'an, although there are allusions to him in the Bible and he does play a significant role. He is designated as "the Man with two horns" (*dhû al-Qarnayn*; Q 18:83–94). The root of the Arabic word *al-Qarnayn* accords with the Hebrew *qaran*. That word, *qaran*, appears in the Bible when Moses is said to come down from Mount Sinai with the two tables of the law that he received from God. Moses does not know that his face is "radiant": "his face was *radiant* because he had spoken with the Lord" (Exod 34:29–30, 35). The Israelites could not look at Moses' face because of the glory that shone out from it (2 Cor 3:7). The Hebrew word used here can mean both "radiant" and "provided with horns." The Greek translation by the Jewish proselyte Aquila from the second century also reads "horned"

---

19. Gowan, *Daniel*, 119.
20. KBS on Dan 8:3.
21. Horsley, *Revolt of the Scribes*, 91.
22. Horsley, *Revolt of the Scribes*, 92.

and the Latin translation by Jerome (ca. 400) also speaks of "horned" (*cornutus*). In accordance with the latter translation, Michelangelo sculpted the famous image of Moses in the Church of San Pedro in Vincoli (Saint Peter in Chains) in Rome with two horns!

In the book of Daniel, the situation after Alexander's death is described as follows.

> Then a mighty king [Alexander] will arise, who will rule with great power and do as he pleases. After he has arisen, his empire will be broken up and parceled out toward the four winds of heaven. It will not go to his descendants, nor will it have the power he exercised, because his empire will be uprooted and given to others. (Dan 11:3–4)

Thus, the *four winds* also allude to the division of the empire among the Diadochi, Alexander's "successors"[23]—his own generals who fought each other.[24] They saw themselves forced after his sudden and premature death to reign over parts of the world empire that fell apart immediately after his death: Ptolemy over Egypt, Seleucus over Mesopotamia (Babylon), and Antigonus over Asia Minor (currently Turkey). Ptolemy and Seleucus founded strong empires that dominated the Middle East for a long time. The *Seleucid* dynasty (with Syria as its center) was founded by Alexander Seleucus, called the "Conqueror" (Nicator). In 301 BC he established Seleucia as a harbor city for his capital Antioch. It is from that harbor that the apostle Paul would leave later for his first missionary journey (Acts 13:4). The Ptolemies ruled Egypt for three centuries from the city of Alexandria. The famous Cleopatra VII would be the last ruler from this dynasty (69–30 BC); her rule was brought to an end by the Romans.

Daniel describes Alexander's sudden death as follows: "The goat became very great, but at the height of its power the large horn was broken off, and in its place four prominent horns grew up toward the four winds of heaven" (Dan 8:8).[25]

---

23. Collins, *Daniel*, 377.
24. Collins, *Daniel*, 331.
25. KBS on, respectively, (1) Egypt; (2) Mesopotamia. Northern Syria, Asia Minor (under the Seleucids); (3) Thracia; (4) Macedonia (Alexander the Great's home country).

ANTIOCHUS IV EPIPHANES AND THE WRITING OF THE BOOK OF DANIEL

The Seleucid ruler Antiochus IV (r. 175–164 BC) reigned over Syria and Palestine. He considered himself equal to God, an "appearance" (epiphany) of God himself—thus his epithet. He is said to have walked incognito—like the caliphs in 1001 Nights—through the streets of Antioch to hear the opinions of his subjects. Antiochus is primarily notorious for his attempt to be worshipped by all peoples in his kingdom as a god. According to Polybius (203–120 BC), however, a Greek historian from the Hellenistic period who was himself also a military man and had held political positions, Antiochus should be called *epimanes* ("insane") rather than *epiphanes*.[26]

Antiochus appears in the Book of the Maccabees and Daniel as evil incarnate. The book of Daniel was written shortly after his death, at that time Judea and Galilee were "a volcanic hotbed of revolutionary violence and zealot hatred."[27] His rule brought great suffering to the Jewish people.[28] The misery and terror reached its high point in 168 BC when Antiochus erected a statue of the Greek god Zeus in the temple in Jerusalem (1 Macc 1:54; cf. Dan 8:11–13). Troops sent by him desecrated the temple fortress and set up a horrifying abomination (Dan 11:31; cf. 8: 11; 9:27; 12:11; 1 Macc 1:59; 2 Macc 5:5–15; 6:26).[29] By introducing the cult of Zeus Olympus into the temple of Jerusalem, he hoped to be able to assimilate the Jews—the goal of his policy was, namely, to make one people out of all the different peoples and have each give up their own customs and teachings (1 Macc 1:41–42). In the New Testament, the *abomination* refers perhaps to the attempt by the Roman emperor Caligula in 40 AD to set up his statue in the temple (Matt. 24:15; Mark 13:14).[30]

Antiochus issued a decree in 167 BC that forbade the Jews from practicing their religion. The effects of that are related in particular in the books of the Maccabees (1 Macc 1:44–61 and 2 Macc 6–7).[31] This event led to the Maccabean rebellion and the guerrilla war. The most famous members of the Hasmonean family are Mattathias and his five sons; they initiated the rebellion in the year 167 BC because they wanted to follow the Torah strictly. After the death of his father, Judas (166–160 BC) assumed leadership and

---

26. Han, *Daniel's Spiel*, 53.
27. Aalders, *De Apocalyptische Christus*, 96.
28. Han, *Daniel's Spiel*, 51.
29. KBS on Dan 8.:13. Gowan, *Daniel*, 117–18.
30. KBS on Matt 24:15.
31. *Dictionnaire encyclopédique du Judaïsme*, s.v., Apocalypse.

THE BOOK OF DANIEL: "THE FLAMING SCRIPTURE OF THE HOLY GOD"

was the first to be given the epithet "Maccabee" ("[sledge]hammer"). Thus began the struggle against political and religious oppression (Dan 11:21–45; 1 Macc 1–6; 2 Macc 3–9). The Hasmonean dynasty ruled Judea from the Maccabean revolt in 167 BC until 37 BC.

After their victory in the year 164 BC, the temple would be dedicated anew by Judas the Maccabean. Their miraculous victory is commemorated in Hanukkah or the "Feast of Lights," which is still celebrated by Jews for 8 days from 10 to 18 December. The Hasmoneans reigned over an independent Jewish kingdom until Judea became a vassal state of Rome in 63 BC. Their political reign came to an end in 37 BC, and in the years that followed, the Herodians would rule the country.[32]

It is clear from the book of Daniel that the author did not at all support the violent resistance advocated and practiced by the Maccabees[33] or what the later Zealots or Sicarii (dagger-wielders) would do in the time of Jesus. The latter saw themselves as the heirs of the Maccabees when they resisted Rome in 66 AD. That kind of violence does not find any support in the book of Daniel.[34] The author is pessimistic about such military resistance, and that resistance is seen only as a "little help" (Dan 11:34).[35] "Whereas the Maccabean vision called for loyalty to *Torah*, Daniel called for loyalty to *God*." Here an element is introduced that was absent with the Maccabees. It is thus revealed that one should be prepared to "fall by the sword or be burned or captured or plundered" (Dan 11:33; cf. 12:3; 7:21–22; 8:10, 24) rather than use violence against the enemy.[36]

THE HEBREW AND GREEK BIBLES

After 70 years of exile in Babylon, a large number of Jews did not return to the "Holy Land" but stayed in the diaspora. This was naturally the case with respect to Babylon, but Egypt was a popular destination for Jews as well. Some also went to the Arab Peninsula. The first are said to have gone there when the first temple was destroyed under Nebuchadnezzar. On the day of Pentecost—the outpouring of the Holy Spirit—"Arabs" came to Jerusalem as well (Acts 2:11). After the second temple was destroyed by the Romans

---

32. https://nl.wikipedia.org/wiki/Hasmoneeën.

33. Cf. Dan 11:34: "When they fall, they will receive a little help, and many who are not sincere will join them."

34. Gowan, *Daniel*, 115.

35. Han, *Daniel's Spiel*, 67. Philip R. Davies gives this suggestion, adding that it is less than a flattering remark.

36. Howard-Brook and Gwyther, *Unveiling Empire*, 52.

in 70 AD and the Jewish rebellion under Bar Kochba in the second century was put down, new waves of Jews would also move to Arabia, including Jewish followers of Jesus.

In the fourth century BC, the use of the Greek language expanded after Alexander's conquests. The expansion of the language kept pace with the growth of the Hellenistic empire. Greek was the language of ecumenism, "the inhabited world." The everyday language of Hellenism, *koine* Greek, was the language of government and high culture and was also the language in which the New Testament was written. In Palestine, people used Aramaic for everyday activities in Jesus' time, but Greek was also widely used. A city like Tiberias, a large center for rabbinic study, had numerous Greek inscriptions and very few Hebrew ones![37]

The city of Alexandria founded by Alexander the Great in Egypt had a large Jewish population. A Jewish community of significant size had allegedly developed there quite quickly after its foundation, thus since about 300 BC. Many of the Jews here were prisoners of war brought by Ptolemy after his campaigns in the Middle East, but many Jews also came to Alexandria of their own free will, attracted by the possibilities that a new city offered to improve their financial or social status. In this period, the Jewish community was explicitly open to Hellenistic influences without, for that matter, letting go of their Jewish faith and way of life. It seems that the Jewish community in Alexandria grew quite a bit when the Maccabean revolt was raging in Judea. Egypt was a logical destination for refugees who wanted to flee the violence.[38]

Because many Jews in the diaspora were unable to speak Hebrew after a few generations, the need for a Greek translation of the Hebrew Bible arose. Most scholars are of the view that the Jewish community in Alexandria had the Pentateuch translated into Greek because Egyptian Jews no longer knew enough Hebrew to be able to read the Tanakh in the original language.[39] This translation came to be called the Septuagint because legend has it that it was done by 73 translators; it was the product of diaspora Judaism, not of the Jews in Palestine but of those in Egypt.[40]

According to Wim Aalders, the Orthodox Jew and linguist J.L. Seeligmann from Amsterdam (1907–1982) demonstrated the historical significance of the Septuagint as a Jewish-Alexandrine translation. The Torah, Prophets, and Writings have thus been passed on in *two forms*: in the

---

37. Han, *Daniel's Spiel*, 43.
38. https://nl.wikipedia.org/wiki/Joodse_gemeenschap_in_Alexandrië.
39. https://en.wikipedia.org/wiki/Septuagint.
40. Aalders, *De Septuagint*, 30–31.

Tanakh, the Hebrew Bible, *and* the *Septuagint*.[41] An important discovery by Seeligmann was[42] that the Septuagint (LXX) arose from the reading of the Pentateuch in the service. It thus had a didactic and liturgical origin and was intended to bring the Scripture closer to the Jewish people in the diaspora. In many respects, the LXX is a *Targum*, a "free" translation of the Scripture, just as the Targum is also a free translation of the Hebrew text in Aramaic.[43] Where it says in the Hebrew text that the prophets spoke to "to our kings, our princes and our ancestors, and to all the people of the land" (Dan 9:6), the LXX simply states that they spoke *to all peoples on earth*!

As a concept, Torah is not translated in the Septuagint as instruction or teaching, as is found in the Hebrew text, but by *nomos*, law. In the LXX, the prophet Isaiah gives the law universal significance by also calling the rulers and people of Sodom and Gomorrah to pay attention to God's *nomos* (law) (Isa 1:10, LXX). The translators of the Hebrew Bible in Alexandria felt compelled to update the biblical documents by demonstrating that the history that was unfolding in front of their eyes was a continuation and fulfillment of the history of the sacred texts: the preaching of the prophets as "education" for encouragement and comfort. In that way, the Septuagint brought the Scripture up to date.[44] "*Paideia* became a central concept for the Greeks' self-understanding, often over against the barbarians and later in particular over against Christianity (W. Jaeger)."[45]

It is striking and particularly telling—one could say programmatic— that the book of Daniel is the last book in the Septuagint. This placement speaks of the apocalyptic view the composers had of the situation of the people, the community in the "Hellenistic period," particularly in the anxious period of the second century BC in which the book of Daniel was written. It was written between the years 165–162 BC in the time of the most cruel successor of Alexander the Great, the above-mentioned Antiochus IV Epiphanes.

While Daniel's stories are placed *in the sixth century BC*, at the court of the Babylonian king Nebuchadnezzar, the world of the author of the book is that of the rule of Antiochus *in the second century BC*. The reading of Daniel developed an alternative to the response of the Maccabees with their armed

---

41. Aalders, *De Apocalyptische Christus*, 14.

42. In his article "Problemen en perspectieven van het moderne Septuagint onderzoek" of 30 October 1940.

43. Summarized by Aalders, *De Septuagint*, 42.

44. Aalders *De Septuagint*, 46–47.

45. *Der Kleine Pauly*, s.v., "Paideia."

resistance.⁴⁶ It is an explicit answer to the persecutions under Antiochus and differs decisively and fundamentally from the character of the books of the Maccabees. No Maccabean "holy war" will end the power of the fourth beast, from Alexander up to and including Antiochus. It is only God's power that removes the oppression from them and will lead to the defeat of their oppressors.⁴⁷ The local Persian imperial court suggests that the stories in the first six chapters (Dan 1–6) originated in circles of Judean writers who served in the Persian imperial court or in in the exilic community that had settled in Jerusalem again when the temple was rebuilt.

The fact that the stories were ultimately connected with the visions of the intellectuals of Jerusalem who were known as *maskilim*, writers, exegetes of the Scriptures (Dan 7–12), indicates that they were also cultivated by writers' circles in Jerusalem.⁴⁸ These "court legends" about Daniel are vehicles of prophetic charges that accused the imperial governments of arrogance.⁴⁹ They translate the belief that the Most High God is in control of history.⁵⁰

DANIEL, INTERPRETER OF MYSTERIES

Apocalyptic texts remain dark until they are interpreted by a messenger. "While I, Daniel, was watching the vision and trying to understand it, there before me stood one who looked like a man. And I heard a man's voice from the Ulai [the Hebrew name for a river near the city of Susa] calling, 'Gabriel, tell this man the meaning of the vision'" (Dan 8:15–16; cf. Luke 1:19, 26). The heavenly interpreter appears for the first time in the visions of the prophet Zechariah: "Then I said, 'What are these, my lord?' The angel who talked with me said to me, 'I will show you what they are'" (Zech 1:9; cf. 4:4).⁵¹ Daniel is thus assisted by the angel Gabriel (Dan 8:16; cf. 9:21; 10:4–5; 12:6). Only in this way can the seer decipher the signs.⁵²

Gabriel will later also be sent to Mary, the mother of Jesus (Luke 1:26), and Zechariah the father of John the Baptist (Luke 1:19). According to the Qur'an, the revelation of God was brought down to Muhammad's heart by Gabriel (Q 2:97; cf. 26:194), the noble apostle, (Q 81:19), whom Muhammad

---

46. Howard-Brook and Gwynter, *Unveiling Empire*, 50–51.
47. Howard-Brook, *"Come Out My People!"* 344.
48. Horsley, *Revolt of the Scribes*, 35.
49. Horsley, *Revolt of the Scribes*, 35.
50. Horsley, *Revolt of the Scribes*, 45.
51. Gowan, *Daniel*, 103.
52. Han, *Daniel's Spiel*, 100.

saw on the manifest horizon (81:23). The messenger is also called the "Holy Spirit" (Q 16:102) and the "Trustworthy Spirit" (Q 26:193).[53] One great in powers visited Muhammad twice (Q 53: 5–7). God does not speak to human beings unless through inspiration or from behind a curtain (*hijâb*) or sends him a messenger (*rasûl*) whom God gives permission to reveal his will (Q 42:51). "Indeed your [Muhammad's] Lord is the All-mighty, the All-merciful. This is indeed [a Book] sent down by the Lord of all the worlds, brought down by the Trustworthy Spirit upon you (so that you may be one of the warners), in a clear Arabic language. It is indeed [foretold] in the scriptures of the ancients" (Q 26:191–196).[54]

The visions are constantly accompanied by physical and psychological effects: "I, Daniel, was troubled in spirit, and the visions that passed through my mind disturbed me" (Dan 7:15). "This is the end of the matter. I, Daniel, was deeply troubled by my thoughts, and my face turned pale, but I kept the matter to myself" (Dan 7:28).[55]

The stories at the beginning of the book of Daniel present him as a new Joseph who also interpreted dreams for the Pharaoh of Egypt and his servants, the butler and the baker (Gen 40–42; cf. Q 12:43–49).[56] Daniel fulfilled a role similar to Joseph's: both lived in exile, respectively Egypt and Babylon; both served foreign masters (the Pharaoh and the king of Babylon). Both were attractive: Joseph was handsome and well-built (Gen 39:6; cf. Q 12:31).[57] When Daniel and his friends had consumed nothing but vegetables and water for ten days, they looked healthier and better nourished than all the other young men who had eaten at the king's table (Dan 1:15). It is said that both Joseph and Daniel had a divine spirit. The Pharaoh asked his officials: "So Pharaoh asked them, 'Can we find anyone like this man, one in whom is the spirit of God?'" (Gen 41:38). The queen mother, Nebuchadnezzar's wife, says to King Belshazzar: "There is a man in your kingdom who has the spirit of the holy gods in him. In the time of your father he was found to have insight and intelligence and wisdom like that of the gods. Your father, King Nebuchadnezzar, appointed him chief of the magicians, enchanters, astrologers and diviners" (Dan 5:11). Belshazzar then turned to Daniel: "I have heard that the spirit of the gods is in you and that you have insight, intelligence and outstanding wisdom" (Dan 5:14).

---

53. Cf. 16:2; 40:15; 97:4.
54. Glassé, *The Concise Encyclopaedia of Islam*, s.v., Gabriel.
55. Gowan, *Daniel*, 103; cf. Ezek 1:28; 3:15.
56. Wessels, *A Stranger is Calling*, chapter V.
57. Speyer, *Die biblischen Erzählungen*, 205–6.

THE DREAM OF NEBUCHADNEZZAR

Nebuchadnezzar II (605–562 BC), the great king of Babylon is known by the Arabic name Bukhtnasar. According to some Muslim sources, he was seen as one of the four rulers who ruled over the whole world in their time (Nimrod, Dahhak, Solomon, and Alexander).[58] Muslim exegetes report that he desecrated the temple in Jerusalem and led the Israelites away into exile to Babylon. He was the king who saw the vision of a large statue that was interpreted by Daniel (Dan 2) and who was changed into a wild animal, a punishment that would last for seven years (Dan 4).[59] He was tortured by a mosquito in his brain, a story that a rabbinic legend transfers to the destroyer of the Second Temple in 70 AD—Titus.[60]

According to the book of Daniel, Nebuchadnezzar saw a large statue in his dream,[61] composed of four metals: the head was of pure gold, the chest and arms of silver, his stomach and thighs of bronze,[62] and feet partly of iron, partly of clay. "The history of the world is depicted in a microcosmos as a human."[63] Because the dream upset him so much, Nebuchadnezzar turned to his magicians, enchanters, sorcerers, and astrologers for an explanation (Dan 2:2). They asked him to tell them his dream first. But the king wanted them to tell him both the dream and its interpretation! The king replied to the astrologers, "This is what I have firmly decided: If you do not tell me what my dream was and interpret it, I will have you cut into pieces and your houses turned into piles of rubble. But if you tell me *the dream and explain it*, you will receive from me gifts and rewards and great honor. So tell me the dream and interpret it for me" (Dan 2:5–6). That the king also asked his astrologers to tell him the dream itself was a precautionary measure against the manipulation of his words so that they could provide an acceptable interpretation: "You have conspired to tell me misleading and wicked things, hoping the situation will change. So then, tell me the dream,

---

58. Dahhak was a Persian king; Noegel and Wheeler, *The A to Z of Prophets in Islam and Judaism*, s.v., Dahhak.

59. Noegel and Wheeler, *The A to Z of Prophets in Islam and Judaism*, s.v., Bukhtnasar.

60. *EI*, s.v., Bukht-Nas(s)ar.

61. Such images recall the gigantic royal figures in the British Museum that radiate oppression and testify to inhumanity, according to Aalders, *De Apocalyptische Christus*, 81–82. Here he also refers to C.W. Ceram's *Goden, graven geleerden*

62. Bronze was used as material for weapons. This is known from Homer's *Iliad*. In later centuries, iron became representative of the most important culture: Rome built up its power in the iron age. Aalders, *De Apocalyptische Christus*, 82.

63. Aalders, *De Apocalyptische Christus*, 82.

and I will know that you *can* interpret it for me" (Dan 2:8–9).[64] The astrologers were not able to do what the king asked of them, however, and he then became angry and, in his anger, ordered all the wise men of Babylon to be executed. That order also included Daniel and his friends, and they were also imprisoned (Dan 2:11–13). Daniel then went to the king with the request to grant him time to inform the king of the interpretation (Dan 2:16). When Daniel was brought before the king, the king asked him: "Are you able to tell me what I saw in my dream and interpret it?" Daniel answered: "No wise man, enchanter, magician or diviner can explain to the king the mystery he has asked about, but there is a God in heaven who reveals mysteries. He has shown King Nebuchadnezzar what will happen in days to come" (Dan 2:25–28). "Your Majesty looked, and there before you stood a large statue—an enormous, dazzling statue, awesome in appearance. The head of the statue was made of pure *gold*, its chest and arms of *silver*, its belly and thighs of *bronze*, its legs of *iron*, its feet partly of *iron* and partly of baked *clay*" (Dan 2:31–33). (The iron recalls the characterization of Alexander's empire by himself as *iron*). But then something happened.

> While you were watching, a rock was cut out, but *not by human hands*. It struck the statue on its feet of iron and clay and smashed them. Then the iron, the clay, the bronze, the silver and the gold were all broken to pieces and became like chaff on a threshing floor in the summer. The wind swept them away without leaving a trace. But the rock that struck the statue became a huge mountain and filled the whole earth. (Dan 2:34–35)

The golden head refers to the king himself. The metals of gold, silver, bronze, and iron are interpreted as, respectively, the Babylonian, the Mede, Persian, and Greek empires. Iron was also identified with the Roman Empire in later exegesis, and one can think of "ironsides" like Julius Caesar, who killed thousands and thousands in Gaul (now France) and, as excavations have shown, reached Brabant—one of the southern provinces of the Netherlands—as well.[65] That image was destroyed by a stone that came loose without any human help, hit the statue, and smashed the feet of iron and clay (Dan 2:34). The stone pulverized the image of iron, clay, copper, silver, and gold. The destruction of these kingdoms does not happen through a violent explosion in a large final battle. It is precisely the opposite that happens. There was no explosion but rather an *implosion*: it collapses of itself.

64. Han, *Daniel's Spiel*. 82.

65. https://www.bd.nl/oss/historische-veldslag-caesar-in-zone-tussen-kessel-en-lith~ac907216/.

The end of oppression, injustice, and violence does not come through violent *jihâd* or holy war. No, injustice punishes itself. The wrong (*zulm*) that one does against oneself is a characteristic expression in the Qur'an. "We [God] did not wrong them, but *they wronged themselves*" (Q 11:101; cf. 3:117; 29:40; 30:9; 16:33,118; 10:44; 11:101; 43:76).[66] That is something one can glean from a good knowledge of history: they had been informed about what happened to others before them: the people of Noah (Q 7:59–64), the overturned cities, Sodom and Gomorrah (Q 7:80–84), the people of Jethro (Shu'ayb) sent to the inhabitants of Midian (Q 7:85–93), the people of the Arab prophets Hûd sent to the people of 'Âd (Q 7:65–72), Sâlih sent to the people of Thamûd (Q 7:73–79). Again and again, messengers came to them with clear proof: "So it was not God who wronged them, *but it was they who used to wrong themselves*" (Q 9:70).[67] The rulers of those peoples and cities simply destroyed themselves.

That is the interpretation that Daniel gives of the dream of the powerful he was confronted with, Nebuchadnezzar and Belshazzar: Be warned—you will fall on your own sword. That is the repeated pattern throughout history: "Your wickedness will punish you; your backsliding will rebuke you" (Jer 2:19). They cause themselves evil just as Sodom and Gomorrah did: they bring misery on themselves (Isa 3:9; cf. Gen 18:20–21; 19:4–11). "Tell Zerubbabel governor of Judah that I am going to shake the heavens and the earth. I will overturn royal thrones and shatter the power of the foreign kingdoms. I will overthrow chariots and their drivers; horses and their riders will fall, each by the sword of his brother" (Hag 2:21–22).

The rock that smashes all metals is the kingdom of God. Precisely like iron that crushes everything and turns it into powder, that kingdom will crush and shatter the previous kingdoms (Dan 2:40; cf. 7:7).[68] The insight that God gives Daniel is that both the king of Babylon and the Hellenistic emperors who destroyed everything will themselves be destroyed when the God of heaven sets up his kingdom that *will not be destroyed*. The God of the Judeans is the true sovereign of history. The wise insight that is given to Daniel is that God dethrones kings.[69] There is a clear connection between the fragile image made by people, obviously shaky on *iron* and *clay* feet, *and* the powerful kingdom that will never be destroyed (Dan 2:44). Nothing remained of the statue, but the rock that had struck it became a large

---

66. Paret on 9:70. p. 207. Cf. Muhammad Kâmil Husain and Kenneth Cragg, "The Meaning of Zulm in the Qurân," *The Muslim World* 49 (1959): 196–212; cited in Paret.

67. Husain and Cragg, "The Meaning of Zulm in the Qurân."

68. Horsley, *Revolt of the Scribes*, 38. The mystery of the dream is that God's kingdom will destroy all empires. Howard-Brook, *"Come Out My People!"* 342–343.

69. Horsley, *Revolt of the Scribes*, 39.

THE BOOK OF DANIEL: "THE FLAMING SCRIPTURE OF THE HOLY GOD"   145

mountain that covered the whole earth (Dan 2:35). With respect to the motif of covering the earth, one can think of the glory (Isa 6:3) and the knowledge of the Lord (Isa 11:3).[70] He reveals to Daniel his divine counsel, his presence as the Lord, as the One who will be there (cf. Exod 3:14). It is he who shows what happens in the darkness, and it is he in whom light dwells (Dan 2:22).[71]

THE WRITING ON THE WALL

King Belshazzar, Nebuchadnezzar's successor, once organized a large feast for a thousand of his nobles. Under the influence of wine, he commanded that the gold and silver goblets his father had plundered from the temple in Jerusalem be brought to him (Dan 5:1–2). The transfer of the goblets from Jerusalem to the temple of his god Marduk invoked the hubris of the city where the "tower of Babel" had been built (Gen 11:1–9). Nebuchadnezzar attempted to change the symbolic meaning of the goblets by placing them in the treasury of *his* gods, those of imperial Babylon, and thus display to the world his own dominion. By drinking wine from them, Belshazzar and his guests were honoring the gods of gold and silver, of bronze, iron, wood, and stone (Dan 5:4; cf. 5:23). Moses had already been told on Mount Sinai: "Do not make any gods to be alongside me; do not make for yourselves gods of silver or gods of gold" (Exod 20:23). The children of Israel transgressed that commandment by fashioning the golden calf (Q 32:2–4, 23–24), a god of gold (Exod 32:31; cf. Q 2:51, 54, 92; 4:153; 7:148, 152; 20:88). Such admonitions can be heard in the Qur'an: "Those who treasure up *gold and silver*, and do not spend it in the way of God, inform them of a painful punishment" (Q 9:34; cf. Q 3:14).

Not worshipping God does not making one atheist; rather, another god is always worshipped instead. This is also the case here. While they were drinking the wine,

> suddenly the fingers of a human hand appeared and wrote on the plaster of the wall, near the lampstand in the royal palace. The king watched the hand as it wrote. His face turned pale and he was so frightened that his legs became weak and his knees were knocking.

The king summoned the enchanters, astrologers and diviners. Then he said to these wise men of Babylon, "Whoever reads this writing and tells me

---

70. Collins, *Daniel*, 165.
71. Aalders, *De Apocalyptische Christus*, 82.

what it means will be clothed in purple and have a gold chain placed around his neck, and he will be made the third highest ruler in the kingdom."

> Then all the king's wise men came in, but they could not read the writing or tell the king what it meant. So King Belshazzar became even more terrified and his face grew more pale. His nobles were baffled. (Dan 5:5–9)

When the queen mother noticed how upset the king and his nobles were, she came into the banquet hall and advised the king to summon Daniel (Dan 5:10). It was Daniel who "was found to have a keen mind and knowledge and understanding, and also the ability to interpret dreams, explain riddles and solve difficult problems. Call for Daniel, and he will tell you what the writing means," the queen mother suggested to Belshazzar (Dan 5:12; cf. Sir 39:1–2).[72]

While all others have failed, Daniel succeeds in interpreting the dream: "Nevertheless, I will read the writing for the king and tell him what it *means*" (Dan 5:17). The Aramaic term *peshar* that is used here means "the interpretation of dreams." The word is used a total of thirty times in the book of Daniel.[73] Just like Joseph, he does make clear that the interpretation of dreams lies solely with God (Gen 40:8; 41:16; Dan 2:28) and that God reveals what will happen through dreams (Gen 41:25, 28; Dan 2:28). Just like Joseph, he will be rewarded. Joseph is given a chain around his neck (Gen 41:42). At Belshazzar's order, Daniel is clothed in purple, is given a golden chain around his neck, and is proclaimed to be the third highest ruler in the kingdom (Dan 5:29).[74]

Why did the writing appear on the wall? Although Belshazzar knew what had happened to his predecessor Nebuchadnezzar, he did not remain humble. He wanted to exalt himself above the Lord of the heavens and to have the goblets fetched and to drink wine out of them with his nobles, wives, and concubines: he had worshipped gods of silver and gold, of bronze, iron, wood and stone who did not see, not hear, and not know, and he did not praise the God in whose hand his breath and his whole life lay. That is why God wrote this on the wall (Dan 5: 22–25).

What was written on the wall? *Mene mene tekel ufarsin*. Daniel interprets these words as follows:

---

72. Horsley, *Revolt of the Scribes*, 35–36.
73. Han, *Daniel's Spiel*, 83.
74. Collins, *Daniel*, 39; cf. Wessels, *A Stranger is Calling*, chapter V: "The Foreign King: Joseph as a Stranger in a Strange Land" and "Joseph as a Role Model for the Prophet Muhammad."

Mene: God has numbered the days of your reign and brought it to an end.

Tekel: You have been weighed on the scales and found wanting.

Peres: Your kingdom is divided and given to the Medes and Persians. That same night Belshazzar was killed (Dan 5).

Rembrandt produced a famous painting of this event with the assistance of his Jewish neighbor, the humanist scholar Menasse ben Israël (1604–1674). Along with Spinoza, Menasse was one of the most well-known figures in the Jewish community at that time. He was personally acquainted with Hugo de Groot.[75] Menasse asked Rembrandt to do the illustrations for his cabbalistic work written in Spanish, *Estatua de Nebuchanassar*. According to Menasse, the rock that destroyed the statue was the same stone Jacob used for a pillow when he dreamed of a ladder reaching from earth to heaven (Gen 28:11–15). It was the same *stone* that David used to kill Goliath (1 Sam 17:54). This "famous stone" is the Messiah at whose coming the kingdom of Israel would be reestablished.[76]

In the late nineteenth century, this rabbi was often viewed as Rembrandt's intimate and highly valued friend, who helped Rembrandt with his biblical scenes and Hebrew inscriptions. *Belshazzar's Feast* is an excellent example of this. Four years after this painting was completed, the rabbi himself published a book in which he cited the story of Belshazzar. In that book, he uses an illustration to show the solution the Talmud provides for the fact that no one could read the writing on the wall. Menasse does that in the form of a magical square in which the words were written not, as is customary, from right to left but from the upper right to the lower left. In his painting, Rembrandt shows us this Talmudic solution that, as far as we know, does not appear in any other painting or print in his time and was included four years later as an illustration in the rabbi's book. It is tempting to think that the rabbi wrote the Talmudic volume in flamboyant letters for his friend Rembrandt and thus, for his part, helped to eternalize this Jewish solution in the painting. The x-ray of the painting shows that Rembrandt first reproduced the inscription flawlessly but ultimately decided to increase the vibrancy of the painting on the one hand by painting the hand while it was writing.[77]

Just like the Jewish wise men who came after him, Daniel knew how the letters could be reordered to produce a meaningful explanation. This

---

75. Schama, *De ogen van Rembrandt*, 609.

76. Hoekstra, "Samenstelling en toelichting," Part 1, 45.

77. Alexander-Knotter, Hilligers, and van Voolen et al., *De 'joodse' Rembrandt*, 44–46.

reinforces the image of the *illiteracy* of the wise men Daniel competes with: none of them could read the writing (Dan 5:8). Daniel is a literate wise man without equal. The narrator of the book does mention his education but focuses interest at once on the divine source of Daniel's wisdom. Due credit is given to God who enabled Daniel to be "lettered." The throne of the king was surrounded by illiterates, who would burst out in useless language and were devoid of any insight into what the future held. Only Daniel was gifted with the spirit of wisdom.[78]

TWO KINDS OF EDUCATION AND TWO KINDS OF DREAMS

Until the rise of the Roman Empire, the Greek or Hellenistic empire had the strongest army in the world. The Hellenistic regime organized education or training—called *paideia* in Greek—for the political consolidation of the empire.[79] Whether it is a question of the explanation of "the writing on the wall" or of the visions that Daniel receives, it is good to know that, fundamentally, it concerns two types of dreams and two types of education or instruction. Does one dream like rulers dream, educated and trained in their view, in their way of looking at the world and how one acts and should act? Or, like the prophet Daniel, does one dream the dream of the exile, the dream of the widow, the orphan, the poor, the oppressed, the refugee? The one dream is dreamed in the royal palace (Dan 2), the worldly center of power, the other on the bed of Jewish exile—it is, in fact the dream of the powerless (Dan 7).[80] What difference does that make? That would depend on one's education or, to say it in Greek, one's *paideia*. Our word pedagogics is derived from this word. Pedagogics is the study of how adults (parents, guardians, educators) raise young people with a certain end in mind. And it is clear that there is an enormous difference with respect to what one is taught and by whom because the purposes are entirely different. There are two kinds of training, two kinds of education: that of the empire, whichever one it is—Babylonian, Chaldean, Persian, Hellenistic, or Roman—or any of the contemporary ones. That is the "imperial education," which is focused only on serving one's own empire. The other is the education rooted in the Torah, in a life dedicated to justice. The education sinks roots in the *oikoumene*—the inhabited world—of Alexander the Great and his successors is the first.[81]

78. Han, *Daniel's Spiel*, 83–84.
79. Han, *Daniel's Spiel*, 39: "Hellenistic Paideia and the Book of Daniel."
80. Aalders, *De Apocalyptische Christus*, 88.
81. Han, *Daniel's Spiel*, 41–42.

What is remarkable and striking about the prophet Daniel is that he had received both types of education, he had enjoyed a *double training*. Immediately upon arriving as an exile in Babylon, he was selected along with his friends from the group of young Israelite exiles of royal blood or prominent family who had been given an all-round education, with wide knowledge and sharp mind; they were given a new imperial education that lasted three years. Afterwards, they would enter the king's service (Dan 1: 4–5). The learned "scribes," whether they served in the imperial government in Babylon or in the "temple state" of Jerusalem, like Daniel and Ben Sirach[82] had to play a role in the imperial court or with the local representative, the Jewish temple state.[83] Their knowledge and insight also entailed their interpretation of dreams and visions. Daniel proved to be more capable than all interpreters of dreams and exorcists from Babylon. To these four young men God gave knowledge and understanding of all kinds of literature and wisdom, and hegave Daniel the ability to understand dreams and visions (Dan 1:17; cf. Gen 40:8; 41:12).[84]

Daniel and his friends are proficient in all wisdom, knowledge, and insight and are thus educated and literate (Dan 1:5, LXX).[85] The arrangement for their education at court does entail that he who pays the piper calls the tune. It is not for nothing that they were placed on a diet (Dan 1:6, 8–16). Nebuchadnezzar's "imperial" education is in the literature and language of the dominant group: they had to learn the language and script of the Chaldeans (Dan 1:3–4). Teaching them the language is the instrument par excellence for indoctrinating the most gifted individuals among the people in imperialistic views. The program was developed to train servants of the government, and thus the wisdom they gained had to be and remain the wisdom of the government. The training reached its peak in a court exam, a test, a conclusion for a "citizenship course" at the highest level.[86] And every time the king asked their advice, he saw that their wisdom and insight was ten times greater than that of all other magicians and enchanters in all his kingdom (Dan 1:20; cf. 1 Kgs 10:3–4).[87]

---

82. The book of Ben Sirach was composed ca 190 BC. *BW*, s.v., Sirach, boek van Jezus.
83. Horsley, *Revolt of the Scribes*, 36.
84. Horsley, *Revolt of the Scribes*, 35–36.
85. Han, *Daniel's Spiel*, 81.
86. Han, *Daniel's Spiel*, 81.
87. Han, *Daniel's Spiel*, 82.

THE SCHOOL OF THE TORAH

Daniel had, however, already undergone an entirely different education—i.e., the instruction, the school, of the Torah. The Septuagint uses the concept of *paideia*, "instruction," for "revelation": for the Lord God does not do anything unless he reveals "instruction" to his servants, the prophets (Amos 3:7). When the Lord was about to go to Sodom, He thought: "Shall I hide from Abraham what I am about to do?" (Gen 18:17).[88]

Jesus Sirach was a professional scribe (Sir 38:25–39:11) who attempted to make a connection between the Hebrew Bible and contemporary events. His agenda consisted of: "Draw near to me, you who are uneducated, and lodge in the *house of instruction*" (Sir 51:23).[89] This reference in the book of Sirach can be understood as a general invitation to education in the house of instruction, *beth midrash*, which can be read as a metaphor. In any case, Sirach presupposes an institutionalized education in the Second Temple period (516 BC–70 AD). Zerubbabel, the grandson of Jehoiachin, the penultimate king of Judah, returned from Babylonian captivity in 538 BC and began rebuilding the temple that had been razed by the Babylonians. The second temple would be destroyed by the Romans in 70 AD.

Daniel's goal is similar to Jesus Sirach's with respect to the encroachment of Hellenism.[90] He thus has already had a completely different kind of education than the officials of Babylon, namely, the school of the Torah. The word *paideia* played a significant role in helping the Jews in the diaspora to lay great emphasis on "learning." For the Greek-speaking Jews, the one who takes that *paideia*, that instruction, to heart is on the road to life (Prov 10:17a). "Those who disregard discipline despise themselves, but the one who heeds an admonition gains understanding" (Prov 15:32). God's word is a lamp for one's feet, a light for one's path (Ps 119:105), for the precepts are a lamp, the teaching is a light, and "correction and instruction are the way to life" (Prov 6:23).

Just like Torah, *shari'ah* can also be translated as "way" or "path." The opening *surah* of the Qur'an, *surah-t-al-Fâtiha*, is a prayer and has a liturgical function for Muslims, just like the Lord's Prayer in the Christian tradition: "Guide us on the straight path" (*sirat al mustaqîm*; Q1:6). Thus, before Daniel came to Babylon with the second deportation of Jews from Jerusalem, he already had a roadmap, had already been given instructions on how to walk the path that God points to for a world of justice and peace. In the

---

88. Aalders, *De Septuagint*, 44.
89. https://nl.wikipedia.org/wiki/Wijsheid_van_Jezus_Sirach; *oikâ paideias*.
90. Han, *Daniel's Spiel*, 47.

book of Daniel, it thus concerns a discourse that targets the imperialistic education that Daniel himself had had during the first years of his stay in Babylon (Dan 1). No book in the Hebrew Bible was so opposed to the Greek empire as that of Daniel.[91] The threat of the Hellenistic training emerged in a particularly dramatic way when the political climate under Antiochus Epiphanes became very hostile. The book of Daniel thus appeared at a critical moment when the Hellenistic political culture became an instrument in the service of imperialist interests. Their *paideia* was the guardian and teacher of the empire. Daniel wanted to deconstruct the friendly facade of the *paideia* and expose the political implications of it[92] in his apocalyptic language.[93]

DANIEL'S DREAM

While Nebuchadnezzar's dream was one about the *ruler* (Dan 2), we also read of the dream of the *exile* (Dan 7). What did Daniel himself see in his nightly dream? That vision again gives a view *of* and insight *into* the history of the rise, flourishing, and speedy decline of the same imperial kingdoms that appeared in Nebuchadnezzar's dream. A group of four is used again. Such a diagramming of history appears nowhere else in the Old Testament except in the book of Daniel (2, 7).[94] In his dream at night he sees a wild, stormy sea churned by the four winds, with four great beasts emerging from it. The sea from which these animals emerge represent *chaos* (cf. Gen 1:2; Job 26:12; Ps 74:13–14; 89: 9–10; Isa 27:1; 51:9–10).[95]

The beasts symbolize imperial and military power. Monumental ports and buildings in Assyria, Babylon, and Persia show reliefs of beasts like winged lions. The Israelite prophetic tradition in which Daniel is deeply rooted presents imperial kingdoms as predatory beasts. Israel's own king threatens to step into the role of a wild lion or bear:

> So I will be like a lion to them,
>   like a leopard I will lurk by the path.
> Like a bear robbed of her cubs,
> I will attack them and rip them open;
>   like a lion I will devour them—

---

91. Portier-Young, *Apocalypse Against Empire*, 223.
92. Han, *Daniel's Spiel*, 41–42.
93. Cf. Han, *Daniel's Spiel*, 95.
94. They are found in different forms in other writings later, such as *The Apocalypse of Abraham* 23–31 and also: *The Assumption of Moses* 2–10; *1 Enoch* 83–90; *Testament of Abraham*; *2 Baruch* 53–74; Gowan, *Daniel*, 103.
95. Gowan, *Daniel*, 105.

> a wild animal will tear them apart.
> (Hos 13:7, 8; cf. 5:14; 2:12; Amos 3:12; Isa 5:29)

This testifies to the standard portrait of Israel's imperial rulers as predatory animals. The kings of Israel who acted so imperially were described by Ezekiel in that way:

> Therefore, you shepherds, hear the word of the Lord: As surely as I live, declares the Sovereign Lord, because my flock lacks a shepherd and so has been plundered and has become food for all the wild animals, and because my shepherds did not search for my flock but cared for themselves rather than for my flock, therefore, you shepherds, hear the word of the Lord: This is what the Sovereign Lord says: I am against the shepherds and will hold them accountable for my flock. I will remove them from tending the flock so that the shepherds can no longer feed themselves. I will rescue my flock from their mouths, and it will no longer be food for them. (Ezek 34:7–10)

Then they will no longer be plundered by the peoples and torn by wild animals (their imperial rulers): "They will no longer be plundered by the nations, nor will wild animals [their imperial rulers] devour them. They will live in safety, and no one will make them afraid" (Ezek 34:28).[96]

The four beasts symbolize the successive unjust kings or kingdoms. They represent *four kings* or *kingdoms*. The schema for the four kingdoms was well known in antiquity.[97]

- It begins again with Babylon, *the first world power*, with Nebuchadnezzar: a lion with eagle's wings, the Babylonian Empire.[98] Both the judge Samson (Judg 14:5–6) and the shepherd David fought lions. David killed both the lion and the bear that attacked his flocks (1 Sam 17:34–37; cf. 2 Sam 23:20). Isaiah sees the time of salvation as a universal peace between the animals: the cow and the bear become friends, their young lie together. The lion eats straw, just like the ox (Isa 11:7).[99]

There are of course the legendary stories of the salvation of the faithful in the lions' den (Dan 6): Daniel is saved from the jaws of the lions because of his innocence (1 Macc 2:60).

---

96. Horsley, *Revolt of the Scribes*, 86.
97. Howard-Brook, *"Come Out, My People!"* 342. Collins, *Daniel*, 168.
98. KBS on Dan 7:4: a symbol for Nebuchadnezzar (gold Dan 2:38). In Dan 4:13 the human heart of Nebuchadnezzar is changed into that of an animal (Dan 4:13).
99. *BW*, s.v., beer.

THE BOOK OF DANIEL: "THE FLAMING SCRIPTURE OF THE HOLY GOD" 153

- The *second kingdom*, that of the Medes, is compared to a *bear*: it was raised up on one side and had three ribs between its teeth. The beast is told to get up and eat its fill of flesh (Dan 7:5).

- The *third world power*, the Persians, is compared to a *leopard* (Dan 7:6; cf. Rev 13:2). The apocalyptic beast that John later sees rising out of the sea does indeed remind one of a *leopard* or a *panther*, but it has the claws of a *bear* and the *jaw* of a lion (Rev 13:2; Dan 7:4–6). With these added characteristics—the claws of a bear and the jaw of a lion—the leopard appears here as an especially cruel predator and thus also as possessing the power of the empires mentioned earlier: Babylon and Medea (Dan 7:4–5)![100]

- It is striking that the animal of the *fourth world power* is not given any name, although it is precisely the most terrifying and is extremely strong: "It had large iron teeth; it crushed and devoured its victims and trampled underfoot whatever was left. It was different from all the former beasts, and it had ten horns" (Dan 7:7). That fourth beast refers to Alexander the Great and his immediate successors! Alexander is like a war machine that trampled the whole Middle East right up to India.

One could ask why it was not given any name. Perhaps it was because the writer did not want to insult any animal by comparing it to Alexander and his successors. Do people not turn out to be worse than animals? The animal is just called "other" or "different," probably because of its destructive activity. Is this more reflective of a European (Macedonian, Greek) empire than an Asian one?[101]

And while Daniel is looking at the horns, he saw an eleventh horn, a small one, appear. That horn had human eyes and a boastful mouth, which reflects the self-deification of King Antiochus IV Epiphanes who wanted to put an end to the Jewish religion.[102] "He will speak against the Most High and oppress his holy people and try to change the set times and the laws. The holy people will be delivered into his hands for a time, times and half a time" (Dan 7:8, 25; cf. 8:1–14, 23–25; 11:36–37).[103]

---

100. *BW*, *s.v.*, pardel.
101. Gowan, *Daniel*, 106.
102. KBS on Dan 7:8.
103. Gowan, *Daniel*, 110.

THE ANCIENT OF DAYS AND THE SON OF MAN

In his nightly vision, Daniel saw someone like *a son of man* coming with the clouds of heaven (Dan 7:13; cf. Mark 14:62). The *clouds* are described as God's vehicle (Isa 19:1; Ps 18:12–13; 104:3), often mentioned in the same context as storms (Ps 18:13–14; 97:2–3; Job 36:29–30; 37:15). The divine revelation is connected with clouds (Exod 13:20–22; 14:19–24; 24:16–17; Deut 4:1–2; 5:22; 1 Cor 10:1–2; cf. Heb 12:18). This is what happened when God appeared on Mount Sinai: "On the morning of the third day there was thunder and lightning, with a thick cloud over the mountain, and a very loud trumpet blast. Everyone in the camp trembled" (Exod 19:16; cf. Q 7:171). The trumpet will sound at the last judgment, according to the Bible and the Qur'an.[104] The connection of the people with a holy place typically becomes clear in the relation of the cloud to the *tabernacle* and to the t*emple* (Exod 40:34–38; Lev 16:2; Num 9:15–23; 10:11–12, 34; Deut 31:15; cf. 1 Kgs 8:10–11; 2 Chr 5:13–14; Isa 4:5). The cloud gives the sign or signal to set up camp (it stands still) or to move on (it itself moves on ahead) (Exod 16:10; 24:15–18; Num 16:42; 1 Kgs 8:11). Day and night, the *cloud* and *column of fire* respectively (Exod 13:21–22) constitute God's leading and protection both going before the people *and* as a rear guard. (cf. Isa 52:12; Wis 10:17). "And We shaded you with clouds, and We sent down to you manna and quails" (Q 2:57; cf. 7:160; Exod 16). The descent of the glory of God is often accompanied by a cloud (Exod 34:5; Num 11:25; 12:5; Ps 18:10–11). Through the cloud, the glory of God is *concealed* and *revealed* at the same time in a special way![105]

But what does Daniel then see in his dream? He sees that thrones have been set in place and the Ancient of Days taking his seat (Dan 7:9). "Indeed your Lord is God, who created the heavens and the earth in six days, and then settled on the Throne, directing the command [*amr*]" (Q 10:3; cf. 25:59). It is God who sits down on the throne (to govern the world) (Q 7:54; cf. 9:129). His Throne was [then] upon the waters (Q 11:7; cf. Gen 1:2; Ps 104:3; Rev 4:6).

The court opens in session and *the books were opened* in which the deeds of people had been recorded (Dan 7:9–10; cf. Ps 56:9. Q 7:8–9). The Ancient of Days symbolizes eternity, his age is, after all, unsearchable (Job 36:26), "He who is enthroned of old" (Ps 55:19), "who outlives all generations" (Ps 102:25). "But you remain the same, and your years will never end" (Ps 102:28). "Who has done this and carried it through, calling forth

---

104. Zeph 1:18; 1 Cor 13:32; 1 Thess 4:15;Q 18:9; 20:102; 23:101; 27:87; 36:51; 50:20; 78:18; 79:13; 69:13; 39:68.

105. *BW*, *s.v.*, wolk.

THE BOOK OF DANIEL: "THE FLAMING SCRIPTURE OF THE HOLY GOD"   155

the generations from the beginning? I, the Lord—with the first of them and with the last—I am he" (Isa 41:4; cf. 44:6; Rev 1:8, 17; 21:6; 22:13). "I am the Alpha and the Omega, the First and the Last, the Beginning and the End" (Rev 22:13). The Qur'an also says, "Yet to God belong the last and the first" (Q 53:25; cf. 92:13).

In his nightly vision, Daniel saw someone coming with the clouds of heaven who looked like a *son of man*. He went to the Ancient of Days and was led into his presence (Dan 7:13). Daniel's vision speaks of a heavenly judgment, the final judgment. The inhuman and godless lust for power of the great king will be condemned.[106] The figure that resembles a human being emerges, appears in the dream in sharp contrast to the violent beasts. This person is completely different from the kings pictured as beasts (lion, bear, leopard, and the unnamed fourth one) that consume people, grind them in their jaws. Nothing in the dream gives an indication that this figure plays a role in defeating and killing the fourth beast that comes up out of the sea. The beast is killed before the son of man appears: "Then I continued to watch because of the boastful words the horn was speaking. I kept looking until the beast was slain and its body destroyed and thrown into the blazing fire" (Dan 7:11; cf. Rev 19:20).[107]

Who is the "son of man" (Dan 7:13)? It is not a Messianic title in Aramaic but simply a designation of a human form, simply the essential characteristic of what it is to be a human being.[108] *Son of man* is a Semitic expression that in itself expresses nothing more than just "man" (cf. Ps 8:5; Isa 51:12), "someone."[109] Just as the beasts were *like* a lion, a bear, or a leopard, so this son of man is *like* a human being. The prophet Ezekiel was called by God and addressed literally as "Son of man" (Ezek 2:1).[110]

There are various theories about the identity of this human figure. Some argue that it is Israel, others Michael, the patron saint of Israel, the Messiah, and still others, God. The Septuagint, for instance, sees the son of man as God. He is also seen as a prefiguration of Jesus.[111] But the "son of man" is not a title; it does not suggest an anointed individual or Messianic figure. It only says that his form is the only conceivable opposite of

---

106. KBS on Dan 7:9.

107. Horsley, *Revolt of the Scribes*, 183.

108. Aalders, *De Apocalyptische Christus*, 91; Fitzmyer, *The Semitic Background*, vol. 2, 153.

109. For the meaning "man," see, for example, also Mark 3:28 (people, literally children of men).

110. KBS on Ezek 2:1.

111. Wink, *The Human Being*, 53, n. 9, 10, 11; cf. Mark 14:62.

the *animal* forms of the kings. Nothing is said about him as a person.[112] Just as the *beasts* are interpreted as symbols of kings (Dan 7:17), so this human figure is a symbol of "the holy people of the Most High" (Dan 7:18, 21, 27).[113] The one who resembled a human, so it appears from what follows, is clearly connected with the people of Israel, or at least the "remnant": the holy people of the Most High will receive the kingdom and possess it forever (Dan 7:18).[114] The human figure who receives the kingship and the dominion is understood to be (plural) *the holy people of the Most High* (Dan 7:27), who were attacked by the *small horn* (Dan 7:21, 25) and who receive the kingship (Dan 7:22).[115] "One like a son of man" is a comparison, not an identification. It is not a title nor is it a name or a role of a person. Given that the figure appears in a nightly vision (in a dream), the symbolism should be seen as ambiguous, deliberately dark and strange. It would be good perhaps to leave the question open as to any identification of the figure.

In any case, Daniel was confused when he woke, and he found the images going through his head disturbing, so he had to seek an interpretation (Dan 7:15–16). It can at least be said that Daniel sees his faith that "nations will be ruled by *human* principles and *humane* leaders rather than by the predatory empires that had so long held sway" reconfirmed.[116]

When authority, glory, and sovereign power are given to the son of man, all peoples, tribes, and languages pay him homage. His dominion is an eternal dominion that will never pass away, his kingdom will never be destroyed (Dan 7:14). The language that is used here very much recalls what was stated earlier about human, divine, and eschatological kingship. "Dominion and power and might and glory" was given to Nebuchadnezzar (Dan 2:37) over all peoples, nations, and languages (Dan 5:19). That dominion, however, was not said to be *eternal*—that characteristic was reserved only for the kingdom of the Most High (Dan 4:2, 34; 6:26). And, according to the dream in chapter 2, the latter is a kingdom that shall never be destroyed and will take the place of all earthly kingdoms. That is the kingdom that is promised here:[117] His kingship is an eternal kingship and all powers will serve and obey him (Dan 7:27). The real royal dominion is—according to the Bible and the Qur'an—solely in the hands of God alone (Q 67:1; 43:85;

---

112. Aalders, *De Apocalyptische Christus*, 91.
113. Gowan, *Daniel*, 107–8.
114. Wink, *The Human Being*, 52.
115. Horsley, *Revolt of the Scribes*, 183–84.
116. Wink, *The Human Being*, 53; italics mine.
117. Gowan, *Daniel*, 108–9.

36:83; cf. 23:88; 3:26). Do you not know that all dominion in heaven and on earth belongs to God?[118]

The son of man, whom Daniel sees coming, is a royal individual: he embodies the believers (Ar. *muminûn*), the just, the devout. The Dutch national anthem includes the text: "Dat ik toch vroom mag blijven, uw dienaar t' aller stond" (That I always brave may be, your servant constantly) The Dutch word *vroom* here means brave, courageous. This person represents the righteous, the pious, the community, the Jewish, the Christian, or the Muslim, either all three or all people. The community of believers, of the righteous, is God's caliph who bears responsibility for the world as it continues to suffer time and again under the abuse of the monsters that arise from the waters of chaos with their death squads and killing machines on land, at sea, and in the air.

This "son of man" (one could say, this true person, this perfect human being; *insân al-kâmil*) receives royal dominion from God's hand—the human being as he/she is intended to be. When Cain kills his brother Abel, God asks him: "Where is your brother Abel?" And Cain asks: "Am I my brother's keeper?" The answer to this is clear and unambiguous: Yes, you are. That is why we were placed on earth—to be the brother, the keeper, the shepherd of our fellow human beings (cf. Gen 4:1–16; Q 5:27–23). Because of that fratricide, according to the Qur'an, God made it a law for the children of Israel, on the tables of the law that Moses was given (Q 7:145; cf. Exod 24:12; 32:15–16): "We prescribed for the Children of Israel that whosoever slays a soul . . . it is as is though he slew mankind altogether, and whosoever saves the life of one, it is as though he saved the life of mankind altogether" (Q 5:32). This explanation is found precisely in this form in the Jewish *Mishna Sanhedrin* IV.5 from the third century AD.[119] God wants to make the human being, man and woman, his representative, his viceroy on earth. The Qur'an uses the word "caliph" for that. But then Satan attempts to seduce the human being to aspire to be a king, rather than a caliph. He offers humankind kingship, that is, instead of being a protector, a shepherd or keeper of his fellow human beings, he offers to make him a *bringer of corruption* and *a shedder of blood*, something that the angels warned God about, when God told them in advance that he was planning to create mankind (Q 2:20; cf. Q 38:69; 37:8, Q 15:28; 38:71). Thus, "son of man" means that every person, man or woman, is created to be God's viceroy on earth.[120]

---

118. Q 2:102; 3:189; 5:17, 40, 120; 6:73; 7:158; 9:116; 17:11; 22:56; 24:42; 25:2, 26; 35:13; 39:6; 39:44; 40:16; 42:49; 43:85; 45:27; 48;14; 57:2,5; 64:1; 67:1; 85:9.

119. Paret on Q 5:32; Speyer, *Die biblischen Erzälungen*, 87–88; Cuypers, *The Banquet*, 202–3.

120. Cf. Wessels, *The Torah, the Gospel and the Qur'an*, chapter III.

But what Daniel then sees in his dream is that that rest was and is disrupted in a harsh way—and how! The monsters from the dark depths are given free rein. But, nevertheless, against this background, this backdrop of atrocities, he suddenly sees a truly apocalyptic, revealing, event, the breaking through of a new age. A new age is dawning, a *new human child* is born. He sees him coming; he is led into the presence of the Ancient of Days, and he is given authority, glory and sovereign power; all peoples, tribes, and languages pay him homage. His dominion is an eternal dominion that shall never pass away, and his kingdom will never be destroyed (Dan 7:13-14; cf. Matt 24:32; 26:64; Rev 1:7; 14:14).

The Ancient of Days, the Only God, certainly does not appear to be preparing for a kind of Armageddon.[121] "Apocalypse" does not refer to that violence and counter-violence in the sense of what has been going on for centuries. The Apocalypse of Daniel reveals, uncovers, unveils what happened then and what will happen: since the time of Nebuchadnezzar up to and including the time of Alexander the Great and his successors, up until the time of the Romans and the time of Jesus, and up to and including the time of the prophet Muhammad. This is not an announcement of a violent end to the world but rather an announcement that there will be an end to all those violent large or small kingdoms. But how and when? Through a great final battle in Syria, where, in the time that this book of Daniel was written, terrible things were happening? No, that is not what Daniel sees happening. How, then, in heaven's name, how on earth, does it then come about? A stone was cut out but not by any human hand (Dan 2:34).

WHEN, OH WHEN?

But perhaps the first to hear or read this text said what many contemporary readers will think: A nice dream. But when will it become reality? Will it ever come about? But when? How long do we have to wait for that wonderful end? (Dan 12:6; cf. Dan 10:5.). It was no different for the prophet Daniel than for the disciples who later asked Jesus:[122] When will that Kingdom of God come? The answer they were given was: "It is not for you to know the times or dates" (Acts 1:7). Muhammad was also asked when the day

---

121. "Then they gathered the kings together to the place that in Hebrew is called Armageddon." (Rev 16:16). The name perhaps means "mountain range of Megiddo." (2 Chr. 23:29-30. Zech 12:11). As a place, Megiddo is connected with several wars (Judg 5:19; 2 Kgs 9: 27; 23:29; 2 Chr 35:22) or connected with God on "the mountains of Israel"(Ezek 38:8; 39:2, 4, 17).

122. The "helpers" (*ansâr*) of 'Isa.

of judgment would be (Q 51:12); the day of resurrection (Q 75:6). "Say, 'Its knowledge is only with God.' / What do you know, maybe the Hour is near'" (Q 33:63; cf. Q 31:34). If the time has arrived, God will reveal it. It will come completely suddenly (Q 7:187; cf. Q 79:42). The day when the sky with its clouds will split open, and the angels will be sent down to herald the last judgment—on that day unlimited true sovereignty will belong to the Merciful (*mulku al-haqqa lir Rahmâni*), and that day will be difficult for unbelievers (Q 25:25-26). This is the dawn of the kingdom of the Merciful. On that day, the Kingship will belong to God. He will judge the people: those who believe and have performed good deeds will then dwell in the gardens of pleasure, and those who are unbelievers can expect a humiliating punishment (Q 22:56-57) on the Day on which the trumpet will sound. The trumpet is mentioned ten times as an instrument that announces the last judgment (Q 6:73).[123]

The evening of history will be a long time in falling.[124] Those who have *persevered* are blessed, the book of Daniel concludes (Dan 12:12). As one "community" all three—*qahal, ekklesia,* and *umma*—are invited to join the ten thousand times ten thousand believers (Dan 7:10). The prophet Daniel also knows what terror and fear is, but we should never forget what this prophet said and continue to dream his dream today, when Daniel writes: "The dream is true and its interpretation is trustworthy" (Dan 2:45; cf. Matt 21:42-44).

Belshazzar saw "history as the flaming scripture of the Holy God"[125] written on the wall. He was unable to read it, but Daniel could explain the graffiti, the placard. The question for our leaders, for ourselves, for believers (Jews, Christians, Muslims, or secular people) is: Can we explain, understand, the flaming scripture of the Holy God for our history?

---

123. Jaber and Jansen, *De Koran*, 106, n. 3; Q 18:99; 20:103; 23:101; 27:87; 36:51; 39:68; 50:20; 69:13; 78:18.

124. Aalders, *De Apocalyptische Christus*, 93.

125. An expression by Groen van Prinsterer, *Ongeloof en revolutie* (1847); cited in: Aalders, *De Apocalyptische Christus*, 80.

VI

Jesus and the Apocalypse

During the night of 8 February 1965, just after he had passed the mark of 140 nights of a life sentence, an angel appeared who spoke to him: "Ask whatever you want." Mandela asked him: "What do the words of Jesus, 'Drink the cup that I drink,' mean?" The angel answered: "The cup of loneliness, thirst, despair, disgust, no longer knowing, a cup as full as a sea." And Mandela asked: "Since you have appeared to me anyway, tell me: Can I do it?" Then the angel lifted his hands as if in prayer; and Mandela then saw, for ten seconds, a raging sea and behind it a mountain range reaching to the clouds. And he knew that he was seeing his own life. "Thank you," he said, "I don't understand, but I know; thank you for coming here." And the angel left him. Twenty-five times three hundred and sixty-five nights later, on 8 February 1990, he had drunk the sea dry and was able to cross to the mainland, the most beautiful country on earth. Then the climb up the mountain began, according to Nelson Mandela.[1]

---

1. Huub Oosterhuis, *Red hen die geen verweer hebben* (Ten Have, 2012), 32.

INTRODUCTION

Palestine—and thus also the city of Jerusalem—was ruled by Rome in the first century of our calendar. Roman governors like Pilate, the procurator of Judea (26–36 AD), and kings were needed for that purpose: representatives of the emperor, like the various figures called Herod. Jesus was born in the time that the Roman emperor Augustus (63 BC–14 AD), issued a decree that a census was to be taken of the whole world under his authority (Luke 2:1). It was under the latter's successor, Tiberius (14–37 AD), that Jesus would be crucified, a usual means for executing rebels. The apostle Paul was tried during the reign of Nero (54–68 AD); unlike Peter, he was not crucified but beheaded because he was a Roman citizen. The punishments that Jesus, Peter, and Paul suffered show that their activities were politically charged and constituted a threat to the public "Roman" order from Palestine to Rome.

CONSTANTINE THE GREAT, FOUNDER OF CONSTANTINOPLE

The first "Christian" emperor, Constantine the Great (ca. 285–337), played a decisive role in the formation of the character of Christianity, particularly in Europe. He convened the first ecumenical council of Nicea (325) in which, under his chairmanship, the significance of Jesus was formulated. In 312 he fought his fellow tetrarch Maxentius (ca. 278–312), whom he defeated after a long civil war at the Battle of Milvian Bridge. Before this battle for Rome, he is said to have seen a cross in the sky, with a message above it in Greek, which, translated into Latin, said *In hoc signo vinces* (In this sign you will conquer).[2] In 313, together with his fellow tetrarch Licinius, Constantine issued the Edict of Milan whereby Roman citizens were free to choose their own religion. That edict ended the persecution of Christians. He was the first Roman emperor to become a Christian, even though he was not baptized until he was on his deathbed.

The first "church historian," Eusebius (ca. 263–ca. 339), bishop of Caesarea, was one of the emperor's counselors for a time.[3] On the occasion of the 30th year of his rule, Eusebius wrote his "Oration in Praise of Constantine," i.e., *Life of Constantine the Great*, in which he develops a "theology" of the "religion of the empire." He presents the emperor as being authorized by God: "His ministers are the heavenly hosts, his armies the supernal powers,

---

2. Beckmann, *Konstantin der Grosze*, 59–60.
3. Howard-Brook, *Empire Baptized*, 200.

who own allegiance to him as their Master, Lord, and King." Timothy R. Barnes concludes that the "greater part of the *Panegyric* consists of variations and elaborations on a single theme: the similarity of Constantine to Christ. The Empire of Constantine is a replica of the kingdom of heaven, the manifestation on earth of that ideal monarchy which exists in the celestial realm."[4] Eusebius thus prepared the way for the following centuries of Christian monarchs, not only in the Roman Empire but also in the later Christian kingdoms. Eusebius's *Life of Constantine* makes multiple comparisons with Moses. "Moses was thus a key figure in Christian apologetics, according to which Mosaic law prepared the world for the Christian dispensation, which reached its culmination in Constantine. Eusebius makes it clear that he now equates Constantine's victories with the Exodus from Egypt.[5] Constantine's opponent, Maxentius, who drowned in the Tiber, is compared with Pharaoh. Constantine was presented not so much as a king but as a divinely sent liberator from tyranny. Eusebius thus wrote a gospel of a "Christian emperor."[6] He draws a parallel between Moses' vision of the burning bush (Exod 3) and Constantine's vision of the *labarum*—or Christogram, the *Chi-Rho*, the Greek initials denoting Christ that Constantine saw in the sky—with the ark.[7]

Eusebius provides us with two reports about the battle. In the first,[8] he records that God helped Constantine but does not make any mention of a vision. In his later version (*Vita Constantini*), Eusebius gives a detailed report that he heard from Constantine himself. According to this version, Constantine was marching with his army (no specification of the precise location of the event is given, but it was certainly not the camp at Rome) when he looked up at the sun and saw a cross of light above it and the Greek words (ἐν τούτῳ νίκα [*en toútōi níka*]). The Latin translation of this means: "In this sign you will conquer" (*in hoc signo vinces*). He was initially uncertain about the meaning of the appearance, but the following night he had a dream in which Christ explained to him that he had to use the sign against his enemies. Eusebius then describes the *labarum*, the military standard on which the *Chi-Rho* sign was placed, that Constantine used in his later wars

---

4. Timothy D. Barnes, *Constantine and Eusebius* (Cambridge MA: Harvard University Press, 1981), 254; cited in: Howard-Brook, *Empire Baptized*, 202.

5. Averil Cameron and Stuart G. Hall, *Eusebius: Life of Constantine* (Oxford: Clarendon Press, Oxford, 1999); cited in: Howard-Brook, *Empire Baptized*, 203.

6. Raymond van Dam, *The Roman Revolution of Constantine* (Cambridge: Cambridge University Press, 2007), 313; cited in: Howard-Brook, *Empire Baptized*, 203, n. 101.

7. Howard-Brook, *Empire Baptized*, 203.

8. In the *Ekklèsiastikè Historia* (IX 11).

against Licinius.⁹ Despite the differences between these versions, they were fused together to indicate that Constantine saw a *Chi-Rho* sign on the evening before the battle. Only later did he make extended use of the *Chi-Rho* sign and the *labarum* in his conflict with Licinius.¹⁰ The later conflict in 324 between Constantine and the other tetrarch was presented by Eusebius as the counterpart of the victory at the Milvian Bridge twelve years prior. Instead of Maxentius, this defeated tetrarch is now presented as a "hater of God" and a "tyrant."¹¹ Maxentius did not persecute Christians. Thus, it was not a religious war.¹²

To mark the final victory, Constantine founded his own "city of victory" (*Nikopolis*), which he named after himself, Constantinople. He moved the capital of Rome to Byzantium on the Bosporus, the boundary between Europe and Asia. Among the most splendid structures Constantine built there was his own mausoleum dedicated to the "Holy Apostles." His primary aim was to ensure that he would rest next to the remains of the apostles that he had brought to this city for that purpose. According to Eusebius's interpretation, Constantine believed that he would be esteemed as an apostle and, by placing his sarcophagus in the circle of the apostles, that he would participate in the veneration accorded to them.¹³

For Eusebius, it was already clear in the fourth century that Constantine did not see himself as a follower but as a leader:

> Just as Christ reigned in heaven and would return to rule on earth, so Constantine "alone of emperors, continued to rule on earth from heaven." Although he was unable to fulfill his wish to be baptized in the Jordan, he had, in Eusebius' view, achieved "a Christ-like majesty." In an oration given shortly before his death, he praised Constantine as Christ's "friend" and "emulator," indeed almost his second coming.¹⁴

Centuries later, in his *Dictionaire philosophique*, Voltaire would call Constantine "a politically not untalented criminal," and, according to Jacob Burckhardt, Constantine was without scruples, a power-hungry Machiavellian who took advantage of the Christian faith for his own purposes, without any inner conviction.¹⁵

9. *Vita Constantini* I, 28–31.
10. https://en.wikipedia.org/wiki/Labarum.
11. Beckmann, *Konstantin der Grosze*, 22.
12. Beckmann, *Konstantin der Grosze*, 66.
13. Beckmann, *Konstantin der Grosze*, 130.
14. Stephenson, *Constantine*, 288–89.
15. Beckmann, *Konstantin der Grosze*, 18.

JERUSALEM AND THE MEANING OF THE CROSS

According to tradition, it was Constantine's mother, Helena, who managed to locate the cross on which Jesus had died: the place where it could be found was conveyed to her in a dream. Helena is credited with having found the holy nails when she discovered the true cross of Jesus. According to Gregory of Tours,[16] two of the nails were used to make a bit for the bridle of Constantine's horse, and another was used to decorate his statue.[17] The legend of the discovery of the "true cross," however, would emerge already, it seems, in the final years of Constantine's reign.[18]

During the ecumenical council of Nicaea (325), the bishop of Jerusalem directed the emperor's attention to his city and returned home with a program for church construction. A new basilica was to be built to honor the newly discovered grave of Jesus. The local Christians saw that as an infringement by Byzantium and did not support the project![19] In other words, since the time of Constantine, a "Christian Roman" imperial claim has been made on Jerusalem and the Holy Land. Jerusalem would become an increasingly important center for the "imperial" Melkite church at the expense of the churches of the East (Syrian Orthodox, Nestorian, Maronite, Armenian, Coptic), and in particular—and not to be forgotten—the Jews!

One aspect of Constantine's embrace of Christianity emerged from the building program under the supervision of his mother Helena. Since the destruction of Jerusalem by the Romans in the year 70, the city had been left in ruins. The local population knew little of the places where the biblical events of three centuries ago had occurred. Constantine revived a feeling for the area as the "Holy Land" by building basilicas and shrines throughout the country. Jerusalem's native Jewish past was replaced by a new Christian presence:

> The juxtaposition of temple ruins and the new Christian basilica (in Jerusalem) serves to justify the Christian colonization of Jerusalem. Constantine's monumental building project constructs imperial presence in Jerusalem and visibly and materially conquers and replaces Jerusalem's native Jewish past with a new Christian present. The contrast between temple ruin and new church "marks the intersection and collusion" of the ecumenical aspirations of Rome and the Christian church.

16. Patrologia Latina, ed. J. P. Migne [Paris 1878–1890] 71: 710.
17. https://www.encyclopedia.com/religion/encyclopedias-almanacs-transcripts-and-maps/nails.
18. Beckmann, *Konstantin der Grosze*, 9.
19. https://nl.wikipedia.org/wiki/Heilig_Grafkerk.

> At the same time that Constantine's new church serves as a visible sign of the supersession of Judaism, however, it is more broadly suggestive of the rejection and defeat of *all* ancestral traditions and their replacement by Christianity.[20]

Constantine creates a "Christian Holy Land" around Jerusalem, even though he himself would never visit that "Holy Land" after his plans had been implemented.[21] Constantine is depicted with the recovered "true cross" along with his mother Helena. The churches of the East celebrate his feast on 21 May.[22]

It is considered one of the great ironies of history that this church is built "on the place where it is proclaimed in the first gospel of Jesus the crucified that 'He is not here'" (Mark 16:6)![23] In other words, Constantine built a church—*on the only place of which the Scripture unambiguously says that Jesus was not there*. "The Gospels remain the strongest witness to the folly and betrayal that are abundantly manifest in the celebration by the Christian leadership of the first 'Christian emperor.'"[24]

In 1009, the Fatimid caliph Hâkim bi Amr Allâh ordered the Church of the Holy Sepulcher to be razed. Al-Hâkim, who believed himself to be an incarnation of God and was very puritanical in his faith could not tolerate the idea that such an important Christian church existed in his realm. He ordered the "Church of Refuse," as it is derisively called by Muslims, to be plundered. The term "Church of Refuse," i.e., *Kanîsat al-Qumâna*, is a wordplay on *Kanîsat al-Qiyâma*, the Church of the Resurrection, as the Arabs still call the Church of the Holy Sepulcher. This satirical term had been used since the seventh century but its usage increased in the twelfth and thirteenth centuries.[25] After his soldiers first robbed the church of all its treasures, it was dismantled stone by stone right down to the bare rock. Even the foundations were hauled away.[26]

Saladin took a completely different approach. In 1187, after capturing Jerusalem from the crusaders, he decided not to destroy the recently rebuilt church. He was apparently persuaded against doing so by those who said

---

20. Jeremy M. Schott, *Christianity and Jewish Society and the Making of Religion in Late Antiquity* (Philadelphia: University of Pennsylvania Press, 2008), 162; cited in: Howard-Brook, *Empire Baptized*, 198.
21. Howard-Brook, *Empire Baptized*, 198.
22. Bleckmann, *Konstantin der Grosze*, 10.
23. Howard-Brook, *"Come Out My People!"* 406.
24. Howard-Brook, *Empire Baptized*, 199.
25. Hillenbrand, *The Crusades*, 317.
26. https://nl.wikipedia.org/wiki/Heilig_Grafkerk.

that "it would not be possible to stop the Franks coming to Jerusalem 'since what they adore is the sanctity of Jerusalem of which the Refuse is only the noblest place.'"[27]

The symbol of the cross and the meaning that was given to it has played a *crucial* role in history since then; in particular, of course, vis-a-vis the Jews and, since the seventh century, the Muslims. But is that meaning in line with the spirit of the New Testament?

CONSTANTIUS II AND THE CROSS

Fourteen years after his death, Constantine the Great's vision of the cross was again brought to the attention of the public, again in connection with an *imperial victory*. On 7 May 351, Cyril, the bishop of Jerusalem (d. 386) sent a letter to Constantine's successor and son Constantius II (emperor from 337–361). Cyril later opposed plans by Julian the Apostate (361–363) to rebuild the Jewish temple. Julian is best known for revoking the privileging of Christians that Constantine the Great and Constantius II had so forcefully advanced.[28]

Shortly after Cyril became bishop, he saw "a cross of light" appear above Jerusalem. Cyril describes this appearance "during the holy days of Pentecost" on the ninth day before the Ides of May, around the third hour of the day (nine o' clock in morning) in a letter to Constantius II: an immense cross of light formed in the sky and stretched above Golgotha, as far as the holy Mount of Olives. Brighter than the sun, it was visible to all in the city for a few hours, and hundreds took refuge in the churches, young and old, men and women, locals and strangers, Christians and others, shouting "the name of Jesus Christ their Lord as if with one voice."

> Cyril offers the vision to Constantius as a greater gift that the earthly crowns with which others had honored him, and as concrete proof of divine favour for his rule, so that he might confront his "enemies with greater courage." The cross is a "trophy of victory," specifically of Christ's victory over death, but also a sign that Constantius has God as his ally, and that he might "bear the trophy of the cross, the boast of boasts, carrying forward the sign shown to us in the skies, of which heaven has made an even greater boast by displaying its form to human beings.[29]

27. Hillenbrand, *The Crusades*, 318.
28. https://en.wikipedia.org/wiki/Julian_(emperor).
29. Stephenson, *Constantine*, 296–97.

Cyril's letter needs to be understood as the first of a series of measures, along with the "true cross" as its central motif, to make Jerusalem the holiest place in Christianity.

> As interpreter of the apparition, therefore, Cyril kept Jerusalem to the fore, praising Constantius' piety as surpassing that of his most God-beloved father of blessed memory, by whose prayers the soterial wood of the True Cross had been found in Jerusalem and the Holy Places revealed. Whereas Constantine was blessed with revelations from Jerusalem's earth, his yet more pious son received his revelation from the heavens above the city, thus fulfilling the evangelist's prophecy (Matthew 24:30) that "the sign of the Son of Man will appear in the sky."[30]

CHRISTIANITY'S FALL INTO SIN

This view of and interpretation of "Constantine" and thus of the faith and practice of the dominant Christianity in Europe and the world since then has rightly evoked a great deal of opposition. Gerrit Jan Heering spoke in this context of "Christianity's fall into sin" ("de zondeval van het christendom").[31] When Constantine converted to Christianity in 312 and raised this religion to the state religion in 324, Christianity turned to the state and reconciled itself with war and with having a military.[32] Heering exposes the pernicious and destructive effect of the act of making Christianity the only religion. With the reprint of his book in 1953—two years before his death—he wrote in the preface:

> We are not creating any political slogans. We are appealing to the Christian conscience and to the thinking guided by this conscience. The strongest powers in the world and life are not violence and weapons but faith and conscience. And the saving deed is not the atom bomb but Christian sacrifice. Whoever doubts this, look to Him who said "I have overcome the world." He has overcome. He shall overcome. His Kingdom is, and it is coming.[33]

---

30. According to J.W Drijvers in Stephenson, *Constantine*, 297.
31. Heering *De zondeval van het christendom*.
32. Heering, *De zondeval van het christendom*, 41.
33. Heering, *De zondeval van het christendom*, 8; https://nl.wikipedia.org/wiki/Gerrit_Jan_Heering.

The Roman Empire did not cease to be an "empire" because Constantine the Great accepted Christianity and later Theodosius I (d. 395) decreed that all Roman citizens had to convert to Christianity. What came into being was an imperialistic Christianity, a *Baptized Empire: How the Church Embraced What Jesus Rejected*[34]—to summarize it in the title of Wes Howard-Brook's study. What followed were "wars, economic exploitation, and countless variations of domination 'in Jesus' name.'" "The history of Crusades and Inquisitions and pillage under the apparent legitimation of 'Christianity,' has led to the hideous muddying and polluting of the crystal clear water of New Jerusalem."[35]

Constantine has had numerous successors in the "Christian history" of Europe. One of the many other examples to imitate Constantine was the Holy Roman Emperor Charles V (1500–1558). The Christian recapturing of the Iberian peninsula from the Muslims, the *Reconquista*, was completed on the eve of his birth, in 1492. It was then that the last Muslim bulwark, Granada, fell, and "America" was discovered. Both Muslims and Jews were expelled from the Iberian peninsula.

Charles V's motto on his coat of arms was *Plus Ultra*: "Still Further." This is a very suggestive variation of the text that Hercules is said to have once chiseled on the pillars on either side of the Strait of Gibraltar to mark the end of the world in classic antiquity: *Non plus Ultra*. Charles's personal motto was thus the direct opposite: *Plus Ultra*, along with the German translation *Noch Weiter*, which would also become the national motto of Spain.[36] The motto was presented for the first time in October 1516 in the Cathedral of Saint Michael and Saint Gudula in Brussels. The idea behind this motto was that Charles would expand his power and influence *beyond the Pillars*, that is, both *toward the West* in order to evangelize the "New World," as well as *toward the East* to combat Islam and to liberate Jerusalem. The original phrase was taken from Dante's *Divine Comedy* (*Inferno*, Canto XXVI): *più oltre non si metta*, in reference to the Pillars that Hercules had set up to prevent people from going any further:

> but forth I put upon the deep
> and open sea with but a single ship,
> and with that little company, by whom
> I had not been deserted. Both its shores

---

34. Howard-Brook, *Empire Baptized*.
35. Howard-Brook, *"Come Out My People!"* 473.
36. https://en.wikipedia.org/wiki/Charles_V,_Holy_Roman_Emperor.

> I then beheld, as far away as Spain,
> Morocco and the island of the Sards,[37]
> and all the rest that sea bathes round about.
> Both old and slow were I and my companions,
> when we attained that narrow passage-way,
> where Hercules set up those signs of his,
> which warned men not to sail beyond their bounds;
> Seville I left behind me on the right hand,
> Ceuta I'd left already on the other.[38]

In contrast, with his *new motto*, Charles V wanted to indicate that the Strait of Gibraltar was no longer the end of the world and that his ambitions reached much farther. His motto referred to the territorial expansions in the New World, which was why the Spanish ships passed beyond the rock of Gibraltar.[39]

The pride and arrogance that the motto expresses is also apparent from the design of his parade shield: *The Apotheosis of Charles V*. This is one of the most excessive glorification scenes that the emperor cult has ever produced. Charles V is crowned by the goddess of victory, Victoria, with a laurel wreath. A shield with the *Plus Ultra* motto is lifted up: "Hercules depicted with the two pillars named after him in his arms." The weapons can be explained as spoils of war, and it is apparent from the turban to which the woman ("Africa") is linked with braids that this is an allegorical presentation of a victory over the Turks![40]

It is important to understand that the crusades that began in the eleventh century brought the Muslims in the Middle East into contact with "Christians" who were fundamentally different from the Christians they were familiar with in their own countries. The cross played a prominent role in the experience of the "Franks" that differed from the faith of the oriental Christians native to that area. If the cross was the symbol for the latter of a minority tolerated by the Islamic majority government, now the cross was the symbol of conquests and occupation by a foreign invader, the "Christian" Franks! The crusaders were seen by the Muslims as "worshippers" of the cross. At that time, the symbol of the cross summarized what the center of Christianity was. A Christian king was called a "servant of the

---

37. The Sards were a south European Romance ethnic group living on the island of Sardinia. https://en.wikipedia.org/wiki/Sardinian_people.

38. Dante Alighieri, *The Divine Comedy*, vol. 1 (Inferno); https://oll.libertyfund.org/titles/alighieri-the-divine-comedy-vol-1-inferno-english-trans.

39. Koldeweij, *Maria van Hongarije*, 236.

40. Koldeweij, *Maria van Hongarije*, 258; see especially p. 259 for the illustration of the parade shield with *The Apotheosis of Charles V*.

cross," *'Abd al-salîb*, a name that was modelled on the way a Muslim name was connected with one of the 99 beautiful names of God, such as "servant of the Merciful"—'Abd al-Rahmân.

The Franks erected crosses everywhere when they conquered a city. Both sides—the Muslims and the Christians—felt a strong need to destroy each other's religious symbols. To break crosses was a symbolic deed whereby Christianity was defeated and Islam triumphant. Saladin "broke their cross violently" at the Battle of Hattin. After the fall of Jerusalem, he brought "the cross of crosses," simply a piece of wood covered with gold and inlaid with precious stones, on which, it was asserted, the Christian God had been crucified. The gilded cross on the Dome of the Rock in Jerusalem was taken down in anything but a gentle fashion: despite its immense size, it was hurled to the ground. After the fall of Jerusalem, Saladin sent the most important trophies of his conquest to the caliph in Baghdad. The cross at the top of the Dome of the Rock was the *pièce de resistance*. Made of copper and covered with gold, the cross was buried in Baghdad under the Nubian Gate and thus trampled underfoot.[41]

The central importance of the cross for the Christian king of Jerusalem became apparent when he was taken prisoner. The Qadi al-Fadil, Saladin's chancellor,[42] realized the central importance of the cross to both the king and his followers: "Their despot was taken prisoner, bearing in his hand the object in which he placed his utmost confidence, the strongest bond by which he held to his religion, namely the cross of the Crucifixion, by which were led to battle the people of arrogance." The counterpart of the cross for Muslims is the Qur'an or the minaret. It was not until much later that the "crescent moon" became that counterpart. It should be stated, however, that when the Armenian Cathedral of Ani was turned into a mosque in the eleventh century, the cross was replaced then already by a crescent moon.[43]

AT THE CROSSROADS

The first words of the gospel of Mark are themselves revelatory, apocalyptic: they give us a window into the dark evil of Roman imperialism. The term *gospel*, with which the book opens, had a familiar ring in that time. The powerful in Rome were constantly announcing the gospel of the Roman peace, the *Pax Romana*, also called the *Pax Augusta* after the adopted son of Julius Caesar, Caesar Augustus (63 BC–14 AD), under whose rule Jesus

---

41. Hillenbrand, *The Crusades*, 305.
42. https://www.orient-institut.org/index.php?id=93.
43. Hillenbrand, *The Crusades*, 306–7.

was born (Luke 2). To properly understand the meaning of this word gospel, one must realize that the Romans called their battlefield victories "gospel." A good illustration of this is the occupation by the Romans of Magdala, a city on the western side of the Sea of Galilee. This was the city where Mary Magdalene, who would be a disciple of Jesus from beginning to end, came from. She witnessed the crucifixion (Matt 27:56), Jesus' burial (Matt 27:61; Mark 16:1), and resurrection (John 20:11–18; Mark 16:9), which cannot be said of the male disciples (with the exception of John in the fourth gospel). When the tenth Roman legion conquered Magdala, they slaughtered 6,700 people. The water of the sea turned red because of the bloodbath that occurred there. After the conquest, the Roman general Titus sent a messenger on horse to tell the emperor in Rome *the gospel* about this bloody conquest.[44]

To properly understand the book of Mark, it is especially important to know *when* and *where* it was written. According to current insights, it was not written in Rome, as was thought earlier, but in Palestine and during the Roman-Jewish War that began in 66, more precisely, probably shortly before or after the destruction of Jerusalem in the year 70.[45] The Zealots revolted against the Romans, and war raged in Galilee and Judea. Only with the capture of Masada did there come an end to the last Jewish resistance.[46] If, knowing that one opens the book of Mark and then reads: "The beginning of the gospel of Jesus the Messiah, the Son of God," then one knows that it contains good news about someone who, it should be noted, was crucified by the Romans. It would take a great deal of courage at that time to call that good news!

In a very striking way, Egbert Rooze has rightly called his commentary on this book of the Bible: *Marcus als tegenevangelie*, i.e., Mark as counter-Gospel.[47] How, precisely, does one discover that Mark is a "counter-Gospel"? That becomes apparent when one pays attention to how Mark has Jesus follow a certain route from Galilee to Jerusalem: via Caesarea Philippi, southwards along the Sea of Galilee, via the Transjordan Perea, and finally Jerusalem. To understand and explain the gospel of Mark, it is very important to look at the "theological" coherence and interaction that Mark indicates at the crossroads: "the way of the cross of the Romans" or "the way of the cross of Jesus."

44. Described by Josephus, *The Wars of the Jews*, III. http://www.isdet.com/_PDF/Complete_Works_%20of_Josephus.pdf, 529–30; cf. Rooze, *Marcus*, 12.

45. Myers, *Binding the Strong Man* (1988), cited in: Howard-Brook, *"Come Out My People!"* 399, n. 2.

46. https://en.wikipedia.org/wiki/First_Jewish–Roman_War.

47. Rooze, *Marcus*; cf. Howard-Brook, *"Come Out My People!"* 400. I am making grateful use of Rooze's comments.

The interaction or the interplay between the two ways is apparent from the comparison between the movement of the Romans to the Transjordan and Jesus' journey to Gadara southeast of the Sea of Galilee. At the beginning of 68 AD, the Romans entered the Transjordan area, occupied the country and invaded the city of Gadara. Mark says Jesus visited that place, which was literally first visited by the Romans. And what a visit that was! The city was taken by storm; a thousand young men who could not escape on time were killed; women and children were taken as prisoners of war; and soldiers were given permission to plunder. Then the houses were set on fire. Whoever could fled, but those were unable to flee were killed.[48] The route that Jesus now followed through the Transjordan thus has to be seen against the background of this bloody Roman campaign.

When Jesus goes to the country of the Gerasenes, the area around Gadara (Mark 5:1–20), he is met by someone who lived among the graves. That was not surprising, for there would have been many graves there, and where else would a person be able to live? The man was possessed, and he was certainly not the only possessed person in a "possessed" land. The Romans were, after all, possessed by the idea of bloody devastations. The people "possessed" by Roman imperialism made them "possessed" in all kinds of ways.[49] This possessed man wandered around crying out, hurting himself and cutting himself with stones. Jesus said to him: "Come out of this man, you impure spirit!" Crying out loudly, the spirit cried: "What do you want with me, Jesus, Son of the Most High God? In God's name don't torture me!" Jesus then asked him, "What is your name?"

"My name is Legion," he replied, "for we are many." And he begged Jesus not to send him out of the region (Mark 5:1–10). The answer to Jesus' question about his name had to ring a bell for those who were listening closely. "My name is Legio, for we are many" (Mark 5:9). *Legio*, legion? A legion, or *legio* in Latin, was the principal unit of the Roman army, and at the end of the first century there were 25 such legions, each containing about 6,000 men. Four legions were sent to the province of Syria. The military headquarters were in Caesarea (Acts 10:1; 27:1), with a small garrison in Jerusalem (John 18:12; Acts 23:17–33).[50] When Jesus was later arrested in Gethsemane by a group armed with swords and clubs, sent by the high priests and elders of the people in accordance with Judas's instruction, "The one I kiss is the man; arrest him," one of his disciples drew his sword and cut

---

48. Josephus, *The Wars of the Jews*, IV, 487–90, 351–52. http://www.isdet.com/_PDF/Complete_Works_%20of_Josephus.pdf.

49. Rooze, *Marcus*, 116.

50. *BW*, *s.v.*, legioen.

off the ear of the servant of the high priest. Jesus then said to him, "Put your sword back in its place, for all who draw the sword will die by the sword. Do you think I cannot call on my Father, and he will at once put at my disposal more than *twelve legions* of angels?" *(*Matt 26:53).

There was a large herd of *pigs* feeding on the hillside. At that time, in the Decapolis, an area that was under foreign control, there were many large herds of pigs (Mark 5:11–13; Luke 15:15–16).[51] And the impure spirits who possessed this man begged him: "Send us among the pigs; allow us to go into them." Jesus assented. To liberate the possessed man from the unclean spirits, he sent them into the pigs, and the whole herd rushed down the steep bank into the sea. About two thousand drowned (Mark 5:11–20).

Some people find this very animal-unfriendly. The pigs had not done anything wrong, had they? But that shows no understanding at all of the "plot" of the narrative and its significance. It cannot be coincidental that the Roman tenth legion that had occupied that area marched under *the sign of the boar* (swine!). Not long after that, this same "legion of the swine" would deal the coup de grace to Jerusalem. Thus, the demon's name "Legion" is a coded expression for the occupying power.[52] Jesus wanted that power to come to an end—but not through embarking on a war of liberation like the one going on when Mark wrote this. Jesus lets the impure spirits go into the pigs, and the legion of pigs kill themselves—make an end of themselves, The demons of the Roman army's "possession" meets their own abyss.[53] That is the "gospel," the good news!

Thus, the message of Jesus the crucified at that time and in that place, Palestine, that was called the "good news" was like a dagger in the heart of imperial propaganda. While "gospel" is used more than seventy times in the New Testament, it only appears once in the Greek translation of the Old Testament (the Septuagint), namely, for the "good news" brought to David of the death of King Saul (2 Sam 4:10).[54] Mark expropriated this term from the Roman empire! The words "evangelize," "proclaim," "preach" refer to a process to actively proclaim Jesus and not Caesar as worthy of one's faith. The Greek word for faith (*pistis*) is also an expropriation of an imperial Latin word for faith (*fides*). Faith in the good news is thus at odds with Roman faith. The eternal gospel is proclaimed. That applies to the message

---

51. *BW, s.v.,* zwijnen.
52. Rooze, *Marcus,* 113.
53. Rooze, *Marcus,* 116.

54. For that matter, this word is connected with respect to content with the Hebrew (and Arabic) words for the good news. Cf. *bashara, bushrâ* in: *A Stranger is Calling,* XI, 2, 4, 11, 41, 77, 98, 101–3, 138, 145, 155, 173, 188, n. 29.

of the Old Testament, i.e., God's exclusive rule over the nations in which the resurrected Lord shares.[55]

Thus, the term "gospel" was especially known at the time as a term for news of a victory, especially a military one and in particular related to Roman political propaganda. Caesar was worshipped in the latter as the "divine man." This is well documented on coins from that period and is primarily apparent in the expanding emperor cult in Asia Minor. A prince's acceptance of power was accompanied by celebrations and sacrifices because this was "good news." The divinization of the emperor gave meaning and power to the good news. The *first* gospel brings the news of the "imperial" birth.

This explains the opening words of Mark. "The beginning of the good news about Jesus the Messiah" is the preeminent challenge to the *imperial propaganda*, a "revolutionary Gospel," a declaration of war on the political culture of the empire. He does indeed tell of a struggle but proclaims an entirely different victory than that gained by the weapons of Rome.[56] Mark thus has the believer's audacity to write a *counter-Gospel* against the *Pax Romana*, the Roman Peace that the Romans attempted to spread to the farthest reaches of the world, the success of which cost a great many "crucified" lives and much property. The gospel of Mark makes clear that the way of the cross, the *via crucis*, the way of suffering that Jesus himself walks, is a completely different path from that of the Romans. Were the "Christian" emperors since the fourth century, beginning with Constantine the Great, the successors of the Roman emperors rather than the successors of Jesus Christ?

THE APOCALYPTIC TRIAD

The gospel of Mark contains *three apocalyptic moments*. The first is at the beginning: the baptism of Jesus, the voice from heaven that declares: "You are my Son, whom I love; with you I am well pleased" (Mark 1:11). Mark does not give any indication that any of those present at the Jordan saw or heard anything. It was "privileged information."[57]

Then there is the episode *in the* middle of the gospel: the transfiguration, Jesus' encounter with Moses and Elijah, to which the three most intimate disciples are witness. "Then a cloud appeared and covered them, and a voice came from the cloud: 'This is my Son, whom I love. *Listen to him!*'" (Mark 9:7). The final episode occurs *at the end*: "*With a loud cry, Jesus breathed his last. The curtain of the temple was torn in two from top to*

---

55. *Fides*; Howard-Brook, *The Church before Christianity*, 130–31.
56. Myers, *Binding the Strong Man*, 123–24.
57. Myers, *Binding the Strong Man*, 128.

bottom" (Mark 15:37–38).[58] Jesus' death is the climax of Mark's symbolic expostulation about the Son of Man. While his enemies look on, he dies and the world "ends." But that is revealed only to those who "have eyes to see."[59]

In some translations, the thirteenth chapter of Mark is given ominous headings like "The Destruction of the World" or "Discourse about the End Times." That already suggests a certain exegesis in line with how the statement "We are living in apocalyptic times" is discussed today. But what precisely is this chapter talking about? What is actually being *revealed*? This final discourse by Jesus has to be placed explicitly within the framework of the apocalyptic purport of the whole gospel.

The central question that the *original hearers and readers of this gospel* were concerned with was: What should we do when the Romans reach Jerusalem? The answer that is put in Jesus' mouth is—decades before this happened—"shockingly specific": "When you see 'the abomination that causes desolation' standing where it does not belong—let the reader understand—then let those who are in Judea flee to the mountains" (Mark 13:14). The expression "the abomination that causes desolation" immediately calls to mind the book of Daniel (Dan 9:27; 11:31; 12:11) that speaks in these terms of God's judgment over the imperial (Seleucid) occupation of the temple in Jerusalem. In Daniel's time, the temple was desecrated by Antiochus IV Epiphanes, who had a statue of Zeus placed there. The expression "abomination that causes desolation" contains a wordplay. "The God of heaven" is corrupted into "The God of desolation." That happens whenever a prince sees himself as the epiphany of God. Such princes and emperors are constantly trampling over bodies, bringing desolation everywhere. Herod the Great was such a prince who heard about the epiphany, the appearance of Jesus in the coming Christmas night, from the wise men from the East. He had asked them to inform him when they had found the place because Herod wanted, so he claimed, to worship him as well. But when the wise men—having been warned in a dream—do not tell him where the newborn king can be found, Herod errs on the side of caution: he pays his "respects" by killing all boys two years old and younger (Matt 2:16). As Joost van Vondel once wrote, Herod could, after all, not endure light coming from anywhere else than himself:

> O Christmas night, fairer than the days,
> How can Herod endure that bright blaze
> That glitters in your darkest night,
> And is lauded and praised aright?

---

58. Myers, *Binding the Strong Man*, 115.
59. Myers, *Binding the Strong Man*, 120.

> His pride rejects firm reason's cries,
> However shrilly it does chastise.
>
> Intent on killing the guiltless one
> He murders instead the innocent sons.
> In town and lane desolation resounds,
> In Bethlehem and in the fields around,
> The spirit of Rachel by sorrow pained,
> Weeping, wanders through meadow and plain.[60]

If, in the book of Daniel, the *abomination* is the altar in honor of Zeus that Antiochus IV put in the temple, now it probably refers to the attempt by Emperor Caligula in the fourth decade to erect his image in the temple. If it was once intended to demonstrate the power of the Greeks, now it is the presence of the eagle, the expression of power and authority of the Romans.[61]

The travel account of Jesus and his disciples began in Caesarea Phillipi (Mark 8:27). This town lay in the proximity of the sources of the Jordan River. Phillip, the son of Herod the Great, had his residence here, and the place was called Caesarea in honor of Caesar Tiberius.[62] *Along the way* Jesus asked his disciples: "Who do people say I am?" (Mark 8:27), to which Peter answered: "You are the Christ" (Mark 8:27–29).[63] Jesus forbade his disciples from telling anyone about him (Mark 8:30). He began to explain to them that the Son of Man had to suffer a great deal (Mark 8:31), to tell them that he is a suffering Messiah, and the fact that he had no ambitions to be a victorious national hero (as Peter apparently expected) is at the heart of the constant misunderstanding of Jesus' mission. It is a particular feature of the gospel of Mark that Jesus forbids the demons that he expels (Mark 1:34; 3:12), the people that he heals (Mark 1:44; 5:43; 7:36; 8:26) and his disciples (8:30; 9:9) to talk about what happened and about his Messiahship.[64] After

---

60. *Liedboek*, Hymn 510: "O kerstnacht, schoner dan de dagen, / hoe kan Herodes 't licht verdragen, / dat in uw duisternisse blinkt, en wordt gevierd en aangebeden? / Zijn hoogmoed luistert naar geen reden, / Hoe schel die in zijn oren klinkt.

Hij poogt d'onnoozle te vernielen / door it moorden van onnoozle zielen, / en wekt een stad- en landgeschrei, / In Betlehem en op de akker / en maakt de geest van Rachel wakker, / die waren gaat door beemd en wei."

Unless otherwise indicated, all translations from incidental texts are the work of the translator of this volume, unless otherwise indicated (see bibliography).

61. Howard-Brook, *"Come Out My People!"* 399; KBS on Matt 24:15.

62. KBS on Matt 16:13.

63. John 6:69: "We have come to believe and to know that you are the Holy One of God"; cf. John 10:36; 17:19.

64. KBS on Mark 1:25.

the three most intimate disciples were witness to Jesus' meeting with Moses and Elijah—the second apocalyptic moment—they were also told not to speak of this. While they were descending from the mountain, he enjoined them not to tell anyone what they had seen before the Son of Man would rise from the dead (Mark 9:9).

For the first time, Jesus' announced that the path he will follow is a path of suffering. Peter, however, thought he knew better what Jesus' path was. He took him aside and began to take him to task. Peter thought that Jesus started out to be a warlike "Messiah." But Jesus turned back not only to Peter but to all his disciples, looked straight at them, and then rebuked Peter in words that can in no way be misunderstood: "Get behind me, Satan!... You do not have in mind the concerns of God, but merely human concerns" (Mark 8:33). To understand Jesus' sharp rebuke of Peter, one must realize that Jesus is not calling people to violent resistance against the Roman empire, like the Maccabees against the Greeks in the second century BC, when that dissenting book Daniel was written. That is what the Jews of the Jewish revolt did in the period when the book of Mark was written, just like the anti-Roman resistance movement of the Zealots and the Sicarii or partisans in Jesus' time wanted to do.[65]

JESUS GOES TO THE OTHER SIDE

Jesus had taught such a large crowd at the sea that he sat in a boat, while the people stood on the shore (Mark 4:1). When evening began to fall, Jesus said to his disciples, "Let us go over *to the other side*." When he boarded the boat, his disciples all followed him into the boat. A severe storm arose, and the waves rolled over the boat so that it was nearly swamped. But Jesus lay in the stern asleep. His disciples woke him and said, "Teacher, don't you care if we perish?" He stood up and rebuked the wind and the waves: "Quiet, be still!" He turned to his disciples, "Why are you afraid? Do you still have no faith?" They were terrified and said among themselves: "Who is this man, that even the wind and waves obey Him?" (Mark 4:35–41).

I was born near the sea myself, the IJssel Sea, on the Frisian coast. I learned already as a child that it can be quite rough on the former Zuiderzee (South Sea). I remember two stories of storms from the children's Bible by W.G. van de Hulst, which I was brought up with. When we were children, we called them the white storm (Mark 4:35–41) and the black storm.[66] The

---

65. One of Jesus' disciples was a Zealot (Luke 6:15).
66. "He makes winds his messengers, flames of fire his servants" (Ps 104:4). "Who maketh his angels winds, And his ministers a flame of fire" (Heb 1:7; ASV); cf. Isa 29:6;

latter storm, in which Jesus walks over the water, was accompanied by an illustration of it in black (Mark 6:45–52). The other storm had no accompanying picture, so for us it became the white storm (Mark 4:35–41).

"Let us go over to the other side." Here as well water and wind are talked about in imagistic language. It is now a question of understanding the metaphorical significance of water and wind. This is not just a story about literally crossing over to the other side of the Sea of Galilee, even though Jesus and his disciples had undoubtedly done that often. This story is full of symbolism that must be interpreted properly. Their destination is *the opposite shore, the other side*. The Sea of Galilee has two sides: a Jewish side and a heathen side. Jesus tells them to go to the other side.

The sea represents threat and danger:

> Woe to the many nations that rage—
> they rage like the raging sea!
> Woe to the peoples who roar—
> they roar like the roaring of great waters!
> Although the peoples roar like the roar of surging waters,
> when he rebukes them they flee far away,
> driven before the wind like chaff on the hills,
> like tumbleweed before a gale.
> (Isa 17:12–13)

The sea crossings that are recorded in the gospels show in a dramatic way the difficulties facing both the disciples and hearers and readers of this story who wanted to make the journey to the other side with Jesus, to walk the path he walked. Then a storm did indeed break. The disciples were terrified on this sea of life, for the waves broke over the boat, threatening to swamp it. What was Jesus doing? He was lying down—asleep!

The attentive hearer and reader will think here of course of the prophet Jonah (Yûnus) who was told by God to go to the city of Nineveh to the *far east*. But what did he do? He attempted to flee as *far west* as he could and boarded a ship bound for Tarshish in Spain to avoid doing what God commanded him. In the ancient world, Tarshish was the Western end of the earth. Jonah paid for his passage and got on board to sail to Tarshish away from the Lord (cf. Q 37:140). But the Lord sent a strong wind on the sea and a *severe storm* broke out, threatening to destroy the ship. And while the crew members were terrified for their lives, Jonah was *sleeping* in the hold of the ship. The captain woke him: "How can you sleep? Get up and call on your god! Maybe he will take notice of us so that we will not perish" (Jonah 1:6).

Jer 51:1.

The sailors wondered who was responsible for this disaster. Jonah told them that he was fleeing in order to avoid doing what God had told him to do. When they asked him "What should we do to you to make the sea calm down for us?" The storm was getting worse in the meantime. Jonah told them: "Pick me up and throw me into the sea . . . and it will become calm. I know that it is my fault that this great storm has come upon you" (Jonah 1:12).

In the Qur'an Jonah is called Yûnus or the Man of the Fish (Q 21:87; 68:48)[67] and is listed among the messengers of God (Q 4:163; 6:86). The Qur'an contains a paraphrase, as it were, of the whole book of Jonah (Q 37:139–148; cf. 21:87–88).

Jonah was one of those who are sent[68] when he fled from his task via the heavily-laden ship.[69] He cast lots with the crew, was found guilty, and was thrown overboard. Jonah needed a strong reprimand, so a large fish swallowed him. It was his own fault. And if he had not been included among those who praise God, he would have stayed in the belly of the fish until the day when all people will be raised. Then God had him thrown up on dry land (cf. Jonah 2:11), where he became sick. God then grew a gourd plant for him (cf. Jonah 4:6–10) and sent him—as a bringer of good tidings and as a warner—to 100,000 people or more who came to faith (cf. Jonah 4:11), and God provided for them for a while (Q 37:139–148). Jonah called out of the darknesses (Q 21:87; i.e., the darkness of the *belly of the fish*, the darkness of the *depths of the sea*, and the darkness of *the night* that surrounded him.[70] Jonah was thus swallowed and then vomited up again as an *example* for others: "Submit patiently to the judgement of your Lord, / and do not be like the Man of the Fish / who called out [only] as he choked with grief" (Q 68:48).

God sent winds (Q 7:57; cf. Q 25:48)—winds with the good news (*al-riyâh bushran*)[71]—as heralds of His mercy by bringing clouds with rain for the scorched earth![72] "Who else guides you in the darknesses of the land on the proper path and who else sends the winds as harbingers of His mercy?" (Q 27:63). God's signs include His sending the winds so that they bring good news (with the prospect of rain), and that bears witness to his mercy.

67. Jonah is one of the twelve "minor" prophets. The Qur'anic surahs are arranged according to length. The second *surah* is the longest, the 114th is the shortest.

68. *Mursalîn*, from which the word *rasûl*, messenger/apostle is derived.

69. That the ship has a full cargo possibly rests on the fact that it is reported that the crew threw all the cargo overboard (Jonah 1:5); Speyer, *Die biblischen Erzählungen*, 408.

70. Tafsîr, al-Tabarî, cited in *EI*, s.v., Yûnus.

71. Here the Qur'anic equivalent for "gospel" is used; *bushra* is the Hebrew word.

72. *EQ*, s.v., weather, 470–71.

Thus, ships sail by his command and his grace may be sought so that He may be given thanks" (Q 30:46).[73]

> The disciples woke Jesus and said to him, "Teacher, don't you care if we drown?"
>
> He got up, rebuked the wind and said to the waves, "Quiet! Be still!" He said to his disciples, "Why are you so afraid? Do you still have no faith?" Then the wind died down and it was completely calm.
>
> They were terrified and asked each other, "Who is this? Even the wind and the waves obey him!" (Mark 4:38–41)

How can Jesus sleep through the storm? When Jesus got up, he rebuked the wind and the sea, just as God reprimanded the Reed Sea during the Exodus from Egypt. The sea then dried up, and the Israelites could pass through the sea as if they were walking across sand flats, and it was *completely still*. Jesus thus stills the storm here as well. Just as—in that other story of the "black" storm—he walks over the waters of chaos, this means that he breaks through the unjust social and economic barriers. He wants to achieve social and political solidarity among people. He wants to both point out and follow a livable path.[74]

The disciples were perplexed. The question had already been raised about Jesus' "identity," the son of Joseph, from Nazareth. "Can anything good come from there?" (John 1:46). Jesus himself had declared that a prophet is not honored in his own country, Galilee (John 4:44).[75] "'Isn't this the carpenter? Isn't this Mary's son and the brother of James, Joseph, Judas and Simon? Aren't his sisters here with us?' And they took offense at him. Jesus said to them, 'A prophet is not without honor except in his own town, among his relatives and in his own home'" (Mark 6:3–4; cf. John 6:42).

The disciples were not asking what kind of divine being Jesus was,[76] but what kind of *man* he was. Jesus was not a God who descended from heaven. It was not in that sense that he was the incarnation of God on earth. There are no texts in the gospels that read: "the son of God walked along the Lake of Gennesaret," "the son of God lay sleeping in the bow of the ship." No, Jesus is a human being; he is the incarnate Torah ("do justice and love"), he is the Torah personified. But that also means that he is a son of man,

---

73. *EQ*, s.v., weather, 470–71.

74. Myers, *Binding the Strong Man*, 186.

75. KBS on John 4:44.

76. The Messiah is declared by the Christians to be God's son and 'Uzayr by the Jews to be God's son (Q 9:30). This is disputed in the Qur'an; cf. Wessels, *De Moslimse naaste*, 127–31 and Wessels, *Islam in Stories*, chapter 8.

someone who has no place to lay his head (Matt 8:20; Luke 9:58). This story shows to his disciples and thus also to the reader and hearer what it means to be a complete and true human being in God's image and likeness.[77]

Willem Barnard wrote a poem summarizing who this human being is:

> To be human on this earth,
> In this age and time,
> Is to emerge from the water
> And in the desert to stand,
> Not a god among the gods,
> Not an angel and not a beast,
> A living and a dead man,
> A being in wind and fire.
>
> To be human on this earth,
> In this age and time,
> It is accepting that we die,
> Accepting peace and struggle,
> the nights and the days,
> the hunger and the thirst,
> the questions and the fears,
> the sorrow and the pain.
>
> To be human on this earth,
> In this age and time,
> Is to accept the Spirit
> That leads to life itself,
> Not abandoning the others,
> To be open to God's word
> It means that we resist
> the devil on this earth.[78]

The call to travel with him to the other side is still being sounded, in a poem by Muus Jacobse as well:

---

77. Wink, *The Human Being*, 30.

78. *Liedboek*, Hymn 538, stanzas 2–4: "Een mens te zijn op aarde / in deze wereldtijd, / is komen uit het water / en staan in de woestijn, / geen god onder de goden, / geen engel en geen dier, / een levende, een dode, / een mens in wind en vuur.

Een mens te zijn op aarde / in deze wereldtijd, / dat is de dood aanvaarden, / de vrede en de strijd, / de dagen en de nachten, / de honger en de dorst, /de vragen en de angsten, / de kommer en de koorts.

Een mens te zijn op aarde / in deze wereldtijd, / dat is de Geest aanvaarden / die naar het leven leidt; / de mensen niet verlaten, / Gods woord zijn toegedaan. / dat is op deze aarde / de duivel wederstaan."

Go on board, You say,
Leave the beach behind;
Sail against the wind and tide,
Sail unto the other side,
Wait there for me.

It's me, You then say,
Come along with Me,
Come to the other side.
You say, no need to be afraid,
I offer you My hand.[79]

THE PURPOSE AND END OF JESUS' WAY

To understand Jesus' last discourse on the end times, the preeminent apocalyptic sermon, one must also understand that it was written against the background of the decline of the city of Jerusalem that was threatening or had just occurred.

When Vespasian was declared emperor in the year 69 AD by the troops in Syria, he transferred command to his son Titus and ordered him to capture Jerusalem. When Titus arrived with his legion in the spring of 70 AD, he set up camp on the *Mount of Olives east* of the city, but they were hard-pressed when the Jewish freedom fighters made an attack, and it was only with difficulty that Titus managed to prevent a defeat. Jerusalem was captured after a siege that lasted five months. Titus razed Jerusalem and set the "house of God" on fire, crucifying 10,000 of the survivors. Flavius Josephus wrote that "There was not enough wood in Judea for all those crosses."[80]

In the so-called "Synoptic Apocalypse" in the Gospel of Mark, "the Discourse on the End Times" is recounted as follows. On the Mount of Olives, from where Titus would later take the city and raze it later along with the temple, Jesus set himself over against the temple. He had just visited the temple before that, and one of his disciples had said to him: "Look, Teacher! What massive stones! What magnificent buildings!" But He said: "Do you see all these great buildings? Not one stone here will be left on another;

---

79. *Liedboek*, Hymn 917. stanzas 1 and 6: "Ga in het schip, zegt Gij, / steek van het strand / Vaar tegen wind en tij, / vaar naar de overkant, / wacht daar op mij."
"Ik ben het, zegt Gij dan, / Kom maar met Mij / mee naar de overkant. / Wees maar niet bang, zegt Gij, / hier is mijn hand."

80. Rooze, *Marcus*, 7.

every one will be thrown down." And after He had sat down on the Mount of Olives and when no one else was around, Peter, James, John, and Andrew asked him: "Tell us, when will these things happen? And what will be the sign that they are all about to be fulfilled?"

The Mount of Olives is one kilometer from Jerusalem, i.e., the distance of one Sabbath's journey. Here Jesus would later be arrested at night (Luke 21:37; John 8:1), and he prays at the foot of the mountain in the garden of Gethsemane (Matt 26:30–46; Mark 14:26–27; Luke 22:39). The place name here, *Mount of Olives*, is charged with meaning, particularly as the place of judgment (Zech 14:4). The first place in the Old Testament where the Mount of Olives comes up is a reference to the place that David fled to from his son Absalom who had rebelled against him (2 Sam 15:30–32). There is an allusion to it perhaps when Ezekiel was brought from Babylon by God's Spirit to Jerusalem "to the gate of the house of the Lord that faces east" (Ezek 11:1): "The glory of the Lord went up from within the city and stopped above the mountain east of it" (Ezek 11:23).[81]

The "Synoptic Apocalypse" is an apocalyptic, thus a revelatory, text about the coming of the day of the Lord, when God will bring all the nations together to fight against Jerusalem:

> the city will be captured, the houses ransacked, and the women raped. Half of the city will go into exile, but the rest of the people will not be taken from the city. Then the Lord will go out and fight against those nations, as he fights on a day of battle. On that day his feet will stand on the Mount of Olives, east of Jerusalem, and the Mount of Olives will be split in two from east to west, forming a great valley, with half of the mountain moving *north* and half moving *south*. You will flee by my mountain valley. (Zech 14:1–5)[82]

It is on this Mount of Olives, then, that Jesus holds his eschatological discourse (Mark 13; Matt 24:2–44; Luke 21:5–33). The question that occupied the Jews in that time of their war against the Roman occupying forces was: What if the Romans later take Jerusalem? Jesus' answer is shockingly specific: he does not urge his disciples to defend the city but to flee to the mountains (Mark 13:14), just as Lot did when Sodom was destroyed: "Flee to the mountains or you will be swept away!" (Gen 19:17; cf. Matt 24:15).[83]

The criterion according to which *all* nations or cities like Sodom and Gomorrah are judged and condemned, and thus now Jerusalem as well, is

81. *BW*, s.v., olijfberg.
82. KBS on Zech 14:5.
83. Howard-Brook, *"Come Out My People!"* 399.

whether they "have slept with" the holders of imperialistic powers. That is the "prostitution" that is at issue here. In this Jerusalem filled with those who are collaborating with Rome spiritually and politically, there is no future for those who want to follow Jesus' path. That is what Jesus wanted to make clear to his disciples when he heard them talking—so full of admiration and awe—about the grandeur of the temple being built by Herod the Great (Mark 13:1–2)—the murderer of the children in Bethlehem.

It has indeed been said that the gospel of Mark had to have been written before the destruction of Jerusalem. The reasoning here is that Jesus *predicts* that not one stone of those beautiful buildings would remain. If it had been written after the year 70 AD, Jesus would have been reported as having said that the temple was burned. That is the reasoning. But that is precisely a weak—if not wrong—argument for dating the gospel. The gospel is not providing a historical report but a "theological" interpretation of what is happening and will happen, inspired by the Torah and the prophets. And it was known that the city of Jerusalem and the first temple were *burned* during the time of Nebuchadnezzar and by his order (Jer 52:13): the Chaldeans laid siege to the city, invaded it, and set it afire, burning it down to ashes (Jer 32:29). Babylon suffered the same fate in the end:

> I will stretch out my hand against [you destroying mountain]
> roll you off the cliffs,
> and make you a *burned-out* mountain.
> (Jer 51:25)[84]

What Jesus announced—the destruction of the Second Temple—is thus entirely in line with the prophets. Therefore, Jesus was *not* making any *predictions* in this "apocalyptic discourse." He gave no answer to the question of when it would happen. Nor could he. Jesus had no certain knowledge about the end: no one could say anything about the day or the hour, not even the angels in heaven, not even the Son, but only the Father (Mark 13:32; Acts 1:7; cf. Matt 24:36). Only God knows the day and the hour, according to the Qur'an as well (Q 31:34; 33:63; 7:187; cf. 41:47; 43:85; 67:26, 79:42, 44). The prophet Muhammad does not know if the hour is near or still far away (Q 21:109; 72:25). The future event is near. There is no unveiler, no revealer other than God (Q 53:57–58).

What Jesus wants to impress upon his disciples is not to let themselves be driven by fear when they hear of wars and rumors of wars. This *has* to

---

84. The human being is a bringer of corruption (*fasâd*) and bloodshed on the earth (Q 2:30; cf Q 7:86). Cf. Wessels, *The Torah, the Gospel, and the Qur'an*, 57, and Index; see chapter V of this book, p. 157, where the human being is called a bringer of corruption (*fasâd*) and shedder of blood.

happen, but it is not yet the end, Jesus says (Mark 13:7; cf. Dan 2:28). The word "end" can be misleading and put the reader/hearer on the wrong track. History does not move purposefully to its end in and of itself. Nor is there any sense of an inexorable course to history. This discourse is not concerned about the end of time but with a certain understanding of time, for the readers then as well as for the readers and hearers now! When those terrible things happen, we are given glasses that allow us to understand and unmask what *had* to happen then and now and happens again and again. It does not concern the end of the world in a literal sense but the question of what all has to stop and be brought to an end and what shall happen.

There is, namely, a different *imperative* that Mark speaks about here. That is what this bringer of the "counter-Gospel" assures his readers. All nations that continue to engage in wars up until the present must first have the good news proclaimed to them (Mark 13:10; cf. 16:15): how an end can be brought to injustice and misery so that a truly new life can certainly begin.

THE THREE DAYS

This generation is not a good one, Jesus says. They desire a sign, but no sign will be given to this generation than the sign of Jonah (Luke 11:29; cf. Mark 8:11,12). Just as Jonah was in the belly of the fish for *three days and three nights*, so the *Son of Man* will spend three days and three nights in the belly of the earth (Matt 12:40; cf. Jonah 2:1). The number three is a very important number in the Old and New Testaments. A new period of salvation will arrive *after three days*.

The Pharisees, who were engaged in a discussion with Jesus, asked him—with a view to testing him—for *a sign from heaven*. In the Jewish tradition, a sign served to give legitimacy to a message of salvation. In his farewell address on the eve of entering into the Promised Land, Moses says: "[God] will raise up for them a prophet like you [Moses] from among their fellow Israelites, and [God] will put [his] words in his mouth. He will tell them everything [God] command[s] him" (Deut 18:18). Both Peter and Stephen apply this to Jesus in their respective sermons (Acts 3:22–23; Acts 7:37). It was also seen later as a reference to Muhammad—he was also asked for signs (Q 6:37, 109–111, 158; 7:203; 10:20; 13:7, 27; 17:90–93; 20:133; 21:5; 29:50). The signs that Muhammad brings is the message of the Qur'an itself. The almost 7,000 *verses* in the Qur'an are also so many "signs" (*ayât*)—that is, after all, what the verses in the Qur'an are called. Muhammad was sent by God to present those signs (Q 62:2) and not to be led away from them (Q 28:87).

In his last apocalyptic discourse, Jesus says, "At that time people will see the *Son of Man* coming in clouds with great power and glory" (Mark 13:26; cf. Dan 7:13–14). *The reader—including the reader today—is told to understand, to pay attention* (Mark 13:14) and is called *to look to* the clouds of heaven (where the epiphany occurs) and to receive the *vision*, the *insight* into the advent of true humanity that will put an end to the present human world order. True humanity will be achieved. Don't be afraid. The reader is called to hold fast to that, to have unshakeable trust in that promise, and never and in no way to be distracted from losing *sight* of that prospect. This is the message that is proclaimed to all creatures under heaven, writes Paul—the Paul who became a servant of the same gospel (Col 1:23)!

The good news of this "counter-Gospel" turns the community into a counter-movement that goes against the destructive martial tendencies of the rulers then and now, in our time. Concretely, this message entails that they will no longer train for war (Isa 2:4), something that Psalm 76 sings about:

> God is acknowledged in Judah, his name is great in Israel,
> his tent is pitched in Salem, his dwelling is in Zion;
> there he has broken the lightning-flashes of the bow, shield and sword and war.
> Radiant you are, and renowned for the mountains of booty
> taken from them. Heroes are now sleeping their last sleep, the warriors' arms have failed them;
> at your reproof, God of Jacob, chariot and horse stand stunned.
> You, you alone, strike terror! Who can hold his ground in your presence when your anger strikes?
> From heaven your verdicts thunder, the earth is silent with dread
> when God takes his stand to give judgement, to save all the humble of the earth.
> (1–9; NJB)

All those rulers follow in the footsteps of the legion of the boar (the herd of swine).

IT'S GOOD, IT'S GOOD, IT REALLY IS GOOD!

I would like to illustrate the above with a personal story. Every now and then I give lectures in Friesland. Some years ago I was in Dokkum four times in as many weeks. I am not Frisian myself, though I was born in Frisia and feel a connection with the Heitelân. Both my parents are buried there. During one of the lectures, I related that my father had been a minister in Lemmer, where he worked until his premature death in 1945 as a result of his role in the Resistance. During the break, a woman approached me and told me something that really touched me. She herself also came from southwest Frisia, where she had been raised on a farm. Two youths about 18 years old went into hiding on their farm during the war. On a certain Sunday in 1944—possibly the darkest year of the war—when she was about 14, she went with the two of them to the church in that village where my father was preaching that morning. I was deeply moved by what she told me. She still remembered the text my father preached on and what the three points (the common structure for sermons at that time) of that sermon were. And that is not all: she also remembered what songs were sung during the service. The text was Lamentations 3. The three points were: It's good, it's good, it really is good.

The first impression most people would have of the book of Lamentations would be a somber one, if only because of the title. This book is ascribed to the prophet Jeremiah. The first line of Lamentations 3 reads: "I am the man who has seen affliction . . . ." Here the Hebrew word *geber* is used, which means a "real man," so to say—a word that has been adopted in Dutch as *gabber*, which also means "a real man." The Hebrew name Gabriel, the name of the angel who brought apocalyptic messages to Daniel and Mary, is derived from this noun. In this lamentation it is not a "softy" who is speaking but a real man, someone who wants to have us share in what he has experienced. He has certainly gone through hard times, and terrible things are still happening to him. He speaks not only of himself but also of countless others.

Lamentations is the first book of the so-called Megilloth or Five Scrolls, that are read on the ninth day of the month of Ab, August. This is the annual fasting and mourning day on which the destruction of the temple is remembered. The songs were written not long after 586 BC.
The Hebrew title of the book of Lamentations is *echa*, which is generally translated into English as "how": "How deserted lies the city,/ once so full of people!" (Lam 1:1). It could also be translated as "oh" or "ah." "Oh, how deserted lies . . . ." The Hebrew term is characteristic of laments:

> See how the faithful city
> has become a prostitute!
> She once was full of justice;
> righteousness used to dwell in her—
> but now murderers!
> (Isa 1:21)

This is a powerful image of the terrible things that the fall of Jerusalem brought with it. This unknown man relates the immense misery that has come about and paints an extended picture of it. But his lament is not private and personal but for and on behalf of the whole community, as one who has been heavily struck by God's rod and is now in distress, doubt, and in the depths of darkness. He feels abandoned by God, cast off, intensely sick, and is wasting away.

That wasting away can be understood in a very literal way. For a number of years, I counseled someone who was suffering from ALS. A case like that shows that wasting away is not a metaphor but a shocking reality. This was someone whose bones were indeed broken, one by one; This was a person who had once climbed mountains and was now coming closer and closer to the death to which he was banished—trapped in his own body, this heap of misery the only thing left.

It is pointless to scream and cry out. The lamenter seeks access but to whom? To a higher power? To God? That path seems completely cut off. Every prayer remains unheard. Has God concealed himself in the clouds? Does the cry for help reach him? "You have covered yourself with a cloud/ so that no prayer can get through" (Lam 3:44). "Has God forgotten to be merciful?" (Ps 77:9). Do we simply have to endure paralysis, numbness, punishment? And if that is not enough, he also becomes the target of mockery—an object of scorn and abuse.

Speaking of mockery, Peter Steinz, a writer who publishes regularly in the NRC, wrote a number of columns for a year and a half about his aggressive muscular disease and his approaching end. His wife took him to the beach once because he wanted to sit one last time on a terrace by the sea. When she went for a swim, he was approached by a waiter who became upset at him: Steinz was not having anything to eat or drink and therefore had no right to sit there. But he was unable to speak, nor could he eat and drink in a normal way. Indeed, one then becomes a stranger on earth, one becomes unwelcome.

The place where this occurred derives its name from Parnassus, the mountain in Greece north of the city of Delphi. The mountain is two and a half thousand meters high, dedicated to the god Apollo and the Muses. When the god Zeus sent a flood to eradicate humankind, only the top of this mountain rose above the waves. Deucalion and his wife were saved by a boat and managed to reach Parnassus when the waters sank. But many do not have a seaworthy boat, and, even if they do reach Parnassus, there is no true rescue—not in Europe and not on the coast of the North Sea.

The accursed host in the book of Lamentations continues to serve the starving guest bitter and harsh food that he cannot consume. He breaks his teeth eating gravel. Want and misery literally poison the lives of peoples. The speaker gives expression here to the situation that a whole community is trapped in. There is no place to catch his breath, to recover, to rest; he is pressed down into the dust, and any expectation of relief is pointless.

Among the students I taught in Beirut were many Sudanese from the southern part of the Sudan. I still correspond with one of them. His country has been repeatedly torn apart by civil wars—between the Arab Muslim north and the Black, partially Christian south, and then also between different tribes. Once, when it was very bad, I asked him how he and his family were doing and what the situation was like for them. *Oh*, he wrote about his family—by which he meant his extended family, thus including uncles, aunts, cousins—with our family it's all right: only 18 deaths. In an email that he wrote about a new peace proposal that was signed, his somber conclusion was: war is better than a bad peace. *Oh*, his name is Zakaria, which means "God has remembered." Has God remembered the South Sudanese? Or the countless other Africans?

The one praying the lament has reached the lowest point of his misery. Having been apparently cast off, he lets the hand he held out to God until now drop. Together with his community, he keeps thinking of his want and his misery. His life has been poisoned by it, and that misery presses down on him like an immense burden.

And suddenly something happens that defies logic. It is not something that one would expect from him. Suddenly, in all that deep heartrending despondency and doubt, words of confidence sound for the first time. The one whom we heard saying: "My hope in God has departed," who has resigned himself to living without hope, now all of a sudden says:

> The Lord *is good* to those whose hope is in him,
>   to the one who seeks him;
> *it is good* to wait quietly
>   for the salvation of the Lord.
> *It is good* for a man to bear the yoke
>   while he is young.

"Good" is mentioned three times. That had to be the source of the three points in my father's sermon in 1944. The one praying this lament wants to pull us out of the pit of doubt and fear. The lines of the poem summon its readers and hearers to this new confidence and new certainty. They call for patience. That can be heard countless times in Arabic in the Middle East: "God is with those who have patience" (*Allah ma'a sabarien*). The poet wants us to believe that all these terrible experiences do not take away the fact that

God's grace knows no limits. The terrible events do not cancel out God's faithfulness. It is experienced every day anew, morning after morning.

More than forty years ago I was in Mahdiyya in Tunisia with my wife and two sons, aged five and three. The name of this place comes from Mahdî, the Muslim name for the Messiah whom Muslims expect will return to earth to restore law and justice. They also associate Jesus' return with this. The city of Mahdiyya is located on a peninsula surrounded by the sea. We stayed then with a priest who was a member of an order that is active primarily in Africa ("White Fathers") and was a great scholar of Islamic theology.[85] He lived in the oldest part of the city, the old "Medina," as it is called.

Early one morning—how coincidental that it was morning!—the four of us walked over the cemetery at the most extreme part of this peninsula, with the sea lapping at its shores. The children ran, as children do, between the graves. And without any one of us suggesting it, they suddenly began to sing spontaneously: "Stil maar wacht, maar alles wordt nieuw!" ("Be still and wait, everything will be made new!"). *Oh, though you lie in your grave, what else can you do but be still and wait?* "Through the praise of children and infants / you have established a stronghold against your enemies" (Ps 8:2).

Lamentations paints a portrait of a believing man, a "real man." He finds strength to avoid being shocked at anything in the fact that he knows that God is his refuge in which he is protected, even when war threatens. It is good for whoever hopes in him, good for those wait in silence for liberation. These are the only explicit words of hope in this book of Lamentations that is full of forsakenness, disconsolateness, and sadness. Despite that forsakenness and sadness, I will remember what gives me hope: the grace of the Lord knows no limits, his compassion is inexhaustible. His mercies know no end, and they are renewed every morning.

It's good, it's good, it really is good! Can we still believe that? Or do we echo the hopelessness of a Moroccan father with his sons who stated so dejectedly: "Everything will be turn out fine"? Were those three points a good division for a sermon in the dark times of 1944? Are they the right division now?

That 14-year-old Frisian girl in 1944 who told me about my father's sermon 70 years later also remembered what was sung in those dark "brown" days of 1944. It was primarily psalms, and when I looked up one of those psalms in the 1773 psalter, which were still sung in the Dutch churches until 1973, I was deeply moved again. I was eight years old when my father died a year after that sermon, in 1945. When I reread those words from that psalter

---

85. Caspar, *Traité de théologie musulmane*.

that I also sang countless times as a child, I was suddenly struck by them. Indeed, that was the piety of my father in which he raised us as children.

> Record my misery;
> > list my tears on your scroll—
> > are they not in your record?
> Then my enemies will turn back
> > when I call for help.
> > By this I will know that God is for me.
> In God, whose word I praise,
> > in the Lord, whose word I praise—
> > in God I trust and am not afraid.
> > What can man do to me?
> I am under vows to you, my God;
> > I will present my thank offerings to you.
> For you have delivered me from death
> > and my feet from stumbling,
> that I may walk before God
> > in the light of life.
> (Ps 56:8–13)[86]

---

86. Cf. Kraus, *Klagelieder (Threni)*, 53–70; O'Connor, *Lamentation & the Tears of the World*, 44–57; Dobbs-Allsopp, *Lamentations*, 109–16.

VII

Paul to the Ends of the Earth

I plan to do so when I go to Spain [the ends of the earth]. I hope to see you while passing through and to have you assist me on my journey there, after I have enjoyed your company for a while. (Romans 15:24)

INTRODUCTION

On Saturday evening, 28 June 2008, on the eve of the feast of the apostles Peter and Paul, Pope Benedict XVI formally opened "the Year of Paul."[1] The reason for this Year of Paul was that it was about 2000 years ago that this apostle and martyr was born. Paul is often viewed as the true founder of the church and Christianity. His letters, especially the one to the church in Rome, have played an enormous role in the development of Christian theology and dogmatics up until the present. One of the elements of those letters has to do with the way in which he speaks of the "law" (*nomos*) that is often explained as directly opposed to the Gospel. That has led to a "one-liner": Jews have the law, Christians have the Gospel. Paul's argument in his letter to the Romans has become one of the reasons for this "Christian" understanding of the "law": "*For Christ is the end [telos] of the law*" (Rom 10:4).

---

1. https://leiden.courant.nu/issue/LLC/1951-09-22/edition/0/page/4?query=1. In cache Paulus herdenking in 1951.

In an otherwise excellent dictionary of the Qur'an, an article on the gospels discusses this alleged fundamental difference between the thinking that arises from the gospels and Paul especially and that of the Qur'an. According to Paul, the Christian is "liberated" from the Mosaic law (Gal 3:25–29). "In contrast, one of the greatest concerns of Islam—the *shari'ah*—is a complete return to the Mosaic law, slightly modified, with an emphasis on the most strict and stern adherence to it."[2]

That, however, is a legalistic view of both the Torah or *nomos* as well as the Islamic law and thus of the whole Qur'an. The complete verse in Paul's letter reads: "For Christ is the end of the law for righteousness to every one who believes." There is a widespread tendency to take this verse out of context and thus to give it a radical interpretation as if it concerns the termination of the "law": Christ as the end of the law (Rudolph Bultmann).[3] The Greek word *telos*, which is usually translated as "end," can, however, be best and most correctly rendered as "fulfillment" or "goal." In English, "purpose" is a good translation. It is precisely the teleological perspective that is primary in this verse: "for righteousness to every one who believes." The objective and purpose of the law was and still is the ultimate uniting of all peoples under the God of Abraham according to the promise. Christ's righteousness is not connected to a certain, specific group but is intended for all who believe, and it ignores the boundaries between the nations, between Greeks, Jews, and barbarians. Its purpose is nothing less than peace and the uniting of the whole world.[4]

In this chapter we will look at the figure of Paul and his apocalyptic understanding of the message that he intended to take to the ends of the earth. He has indeed been called "Paul the Apocalypticist."[5] Already as a Pharisee, he lived in the hope of the fulfillment of the Messianic promises.[6] Contemporary Arabic apocalyptic literature contains conspiracy theories that depict Paul as the one who successfully perverted Jesus' teachings and corrupted the New Testament. These authors are convinced that this Jewish conspiracy led directly to the confrontation of Muhammad with the Jews who lived in Medina.[7] We will not look at such gratuitous, unfounded assertions but attempt to probe Paul's real intent.

---

2. *Dictionnaire du Coran, s.v*, Évangiles, 290.

3. Jewett, *Romans*, 619, n. 125.

4. Jewett, *Romans*, 619–20.

5. Beker, *Paul the Apostle*, chapter 5: "Paul's Apocalyptic Theology: Apocalyptic and the Resurrection of Christ," 135–81.

6. Beker, *Paul the Apostle*, 143.

7. Cook, *Contemporary Muslim Apocalyptic Literature*, 20–21.

Paul introduced himself as an *apostle to the Gentiles* or all nations (Rom 1:5; 11:13). The prophet Jeremiah, with whom Paul is compared, was called a prophet for the nations. Paul talks about his call in same terms as those used for the ancient prophets when they were called (e.g., Jer 1:5).

> But God in his grace chose me even before I was born, and called me to serve him. And when he decided to reveal his Son to me, so that I might preach the Good News about him to the Gentiles, I did not go to anyone for advice, nor did I go to Jerusalem to see those who were apostles before me. Instead, I went at once to Arabia, and then I returned to Damascus. (Gal 1:15–17)

Paul was called (Rom 1:1), while on the road to Damascus (Gal 1:16) and was recognized by the other apostles who were esteemed as pillars of the faith. (Gal 2:7, 9).[8]

Having now introduced Paul, I will now look particularly at the meaning of specifically two visions he had. The *first* was when he was on his way to Syria as a persecutor of Jesus' followers. This was not so much a conversion experience as often stated, but a *call*.[9] The *second* was the vision that he had in Troas or Troy on the eve of his journey as a Jew to Europe, which led to his going to the ends of the earth—to Tarshish in Spain.

PAUL'S BACKGROUND AND HIS WORLD

Paul was born around the year 8 in Asia Minor in Tarsus. This city had been part of Syria since the death of Alexander the Great. His Hebrew name was Saul, after King Saul (Tâlût; Q 2:247–250);[10] like him, he came from the tribe of Benjamin. In addition, he also had the Latin name Paul or Paulus. Tarsus should not be confused with Tarshish, the destination of the ship on which Jonah (Yûnus; cf. Q 37:139–148) sought to flee (Jonah 1:3; cf. Ps 139:7).[11] Paul also sought to go to Tarshish, but with the goal of his mission, rather than flight.

Paul was born and raised in a very different setting than Jesus had been. He grew up between two cultures—the Jewish culture on the one hand and the Greek or Hellenistic on the other—and he was proud of counting as home a city with a mixed population of people from Asia Minor—Greeks and Jews. It was a prosperous Greek city famous as a center of science and

---

8. Jewett, *Romans*, 678–79.
9. Krister Stendahl, cited in Elliot, *Liberating Paul*, 140.
10. Cf. Wessels, *The Torah, The Gospel, and the Qur'an*, 154–57.
11. https://en.wikipedia.org/wiki/Tarsus,_Mersin.

philosophy[12] and had an active intellectual life in which *philosophers* and *poets* played a prominent role. It was even said that it exceeded Athens and Alexandria in such culture. Because of that, he could interact with Epicurean and Stoic philosophers (Acts 17:18). Paul quoted, for instance, from the poem *Phaenomena* by the Greek poet Aratus (ca. 315–ca. 245 BC), who came from his area of Cilicia and had lived in the court of the Ptolemies in Egypt:[13] "'In him we live and move and have our being.' As some of your poets have said, 'We are his offspring'" (Acts 17:28). This quote is also found in a hymn to Zeus by Cleanthes (ca. 330–232 BC), a Greek philosopher from the same Hellenistic period.[14]

Paul was a Roman citizen. As a strict religious Pharisee, he followed the Jewish laws much more stringently than many people his age and was completely devoted to the traditions of his ancestors (Gal 1:13–14). He learned to be a tentmaker in order to support himself. Cilicia was well known for its canvas made from goat hair.[15] Paul lived in the Roman Empire over which Augustus (63 BC–14 AD) ruled when Jesus and he himself were born, and Tiberius (42 BC–37 AD) when Jesus was crucified. Nero was emperor (54–68 AD) when Paul was put on trial and, according to the tradition, executed.

Although Paul was probably already living in Jerusalem during the last years of Jesus' life, there is nothing to indicate that he ever knew Jesus personally or heard him speak. Even though Paul probably never knew Jesus himself, he certainly was no stranger to Jerusalem. He was obviously in total agreement with Jesus' opponents that this man constituted a great danger to the Jewish people. The quick growth of his movement incited Paul's great fear and concern, and he stood approvingly by as a witness to the execution of the first "Christian" martyr, Stephen, a Jew from the diaspora like himself. When Stephen was dragged out of the city to be stoned, the witnesses placed their cloaks in the care of a young man called Saul (Acts 7:58). Here Paul was introduced by his Hellenized name, Saul:[16] "And when your witness Stephen was put to death, I myself was there, approving of his murder and taking care of the cloaks of his murderers" (Acts 22:20). In the book of Acts, Paul is first called Saul, but his Latin name Paulus/Paul is used as soon as he interacts with a Roman for the first time in the book (Acts 13:9).[17]

12. Küng, *Grosze christliche Denker*, 17.
13. https://en.wikipedia.org/wiki/Aratus.
14. Stählin, *Die Apostelgeschichte*, 236; Haenchen, *Die Apostelgeschichte*, 462.
15. *BW*, s.v., tentenmaker; cf. Heb 18:3.
16. KBS on Acts 7:58.
17. KBS on Acts 13:9.

PAUL AS PERSECUTOR ON THE WAY TO SYRIA AND HIS CALL VISION

For Saul, the followers of Jesus constituted a threat to everything that was dear to him: the law, the temple, and the traditions of his people. This was, after all, a sect that declared a man hanging on a cross to be the Messiah, whereas the Torah nevertheless clearly teaches that a man hanging between heaven and earth is cursed by God (Gal 3:13; cf. Deut 21:23).[18] He was the persecutor par excellence of the first disciples of Jesus: "I persecuted without mercy the congregation of God and did my best to destroy it" (Gal 1:13). He raged against the assemblies and went from house to house, dragging out both men and women and throwing them into prison (Acts 8:3).[19] His first target was apparently the "Christian" Jews from the diaspora who had come to Jerusalem, which is why many of them fled to other cities like Damascus and Antioch. That is why he asked the high priest for letters for the Damascus synagogues giving him permission to arrest *all followers of the Way* he found and bring them back to Jerusalem. (Acts 9:1-2).[20] I have deliberately placed "Christian" between quotation marks because this is in fact an anachronistic term. The book of Acts refers six times to the movement or way of life of the followers of Jesus as "the people of the Way" (cf. Acts 19:9, 23; 22:4; 24:14, 22)!

About five years after the crucifixion of Jesus, when Paul himself was around 30 years old, he went to Syria with those letters. But then something special happened to him on the way there, which is related three times in the book of Acts (Acts 9:1-22; 22:1-21; 26:15-18). As he nears Damascus, he is suddenly surrounded by a blinding *light*. When Paul is on trial later, he tells King Herod Agrippa II, the great-grandson of Herod the Great, about this experience as part of his defense: "'It was on the road at midday, Your Majesty, that I saw a light much brighter than the sun, coming from the sky and shining around me and the men traveling with me. All of us fell to the ground, and I heard a voice say to me in Hebrew, 'Saul, Saul! Why are you persecuting me?'" (Acts 26:13-14; cf. 9:3-4).

> "Who are you, Lord?" I asked. And the Lord answered, "I am Jesus, whom you persecute. But get up and stand on your feet. I have appeared to you to appoint you as my servant. You are to tell others what you have seen of me today and what I will show you in the future. I will rescue you from the people of Israel and

---

18. Cf. Josh 8:29; 10:26-27; John 19:31.
19. Cf. Acts 22:4-5,19; 26:10-11; 1 Cor 15:19; Gal 1:13; Phil 3:6; 1 Tim 1:13.
20. KBS on Acts 9:2.

from the Gentiles to whom I will send you. You are to open their eyes and turn them from the darkness to the light and from the power of Satan to God." (Acts 26:15–18)

Paul's fellow travelers were struck dumb: they *heard* the voice but *saw* no one (Acts 9:7). Another retelling says that his fellow travelers *saw* the light but did not *hear* the voice of the one who spoke to him (Acts 22:9), and in the third retelling, the light also shone around his traveling companions (Acts 26:13). Did Paul see the risen Lord? Or does it mean that he was blinded by the light? Ananias, a Jewish follower of Jesus in Damascus was commanded by God in a vision to lay hands on him so that he would be able to see again (Acts 9:10–18).

In the *second* report of his experience, the content of what the heavenly voice said to him is also supplemented: "He said, 'The God of our ancestors has chosen you to know his will, to see his *righteous Servant*, and *to hear him speaking with his own voice*. For you will be a witness for him to tell everyone what you have *seen and heard*'" (Acts 22:14–15).

The *voice* speaks even more completely in the *third retelling*:

> But get up and stand on your feet. I have appeared to you to appoint you as my servant. You are to tell others what you have *seen* of me today and what I will show you in the future. I will rescue you from the people of Israel and from the Gentiles to whom I will send you. You are to *open their eyes* and turn them *from the darkness to the light*. (Acts 26:16–18a; cf. Isa 42:7; Col 1:12–14; 1 Pet 2:9)

In this final version of what happened, which is part of his legal defense before King Agrippa, Paul uses the genre of the *prophetic vision*. This is similar to the vision call of the prophet Ezekiel, where God says to him: "Son of man, stand up. *I want to talk to you*" (Ezek 2:1) and to the prophet Daniel: "The angel said to me, 'Daniel, God loves you. Stand up and listen carefully to what I am going to say. I have been sent to you'" (Dan 10:11).

If Luke, the author of the book of Acts, speaks of a *blinding light* that Paul saw on the way to Damascus (Acts 9:1–22; 22:6–16; 26:9–23), Paul himself is somewhat more restrained about this in his letters, saying nothing more than that God decided "to *reveal* [*apokalyptein*] his Son to me, so that I might preach the Good News about him to the Gentiles" (Gal 1:16). Specific to Paul's experience is his emphasis that he saw Jesus Christ in heaven (Gal 1:15–16; 1 Cor 9:1): "*This insight into the apocalyptic content of Paul's vision is the key to understanding the force of his 'conversion'.*"[21]

---

21. Elliot, *Liberating Paul*, 142; italics his.

What did that insight mean for this Pharisee who thought in such apocalyptic terms, who persecuted the assemblies of the crucified Messiah?[22] Paul attempted to suppress the Messianic movement in Damascus because their preaching constituted a danger to the precarious position of the Jewish community there. His zeal for ancestral traditions (Gal 1:14; cf. Phil 3:6) was not focused on keeping the law but on political considerations; his concern was that each Jew would be able to survive Roman rule. In fact, Paul's motives were formed by apocalyptic traditions that were operative in the political climate of Judea under Roman occupation. Apocalyptic was the medium by which the Jews held to their faith under foreign oppression.[23]

There are always two things that happen to prophets when they are *called*: they *see* something and they *hear* something. Moses *sees* a burning bush and *hears* a voice. Then the angel of the Lord appeared to him in a flame that flared up out of the bush. Moses saw that the bush was on fire but that it did not burn up. "This is strange," he thought. "Why isn't the bush burning up? I will go closer and see." When the Lord saw that Moses was coming closer, he *called* to him from the middle of the bush and said, "Moses! Moses!" He answered, "Yes, here I am" (Exod 3:2–4).

There is a similarity here to the *call* of the prophet Samuel (Samwîl; cf. Q 2:246).[24] While the young Samuel is asleep in the sanctuary of the Lord, where the ark of God was, he heard someone call *three times* and each time he went to the priest Eli because he thought Eli was calling him. When Samuel did this the third time, Eli then understood that it was the Lord who was calling the boy. He then told Samuel: "Go back to bed, and if He calls you again, say: 'Speak, Lord, your servant is listening.'" Samuel went back to bed, and then the Lord appeared to him and called, just like the previous times. "Samuel, Samuel!" And Samuel answered, "Speak, your servant is listening" (1 Sam 3:1–10).

What is the characteristic moment at which the call begins, the central moment in the case of all three—Moses, Samuel, and Paul? Their names are called twice in succession! The use of the proper name indicates the person, indicates who he is. "A person is his name." This was the case, for instance, with a certain man who was called Nabal: his name means "fool" and that is what he truly was (1 Sam 25:25). One's name expresses one's being and the core of what one is, one's existence. Calling someone flat out by his name is asking for access to someone's heart.

22. Elliot, *Liberating Paul*, 143.
23. Elliot, *Liberating Paul*, 148–49.
24. This prophet is mentioned in the Qur'an but not by name. Q 2:246 (the request for a king; cf. 1 Sam 8; in connection with Goliath (Jalût). Cf. 1 Sam 7:14; Q 2:248 (the ark will be brought to Samuel as sign of his kingship; cf. 1 Sam 5–9).

A striking illustration in literature can be found in Charles Dickens's well-known *Christmas Carol* about the miser Scrooge who was visited in one night by three ghosts—those of Christmas past, present, and future—and as a result comes to *new insight* about himself and the world. The most important moment when it truly begins is when Scrooge is called by his full name![25] *Ebenezer Scrooge*. Who are you? What are you doing, for God's sake? Thus, it follows that Paul's name would be spoken twice, just as Moses' and Samuel's were: "Saul, Saul! Why do you persecute me?" (Acts 9:4).[26] The only thing Paul can manage to say is: "Who are you, Lord?" What he then receives as an answer causes his whole world to collapse, as a result of which he becomes a new man: "I am Jesus, whom you persecute" (Acts 9: 5; 22:8; 26:15). He suddenly realizes, suddenly gets it, understands that this heavenly light is from God, whom he thought he had served his whole life but until now has obviously completely misunderstood. The blinding light shows how *blind* he was when he persecuted the followers of Jesus.

PAUL'S CALL AND MUHAMMAD'S

Comparisons are often made between Christianity and Islam. The Bible and the Qur'an, for instance, or Jesus and Muhammad are often compared with each other. But that is not very helpful. If one wants comparisons with respect to content, Jesus should be compared not with Muhammad but with the Qur'an. In the Qur'an, Jesus is called the Word of God and the Spirit of God (Q 4:171). Muhammad is also compared to Mary. Just as she received Jesus, so Muhammad received the message in his heart (Q 2:97): "This is indeed [a Book] sent down by the Lord of all the worlds, brought down by the Trustworthy Spirit upon your heart in a clear Arabic language" (Q 26:192–195).

Paul and Muhammad can be compared as well. Both are messengers of God and are sent to the nations as apostles. In both cases, we hear of a heavenly journey and the way in which both are called. One could think of the parallelism between both *experiences* of revelation. They include both an *auditory* and a *visual* experience—*hearing* and *seeing*. It is fascinating to look at two strophes from the longest Psalm, i.e., Psalm 119, which is ultimately about the Torah. In Huub Oosterhuis's reworking of this Psalm, the refrain is: "Ik heb u lief mijn Thora zal altijd aan u denken" (I love you, my Torah, I will always think of and meditate on you). The two strophes in this

---

25. Roes, *Dickens*.

26. Gen 22:10–11: "Then he picked up the knife to kill him. But the angel of the Lord called to him from heaven, 'Abraham, Abraham!' He answered, 'Yes, here I am.'"

psalm, one beginning with the Hebrew letter Qoph of the word for *call* and the next with the letter Resh of the Hebrew word for *seeing*, read as follows:

> *Qoph*:
> I call with all my heart; answer me, Lord,
> and I will obey your decrees.
> I call out to you; save me
> and I will keep your statutes.
> I rise before dawn and cry for help;
> I have put my hope in your word.
> My eyes stay open through the watches of the night,
> that I may meditate on your promises.
> Hear my voice in accordance with your love;
> preserve my life, Lord, according to your laws.
> Those who devise wicked schemes are near,
> but they are far from your law.
> Yet you are near, Lord,
> and all your commands are true.
> Long ago I learned from your statutes
> that you established them to last forever.
> (Ps 119:145–152)
>
> *Resh*:
> Look on my suffering and deliver me,
> for I have not forgotten your law.
> Defend my cause and redeem me;
> preserve my life according to your promise.
> Salvation is far from the wicked,
> for they do not seek out your decrees.
> Your compassion, Lord, is great;
> preserve my life according to your laws.
> Many are the foes who persecute me,
> but I have not turned from your statutes.
> I look on the faithless with loathing,
> for they do not obey your word.
> See how I love your precepts;
> preserve my life, Lord, in accordance with your love.
> All your words are true;
> all your righteous laws are eternal.
> (Ps 119:153–160)

On the way to Damascus, Paul *sees* the light and *hears* a voice. something similar happens to the prophet Muhammad: he hears a voice that tasks him to speak, perhaps the first or oldest revelation he receives: "*Speak* in the name of your Lord who created man from an embryo" (Q 96:1–2).[27] In Arabic, the word *iqra'* is used, which—just like its Hebrew cognate—means "to speak," "to call." Muhammad is not called to read, as the verb is often incorrectly translated, but *to recite, to read aloud*. And what he has to call out, present, recite is the *qur'an*, thus, the Qur'an.

Muhammad, therefore, had *visionary* experiences, just like Moses, Samuel, and Paul. There are two visions (Q 53:1–12, 13–18). God (or is it the angel of God, Gabriel?) also appears to him: "Certainly he [Muhammad] saw him [God or Gabriel] on the manifest horizon, and he [Muhammad] is not miserly concerning the Unseen" (Q 81:23–24).[28]

THE PARABLE OF THE UNBELIEVING CITY: "ANTIOCH"

A later collaborator of Paul was Joseph, one whom the apostles called Barnabas, "Son of Consolation" (Acts 4:36), a Levite from Cyprus. He was an early convert of the temple community in Jerusalem and supported the church by selling some land (Acts 4:37). Barnabas was an important link between the Jewish and non-Jewish believers and defended Paul who was viewed with suspicion by those whom he had earlier persecuted (Acts 9:27). Under his leadership, the church in Antioch grew so quickly that Barnabas went to Tarsus to ask for Saul's help. They collaborated for a full year in Antioch, and it was also in Antioch that the disciples were called "Christians" for the first time, after Christ (Acts 11:26). In Judea, they were called Nazarenes, after Jesus the Nazarene.[29] Barnabas managed to further the unity between Jews and non-Jews during a severe famine (Acts 11:30). That happened during the reign of Emperor Claudius (41–54 AD) when there was a shortage of food in many provinces. Barnabas was sent out with Paul (Acts 13:1–3) and built up the mission work with Paul on Cyprus and the cities of Asia Minor, Cilicia, and Lycaonia (Acts 13–14).[30]

In Antioch, Paul was included among the prophets and teachers there (Acts.13:1; cf. 11:27; 15:32; Eph 2:20). Situated on the Orontes River, Antioch was once the residence of the Seleucids (1 Macc 3:37). Seleucus I Nicator, one of Alexander the Great's generals, founded the city around 300 BC,

27. My translation; the book of Leviticus begins with the same word: The Lord called Moses (Lev 1:1: *wayiqra*). The Qur'an draws its name from that recitation.

28. What the name "Gabriel" means is a question of interpretation. The oldest view is that it was God who appeared to Muhammad.

29. Cf. Acts 24:5; KBS on Acts 11:28.

30. *Alle Bijbelse personen*, s.v., Barnabas; *BW*, s.v., Barnabas.

and it was occupied in 64 BC by Pompey the Great, a military and political leader of the late Roman Republic. It became the largest and most important Roman city in Asia and the capital of the Asian provinces of the Roman Empire. It later became the third city of the world, after Rome and Alexandria, the capital of the Roman province Syria. Ten per cent of the population were Jewish.[31] The mission among the Greeks, i.e., the non-Jews, began there. It was the springboard for the missionary work among the Gentiles, especially that of Paul (Acts 11:25; 13:1–3, 14:26; 18:22).[32]

The only important Muslim monument is the sanctuary below the former citadel, called Habîb al-Najjâr, the "Carpenter," identified in Muslim tradition with the unnamed believer referred to in the Qur'an (Q 36:12–26). This legendary character was put to death for having urged the city's inhabitants not to reject the three apostles who had come to proclaim the divine message to them.[33]

The Qur'an tells a parable of an "unbelieving city," which Muslim tradition identifies with Antioch.[34] The parable coheres with the activities of Paul in Lystra and Derbe, which are related in the books of Acts. Paul and his companion Barnabas had to deal with leaders of Gentiles and Jews who attempted to use violence against them and to stone them. They fled elsewhere.

> In Lystra there sat a man who was lame. He had been that way from birth and had never walked. He listened to Paul as he was speaking. Paul looked directly at him, saw that he had faith to be healed and called out, "Stand up on your feet!" At that, the man jumped up and began to walk.
> When the crowd saw what Paul had done, they shouted in the Lycaonian language, "The gods have come down to us in human form!" Barnabas they called Zeus, and Paul they called Hermes because he was the chief speaker. The priest of Zeus, whose temple was just outside the city, brought bulls and wreaths to the city gates because he and the crowd wanted to offer sacrifices to them. (Acts 14:8–13)

To understand what is going on in the above account, we need to look at the following story. One day, Ovid relates, an old couple, Philemon and Baucis in Tyana, were visited by two strangers. Despite their poverty, they

---

31. KBS on Acts 11:19; *EI, s.v.*, Antâkia.
32. *BW, s.v.*, Antiochië.
33. *EQ, s.v.*, Antâkiya; Habib al-Nadjdjâr.
34. Watt, *Companion*, 201.

welcomed their guests with open arms[35] and prepared an excellent meal for them. It becomes clear in the story that there is something special about the visitors. For example, the pitcher containing wine remains full. To pamper their guests even more, Philemon and Baucis decide to slaughter their goose. Baucis chases it, but it constantly eludes her. When the goose sits on the lap of the chief god, the visitors introduce themselves as Zeus and Hermes. Out of thankfulness for their generous reception, which the rest of the village has not offered, the gods take their host and hostess to a hill, and the whole village is punished by a flood.

Zeus and Hermes ask if Philemon and Baucis have a wish that they can grant as gratitude for their hospitality. They wish for nothing more than to worship the two gods their whole lives. Their small hut suddenly changes into a large temple. They also wanted nothing more than to stay with each other, and, when the time came for one of them to die, it was their wish that the other would die as well. It thus happened that one day in front of the temple Philemon and Baucis are changed into an oak and a lime tree. They stood there for many years, their trunks intertwined.[36]

In the Acts of the Apostles, the exuberant reception of Paul and Barnabas—two generations after Ovid—following the healing is described as follows: "they shouted . . .: "The gods have come down to us in human form!" (Acts 14:11). The inhabitants of Lystra believed that Zeus and Hermes had taken human form, in the older Barnabas and Paul, respectively, and wanted to make sacrifices to them in the temple of "Zeus outside the walls."[37] When the apostles heard that, they tore their clothes and rushed out into the crowd: "Friends, why are you doing this? We too are only human, like you. We are bringing you good news, telling you to turn from these worthless things to the *living* God, who made the *heavens* and the *earth* and the *sea* and everything in them" (cf. Exod 20:11; Neh 9:6; Ps 146:6; Rev 10:6). But not even this could prevent the people from making an offering to them. However, Jews from Antioch and Iconium came who managed to talk the people round. So they *stoned* Paul and dragged him outside the city, thinking he was dead. But when the disciples had gathered around him, he stood up and went into the city (Acts 14:5–20).

In connection with this story, the Qur'an tells the following parable about two messengers (*mursalûna*)[38] of Jesus who visited Antioch, possibly

---

35. *Xenia*, the Greek term for hospitality.

36. https://en.wikipedia.org/wiki/Baucis_and_Philemon; Ovid, *Metamorphoses*, VIII, 611–724. pp. 195–98.

37. *BW*, s.v., Zeus.

38. The noun is *rasûl*, which means apostle, the sent one. The prophet Muhammad is both prophet (*nabi*) and envoy, apostle, messenger (*rasûl*).

in connection with the story just related above. When God sent two of them, they called them liars. Then God sent them a third, and they said: "We have been sent to you." But the city's inhabitants said: "You are just people like us, and the Merciful has not revealed anything to you. You are telling us nothing but lies." The messengers said: "Our Lord knows that we have been sent to you. We are duty-bound to warn you." The inhabitants of the city replied: "We see you as a bad omen. If you don't stop, we will certainly stone you, and you will certainly be severely punished by us. The messengers said, "You yourselves bear your own bad omens. If you don't want to be admonished. No, you are a sinful people!" (Q 36:13-19).[39]

The purpose of stoning is not only to kill someone; it can also be a means to chase them away (Q 11:91).[40] Abraham's father, who worshiped idols, says to his son: "Abraham! Are you renouncing my gods? If you do not relinquish, I will stone you" (Q 19:46; cf. 18:20). Here this means chasing him away by stoning him. Then the story about the messengers continues as follows:

> There came a man from the city outskirts,[41] hurrying [cf. Q 28:19]. He said, "O my people! Follow the apostles! Follow them who do not ask you any reward and they are rightly guided. Why should I not worship Him who has *originated* me, and to whom you shall be brought back? Shall I take gods besides Him? If the All-beneficent desired to cause me any distress their intercession will not avail me in any way, nor will they rescue me. Indeed then I would be in manifest error. Indeed I have faith in your Lord, so listen to me." (Q 36:20-25)[42]

THE VISION OF THE MACEDONIAN MAN IN TROY

There is a second moment in Paul's life in which he has a vision that sends him to "the ends of the earth" (Acts 15:36-28:31). The *second journey* (Acts 15:36—18:22) brings him to Europe, to cities like Athens, Corinth, and Ephesus. This journey is an independent undertaking by Paul, given that he does not report on his journey after returning to Antioch—in contrast to before, when the church was called together after he returned and he

---

39. Paret on Q 11:91f., 242.
40. Paret on Q 11:91f., 242.
41. Speyer, *Biblische Erzählungen*, 248.
42. *EQ*, s.v., parable; most identify the town with Antioch, though this identification cannot be verified. Cf. Nasr, *The Study Quran*, 1073.

did report on the fact that God had opened the door for the faith of the Gentiles (Acts 18:22–23). A *third journey* brought him again to Macedonia and Achaea (Acts 18:23—21:14). Upon arriving in Jerusalem after that trip, he was taken prisoner (Acts 21:15–23; 35). Just like Jesus, he not only had to answer to the *Sanhedrin* in Jerusalem (Acts 22:30—23:11), but he also had to appear in Caesarea before the *Roman governor* as well as before a Jewish king (Acts 24:1—26:32). Because he then appealed to Caesar, he was brought to Rome as a prisoner (Acts 27:1—28:16). In the capital of the empire, he was, however, free to proclaim the Gospel without hindrance—so ends the book of Acts.[43]

Some editions of the Bible include maps of these journeys, which ultimately end in Rome where Paul was executed by the sword. This is not reported in the book of Acts but is known only from the tradition. The various trips did not occur in line with, so to say, any fixed marching orders in which he knew beforehand where precisely he would be led. There did not seem to be any clear and defined plan. And if there was, everything seemed to go against him. Paul and his companions felt hindered and thwarted in their work. His original goal was apparently Ephesus, the capital of the Roman province of Asia (the *western* part of Asia Minor). The route he follows goes *northward* first (Galatia, north of Lycaonia where Iconium was[44] and then westward through Phrygia and Mysia until Troas at the Hellespont):[45] they "traveled throughout the region of Phrygia and Galatia, *having been kept by the Holy Spirit from preaching the word in the province of Asia*. When they came to the border of Mysia, they tried to enter Bithynia, but *the Spirit of Jesus would not allow them to*. So they passed by Mysia and went down to Troas" (Acts 16:6-8). They cannot follow the route they had planned precisely. It does not work. Or, as the text states much more sharply: *He did not want it. The Spirit of Jesus* would not allow them to.[46] The Spirit of Jesus clearly blocked the way of Paul a few times in succession. He cannot go any further and is stranded in Troas.

In the end, Paul arrives in a Asiatic port city, Troas, a name that says little at first to most people but should ring a bell if one realizes that the city is called Troas because it is close to the famous city of Troy that was destroyed by the Greeks in the Trojan War. In other words, they did not end up just anywhere. After all, whoever says "Troy" says "Homer." The *Iliad* is the

---

43. Schneider, *Die Apostelgeschichte*,193.
44. The current Konya where the famous mystic Jamal al-Din al Rûmî is buried.
45. KBS on Acts 16:6-8.
46. Jesus is called "the Spirit of God" (*Rûh Allâh*) in the Qur'an; cf. Q 19:17; 21:91; 66:12; 4:171.

story of the tragedy about and around the city of Troy. The Greeks fought with the Trojans over that city, and countless people were killed during that ten-year war. The story of Odysseus's return after twenty years' absence to his home in Ithaca is told in Homer's *Odyssey*. According to myth, the war arose out of a dispute between the goddesses Hera, Athena, and Aphrodite, after the goddess of strife, Eris, gave them a golden apple intended "for the fairest." The chief god, Zeus, sent the women to Paris, the son of the Trojan king, who concluded that Aphrodite was the fairest. In return, Aphrodite had the beautiful Helen, wife of the Spartan king Menelaus, fall in love with Paris. After Paris had kidnapped Helen and brought her to Troy, all the Greeks joined in battle against Troy.

The *Iliad* begins with singing of the revenge of the greatest Greek hero of the that war—Achilles:

> The Wrath of Achilles is my theme, that fatal wrath which, in fulfilment of the will of Zeus, brought the Achaeans so much suffering and sent the gallant souls of many noblemen to Hades, leaving their bodies as carrion for the dogs and passing birds. Let us begin, goddess of song, with the angry parting that took place between Agamemnon King of Men and the great Achilles son of Peleus.[47]

Just as on the road to Damascus, something very particular happened to Paul again. There in Troas, he had a *vision* at night: a Macedonian man stood before him, from across the sea, from what we now call Europe, begging him: "Come over to Macedonia and help us" (Acts 16:9).[48] The identity of that Macedonian man is not given. But there is actually only one great figure that is called that in history: a man who influenced world history in antiquity like no other. This was "the Macedonian"—Alexander the Great! Paul has thus arrived, during this missionary journey, where the Greeks once crossed from the other side to destroy Troy! That was, by the way, not the only time they did so. They returned later to fight other enemies in Asia, particularly of course the Persians.

It was there at Troy that Alexander crossed the Hellespont. Alexander was given the epithet "the Great" for the first time in a comedy by the Roman playwright Plautus (d. 184 BC).[49] Alexander's father appointed Aristo-

---

47. Homer, *The Iliad*, 23.

48. Wilder writes that when Paul's campaign was directed across the Bosporus to Europe by his dream of a man from Macedonia asking him to come and help them (Acts 16:9), it concerned, in his view, a mysterious oracle that needs explanation (*Jesus' Parables and the War of Myths*, 105).

49. Wirth, *Alexander der Grosze in Selbstzeugnissen und Bilddokumenten*, 116, 118.

tle as his teacher, to whom his fondness for Homer can be traced. According to Robert Graves, Homer had, however, "an inveterate hatred of war" that "appears throughout the *Iliad*" and treated his heroes, even Achilles, the greatest of them all, with irony.[50]

In the myths and folklore of many peoples, Alexander is seen as the embodiment of Hellenistic rule, the scourge of God, a conqueror, who had the holy books of the Persians burned in Persepolis; he is viewed as a superhuman violent ruler who embodied evil as such.[51]

Alexander then carried out his father's plans in the East-West conflict of the time: to take vengeance on the Persians who wreaked extensive havoc in Greece. When Alexander crossed to Asia Minor to persecute the Persian king Darius who had threatened the Greeks, the first thing he did when he set foot on Asian soil was to visit the ruins of Troy. He then offered up a sacrifice on the grave of his great example Achilles, the most famous and bravest Greek hero from whom he claimed to have descended. After his visit to Troy, he took Achilles's shield with him on his world-conquering and city-destroying campaigns![52] That shield would save his life once. It bore the images of the terrifying faces of the Gorgons, including Medusa, a monster-like figure from Greek mythology, whose look turned people to stone. According to Homer, however, Achilles's shield is covered with images of peace, abundance, and everyday life, rather than war![53]

Alexander's conquest of a large part of the then known world began with this *crossing*. It led to the spread of "Hellenistic culture," from which Paul of Tarsus would greatly benefit. Later, "Alexander was portrayed at the Forum of Augustus as the prototypical human-become-divine by world conquest." The *Macedonian* globalization *in the fourth century BC* was the model for the later Roman globalization in the first century of the Christian calendar.[54]

THE NATURE OF PAUL'S CROSSING TO EUROPE

What was the nature and content of Paul's dream, his vision, in Troas? To *conquer* Europe? To go on a *crusade, fight a holy war*? If one looks at the later history of Christianization, that is what one might think.

50. Cited in Gittings, *The Glorious Art of Peace*, 41–42.
51. Wirth, *Alexander der Grosze in Selbstzeugnissen und Bilddokumenten*. 97.
52. Napoleon read the Iliad on St. Helena and concluded that Homer himself must have been a military man; Gittings, *The Glorious Art of Peace*, 41
53. Gittings, *The Glorious Art of* Peace, 44; *Iliad*, XVIII, 541–49.
54. Crossan and Reed, *In Search of Paul*, 127–28.

Erasmus wrote a book about Julius II, who was pope from 1503 to 1513, one of the most well-known Renaissance popes, and was called "il terribile," ("the terrible"), which he was indeed. In Erasmus's book, when Julius, who wielded the sword in a literal sense as pope, meets Peter at the gates of heaven, he proudly tells Peter about his military triumphs. Peter tells him about his "colleague" Paul: When he lists his achievements, he does not talk about cities that were captured by force, about legions that were massacred, about world rulers who are incited to go to war with each other, or about a despotic display of splendor and opulence; we hear only about shipwreck, imprisonment, torture, dangers, and betrayal (cf. 2 Cor. 11:23–33).[55]

How different Paul's activity was from this later pope and "successor of Peter" in Rome after his vision. From this moment on, there is a striking use of "we" in the book of Acts: after this vision, *we* immediately sought for an opportunity to depart for Macedonia because *we* concluded that God had called *us* to bring them the good news (Acts 16:10). Suddenly, therefore, the narrator of this travel story himself emerges, namely, Luke, the writer of the Acts of the Apostles, the same one who wrote the gospel named after him. Thus, in this report, Luke draws on his own memory—he was there, after all. Here in this crucial episode he is also suddenly present.

There was a major exhibition in Paderborn, Germany, from 26 July until 3 November 2013, called *Credo: The Christianization of Europe in the Middle Ages*.[56] It consisted of three successive exhibitions at three separate locations in the city, indicated by Latin titles: *Lux mundi: The Light of the World*; *In hoc signo: In that sign*; *Quo vadis? Where Are You Going?* The first exhibition, *Lux mundi*, was about the beginning of Christianity in Rome and Byzantium (or Constantinople, now called Istanbul).[57] Willibrord and Boniface and their mission to the Germanic lands. Both are also associated with the Christianization of the Netherlands. But the second exhibition, *In hoc signo*, was more gruesome: "Europe became Christian through word and sword." After all, Charlemagne subjected the Saxons, to whom he gave a choice: baptism or death. The pope and emperor represented a Christianization by all means available and also carried it out. The title of the third exhibition was *Quo vadis?* When the apostle Peter fled Rome because of the persecution of Christians, he met Jesus, the legend says, on the Via Appia Antiqua. When Peter asked, "Lord, where are you going?," Jesus answered:

---

55. Erasmus, *Hoe paus Julius II bij de hemelpoort aanklopt*, 77–78.

56. Stiegemann et al., *Credo*.

57. The capital of the Ottoman Empire from 1453 on. The word play in Islâm-bol ("where Islam abounds") was, according a contemporary Armenian source, given to the city by its conqueror Mehmed II. *EI, s.v.*, Istanbul.

"I'm going to Rome to be crucified anew."[58] This answer made Peter change his mind, and he returned to Rome where he was taken prisoner and crucified upside-down in Nero's Circus.

The content that the third exhibition gave can be paraphrased as follows: What has come of Christianity? I found this last exhibition the most shocking. National socialism's view of Christianization is also presented: some Nazis were awarded the Iron Cross, a German military decoration instituted by the Prussian king in 1813. Hitler reintroduced it during the Second World War, this time not as a military distinction but as a knightly order. The cross was somewhat thicker and showed a swastika in the middle with the year 1939 on the front and 1813 on the back.[59]

For no specific reason, I visited the exhibition in the reverse order and began with this last one. That is why it affected me so deeply when I entered the first exhibition, *Lux mundi*, and saw how it all began: at the beginning of the exhibition was a papyrus from the second century hanging in a display case. It had been found in Egyptian sand and was a fragment of the letter Paul wrote to the congregation in Rome, probably in 57 AD, with these words: "What shall separate us from the love of God?" (Rom 8:35):

> What, then, shall we say in response to these things? If God is for us, who can be against us? He who did not spare his own Son,[60] but gave him up for us all—how will he not also, along with him, graciously give us all things? Who will bring any charge against those whom God has chosen? It is God who justifies.[61] Who then is the one who condemns? No one. Christ Jesus who died—more than that, who was raised to life—is at the right hand of God and is also interceding for us.[62] Who shall separate us from the love of Christ? Shall trouble or hardship or persecution or famine or nakedness or danger or sword? As it is written:
>
> > For your sake we face death all day long;
> > we are considered as sheep to be slaughtered." [Ps 44:23]
>
> No, in all these things we are more than conquerors through him who loved us. For I am convinced that neither death nor life, neither angels nor demons, neither the present nor the future, nor any powers, neither height nor depth, nor anything

---

58. Cf. *Acts of Peter*, (*Acta Petri*), 35; cf. *Buiten de Vesting*, 518.
59. https://en.wikipedia.org/wiki/Iron_Cross.
60. An allusion to the "binding of Isaac" (Gen 22:16); cf. John 3:16; 1 John 4:9–10.
61. Isa 50:8: "He who vindicates me is near. / Who then will bring charges against me? / Let us face each other! / Who is my accuser? / Let him confront me!"
62. Cf. Ps 110:1.

else in all creation, will be able to separate us from the love of God that is in Christ Jesus our Lord. (Rom 8:31–39)

What did Paul come to *help* Europe with? When Paul went to Syria to persecute Jewish followers of Jesus, he was operating in that "violent" spirit in a certain sense. If one looks at the history of Christianity in later centuries, one could say that something similar happened: the Christianization of Europe via a kind of holy war of conquest. Clovis (ca. 466–511), the king of the Franks, swore that if he was victorious, he would become the servant of the god of the Christians. He kept his promise. In 506, at Christmas, he was baptized along with 3,000 of his men. This number, however, seems to have been inspired by the Bible. Those who accepted Peter's word on Pentecost and were baptized and joined the followers of the Way on that day were about *three thousand* (Act 2:41). Clovis was the first king of all Frankish tribes, the first *Catholic king*. His conversion to Catholic Christianity has been of great political importance. While all German princes were either Arians or pagans, this made him the hero of the Catholic Gallo-Roman population. His cruelty remained as great as ever, and his followers would not fail to match him as best they could. The history of the Merovingians was a succession of murders and cruelty.[63] The legend says that, during their immersion in the baptism ceremony, his men held their right arms above their heads in order to symbolize that the god of the Christian could have everything but their sword arm. We do not know whether or not this legend is based in fact or not, whether it truly happened. But does that matter? Is it, in light of the history of Europe, not one of the truest stories that characterizes our European "Christian history"?

But Paul's mission began so differently from that, and its end was also very different, for him personally![64] The true beginning is: LUX MUNDI— the light of the world, the light that overcame Paul himself, overwhelmed him on the road to Damascus. This light was expressed in the insights that this experience, this call, brought with it and the vision that he saw in Troy, and what he recorded in his letter to the church in Rome, in that fragment that the exhibition in Paderborn opened with: *Who shall separate us from the love of Christ?*

Paul's journey to Europe was not a victory march like Alexander's crossing to Asia. From that moment on the road to Damascus and that vision in Troas, Paul followed an entirely different path—the same path on

---

63. Otten, *Hoe god verscheen in Saksenland* p. 31; https://nl.wikipedia.org/wiki/Clovis_I.

64. That is what the first exhibition in Paderborn shows (which one can still view via the comprehensive [illustrated] catalogues (851 pp.).

which Jesus preceded his disciples on the road from Galilee to Jerusalem, the *via crucis*, the way of the cross. Paul wrote to the church in Corinth: "For I resolved to know nothing while I was with you except Jesus Christ and him crucified" (1 Cor 2:2). He had also walked that road before his crossing in Asia Minor: "You foolish Galatians! Who has bewitched you? Before your very eyes Jesus Christ was clearly portrayed as crucified?" (Gal 3:1); "May I never boast except in the cross of our Lord Jesus Christ, through which the world has been crucified to me, and I to the world" (Gal 6:14). Paul follows a *via crucis*, just like his master. He is spared nothing on that road.

> I have ... been in prison more frequently, been flogged more severely, and been exposed to death again and again. Five times I received from the Jews the forty lashes minus one. Three times I was beaten with rods, once I was pelted with stones, three times I was shipwrecked, I spent a night and a day in the open sea, I have been constantly on the move. I have been in danger from rivers, in danger from bandits, in danger from my fellow Jews, in danger from Gentiles; in danger in the city, in danger in the country, in danger at sea; and in danger from false believers. I have labored and toiled and have often gone without sleep; I have known hunger and thirst and have often gone without food; I have been cold and naked. (2 Cor 11:21–27)

In all those individually shocking circumstances, he travels with the deep, indestructible conviction that nothing could separate him from the love of Christ: adversity, misery, persecution, hunger, poverty, danger, the sword. He had already experienced *six of the seven* things that he sums up in the fragment of this letter. The *seventh*, the sword, was waiting for him as he wrote this: the Roman emperor, Nero, would execute him by the sword. The only privilege, the only advantage of his Roman citizenship, was that he was executed with the sword; otherwise, he would have been crucified like Peter. Paul was and remained convinced that neither death nor life, nor any other creature could separate Christians from the love of God that is in Christ Jesus (Rom 8:38–39). After all the threats by people (Rom 8:35–36), Paul lists the cosmic powers that could be personified and determine the fate of people (cf. Gal 4:3,9; Eph 1:11; 2:2–3; Col 2:8, etc.). That is why he erupts in that crescendo: "We are more than conquerors!" How different that is from the conquest of Alexander before him, as well as, later, from that of Constantine, Clovis, Charlemagne, or Charles V. His only certainty was and remained *Lux mundi*, God's light, his love, which Paul had experienced, the message that he passed on and continues to pass on to his readers today.[65]

65. Cf. Stiegemann et al., *Credo*.

That face, that vision of Paul in Troy, brings him again—after the experience on the road to Damascus—to the understanding of his destiny, his actual calling. And then it happened. In this "missionary journey" of Paul, the Gospel penetrates from the East into the world of Europe: *ex oriente lux: light* from the East that was revealed to him on the road to Damascus, and then after his second vision in the important cities, the major centers of civilization, especially Athens (Acts 17), and finally Rome. But his vision reached even further, to the ends of the earth.

PAUL THE HEBREW: THE MAN FROM THE OTHER SIDE

The term "Hebrew" is *first* used in the Bible in reference to Abra(ha)m, to distinguish him from the Amorites.[66] In Palestine, Abraham is still explicitly called "the Hebrew" (Gen 14:13).[67] Abraham is the grandson of Shem (Gen 11:26–27), and Shem was the ancestor of the sons of *Eber*; this includes Aramean and Arabic tribes in Mesopotamia, Syria, and the Transjordan, especially also the family of Abram (Gen 10:21–30).[68] The name Eber means "one passing by," "nomad," "on the other side of." Eber also occurs in Jesus' family tree (Luke 3:35).[69] The *second time* the name appears as an adjective in the words of the wife of the Egyptian Potiphar. She calls Joseph "that Hebrew slave" (Gen 39:17). Joseph declares to the Egyptians that he has been carried off "from the land of the Hebrews" (Gen 40:15). It was an abomination for Egyptians to dine with the Hebrews: "They served [Joseph] by himself, the brothers by themselves, and the Egyptians who ate with him by themselves, because Egyptians could not eat with Hebrews, for that is detestable to Egyptians" (Gen 43:32). The Israelites were originally called Hebrews because they invaded Canaan from the Desert of Sinai. It is quite possible that the inhabitants of Canaan and of Egypt used the term

---

66. Gen 14:13: "A man who had escaped came and reported this to Abram the Hebrew. Now Abram was living near the great trees of Mamre the Amorite, a brother of Eshkol and Aner, all of whom were allied with Abram." This man reported that Abram's nephew Lot had been taken prisoner in connection with a war between a number of kings against Sodom and Gomorrah, where Lot was living.

67. The word *'ibrî* appears 13 times in Exod 1–10.

68. It is important to mention the table of nations here because we are also concerned with land, the earth, the people of Israel and the nations. KBS on Gen 10:1–32. That chapter groups all known nations then according to their history and places where they live. The sons of Japhet lived in Asia Minor and the islands of the Mediterranean Sea. The sons of Ham settled in Egypt, Ethiopia, Arabia. Between these two groups are the "sons of Shem," Elamites, Assyrians, Arameans, in addition to the ancestors of the Hebrews.

69. *BW*, s.v., Eber.

"Hebrew" for people who, like Abraham, came from the other side of the Euphrates: the name was then used in connection with *eber*, i.e., the other side, thus: people from the other side,[70] those who "go to the other side." The noun means "the opposite side,"[71] "someone from the other side," as a way of referring to an immigrant from the other side of the Euphrates River.[72]

God appeared to the prophet Elijah on Mount Horeb (1 Kgs 19:9) in a way that can only be comparable to the appearance of God to Moses (Exod 31:1; 33:18–23). Just like Moses, he stayed there 40 days and 40 nights (1 Kgs 19:8; cf. Exod 24:18). But then we read: "The Lord said, 'Go out and stand on the mountain in the presence of the Lord, for the Lord is about to pass by'" (1 Kgs 19:11). Then the Lord passed by. That recalls the scene of God passing by on the night of the Exodus,[73] the God who *passes by*, passes on, the God who does not accept the status quo, who points to a liberating exit (Exodus, *hijra*). A Hebrew man goes with this God, seeking an alternative to what the unjust authorities have to offer.[74]

It is telling that Paul presents himself as a "Hebrew": "Are they Hebrews? So am I. Are they Israelites? So am I. Are they Abraham's descendants? So am I" (2 Cor 11:21–22). I was "circumcised on the eighth day, of the people of Israel, of the tribe of Benjamin, a *Hebrew of Hebrews*; in regard to the [Torah], a Pharisee; as for zeal, persecuting the church; as for righteousness *based on the law*, faultless" (Phil 3:5–6).[75]

As soon as Paul had *crossed over*, he went to Philippi, the most important city in Macedonia. Philippi owed its existence to the silver and gold mines in the area, which were no longer profitable. The Roman colonists living there controlled the city.[76] Paul followed the same procedure there that he followed elsewhere, i.e., first seeking contact with the Jews. On the Sabbath, he wanted to attend the synagogue, but probably there was none there—at least in the sense that there were not enough men; ten were needed—to hold a service. That is why Paul went outside the city to the river, where there was a place of prayer and met some women who had come there. One person who attracted their attention was Lydia: she was apparently rich, from a town in

---

70. BW, s.v., Hebreeën.

71. Jenni and Westermann, *Theologischer Handwörterbuch zum Alten Testament*, II, 200, 201.

72. BW, s.v., Eber. Hebreeën.

73. Naastepad, *Elia*, 75. Rooze, *Marcus*, 234, 264, n. 227.

74. Rooze, *Marcus*, 255, n. 71.

75. Acts 22:3: "I am a Jew, born in Tarsus of Cilicia, but brought up in this city. I studied under Gamaliel and was *thoroughly trained in the law of our ancestors*. I was just as zealous for God as any of you are today."

76. Stählin, *Die Apostelgeschichte*, 217.

Asia Minor that was the center for the purple cloth trade. We can read about the purple cloth of Philippi already in Homer's *Iliad*.[77] Purple cloth was a luxury item in the Roman world. Lydia, a Greek woman, feels attracted to the Jewish religion. She is a "worshipper of God," a "God-fearing" woman, which is what people who sympathized with the Jewish religion were called, though they did remain outsiders, pagans. Apparently, she listened to Paul on several occasions.

And then Jesus *opened* her heart. In the Lucan narratives, Jesus is the one who opens the *understanding* (Luke 24:45); the *eyes* of the travelers to Emmaus are *opened* when Jesus breaks bread and he disappears immediately from their sight. "They asked each other, 'Were not our hearts *burning* within us while he talked with us on the road and opened the Scriptures to us?'" (Luke 24:20–33). Paul *opened* the Scriptures on three Sabbath days in succession and explained that the Messiah had to suffer and rise from the dead: "This Jesus I am proclaiming to you is the Messiah" (Acts 17:3). God opens the doors of the prison in Philippi that Paul and Silas had been put in (Acts 16:26–27). God opens the door of faith to the nations (the Gentiles) in Phoenicia (Lebanon) and Syria with its capital of Antioch (Acts 14:27), and now for the first time in Europe.

"*Come over . . . and help us.*" The work of salvation can, apparently, be described in various ways as *opening*. With Lydia, the heart, the center of feelings, thinking, and decisions, is opened with the result that she pays attention to what Paul says. She and all those who were part of her household, i.e., those who worked for her, children, husband, slaves, assistants in the business, were baptized. She became the heart of the first church on European soil. She then shows hospitality to the apostles. After being beaten and thrown in prison and then set free by supernatural means, Paul and Silas went again to Lydia's house (Acts 16:11–40). Lydia's home was the first "support center for the mission" and the first European "house church."[78]

PAUL, APOSTLE TO THE GENTILES TO THE ENDS OF THE EARTH

To properly understand Paul's missionary journey to the Gentiles, Psalm 72 is very important as a source of inspiration. This psalm is attributed to King Solomon, even though he himself was not a personification of the Messianic king who is celebrated here and promised:[79] the rule of this king extends

---

77. *Alle Bijbelse personen, s.v.*, Lydia.
78. Stählin, *Die Apostelgeschichte*, 217–18.
79. Cf. 1 Kgs 11; Wessels, *The Torah, the Gospel, and the Qur'an*, chapter VI.

from sea to sea, from the great river to the ends of the earth (Ps 72:8), i.e., he rules from the Mediterranean Sea to the Persian Gulf. The Euphrates was located between both bodies of water and was considered the center of the inhabited world.[80]

The profile of this king of peace in the prophet Zechariah corresponds with that in this psalm:

> Rejoice greatly, Daughter Zion!
>   Shout, Daughter Jerusalem!
> See, your king comes to you,
>   righteous and victorious,
> lowly[81] and riding on a *donkey*,[82]
>   on a colt, the foal of a donkey.
> I will take away the chariots from Ephraim
>   and the warhorses from Jerusalem,
>   and the battle bow will be broken.
> He will proclaim peace to the nations.
>   His *rule will extend from sea to sea*
>   and *from the River to the ends of the earth.*
> (Zech 9:9–10; cf. Matt 21:5)

The donkey was the primary mount for a new king *and* the Messiah. At the command of David, his son Solomon was seated on his own female donkey and brought to a well at the foot of the *southeastern* hill of Jerusalem. There the priest Zadok and the prophet Nathan anointed him king of Israel (1 Kgs 1:33–34).

It was King Solomon who would later introduce—in imitation of Egypt—the *horse* as a mount (1 Kgs 10:26, 28–29)![83] The horse was expressly not used in Israel for the establishment of the state. David had the horses that were captured in war hamstrung (2 Sam 8:4), but horses and chariots were, however, already included in the royal army in his time (2 Sam 15:1; 1 Kgs 1:5). Solomon in particular saw the military importance of the horse and equipped his army with chariots (2 Kgs 134:7; cf. Rev 9:9), importing them—of course—from Egypt (1 Kgs 10:28), and built cities for his chariots with stalls (1 Kgs 9:17–19).

---

80. KBS on Zech 9:10.

81. KBS on Zech 9:9. The expected Messiah will be humble like the people in the future: "But I will leave within you / the meek and humble. / The remnant of Israel / will trust in the name of the Lord. (Zeph 3:12); cf. Isa 57:15.

82. Cf. John 12:15.

83. Wessels, *The Torah, the Gospel, and the Qur'an*, chapter VI.

In the "King's Law" in the Torah, to which a just king had to adhere, it is stated that a king must not acquire many horses, for that would mean bringing the people back to Egypt, thus negating the Exodus: "You are not to go back that way again" (Deut 17:16). The prophets are strongly critical of horses:

> "In that day," declares the Lord,
> "I will destroy your horses from among you
>   and demolish your chariots."
> (Mic 5:9; cf. Isa 2:7; Hos 14:4; Zech 9:10)[84]

A similar "king's law" arose in the European genre tradition called "Mirrors for Princes." Erasmus wrote one for the newly crowned Charles V. These were works written to be held up to a prince as a mirror that he should follow. The Muslim tradition also includes such "advice for princes and people in government (*Nasihat al-muluk*)."[85]

The Messianic king is the *savior of the poor* and their *liberator from violence and deadly threats* (Ps 72:2-4, 12-14). His dominion is universal, and this king thus brings Israel and the nations together in peace (Ps 72:8-11).[86] That promise was already made to Abraham: "To your descendants I give this land, from the Wadi of Egypt [southern border of Judah] to the great river, the Euphrates" (Gen 15:18; cf. 1 Kgs 5:1). Land and earth are part of the same continuum. "Through the work of this Messianic king, the history of Israel *and* the nations that began in and with Abraham as a blessing and history of salvation effected by God become reality."[87]

The king does not establish and maintain his rule by wielding a rod of iron (Ps 2:9; cf. Rev 19:15; 2:27) nor through war (cf. Ps. 110:5-7). In the universal recognition of this royal dominion (Ps 73:9-11), it is the pilgrimage of the nations and the tribute of the nations that flows to him that is in mind here. The world becomes fascinated with the "king of righteousness." And thus all come, *the tribes who dwell in the desert and those who live by the sea*, i.e., kings and peoples *from all regions right up to the ends of the inhabited earth* to pay homage to this king, to bring him gifts and tribute and to serve his dominion of peace. These are therefore the representatives of the whole earthly sphere from the most extreme western point of the world, Tarshish (Ps 72:10; cf. Jonah 1:3), to the extreme east, Sheba and

---

84. W. B., s.v., paard.
85. EI, s.v., Nasihat al-muluk.
86. Zenger, *Psalmen: Auslegungen in zwei Bänden*, 651-52.
87. Hossfeld and Zenger, *Psalmen 51-100*, 322-24; cf. Gen 12:1-3, 2:18; Ps 72:17: "Then all nations will be blessed through him, / and they will call him blessed."

Seba, Ethiopia and South Arabia (cf. Gen 10:7; 1 Kgs 10), so that they also will share in the righteousness of God.[88]

ON THE WAY TO SPAIN

In connection with the importance and significance of the missionary journeys of Paul, it is important to pay attention to how the ends of the earth are indicated: Tarshish in the west, Sheba in the east. These are used more often in the Bible. It is striking that the prophet Jonah, precisely to flee from his task to go to Nineveh in the far *east* on the opposite side of the Tigris River in the vicinity of what is now Mosul, boards a ship for the farthest point *west*, Tarshish, which, at that time, was the furthest west one could go. Because the sun sets in the west, this place was the symbol of darkness, and darkness, in turn, symbolizes God-forsakenness.[89]

In his letter to the Romans, Paul makes a remark that can easily be casually passed over—namely, that he has for years wanted to visit the church in Rome "when I go to Spain" (Rom 15:24; cf. Rom 1:10–15; 23:11; Acts 19:21). Thus, he apparently planned to visit the church in Rome only while passing through and to continue his journey to Spain with their support (Rom 15:22–24). This mention of his intention to go to Spain must have made it clear to the first readers of Paul's letter that he did not intend to stay in Rome for an extended time. He was only planning to "drop by."[90]

On ancient maps, Spain lies at the end of the northern circle of the Mediterranean world, thus the arc from Jerusalem via Illyricum, the western part of the Balkans northwest of Macedonia and Greece to Spain. By announcing he is planning to go to Spain, he indicates the extent of his preaching of the Gospel from Jerusalem and the surrounding areas to Illyricum (Rom 15:19; cf. 2 Cor 10:14–16; 1 Thess 1:8). He wants to visit the church in Rome while on his way to Spain and then finally to go to the ends of the known earth at that time. Given this geographical framework, it is not strange that Paul thought of Illyricum as situated halfway in the circle. God placed Jerusalem in the middle and grouped all the countries around it. "This is Jerusalem, which I have set in the center of the nations, with countries all around her" (Ezek 5:5).[91] Jerusalem is seen as "the navel of the earth, the center of the

---

88. Hossfeld and Zenger, *Psalmen 51–100*, 324.
89. KBS on Jonah 1:2 and 3.
90. According to Paul Käsemann, "Paul must avoid the suspicion that he wants to make the world capital his new domain, and he does not want to say brusquely that he regards it merely as a bridgehead." Cited in Jewett, *Romans*, 923–924, n. 23.
91. Jewett, *Romans*, 913, n. 113, where he cites James M. Scott. He quotes Gen 10

world (Ezek 38:12). In the Old Testament (the Septuagint) the term "circle" is used for Jerusalem.[92] The intended mission was meant to complete the geographical circle in the Mediterranean area before the appearance or coming of the Messiah. The places where Paul preached were Damascus, Arabia, Sicily, Antioch, Cyprus, Galatia, Asia, Macedonia, and Greece, which are located along the northern side of the Mediterranean Sea between Jerusalem and Illyricum.[93] In addition, Spain was the furthest western point in the then known world where he thus ultimately wanted to go.[94]

It is very probable that Paul saw Tarshish as the western end of the Mediterranean Sea, where, according to the prophet Isaiah, *the final sacrifice* would be made, as written in the conclusion of the book of Isaiah:

> I am coming to gather every nation and every language. They will come to witness my glory.
>
> I shall give them a sign and send some of their survivors[95] to the nations: to Tarshish,[96] Put [Somalia, point on the African coast of the Red Sea],[97] Lud,[98] Meshech,[99] Tubal and Javan, to the distant *coasts and islands* [the Greek archipelago] that have never heard of me or seen my *glory*. They will proclaim my glory *to the nations*, and from all the nations they will bring all your brothers as an *offering* to Yahweh, on horses, in chariots, in litters, on mules and on camels, to my holy mountain, Jerusalem,

---

(the table of nations) and 1 Chr 11–2:2, which Israel places in the center of the world, a conception that is found in Ezek 38–39 and Is 66:18–20. The later impact of that conception of the world is reflected in Jub 8:9; cf. Josephus, *Ant*, 1:120–47, who describes the journeys to surrounding peoples, using schemes from the Garden of Eden and locations of the sons of Jacob, holding on to the idea of the centrality of Israel and the cities in Spain as the most extreme points of the world.

92. *Kuklos*; this is the Jewish variant of the circular image, according to James M. Scott; see Jewett, *Romans* 913, n. 113.

93. Jewett, *Romans*, 913.

94. Jewett, *Romans*, 913, n. 113. The *Acts of Peter*, an apocryphal work from the second century, speaks of Paul's trip to Spain. According to this work, Paul had a vision and had to go to Spain at the behest of the Lord to work there as a doctor.

95. KBS on Isa 66:19.

96. Spain. Next to the fleet of Hiram, the king also operated a Tarshish fleet and every once in three years they came to port with a cargo of gold, silver, ivory, monkeys, and peacocks. 1 Kgs 10:22. "Trembling seized them there, / pain like that of a woman in labor. / You destroyed them like ships of Tarshish / shattered by an east wind" (Ps 48:6–7). KBS *Schepen van Tarsis*: The Phoenicians were a seafaring people who even reached Tarshish in Spain.

97. *BW*, *s.v.*, Put.

98. Lud. Libya.

99. A people in Asia Minor.

Yahweh says, like Israelites bringing offerings in clean vessels to Yahweh's house. (Isa 66:18–20; NJB)

The language used here is "epiphanic," on the verge of being *apocalyptic*. This is the divine language the Lord uses, who gathers Israel from the diaspora: "I will gather still others to them besides those already gathered" (Isa 56:8).[100] Paul saw himself as called by God for this *priestly duty* (Rom 15:16). He compares his apostolate with a priestly service where he presents himself and the faith of the Gentiles as an *offering*.[101]

GREEKS AND BARBARIANS: THE EDUCATED AND THE ILLITERATE

"Greeks and barbarians" is a stereotypical formula whereby the Greeks are mentioned first and the barbarians—of course—are mentioned last. In the bilingual context of Rome, Greek meant Greco-Roman, while barbarian referred to someone who did not speak any Greek or Latin, was uneducated, wild, savage, fundamentally uncivilized. The Romans saw the barbarians as "inhuman, savage, arrogant, weak, belligerent, quarrelsome, and unstable."[102] The Roman authorities celebrated their *victoria* over the barbarians in monuments and on coins, public inscriptions, in triumphal parades, public games, and other means of propaganda. That reveals, discloses, the worldview of the Roman Empire. That is their "apocalyptic" thinking! The developed people saw the barbarians as *Untermenschen*.[103] In the Eastern and Western Roman Empire, the view prevailed that the barbarians were excluded from salvation. The Greeks/Romans saw themselves as the sole representatives of the *human race*. Barbarians were only there to be subordinated. And the inhabitants of Spain were seen at that time as prime examples of barbarians because many of them continued to oppose Roman dominion. Cicero classified the Spaniards as uncivilized, just like the Africans and the Gauls.[104]

The educational system of the Romans was directed at training the youth of the elite for public service in the empire, with the understanding that an uncivilized person, a barbarian thus, was not considered to have the ability to be trained for those tasks. The word "illiterate" does not only mean

---

100. Brueggemann, *Isaiah 40–66*, 258.
101. KBS on Rom 15:16. Cf. Phil 2:17; 2 Tim 4:6
102. Jewett, *Romans*, 130–31.
103. Jewett, *Romans*, 132.
104. Jewett, *Romans*. 131.

unwise, irrational, and foolish but ultimately *not completely human*. Barbarians are by nature *foolish*, whereas the Greeks/Romans are by nature *wise*. Nothing can be expected from illiterate barbarians. By definition, barbarians are not able to contribute to a human undertaking. And that was fine as such and had to remain so always.

When Paul wrote in his letters to the Romans: "I am obligated both to Greeks and non-Greeks, both to the wise and the foolish" (Rom 1:14), he says something completely unprecedented and, for the so-called "civilized" Romans, something inconceivable and revolutionary: How could someone be obligated to barbarians!? That was a complete *Umwertung aller Werte*—turning all recognized values upside down—an inversion of the honor and shame system in which one felt obligated to the uneducated, illiterate masses. Paul sees his mission as a joyful message that completely reverses the stereotypes of the old world. It is by this conviction, by this faith, that the human being, Greek or barbarian, will live: "The righteous will live by faith" (Rom 1:17; cf. Hab 2:4; Gal 3:11; Heb 10:38).[105] That Paul feels indebted to those in both categories is indeed seen as the key to unlocking the whole letter to the Romans, including his intention to go to Spain, which lay at the end of the northern sphere of the Mediterranean Sea.[106] Spain was, namely, both "heathen" and "barbarian." There was no Jewish population there, and it continued to stubbornly resist Greco-Roman culture. For that reason, it was logical for the apostle to the Gentiles to go there.

In connection with the faith that Paul is talking about—the righteous will live by faith—one should not think of the dogma that his words would later be loaded with. The first hearers and readers of this letter certainly understood, saw, and experienced the connection Paul makes between faith/trust and true life. The question that Paul asks his reader is not: Are you *saved* in the dogmatic sense as understood for centuries—saved from the guilt of personal sins, but how do you manage in the unrighteous society that Roman society is? How can you live and survive so that you can live righteously in Roman society with your faith, with trust? Paul is not ashamed of *this* Gospel he preaches. "It is the power of God that brings salvation to *everyone* who believes," who trusts in it (Rom 1:16). The purpose of God's righteousness is to bring about redemption, liberation, salvation so that just societal, social, and economic relations can permanently arise. More than the individual (which it includes of course), it concerns the group, the nation, the whole world. It concerns the establishment of communities of faith that are just as far as the ends of the earth. This is not

---

105. Jewett, *Romans*, 132.
106. Jewett, *Romans*, 924, n. 28.

an imperialistic subjection of the world. The goal of Paul's letter is to spread this new form of salvation to the ends of the earth, not by force or violence, but by conviction, by faith or trust in God's justice.

Precisely in this context, it is good to understand what it means that the apostle Paul had taken the obligation upon himself at the Apostolic Council in Jerusalem to hold *collections* in his churches among the nations, such as Galatia in Asia Minor (1 Cor 16:1–2) for the mother church in Jerusalem: "All they asked was that we should continue to remember the poor, the very thing I had been eager to do all along" (Gal 2:10). The disciples decided that each of them would contribute according to their ability to the support of their brothers and sisters in Judea. They did that and sent Barnabas and Saul to the elders to give them what had been collected (Acts 11:29–30).[107] Paul handed over the gifts he brought with him during the last time he was in Jerusalem. "After an absence of several years, I came to Jerusalem to bring my people gifts for the poor and to present offerings" (Acts 24:17).[108] He attached great value to this service of love for the poor in the community of Jerusalem and Palestine, also as a sign of unity between Gentiles and Jewish believers. Thus, it was more than simply organizing some sort of aid. In his feverish activities in Asia Minor, Macedonia, Achaia, and Italy, he intended to organize a caravan of the first fruits of the nations, holy men and women from out of the nations who marched to Jerusalem in fulfillment of the prophetic scenario of the final days (Isa 2:2–4; 12:3; 25:6–8; 60:3; 66:18; Jer 16:19; Mic 4:1–3; Zech 8:20–23). Paul understood these gifts not only as a return of the Jews from the diaspora but as a coming of the nations themselves![109]

This collection for the poor among the saints in Jerusalem was also done in Achaia (the largest southern part of what is now Greece) and Macedonia. It was a good decision, but they were now *obligated to them as well*: because the nations had received a share in *their spiritual blessings*, they were obligated on their part to help with *material blessings* (Rom 15:26–27). Here Paul uses the same verb that he used at the beginning of his letter, namely, that he *was obligated to both Greeks and barbarians, to both the wise and the foolish* (Rom 1:14). Paul was and remained intrinsically bound to the community in Jerusalem.

---

107. KBS on 1 Cor 16:1.
108. *BW*, s.v., collecte.
109. Elliot, *Liberating Paul*, 274, n. 133.

VIII

The First and the Last Things: The End of Violence

Too often in the history of religion, people have killed in the name of the God of life, waged war in the name of the God of peace, hated in the name of the God of love and practiced cruelty in the name of the God of compassion. When this happens, God speaks, sometimes in a still, small voice almost inaudible beneath the clamor of those claiming to speak on his behalf. What he says at such times is: "Not in My Name." (Rabbi Jonathan Sacks)[1]

Jesus does not call us to a new religion, but to life. (Dietrich Bonhoeffer)[2]

Today, there's nothing left of religion but a machine of extermination. Daesh (Islamic State) represents this transformation of the divine into a machine that exterminates. (Syrian poet Adonis)

---

1. Sacks, *Not in God's Name*.
2. Bonhoeffer, *Letters and Papers from Prison*, 362.

INTRODUCTION

The theme of the apocalyptic times we are living in today is often paired with the increasing violence that prevails in the world, the wars that are fought, and the terror that reigns in so many places. It is associated with the Armageddon that is thought to be imminent, the appearance of Gog and Magog, and the fear that our planet will be destroyed. Is that what the Bible and the Qur'an announce or "predict"? Is God a God of vengeance? How should we understand the three books' numerous references to violence, vengeance, and retribution? Are we being invited to sing psalms of vengeance?

In this last chapter we will show that we can understand the "last things," such as the final judgment, clearly only if we see how those last things are indissolubly connected with the "first things." This chapter consists of two connected parts. In the first part, it will be made clear that the Bible and the Qur'an—and in particular the Old Testament on which both the New Testament and the Qur'an are based—never call humans to take up violence in their own hands, to bring the end closer through fighting, to go to war against Gog and Magog. The Scriptures do not tell us how the earth will be violently destroyed but how it is God who will put an end to all violence. In the second part, we will look at the integral connection between the last things—eschatology—and the first things—protology. If we do not see or understand that connection, then we will not understand what is meant by apocalyptic, by revelation. This is not at all a question of a chronological order between the first and the last things. The so-called "first things" described at the beginning of the Bible do not relate *how* it began but *why* it all began.[3] The clue, the key, to understanding the last things is given at the beginning. And God saw then, already at the beginning, that creation was very good. It was evening and it was morning. That is true for every new day, up until the last day.

RETRIBUTION AND REVENGE

It is (has been) almost universally accepted among Christians that, with respect to retribution, revenge, and war, there is a great difference between the New Testament on the one hand and the Old Testament and the Qur'an on the other. It is generally thought that, whereas Jesus talks in the Sermon on the Mount of turning the other cheek (Matt 5:38) and says that whoever lives by the sword will perish by the sword (Matt 26:52), the Old Testament and the Qur'an are full of violence. According to one biblical scholar,

---

3. Deurloo, *Schepping van Paulus tot Genesis*, 161.

"there are six hundred passages of explicit violence in the Hebrew Bible, one thousand verses where God's own violent actions of punishment are described, a hundred passages where Yahweh expressly commands others to kill people, and several stories where God irrationally kills or tries to kill for no apparent reason."[4]

The root *nqm*, which is usually translated as "avenge" or "vengeance," is identical in Arabic and Hebrew.[5] In Semitic languages, one always has to pay attention to the three consonants of the verb. God is called "vengeful" (*dhû intiqâm*) in the Qur'an, a God who unleashes his vengeance.[6] The word is used to describe God's vengeance on or retribution carried out against sinners: God previously sent prophets to the various peoples. If they rejected the message, God took vengeance on them (Q 30:47), on the people in Sodom and Gomorrah to whom Lot was sent (Q 15:79), the people of Pharaoh in Egypt (Q 7:136; cf. Exod 14:28; 32:22).[7] Moses sings his song at the Sea of Reeds:

> The Lord is a warrior;
> the Lord is his name.
> Pharaoh's chariots and his army
> he has hurled into the sea.
> The best of Pharaoh's officers
> are drowned in the Red Sea.
> The deep waters have covered them;
> they sank to the depths like a stone.
> (Exod 15:3–5)

The prophet Jeremiah gives the staff officer Seraiah a task. Seraiah had gone with King Zedekiah of Judah to Babylon. He was the brother of Baruch, Jeremiah's scribe,[8] who had sacrificed a promising career as secretary to King Zedekiah to help his friend the prophet Jeremiah. In 605 BC, Jeremiah dictated the first series of prophecies. Baruch read them aloud before the entrance to the temple because Jeremiah himself had been banned by the king from entering the temple.[9] Jeremiah uses the image found in Moses' song in the task he gives to Seraiah: "When you get to Babylon, see that you

---

4. Raymund Schwager, cited in Wink, *The Powers that Be*, 84, and Houtepen, *Geloven in gerechtigheid*, 134, n. 166.

5. Mendenhall, *The Tenth Generation*, 71; in Hebrew and Arabic: the verb *naqam* or the noun *neqamah*.

6. So paraphrased by Rudi Paret in his translation of the Qur'an.

7. *EQ*, s.v., vengeance

8. *BW*, s.v., Seraja.

9. *Alle Bijbelse personen*, s.v., Baruch.

read all these words aloud. Then say, 'Lord, you have said you will destroy this place, so that neither people nor animals will live in it; it will be desolate forever.' When you finish reading this scroll, tie a stone to it and throw it into the Euphrates. Then say, 'So will Babylon sink to rise no more because of the disaster I will bring on her'" (Jer 51:61–64). The theme returns in the Apocalypse of John: "Then a mighty angel picked up a boulder the size of a large mill*stone* and threw it into the sea, and said: 'With such violence the great city of Babylon will be thrown down, never to be found again'" (Rev 18:21; cf. Ezek 26:12). Here Babylon refers to Rome.

In the Jewish tradition, the texts of violence in the Old Testament are never used to legitimate *human* violence. George E. Mendenhall is right when he says that the normative value system of the early biblical society never tolerated individual violence to redress a wrong: God "was the sovereign to whom alone belonged the monopoly of force":[10] The Lord is king forever and ever (Exod 15:18). That is what we hear in the song of Moses at the Sea of Reeds, in which the refrain is sung by Moses' sister, Miriam:

> Sing to the Lord,
> for he is highly exalted.
> Both horse and driver
> he has hurled into the sea.
> (Exod 15:21)

The "Song of the Sea" concerns not only the Israelites' journey but also their entrance into, the conquest of, Canaan![11]

> You stretch out your right hand,
>   and the earth swallows your enemies.
> In your unfailing love you will lead
>   the people you have redeemed.
> In your strength you will guide them
>   to your holy dwelling.
> The nations will hear and tremble.

And then Israel's enemies are listed one after the other:

> Anguish will grip the people of Philistia.
> The chiefs of Edom be terrified,
>   the leaders of Moab will be seized with trembling,
> the people of Canaan will melt away;
>   terror and dread will fall on them.
> By the power of your arm

---

10. Mendenhall, *The Tenth Generation*, 95.
11. KBS on Exod 15:1.

> they will be as still as a stone—
> until your people pass by, Lord,
> until the people you bought pass by.
> (Exod 15:12–16)[12]

A better and more accurate translation of the Hebrew word—and thus also of the Arabic word—is *retribution*. But actually, it is best, with Erich Zenger, to paraphrase the stem *nqm* in line with its actual meaning as "to make good" or "to redress."[13] The purpose of God's retribution is to restore the order of his justice. It is not a question of irrational vengeance, as understood by countless readers throughout the ages and often still by many today. A just punishment for injustice is imposed, not with a view to destruction but to proper punishment for the nations (Ps 149:7b), in the sense of correction and transformation, a concept borrowed from raising children.[14]

It is not a matter of coincidence that these words and expressions appear in *songs*, such as Moses' (Exod 15), the song of the prophetess Deborah (Judg 5), and in the Psalms. It is poetic language, which must be read figuratively. One of the psalms begins:

> The Lord is a God who avenges.
>   O God who avenges, shine forth.
> Rise up, Judge of the earth.
> (Ps 94:1–2a)

If this translation of "vengeance" is used, then we must avoid any connotations of caprice and emotion that are often heard in that word. If one listens properly, the "songs" give insight into the way in which justice is carried out: "Now what have you against me, Tyre and Sidon and all you regions of Philistia? Are you repaying me for something I have done? If you are paying me back, I will swiftly and speedily return on your own heads what you have done" (Joel 3:4). The nations fall into the pit they have dug, their foot gets trapped in the net they have hidden (Ps 9:15). Evil punishes itself: doing evil brings death to the evildoer (Ps 34:21a).[15] Those who dig pits fall into them themselves; those who roll a stone will have it roll back on them (Prov 26:27; Eccl 10:8).[16] Digging a pit to trap someone else means digging a pit

---

12. God is the father of Israel, as stated in the song of Moses (Deut 32:18; Ps 74:2).
13. *Wiedergutmachung*; Zenger, *Das erste Testament*, 64.
14. Hossfeld and Zenger, *Psalms 3*, 652.
15. KBS on Ps 34:22.
16. "Repay them for what their hands have done / and bring back on them what they deserve" (Ps 28:4; cf. Jer 50:29). Cf. "Pay them back what they deserve, Lord, / or what their hands have done" (Lam 3:64).

for oneself (Ps 7:15). Any evil a person does will come back on him, and he will not even know where it comes from (Sir 27:27).

The story of the judge Samson recounts that he took vengeance on the Philistines after he had been captured through Delilah's scheming and his eyes had been gouged out. He was taken as a prisoner of war to the temple of Dagon, the Philistine god of fertility, and was made to stand between the pillars. The temple was full of men and women and all the rulers of the Philistines, and there were another more or less 3000 people on the roof. They were all laughing at him and mocking him. Then Samson called on the Lord: "Sovereign Lord, remember me. Please, God, strengthen me just once more, and let me with one blow *get revenge* on the Philistines for my two eyes" (Judg 16: 27–28).

This prayer for vengeance is directed to the "God of retribution," the one who carries out retribution in the world in the right way: the ultimate restoration, redressing all wrongs. "Here Samson, beyond all hope of ever seeing procedural justice done him for his injuries, entreats God to empower him to exact extraordinary retribution for himself—for him, there can be no other kind; and the God of *nqm* complies."[17] It is God who retaliates against the Philistines, not Samson. We should keep in mind when reading this story that it is not a description of what actually happened, as is also true in a particular way for the story of the Flood (Gen 6–9). The "medium" of the story is used to convey the message: God alone is the one who "redresses" the wrong.

Actually, Erich Zenger thinks that retribution is not a good translation of *nqm* either, given that that word is also loaded with anti-Jewish biblical clichés ("eye for an eye"; "tooth for a tooth" [Exod 21:24]).[18] He explains what the expression that is often translated as "vengeance" and "retribution" really means with the help of Psalm 99. That psalm states who God is:

> Lord our God,
> > you answered them;
> you were to Israel a forgiving God,
> > though you punished their misdeeds.
> (Ps 99:8)

Zenger states correctly that Ps 99 alludes to Exod 34:6–7 and the meaning given to God's name there:

---

17. According to Moshe Greenberg, *Biblical Prose Prayer*, 13, cited in Miller, *They Cried to the Lord*, 119.

18. The *lex talionis* aims at equal retribution (Lev 14:19–20; Deut 19:21), in order to control the extent of revenge taken (cf. Gen 4:23–24; Matt 5:38–39). KBS on Exod 21:24–25.

> The Lord, the Lord, the compassionate and gracious God, slow to anger, abounding in love and faithfulness, maintaining love to thousands, and forgiving wickedness, rebellion and sin. Yet he does not leave the guilty unpunished; he punishes the children and their children for the sin of the parents to the third and fourth generation. (Exod 34:6–7)[19]

A variation on the translation of this confession is found in the Revised Standard Version: "O Lord our God, thou didst answer them; / thou wast a forgiving God to them, / but an *avenger* of their wrongdoings" (Psalm 99:8).[20] This translation embraces the idea of a punishing God that paves the way to the above-mentioned cliché of the God of vengeance. Zenger even speaks of *An Eternal Cliché: The God of Vengeance and Violence?* The God of the Old Testament is said to be violent and vengeful, not only justifying but also demanding violence, murder, and war. Zenger calls that "the anti-Old Testament or anti-Jewish stereotype."

But the aggressive conquest of the land of Canaan, as related in the book of Joshua, and the so-called ban, i.e., the destruction of men and animals never actually took place! Israel shared the *style* of the war stories in Joshua with those nations around it. If one is to understand this "history" from the perspective of the Tenach, then one must place it alongside the critique of arms and war found in prophets like Isaiah and Hosea. Arms and war are idolatry (Isa 2:6–21; cf. Isa 30:15–17; 31:1–3). Zenger believes that the psalm text emphasizes almost the opposite and translates it into German as follows: "JHWH, unser Gott, du, ja du hast ihnen geantwortet: / Ein vergebender Gott warst du ihnen und ein ihre Taten ausgleichender Gott" (YHWH, our God, indeed, you have answered them: You were a forgiving God to them and a God who redresses, makes up for, their actions) (Ps 99:8). Thus, he is a God who redresses their (evil) deeds and wins the day.

The view that the translation as "vengeance" leads to misunderstanding has become almost universal among exegetes, according to Zenger. What verses like this intend to say is that "God restores the disrupted order of life by helping the victims in the first place." In this psalm, as in Exodus 34:6–7, it is not a matter of a tense relationship with the both merciful and at the same time punitive God, but one of the renewing God of the covenant

---

19. KBS on Exod 34:6–7. This is one of the few confessions of faith in the Bible that is not a listing of salvific facts. Cf. also Neh 9:17; Ps 103:8; 145:8; Jonah 4:2.

20. ISV: "Lord our God, you answered them; / you were their God who forgave them, / but also avenged their evil deeds." ASV: "Thou answeredst them, O Jehovah our God: / Thou wast a God that forgavest them, Though thou tookest vengeance of their doings"; CJB: "*Adonai* our God, you answered them. / To them you were a forgiving God, / although you took vengeance on their wrongdoings."

who goes beyond forgiving the sin that the sinners have brought about. "The Lord is indeed a merciful God because he continually restores the disrupted order of life."[21]

What this example shows is that translating the metaphorical language of the Bible requires great care so that the nuances are properly understood and the old prejudices about the "violent God of the Old Testament are not again repeated or even invoked anew."[22] On the one hand, God is the God who forgives guilt *and*, on the other, the God who punishes sin. The asymmetry is certainly emphasized, however, in that his will to forgive is stronger than his readiness to punish, and the purpose of this punishment is to reinforce his saving power. That is the answer to the tension-filled reality of God's turning to and turning away from Israel. It is precisely there that we see *this* King's specific love for justice. Retribution has nothing to do with vengeance but with justice: it is a matter of going on and again restoring the disturbed just order, where the final word is forgiveness. God certainly proves himself to be a "God who takes away—forgives—sin but at the same time, what is also present here is that he is the good shepherd [a metaphor par excellence for a king!], who carries his people like wounded lambs" (cf. Isa 40:11; 46:3–4).[23]

> *In that day* I will make a covenant for them
>   with the beasts of the field, the birds in the sky
>   and the creatures that move along the ground.
> Bow and sword and battle
>   I will abolish from the land,
>   so that all may lie down in safety.
> (Hos 2:18)

Peace between humans and animals is an image for happiness. It is the situation at the beginning of creation as it was intended (Gen 1:29). This often appears in the Messianic texts (cf. Isa 11:6–8; Ezek 34:25–28; Isa 35:9; 65:25).

IF I FORGET YOU JERUSALEM

The last verses of Psalm 137, which was written during the Babylonian exile, are perhaps the most shocking example of a violence or curse psalm, of a plea for an extreme form of revenge:

---

21. Zenger, *Das Erste Testament*, 62–64.
22. Zenger, *Das Erste Testament*, 64.
23. Zenger in: Hossfeld and Zenger, *Psalmen 51–100*, 703.

> Daughter Babylon, doomed to destruction,
> > Happy is the one who repays you
> > according to what you have done to us.
> > Happy is the one who seizes your infants
> > and dashes them against the rocks.
>
> (Ps 137:8–9)

The city of Babylon is imagined as a woman and its inhabitants as her children. To the extent that small children are intended here, they are viewed as the soldiers of tomorrow.[24] It concerns the city whose fall Jeremiah prophesies (Jer 50–52). The prophet Hosea speaks in such shocking terms about the fate of the city of Samaria, which has to pay for its sin because it rebelled against God: "They will fall by the sword; / their little ones will be dashed to the ground, / their pregnant women ripped open" (Hos 13:16). The Revelation of John also speaks of the destruction of Babylon, even thought it means the city of Rome:

> Then I heard another voice from heaven say:
> "Come out of her, my people" [cf. Isa 48:20; 52:11; Jer 51:6, 45],
> > so that you will not share in her sins,
> > so that you will not receive any of her plagues;
> > for her sins are piled up to heaven,[25]
> > and God has remembered her crimes.
> *Give back to her as she has given*;
> > *pay her back double* for what she has done.[26]
> > Pour her a double portion from her own cup.
>
> (Rev 18:4–6; cf. 18:8)

It is necessary "to give an eschatological explanation when Babylon becomes a symbol of a multifarious and endless engagement in war": "The name written on her forehead was a mystery: / Babylon the great / the mother of prostitutes / and of the abominations of the earth" (Rev 17:5). Rome was seen by Jews and Christians at the time as a godless and wicked world power.[27]

The context of Psalm 137 is the destruction of Jerusalem and the temple. It was composed at the beginning of the sixth century BC, and the

---

24. KBS on Ps 137:8–9. On the fall of Babylon, cf. Jer 50–52.

25. Cf. Gen 18:20; "Then the Lord said, "The outcry against Sodom and Gomorrah is so great and their sin so grievous"; and Jer 51:9: "We would have healed Babylon, / but she cannot be healed; / let us leave her and each go to our own land, / for her judgment reaches to the skies, / it rises as high as the heavens."

26. Cf. Jer 50:15.

27. KBS on Rev 17:5; 1 P 5:13.

curses in this song are directed against Edom and Babylon. The "emperor" of Babylon, Nebuchadnezzar, had used Edomite mercenaries, who were the descendants of Jacob's brother, Esau. The hostility of Edom toward Israel and vice versa began already at the time of the patriarchal narrative of the two brothers. Nebuchadnezzar encouraged the complete destruction of the holy place of Israel.[28] *The first curse* is addressed to the southern neighbor Edom, who, as auxiliary troops for the Babylonians, had helped in initiating this complete destruction of Jerusalem:

> *On the day* you stood aloof
>   while strangers carried off his wealth
> and foreigners entered his gates
>   and cast lots for Jerusalem,
>   you were like one of them.
> You should not gloat over your brother
>   in the day of his misfortune,
> nor rejoice over the people of Judah
>   in the day of their destruction,
> nor boast so much
>   in the day of their trouble.
> You should not march through the gates of my people
>   in the day of their disaster,
> nor gloat over them in their calamity
>   in the day of their disaster,
> nor seize their wealth
>   in the day of their disaster.
> You should not wait at the crossroads
>   to cut down their fugitives,
> nor hand over their survivors
>   in the day of their trouble.
> (Obad 11–14)[29]

The second curse concerns "Daughter Babylon." She would, by the principle of the *ius tallionis*—"eye for an eye, tooth for a tooth"—have to suffer precisely what she did to Jerusalem, for which the dashing of children is mentioned pars pro toto. The children of Daughter Babylon can also refer to the children of the dynasty ruling in Babylon: "Blessed be those who bring your constantly revived dynasty to an end."[30] The psalm should be

---

28. Ezek 25:12–14; Obad 8–15; cf. 2 Kgs 24:10–17; Lam 1:20–22; 3:64–66; Ezek 35:5–9; Terrien, *The Psalms*, 867.

29. Zenger, *Stuttgarter Psalter*, 375.

30. Zenger, *Stuttgarter Psalter*, 376.

understood primarily as a cry of protest and a desire for law and justice.[31] These verses are not meant as a blessing for child murderers. They are a heartfelt, passionate cry by the powerless who ask for justice. This is not a song of people who have the power to bring about a violent change in their situation of suffering, nor is it the war cry of terrorists. It is an attempt—in the face of the deepest humiliation and helplessness—to suppress precisely the primitive human lust for violence in one's own heart by leaving everything to God.

In contrast to the first impression one has of this psalm, these concluding verses are not based on feelings of hate or irrational revenge. Precisely this initially shocking image expresses primarily Israel's experience of powerlessness in their confrontation with the Babylonian war machine and the ideology of world dominance. It can be called a "political" psalm that revolves around the end of the Babylonian reign of terror. This terrible image is intended to express that this dynasty of terror needs to be completely eliminated—root and branch. It is an appeal to God to protect a just world order.[32]

In the following retelling, against the background of this explanation just given above, in which I have followed Erich Zenger, Zenger translates the problematic section of the psalm by staying as close as possible to the original text:

> O daughter Babylon, you devastator!
> Happy the one who brings you to judgment
> > because of what you have done to us!
> Happy the one who seizes you
> and puts an end to your rule forever![33]

In contrast to *that day*, when Edom did not support the nation that was its close kin, however, there is *the day of the Lord*:

> The day of the Lord is near
> > For all nations.
> As you have done, it will be done to you;
> > your deeds will return upon your own head.
> (Obad 15)

But, in the end, the deliverers (Judg 3:9–11)—as the *judges* of old were also called—would pronounce justice on Mount Zion over the mountain country of Edom: "And the kingdom will be the Lord's" (Obad 21).[34]

---

31. Zenger, *A God of Vengeance?* 93.
32. Zenger, *A God of Vengeance?* 47–50.
33. Zenger. *A God of Vengeance?* 91.
34. Cf. Ps 22:9; 47:9; 93:1; 97:1; 99:1; 103:19; 145:11–13.

IMPRECATORY PSALMS/PSALMS OF VENGEANCE?

One of the most moving psalms about the individual who wants to follow God's path is Psalm 139:

> You have searched me, Lord,
>   and you know me.
> You know when I sit and when I rise;
>   you perceive my thoughts from afar.
> You discern my going out and my lying down;
>   you are familiar with all my ways,
> Before a word is on my tongue
>   you, Lord, know it completely.
> You hem me in behind and before,
>   and you lay your hand upon me.
> Such knowledge is too wonderful for me,
>   too lofty for me to attain.
> (Ps 139:1–6)

The psalm ends with the prayer:

> Search me, God, and know my heart;
>   test me and know my anxious thoughts.
> See if there is any offensive way in me,
>   and lead me in the way everlasting
> (Ps 139:23–24)

But then suddenly we see a few verses that we feel mar this psalm and that we would rather skip:

> If only you, God, would slay the wicked!
>   Away from me, you who are bloodthirsty!
> They speak of you with evil intent;
>   your adversaries misuse your name.
> Do I not hate those who hate you, Lord,
>   and abhor those who are in rebellion against you?
> I have nothing but hatred for them;
>   I count them my enemies.
> (Ps 139:19–22)

There is indeed no suggestion that the psalmist wants to take the law or sword into his own hands and engage in violence himself. Nevertheless, the question remains: Does the book of Psalms, even such a beautiful psalm as this, speak of a "God of vengeance"?[35]

---

35. Zenger, *A God of Wrath*, 28–34.

In his beautiful reworking of the psalms, *150 Psalmen vrij*, the Dutch poet Huub Oosterhuis skipped such passages,[36] and he is not the only one. But are we free to do so, just like the "Vatican" also did with respect to the use of the psalms in prayers in monasteries?[37] "Rome" adapted, as it were, the Psalter to "Christian" standards that are thought to be far exalted above the Jewish ones (sic!)—that is the idea behind their choices here. The latter is a serious misunderstanding of this psalm, as well as a wrong understanding with respect to what should be understood by revenge or retribution, as we saw above.

This psalm is a prayer by someone wrestling with his own life, suffering, and fears. He is looking for hope in the midst of this wrestling and asks God to let him personally experience that the path in life that he has to and will follow will prosper: Lead me in the way that has a future (Ps 139:24). In the midst of a world full of riddles, of such threatening chaos and violence, the one praying is looking for light and strength: "Show me your ways, Lord, / teach me your paths. Guide me in your truth and teach me" (Ps 25:4–5a). The psalmist is certainly not a naïve optimist. He does not swear by the old "wisdom" that says "Do good to others and good will come back to you," that says that the good will prosper and the wicked fail. He does not subscribe to such a philosophy. After all, we often experience the opposite—just as was the case undoubtedly then. The powerhouses, the doers of violence, are the ones who are successful, who have influence and power. Those with the biggest mouths say what goes; those are the ones who are heard, and, yes, they are seen. The psalmist has difficulty with that, with the fact that the bad people seem to prosper. He wrestles with the question of the truth concerning God and longs passionately for the assurance of God's nearness that he cannot live without. That alone gives him the strength to endure. "You have searched me, Lord, / and you know me, don't you?"

This psalm is sometimes explained in such a way that it portrays a God who only inspires fear. In the past, many homes included a portrait of the "All-seeing eye," with the text below "God sees you." That "All-seeing eye" can still be seen in Saint John's Cathedral in 's Hertogenbosch. Is this a God who watches people day and night, spies on them, checks out what they are doing in order to catch them at a thousand minor infractions? Is this a God who is so easily insulted, so easily irritated, and responds to that by punishing people? Is he a "Big Brother" who is watching us, who enjoys controlling us?

---

36. Oosterhuis, *150 psalmen vrij*, 248–49.

37. D. Sölle does that as well in her *Death by Bread Alone*; cf. Zenger, *A God of Wrath*, 30.

Philosophers have written about the *human* eye, the human gaze. The gaze of another can be positive, but the unfavorable look can also mean the loss of freedom. The other can trap someone with his "I saw you" (Sartre). And that look can be that of a predator (Walter Benjamin). The look then has no meaning for the other because the other is seen as a stranger. The look itself can be alienating. People who no longer see each other can no longer notice each other.

In his moving and haunting work, *The Evenings: A Winter's Tale* (Dutch, 1947), the well-known Dutch writer Gerard Reve wrote a story about a young boy from an extremely suffocating, petit-bourgeois environment—undoubtedly containing many autobiographical details from Reve's own early life—who became an office clerk in Amsterdam during the last ten days of 1946. The first words of *The Evenings* are: "It was still dark in the early morning hours . . ." And the book ends with the immortal words: "'It has been seen,' he murmured, 'it has not gone unnoticed.' He stretched himself out and fell into a deep sleep."

I think that it can in all certainty be said that Reve understood how God looks at people in this psalm, how he notices them: "Lord, who sees me as I am" ("Heer die mij ziet zoals ik ben"), as the rhymed version in Dutch begins. God sees and knows us truly. The God who is intent on loving humanity (Schillebeeckx)[38] ensures the dignity and honor of people: the human dignity of the poor. He ensures the preciousness of the vulnerable human being (Okke Jager)[39]: "What is mankind that you are mindful of them, / human beings that you care for them?" (Ps 8:4). "Lord, what are human beings that you care for them, / mere mortals that you think of them?" (Ps 144:3). It is out of true interest in them that God wishes to guide people when they sit and when they stand, when they think and when they work, when they sleep and when they are awake. He wants to protect, lay his hand in blessing upon, them. This is not a complaint from a doubting person who cannot escape the piercing glance of God. To the contrary, the psalmist traverses the whole of reality, as it were, the heavens above and the earth below, and even deeper; he travels from east to west. And always the comforting line is heard: "You are there." Even if it is pitch-black, and the light changes into darkness around me—even then, "the darkness will not be dark to you" (Ps 139:7–8, 11–12, 17). This is deep trust!—for the darkest of nights, "the dark night of the soul" when one feels abandoned by everyone, without hope for a better future. O God, your thoughts are far too lofty for me.

---

38. "De op menslievendheid bedachte God."
39. "Hoe kostbaar is een kwetsbaar mens."

But is this not all too beautiful—too beautiful to be true? Isn't every new morning a rude awakening for countless people? Wouldn't it be difficult to find God's loving presence there? Do you reign, God? Are you there? Do you notice how humankind suffers today? Do you truly look "*after humankind and its woe*"?[40] It seems much more often the case that those who do not take God into account at all say what goes, those who have blood on their hands, who live by torture and exploitation, who mock God and his commands, who do not bother about God at all. This is what the psalmist is thinking about. And suddenly we hear him strike a completely different key:

> If only you, God, would slay the wicked!
>   Away from me, you who are bloodthirsty![41]
> They speak of you with evil intent;
>   your adversaries misuse your name.
> Do I not hate those who hate you, Lord,
>   and abhor those who are in rebellion against you?[42]
> I have nothing but hatred for them;
>   I count them my enemies.
>
> (Ps 139:19–22)

Are these verses simply not incongruous with the rest? Are they not at odds with the rest of the psalm? Does this psalm suddenly turn to hatred and violence as well? These parts of the psalms that seem so reflective of hatred and violence, such as what we see here in Psalm 139, should not, however, be viewed as a call to or legitimation for engaging in *personal* vengeance or retribution. That is not what is actually being said here nor what is intended. Instead, these verses very clearly and emphatically place one in the reality of the world's violence: far away and close by—then and now and still for those who sing this psalm. The spiritual and physical terror and violence that occurs every day and night cannot and must not be trivialized. We cannot close our eyes to that, smooth it over, ignore it, or forget about it. We cannot overlook the suffering that people continually undergo in this world. That is what the psalm is calling us to. If these verses are omitted or removed in order to preserve a "nice" psalm, then one cuts out the complaint, losing the whole intention and even the point of the psalm. The poet of Psalm 139

---

40. "De mensheid en haar weedom." *De kleine Johannes* (by Frederik van Eeden); at the end of the book, he accompanies a Christ-like figure to humankind and its woe. https://nl.wikipedia.org/wiki/De_kleine_Johannes.

41. Cf. Ps 119:115: "Away from me, you evildoers, / that I may keep the commands of my God!"

42. Cf. Ps 119:158: "I look on the faithless with loathing, / for they do not obey your word."

feels obligated to offer concrete resistance and to fight against the enemies of reality as God intended it, namely, a world of justice and love.

That does not make him a religious fanatic, nor do those words turn him into someone bent on a "holy war." These verses cannot stimulate us in any way to despise and hate people hostile to us. Instead, what we hear is a passionate struggle against *structural* violence, against the injustice that corrupts society. We cannot close our eyes to social injustice and be blind to it. This psalm does not provide us with a doctrine about God's omniscience. It is a poetic psalm that is intended to hold up a mirror to those who cause violence. It is a poetic prayer that is intended to help the *victims* of violence, by putting this *cry* for justice in their mouths: to ask God to maintain their human dignity. It is therefore incorrect to speak here and elsewhere of psalms of vengeance in the usual sense of the term. All these imprecatory psalms to God rest on the recognition that *vengeance or retribution*—or, as we saw, redress—*belongs to God alone* (Deut 32:35;1 Sam 24:13; Ps 94:1; Isa 26:21; 63:4; cf. Ezek 23:3:7, 8; Rom 12:19; Heb 10:30). Vengeance is not something left to human hands: human beings need not concern themselves with vengeance or retribution but can leave it safely in God's hands. To assert that vengeance is the Lord's is an act of deep faith.[43]

PRAISING GOD AND WIELDING THE SWORD?

In the church services where I preach, I like to choose the Dutch rhymed version of Psalm 149 as the opening hymn. I usually choose the first two verses before the Votum and Greeting and two verses (3 and 5) after. "For convenience's sake" (?) I skip the fourth verse which, in the rhymed version, is translated as follows:

> God's praise shall in their song resound
> And in their right hand the sword be found
> That to God's vengeance will give voice
> To punish the pride, the nations' choice.
> They will cast in chains and cell
> The tyrants who against God rebel
> They can rejoice because forever quelled
> Are the brutish deeds; they are felled.

The verses in the original text on which the above is based reads:

> Let his faithful people rejoice in this honor
> and sing for joy on their beds.

43. According to Zenger, *A God of Vengeance*, 31–33.

> May the praise of God be in their mouths
>   and a double-edged sword in their hands,
> to inflict vengeance on the nations
>   and punishment on the peoples,
> to bind their kings with fetters,
>   their nobles with shackles of iron,
> to carry out the sentence written against them—
>   this is the glory of all his faithful people.
> (Ps 149:5–9)

What does the Hebrew text say? It says that God will put an end to violence. But how will he do that? What is the role of the pious individual, that is, the "righteous individual," in that? Can we speak here of collaboration between the human being and God? Do both have a part to play in this? Is this an invitation to praise God and at the same time to take up the sword to take vengeance for themselves? Does the verse that I prefer to leave out invoke that?

If this psalm had been written in the second century before the Christian calendar—thus in the same period as the book of Daniel—then it could be suggested that it would have to do with the victory that Judas Maccabee (the Hammer) enjoyed over the well-trained battalions of the tyrant Antiochus IV Epiphanes (168–165 BC), who wanted to eradicate the Jewish religion. The Maccabees engaged in a holy war, a *jihâd*, against the Greek occupiers and made liberal use of violence in doing so. They did so in God's name. Fighting with their hands, they prayed to God in their hearts. They killed no less than 35,000 men, overjoyed at God's visible help (2 Macc 15: 27).

The Psalms have indeed often been read, exegeted, and used that way until the present by Christian exegetes, Military success has been understood as a sign of God's nearness, and it is still thought that one can and should wage wars in God's name. This psalm could be sung enthusiastically as support for that idea. Such an explanation of the psalms is what incited Thomas Müntzer (d. 1525) in the German Peasants' Revolt. Müntzer was a German evangelical theologian who broke with the ideas of Martin Luther, whom he initially admired, and, in opposition to Luther, called for military resistance to feudal oppression, taking the lead in the German Peasants' Revolt, which ended with his own beheading in 1525.[44]

This psalm was a battle song of both Catholic rulers and the soldiers of the Protestant Swedish king Gustav Adolph (1611–1632) in the Thirty Years' War (1618–1648, which took place during the Dutch Eighty Years' War). Gustav Adolph was viewed as one of greatest military leaders of all

---

44. Zenger, *Mit meinem Gott überspringe ich Mauern*, 49.

time. According to Johannes Burckhardt, the king began the Thirty Years' War precisely 100 years after the publication of the Lutheran confession of faith[45] and had himself extolled as a savior. In his own war manifesto, however, the king did not speak of religious motivations but only of political and economic issues.[46]

But does this use fit the spirit of the psalms? It is instructive to compare these psalms with the song of Judith. Both "songs" are called "new songs," like Psalm 149: "Sing to the Lord a new song" (Ps 149:1; cf. 33:2; 144:9). This is the case with the song of Judith:

> I will sing to my God a new song:
> O Lord, you are great and glorious,
> > wonderful in strength, invincible.
> (Jdt 16:13)

This song is similar to the song of Moses (Exod 15:1–18); and the song of the prophetess Deborah (Judg 5:1–31). Deborah was indeed the only female judge, but there were other Israelite women who were prophets, such as Miriam and Huldah (2 Kgs 22:16–17). Deborah has been called one of the oldest examples of charismatic leadership.[47]

Judith is the chief character of the apocryphal biblical book named after her. She was probably a fictional figure, intended as a model of heroic courage. There are serious historical errors in the book, which led to the book being put aside as an incredible fairy tale, though it is possible that the errors were intentional to avoid trouble with the authorities.[48] The writer was probably a Palestinian Jew who wrote the book toward the middle of the second century BC, after the Maccabean revolt. Judith is a Jewish widow who manages to win the trust of Holofernes, Nebuchadnezzar's general, seduces him, and then kills him. Her act causes the enemy to take flight. Hundreds of artists, poets, and playwrights have told her story.[49]

Her song of praise begins as follows:

> Begin a song to my God with tambourines,
> > sing to my Lord with cymbals.
> Raise to him a new psalm;
> > exalt him, and call upon his name.
> (Jdt 16:1)

---

45. *Confessio Augustana.*
46. https://historipediaofficial.wikia.org/wiki/Gustavus_Adolphus_of_Sweden.
47. *Alle Bijbelse personen*, s.v., Debora.
48. *Alle Bijbelse personen*, s.v., Judith.
49. *Bijbelse Encyclopaedie*, s.v., Judith; *BW* s.v., Judit.

Already before the actual praise of God (Jdt 16:13–17), the hymn first describes what happened (Jdt 16:2–12):

> For the Lord is a God who crushes wars;
> he sets up his camp among his people;
> he delivered me from the hands of my pursuers.
> (Jdt 16:2)

> But the Lord Almighty has foiled them
>   by the hand of a woman.
> For their mighty one did not fall by the hands of the young men,
>   nor did the sons of the Titans strike him down,
>   nor did tall giants set upon him;
> but Judith daughter of Merari
>   with the beauty of her countenance undid him.
> For she put away her widow's clothing
>   to exalt the oppressed in Israel.
> She anointed her face with perfume;
>   she fastened her hair with a tiara
>   and put on a linen gown to beguile him.
> Her sandal ravished his eyes,
>   her beauty captivated his mind,
>   and the sword severed his neck!
> (Jdt 16:5–9)

In her prayer preceding that, Judith says:

> Look at their pride, and send your wrath upon their heads. Give to me, a widow, the strong hand to do what I plan. By the deceit of my lips strike down the slave with the prince and the prince with his servant; crush their arrogance *by the hand of a woman*.[50] For your strength does not depend on numbers, nor your might on the powerful. But you are the God of the lowly, helper of the oppressed, upholder of the weak, protector of the forsaken, savior of those without hope. (Jdt 9: 9–11)

The story of Jael, who killed Sisera, the Canaanite army commander while he slept by hammering a tent peg into his temple (Judg 4:21–23), also shows a scornful view of women as executors of justice. Jael's husband was descended from Jethro, Moses' father-in-law, and belonged to the nomadic Kennite tribe of metal workers who were said to have descended from Cain. The song of Deborah gives a poetic summary of the story of that final battle

---

50. KBS on Jdt 9:10.

(Judg 4): "Most blessed of women be Jael, . . . / most blessed of tent-dwelling women" (Judg 5:24).

It was said about Judith centuries later,: "O daughter, you are *blessed* by the Most High God above all other women on earth; and blessed be the Lord God, who created the heavens and the earth, who has guided you to cut off the head of the leader of our enemies" (Jdt 13:18). Exegetes tell us that, while the book of Judith is full of chronological, historical, and geographical mistakes and improbabilities, as a narrative it is exciting, realistic, logical, and very well composed.[51] But just as the song of Deborah does not give a historical description of the event, so it is also not the intention of this book of Judith to narrate a *historical* event, but to indicate to whom all power actually belongs.

But after these songs and hymns, Psalm 149 still leaves us with the question: Is there collaboration between the human being and God? Walter Brueggemann states in his exegesis of Psalm 149 that the psalm does call for human cooperation on the basis of praising God (sic!). People are urged to an act of war that entails vengeance, punishment, putting the enemy in chains, and carrying out judgment (Ps 149:8–9). He calls this a statement of sober historical realism. In its songs, Israel does not try to escape historical reality but plays an active role in that reality.

Brueggemann is perhaps not completely happy with his exegesis—at least that is the impression I get when he says that the psalm is very difficult to explain because the proposed action can have different intentions.[52] In another commentary on the psalms that he wrote with Bellinger, he discusses these verses (Ps 149:7–9a) about the double-edged sword as an effective instrument. It is a sword in the hands of Israel that will execute vengeance and punishment, will put kings and nobles in chains, and will implement justice. "These phrases portray an act of great savage power by which the adversaries of Israel are overpowered and punished, thus establishing the supremacy of *Israel's power* as a result of YHWH's victory. The psalm moves from a celebration of YHWH's power to an affirmation of Israel's military capacity (sic!)."[53] He then refers to an expression in the American army from the Second World War: "Praise the Lord and pass the ammunition." Both exegetes then conclude by saying that "God bless America" is a compelling echo of Israel's old and "theo-military claim."[54]

---

51. *BW*, s.v., Judit.
52. Brueggemann, *The Message of the Psalms*, 166.
53. Brueggemann and Bellinger, *Psalms*, 616.
54. Brueggemann and Bellinger, *Psalms*, 617.

Is that what we find in the psalms and what is truly intended? Is that how these psalms must be interpreted and applied in the modern period? Or is there another possibility or, in my view, even a necessity to explain the lines "Let the high praises of God be in their throats / and two-edged swords in their hands" in an entirely different way? What is meant by the Hebrew conjunction *waw* (and) that is present in the text? In my view, it is crucial for exegesis to not understand that word in the usual sense of "both the one and the other." Here it has to be understood as a *waw adequationis*, suggesting thereby an equivalent, which means "equal to."[55] Thus, praising God is like having a double-edged sword.

The Targum, an old Jewish translation or paraphrase of the Old Testament in Aramaic, already provides this interpretation. In the synagogue service the Hebrew Bible readings were translated in sections by an interpreter.[56] The psalms of praise that were sung by the faithful are thus to be understood as the sword by which God's judgment was carried out, how his order of justice comes about. That allows for the following translation: the praise of God is the double-edged sword in their hand.[57] The conjunction "and" can best be rendered by a colon. The second line is intended precisely—as in countless psalms—to explain what has been stated in the first line of the verse; that is how biblical poetry works. According to this psalm, judgment is and remains a work of God *alone*. He is the one who carries it out. What the poor, the faithful, the just must do here is praise God—that is their sword.[58] In that sense, it is not in any way a battle song as used by Catholic rulers and Gustav Adolph's soldiers![59]

I found the intention of this psalm concisely expressed in a beautiful preface to a biblical journal devotional:

> While strongmen and he-men fight their whole lives long on the razor's edge, the weapon they [the pious] use is their songs to the glory of God. That is where they put their trust. They would prefer to go singing through life than fighting. Their power lies in keeping the song of praise going.[60]

The final psalm of the Psalter (Ps 150), which follows as a conclusion to Psalm 149, is recast by Dorothy Sölle in poetic form as follows:

---

55. Cf. https://www.deepdyve.com/lp/brill/further-examples-of-the-waw-explicativum-WhdTHzUsoS.
56. *BW*, s.v., Targum.
57. Hossfeld and Zenger, *Psalms 3*, 643.
58. Zenger, *Mit meinem Gott überspringe ich Mauern*, 53.
59. Zenger, *Mit meinem Gott überspringe ich Mauern*, 49.
60. Dekker, *Verborgene die bij ons zijt*, 214.

Praise God no longer everywhere,
Seek him not in power and numbers,
Conceive of him not in pomp and splendor,
Give him no royal hall.
File him off the circled guilder.[61]
Do not make him a star,
up in the clouds, high and wild.
He turns his back on all that homage!
Praise God as the least of men,
outlawed and with no homeland,
constantly besieged around,
a life despised and forgotten,
deeply ignored and rudely treated.
He looks for those
who seek him in the minor things,
where he calls for peace and justice![62]

GOD IS MERCIFUL

Who is God? What are his characteristics, his attributes (*sifât* in Arabic)? The Christian and Muslim theological traditions have devoted a great deal of thought to this. Judaism does not actually speak of "Jewish theology."[63] Islam speaks of the 99 beautiful names of God that play an important role in the daily pious ritual of the *subha*, or "rosary." The "Names" were extensively discussed[64] in Muslim theology (*'ilm al-kalâm*) like the attributes of God in Christian theology. When I was young, dogmatics was the most important discipline in the faculty of theology and its final exam was the most exacting. Theology was actually thought to be more or less limited to dogmatics. In his *The Muslim Creed*, A.J. Wensinck gives a general overview of Muslim dogmatics and confessions of faith, that is, the later developments of Muslim theology.[65] In the Anglo-Saxon world, dogmatics falls under systematic theology. In my view, that is a *contradictio in adjecto*: the contradiction is found in the adjective. As I see it, theology cannot be systematized, turned into a system, if one wants to deal with the Scriptures—here the Tanakh,

---

61. The phrase "God met ons" (God with us) was engraved on the side of the Dutch guilder, and now on the Dutch two-euro coin. https://www.digibron.nl/viewer/collectie/Digibron/id/7a42bc984116be6a447b11f4bd12c77c.

62. https://docplayer.nl/23439805-Dorothee-solle.html.

63. There is no entry for this in *The Eerdmans Dictionary of Early Judaism*.

64. Cf. Gimaret, *Les Noms divins en Islam*.

65. Wensinck, *The Muslim Creed*.

the New Testament, and the Qur'an—in a responsible way and wants to use these Scriptures as the starting point for an understanding of God. It is striking that, in his brilliant and thorough study of the divine names in Muslim theology (*ilm al-kalâm*), Daniel Gimaret indicates that the love of God is stronger than his punitive righteousness.[66] Mercy triumphs there as well over judgment, as James, Jesus' brother, already wrote in his letter (Jam 2:13).[67]

Who is God then? What is our image of God as based on the Bible and the Qur'an? Christians have had (or still have?) the idea that the Old Testament portrays the God of vengeance and the New Testament the God of love. But that is a fundamentally wrong understanding of how the three books fit together. The God of love cannot be played off against the God of anger. Both these ways of acting on God's part belong together in an inseparable yet tension-filled way. Nevertheless, the Old Testament, according to Rabbinic Judaism, attempts to keep both aspects together in such a way that, when it comes down to the wire, justice moves into the background because God's actual work is to show mercy.[68]

In both the Bible and the Qur'an, God is called the Merciful or Compassionate, *Rahmân*. All chapters in the Qur'an, with the exception of the ninth, begin with the words: "In the name of God the Merciful, the Compassionate," both words being two different forms of the root of the word "merciful" (*rhm*). God is spoken of metaphorically both in the Bible and in the Qur'an, and God can be spoken as both father and mother. The maternal side comes to expression, as it were, in the divine name "Merciful." This name Merciful, *Rahmân*, is related to both the Hebrew word *rehem* and the Arabic word *rahîm*, both of which mean "womb." According to Hosea, God has a feminine, maternal side:

> How can I give you up, Ephraim?
> How surrender you, O Israel? . . .
> I have had a change of heart,[69]
> All my tenderness is stirred.
> I will not act on My wrath,
> Will not turn to destroy Ephraim.
> For I am God, not man—
> The Holy One in your midst:
> I will not come in fury.
> (Hos 11:8–9; JSB)

66. Gimaret, *Les Noms divins en Islam*.
67. Oussoren, *De Naardense Bijbel*.
68. Zenger, *Das Erste Testament*, 72–73; Rahbar, *God of Justice*.
69. *De Naardense Bijbel*: "Mijn hart zal zich in mij omdraaien" ("My heart will turn over in me.")

What motivation does God have for not carrying out his fierce anger and instead expressing his "maternal" love? *For I am God, and not man* (Hos 11:9).[70] The prophet Samuel says to King Saul that, because he did not obey the command of the Lord, the Lord had rejected him as king over Israel: "He who is the Glory of Israel does not lie or change his mind; for he is not a human being, who should change his mind." (1 Sam 15:29). God is not a human being that he *regrets* something he does. If God says he will do something, will he not do it? And he promises something, will he not bring it to pass? (Num 23:19. Job 9:32).[71] After all, God has no regrets about his gifts or calling (Rom 11:29).

The background of this negation is the fact that God does change his mind. One can think here of the flood: "The Lord regretted that he had made human beings on the earth, and his heart was deeply troubled. So the Lord said, 'I will wipe from the face of the earth the human race I have created—and with them the animals, the birds and the creatures that move along the ground—for I regret that I have made them'" (Gen 6:6–7). When Moses stayed for such a long time on the mountain, the children of Israel forged the bull calf, bowed before it and cried out: "These are your gods, Israel, who brought you up out of Egypt" (Exod 32:8). God then said to Moses: 'They are a stiff-necked people. Now leave me alone so that my anger may burn against them and that I may destroy them. Then I will make you into a great nation" (Exod 32:9–10). But Moses pleaded with God and persuaded him to forego his punishment of his people (Exod 32:14; cf. Deut 32:26). God also *regretted* that he had made Saul king because Saul had turned away from him. The prophet Samuel who had anointed him was deeply distressed about this and cried out to God all night (1 Sam 15:11). He continues to mourn for Saul because the Lord regretted that he had made him king over Israel (1 Sam 15:35; cf. Q 2:247–248). But when the people of Israel to whom God turned repent, God regrets the disaster he threatened them with (Jer 18:8). "If it does evil in my sight and does not obey me, then I will reconsider the good I had intended to do for it" (Jer 18:10); "Now reform your ways and your actions and obey the Lord your God. Then the Lord will relent and not bring the disaster he has pronounced against you" (Jer 26:13). The best-known example is the change that occurs with respect to Nineveh against the expectations (and even the wishes) of the prophet: "When God saw what they did and how they turned from their evil ways,

---

70. Cf. Num 23:19; 1 Sam 15:29.

71. Eccl 6:10: "That which hath been is named already, and it is known that it is man: neither may he contend with him [God] that is mightier than he" (KJV). In the given order, the human being can do nothing but resign himself; over against God he means nothing. Cf. Isa 45:9; Job 9:12; Rom 9:20.

he relented and did not bring on them the destruction he had threatened" (cf. Q 10:98; 37:147–148).[72]

Nevertheless, the unconditional love of the Merciful does not want the children of men to die but to live: "Do I take any pleasure in the death of the wicked? declares the Sovereign Lord. Rather, am I not pleased when they turn from their ways and live?" (Ezek 18:23; cf. 33:11; Wis 11:26; Luke 15:7, 10, 32; John 8:11; Rom 11:32).

THE EARTH WAS WITHOUT FORM AND VOID

In the second part of this final chapter of this book on apocalyptic, which actually concerns the last things, we will argue that we cannot actually say anything sensible about the last things if we do not see that they are inseparable from the first things, with what the creation of humankind concerned in the beginning and still does, every day anew. Unfortunately, the creation narratives have been incorrectly understood for centuries, which has led to interesting, fascinating, and perhaps also important discussions but which have little to do with Genesis 1.

We can begin with the question: Does the Old Testament present God's creation as *creatio ex nihilo*, as creation out of nothing? There is no unambiguous "evidence" for that before the very late apocryphal text of 2 Maccabees. In that work, the mother of the seven Maccabee brothers saw all her seven sons die in one day at the hands of King Antiochus. Animated by noble sentiments, she encourages each of them in their mother tongue. She hardens her womanly sensitivity with manly courage and says to them:

> I do not know how you came into being in my womb. It was not I who gave you life and breath, nor I who set in order the elements within each of you. Therefore the Creator of the world, who shaped the beginning of humankind and devised the origin of all things, will in his mercy give life and breath back to you again, since you now forget yourselves for the sake of his laws. (2 Macc 7:22–23)

To her youngest, the only one still left alive, she says, mocking the cruel despot in her native Hebrew:

> My son, have pity on me. I carried you nine months in my womb, and nursed you for three years, and have reared you and brought you up[73] to this point in your life, and have taken care

---

72. Jewett, *Romans*, 709, n. 144.
73. Here an important key word is again found that was discussed in chapter V:

of you. I beg you, my child, to *look at the heaven and the earth and see everything that is in them, and recognize that God did not make them out of things that existed.* And in the same way the human race came into being. (2 Macc 7:27–28)

But here is almost no mention of a *creatio ex nihilo* in the canonical texts. Neither the Bible nor the Qur'an speak about it, even though both the Christian and the Muslim tradition still hold to it.[74] An *Encyclopedia of the Qur'ân* that was published at the beginning of this century still pays extensive attention to this idea.[75] The notion of a *creatio ex nihilo* arose in Christianity at the beginning of the third century, and only later in Judaism. Both the Bible and the Qur'an speak of the creation of heaven and earth in six days. Despite the fact that this idea is widespread, it is given scant attention in the Bible itself (Gen 1:2; 2:3; Exod 20:11; 31:17). It was believed to be literally true and explained in that way for centuries. That God completed the creation in six days (Q 7:54; 10:3; 11:7; 57:4; 25:59; 32:4; 41:9–12; 50:38) led to calculations that the world was created six or seven thousand years ago. If that is a "fact," how does that relate to the theory of evolution (Darwin and others), to the idea that the earth has existed for billions of years since the Big Bang?

If the book Genesis begins with the story of the creation of heaven and earth, of animals and human beings, it is not concerned with those questions that have been at the heart of usually fruitless discussions: the theme of creation over against evolution. However captivating that issue might be, in any case the Bible and the Qur'an are not concerned with that, and they do not give any indication of that if they are read properly. The subject of Genesis 1 is not creation versus evolution. The story of creation does not give any literal information that God created the earth out of nothing in six 24-hour days. That is not the issue for this mythological, poetic narrative, which instead must be read with a sense of the late-Jewish and early Christian mythological mentality, as Amos Wilder correctly observed.[76]

Because the creation narrative is found at the beginning of the Bible, we readers are usually not aware that it was written after the books of prophets like Isaiah and Jeremiah. Those are the books that we must first read and understand to have a good understanding of what the first chapters of Genesis are concerned with. The Bible opens as follows:

---

paidaia.

74. *EQ* s.v., creation, 475–79.

75. *EQ*, s.v., creation, 475–79; *EI*, s.v., Kalk, for a discussion of *creatio ex nihilo*.

76. Wilder, *Jesus' Parables and the War of Myths*, 135.

> In the beginning God created the heavens and the earth. Now the earth was formless and empty [*tohu wabohu*], darkness was over the surface of the deep, and the Spirit of God was hovering over the waters.
>
> And God said, "Let there be light," and there was light. God saw that the light was good, and he separated the light from the darkness. God called the light "day," and the darkness he called "night." And there was evening, and there was morning—the first day. (Gen 1:1–5)

How a translation can put the reader on the wrong track already in the second line (!) of the Bible becomes clear in the second verse of some translations, such as the new Dutch translation of the Bible. There the text reads that the earth was "still (*nog*)" formless and deathlike. That word *nog* is not found at all in the Hebrew text. But if the verse is translated in this way, it is then being read in a *chronological* sense. *At first*, at the primal moment, everything was formless and empty, but *since then* a change has occurred. If that is what is said or meant, then there would be no reason to speak elsewhere in the Bible of something being "formless and empty." But we do find the expression "formless and empty" a few times in the prophets! And it is crucial and very enlightening therefore to see the context in which that expression is used.

The prophet Jeremiah describes the destruction of Jerusalem and the land of Canaan by the Babylonians under King Nebuchadnezzar, whom we have already encountered a number of times in this book.

> I looked at the earth,
>   and it was formless and empty;
> and at the heavens,
>   and their light was gone.
> . . .
> I looked, and the fruitful land was a desert;
>   all its towns lay in ruins
>   before the Lord, before his fierce anger.
> (Jer 4:23, 26)

Jeremiah sees total devastation around him: he sees towns in ruins,[77] no more lights in the sky, mountains and hills quaking[78] and swaying,[79] no

---

77. With respect to Ammon: It would become a mound of ruins and all its towns would go up in flames (Jer 49:2). Jerusalem is called a city of deception and oppression (Jer 6:6).

78. Jer 8:16; 10:10; 25:16; 49:21 51:29.

79. Jer 4:24.

human being anywhere to be found. The vineyard,[80] the garden, the paradise of the promised land had become a desert.[81] In short, all is summarily expressed as *tohu wabohu*—formless and empty.[82]

Another example can be found in (Deutero-)Isaiah (40–55), who prophesied during the Babylonian captivity. The situation in which the children of Israel found themselves is the opposite of the promised land, but Isaiah makes clear that it did not begin this way. God did not create the world as *empty* (*tohu*) but formed it to be inhabited (Isa 45:18). In this situation, however, the peoples of the earth are viewed by God as worthless and less than nothing (*tohu*) (Isa 40:17; cf. Ps 62:10; Dan 4:32), just like the rulers of the earth (Isa 40:23) and their images are as wind and emptiness (Isa 41:29). Everything has become *formless and empty*. The images (i.e., the idols) express that *ideologically*. But that is not what God *intended* for the earth.[83]

Thus, if one keeps in mind that the creation narrative in Genesis was written after Isaiah and Jeremiah, it will be discovered—speaking apocalyptically!—that the characteristic of being formless and empty is not a description of a kind of moonscape. Rather, already at the beginning of the Bible, the phrase is intended to provide insight into the disastrous situation in which humans and the world exist, with the exile after the devastation of Jerusalem as the example par excellence.

"Formless and empty/void" describes the despair, the chaos, the dream of a city of peace (Jerusalem) and a land of promise cruelly destroyed.[84] The "primal flood" is characteristic of all kinds of threats that wash over the earth again and again—the flood story revisited: on that day all the springs of the deep broke loose, the floodgates of the heavens were opened (Gen 7:11; cf. Q 11:36–48), and the chaos returned.[85] Jonah—strikingly called the "Man of the Fish" (!) (Q 21:87; 68:48)—prays in the belly of the fish: "You hurled me into the depths, / into the very heart of the seas, / and the currents swirled about me; / all your waves and breakers / swept over me" (Jonah 2:3; cf. Ps 42:8). Jonah is talking here about the waters of the great deep, the sea that

---

80. Jer 12:10.

81. Jer 6:8: "Take warning, Jerusalem, / or I will turn away from you / and make your land desolate / so no one can live in it."

82. Rooze, *Schepping is bevrijding*, 22–24.

83. Rooze, *Schepping is bevrijding*, 24–25.

84. Rooze, *Schepping is bevrijding*, 25.

85. KBS on Gen 7:11.

surrounds the earth (Isa 51:10).⁸⁶ It is constantly maintained that the primal flood can (and will) be suppressed; the threat will be overcome!⁸⁷

THE BIBLICAL COUNTERNARRATIVE TO THE BABYLONIAN

The creation story comes from Babylon, indeed the same time and place where Ezekiel's visions were revealed to him! It is crucially important that we understand the immediate political context in which both Ezekiel received his visions and in which the creation story was told. A Jewish exegete in the Middle Ages already established the connection between Ezekiel's call vision (Ezek 1) and Genesis 1: "Let us make man in the very image that the Holy One, blessed be He, showed to the prophets in the form of an anthropos."⁸⁸

What does it mean that God reveals himself as human? Why does God turn to Ezekiel with a human face?⁸⁹ The story of the creation of the human being is completely at odds with the Babylonian creation narrative (*Enûma Eliš*). The creation narrative in the Bible explicitly concerns, as does Ezekiel's message, a "counternarrative" that is directed against the Babylonian "mythical" stories that are intended to create an ideology of inhumanity. This counternarrative, like that of the gospel of Mark,⁹⁰ is thus incredibly politically charged and subversive. After all, people live in social and political contexts and are, also according to the biblical creation narrative, not created to live as slaves of the state, as the god Marduk wanted. Given such a god, people would continue to suffer under the yoke of unjust rulers and the blood of fellow human beings would continue to be shed (cf. Gen 9:6). In the *counternarrative*, people are made for "freedom and responsibility."⁹¹ Being created in the image of God has ethical consequences.⁹² And if the *shedding of blood* continues, then one loses one's good land and the good earth (Ezek 33:25; cf. Lev 17:10–14).⁹³

---

86. KBS on Isa 51:10.
87. Rooze, *Schepping is bevrijding*, 25.
88. Wink, *The Human Being*, 290, n. 40.
89. Wink, *The Human Being*, 26.
90. Cf. chapter VI.
91. Bill Wylie Kellermann according to Wink, *The Human Being*, 28. 279, n. 35.
92. Wink, *The Human Being*, 28.
93. Wink, *The Human Being*, 28.

In the struggle between the gods that ends in the supremacy of Marduk, people are seen as destined for slavery to the gods of Mesopotamia.[94] In contrast, the climax of the biblical story of the creation of people is that they are created in God's image and likeness (Gen 1:26). In the Babylonian creation epic, people are the slaves of the gods, created from the blood of a murdered god, which means that people must be viewed as always subjected to the rulers of this world, and this was to be the primary characteristic of their existence throughout all time. These rulers saw themselves as supermen, the "big bosses,"[95] people who think they will hold on to power their whole lives and believe they are equal to God. This was the case in the Bible *and* the Qur'an for Nimrod in the time of Abraham, the Pharaoh at the time of Moses, and that of Nebuchadnezzar, Alexander the Great and his successors, such as Antiochus IV Epiphanes, and in the New Testament time for emperors like Augustus and his successors. Julius Caesar and the following Roman emperors were divinized after they died: Augustus, Claudius, Vespasian and Titus, the destroyer of Jerusalem! "While at life's end ordinary mortals entered the world of the dead, the divinized Emperor joined the gods."[96] Although the general public greeted the death of Caesar Domitian with indifference, the troops grieved and began to speak immediately of Domitian as a god.[97]

The Qur'an speaks very clearly and poignantly about the Pharaoh's arrogance when he says, "I do not know of any god that you may have other than me" (Q 28:38; 26:29).[98] Pharaoh says to Moses "I am your exalted lord!" (Q 79:24). What is characteristic for rulers of that time—just as much as for the rulers of today, according to the apocalyptic reading!—is their absolute faith in the power of money (gold), lies ("fake news"), and the military power of destruction.[99] But the complete opposite is revealed to Moses in the holy valley Tuwâ: "I am God / —there is no god except Me" (Q 20:14). God reveals his Name to Moses: "I am who I am" (Exod 3:14). Then the One says: "I have indeed seen the misery of my people in Egypt. I have heard

---

94. https://en.wikipedia.org/wiki/Enûma_Eliš.

95. *Heer Bommel en de bovenbazen* (Mr Bommel and the Big Bosses) is a story from the Bommel saga, written and illustrated by Marten Toonder. The story was first published on 12 August 1963 and ran until 7 December of that year: Bommel's first encounter with the very top people in stock exchange circles. https://nl.wikipedia.org/wiki/De_bovenbazen.

96. Suetonius, *The Twelve Caesars*, 259.

97. Suetonius, *The Twelve Caesars*, 272.

98. Moses hears: "Indeed I am God /—there is no god except Me. (Q 20:10–14; 79:17; Deut 6:45).

99. Moloch and mammon; see Wessels, *The Torah, the Gospel, and the Qur'an*, index.

them *crying out* because of their slave drivers, and I am concerned about their suffering" (Exod 3:7).

What does the biblical creation story say? What is the biblical vision? And God says:

> "Let us make mankind in our image, in our likeness, so that they may rule over the fish in the sea and the birds in the sky, over the livestock and all the wild animals, and over all the creatures that move along the ground." So God created mankind in his own image, / in the image of God he created them; / male and female he created them. (Gen 1:26–27)

It is not about just two people (Adam and Eve) but about all of *humankind*: we are all created in God's image and not just the rulers.

In the same period that this creation narrative was written in Babylon, Ezekiel sees someone on a sapphire throne who seems to have a *human form* (Ezek 1:26). It is important to understand that this is a "figure of speech." It is an *anthropomorphic* way of speaking of God's appearance, with which Israel was familiar.[100] Many of the texts are written in poetic language, which requires a non-literal reading of the texts. This is true of both the Bible and the Qur'an.

God's *feet* (Exod 24:10; Zach 14:4) and his *hand*, primarily an image of his strength, his power in creation and history, are described (Ps 8:7; Deut 5:15). The righteous person is held in God's right hand (Ps 73:23).[101] The Qur'an also speaks of the *hand* of God (Q 3:73; 5:64; 48:10; 23:88; 36:83).[102] All gifts are in God's hand ((Q 3:73; 5:64; 48:10). The good is in God's hand (Q 3:26), just as grace is (Q 3:73; cf. 57:29; 5:54). Moses sees God's *back*: "[Y]ou will see my back; but my face must not be seen" (Exod 33:22–23). The Lord appeared to Abraham once, in the heat of the day, while he was sitting at the entrance to his tent. He raised his eyes and saw three men suddenly standing in front of him (Gen 18:1–2; cf. Gen 18:16, 22). Three *strangers* visited Abraham; he showed them hospitality, and one of them in particular revealed himself to be God (Gen 18:2; Gen 18:16, 22). The Qur'an calls these visitors "messengers"[103] who announce to Abraham the birth of Isaac and then Jacob (Q 11:71). The prophet Daniel sees God as an "Ancient of Days," sitting on a throne, with his hair as white as wool (Dan 7:9), his *eyes* flaming like fire (Rev 1:14). In another vision, Daniel sees him standing

---

100. Kuitert, *De mensvormigheid Gods.*
101. *BW*, s.v., hand.
102. *EQ*, s.v., antropomorphism.
103. Gabriel and Michael are mentioned by name (Q 2:98).

before him, looking *like a man*, and he heard a *human voice* calling: "Gabriel, tell this man the meaning of the vision" (Dan 8:15–16; cf. 9:21–23).

The Qur'an also speaks of God in an anthropomorphic way, despite the fact that there is nothing like Him (Q 42:11). This notion is also found in the Bible: "'To whom will you compare me? / Or who is my equal?' says the Holy One" (Isa 40:25; cf. Isa 44:7).[104] Dominion over all is in God's hand (Q 23:88). That hand is thus not literally intended but also refers here to God's power. The Qur'an speaks of God's *eyes* (Q 20:39; 52:48; 54:14): Noah sails in the ark before God's eyes (Q 54:14). God's love was poured out over Moses in his basket made of rushes so that he would be brought up under God's eyes (Q 20:39; 52:48), which means under his protection and his will. God sits on the throne (Q 7:54; 10:3; 13:2; 25:59; 32:4; 57:4), a symbol of his power and majesty.[105] After creation, God *sat* on his throne[106] to govern the world (Q 7:54).[107]

The prophet Ezekiel gives us a view of and insight into the history of a God-human drama that is portrayed against the backdrop of how it all *began* with humankind and the world. Thus God said at the beginning: "Let there be light." "And God separated the light from the darkness" (Gen 1:3). The creation of humankind happens on the sixth day. The narrative repeatedly declares concerning the acts of creation on the previous days that *God saw that it was good*. At the end of that sixth day, on which humankind was created, he himself says that *it was very good* (Gen 1:3–31)! And humans, both male and female, live in the Garden of Eden (Q 9:72; 13:23; 16:31; 19:61; 20:76; 35:33; 38:50; 40:8; 61:12; 98:8).

When the Bible and the Qur'an speak of the last things (*eschata*; *eschatology*), such language goes back to the first things, to how it all began. There is a close connection between *protology* and *eschatology*. The term "protology"—literally, "the doctrine of the *first things*," is used primarily when the beginning of the world is discussed in a religious context. It then refers to the "doctrine of creation."[108] The counter to protology is "the doctrine of

---

104. Is 46:5: "With whom will you compare me or count me equal? / To whom will you liken me that we may be compared?" Ps 89:6: "For who in the skies above can compare with the Lord?"

105. *EQ*, s.v., Literary Structures, 201–2; s.v., hand, 401.

106. His throne was on the water (Q 1:7. Gen 1:2; Ps 104:3; Rev 4:6; KBS). This is the image of the firmament and the "waters above the firmament" (Gen 1:7); it was thought that God's throne was located above the waters above the firmament Cf. Exod 24:10; Ps 29:10.

107. In the Jewish Sabbath liturgy it appears as follows: "On the seventh day he exalted Himself and sat on the throne of His glory" According to the midrash, he did not do that before the Sabbath; Speyer, *Die biblische Erzählungen*, 24.

108. https://nl.wikipedia.org/wiki/Protologie.

the *last things*." If "we people" are made in God's image, male and female (Gen 1:27), this therefore means that we humans are therefore, in one way or another, like God in our human existence. But how? And are we humans truly the image of God, as the Creator himself intended?

"We humans" are put into the Garden of Eden. We were (and are!) intended to live in that Paradise not only at the beginning but for always—a paradise on this earth already, here and now. From the beginning of the Bible to its end, that paradise is held out as a prospect, promised, assured because God, who himself resembles "the human being," breathed his breath, his divine Spirit, into us and wants to breathe it into us again and again! That is why it can and will turn out alright with humans here on earth, even very well—that is the good news!

Ezekiel provides the most powerful example one can think of in this context when he had a vision—probably in the same valley where he received his great call vision. Now, however, he sees the valley as full of dry bones. The *hand of God*—which refers to a specific prophetic experience[109]—came over the prophet Ezekiel, and he was transported by the Spirit of God to that valley (Ezek 37:10). The Spirit of God is often mentioned in connection with Ezekiel's visions (cf. Ezek 3:12, 14, 24; 8:3; 11:1; 5:24; 37:1; 43:5).[110] God then asks Ezekiel:

> "Son of man, can these bones live?"
> I said, "Sovereign Lord, you alone know."
> Then he said to me, "Prophesy to these bones and say to them, 'Dry bones, hear the word of the Lord!' This is what the Sovereign Lord says to these bones: I will make breath enter you, and you will come to life." (Ezek 37:3–5)

Then he said to Ezekiel:

> "Prophesy to the breath; prophesy, son of man, and say to it, 'This is what the Sovereign Lord says: Come, breath, from the four winds and breathe into these slain, that they may live.'" So I prophesied as he commanded me, and breath entered them; they came to life and stood up on their feet—a vast army. (Ezek 37:9–10)

---

109. KBS on Ezek 1:3; cf. Ezek 3:14, 22; 33:22; 37:1; 1 Kgs 18:46; 2 Kgs 3:15; Isa 8:11; Jer 15:17.

110. The spirit of the Lord is mentioned in connection with the judge Othniel, a special power that is at work in someone and is viewed as a gift of God. KBS on Judg 3:10

THE FIRST AND THE LAST THINGS: THE END OF VIOLENCE 255

The revival of Israel is depicted in the image of the resurrection.[111]

A verse in the Qur'an that speaks of God who kills thousands of people and then raises them again links up with this:

> Have you not regarded those who left their homes
> in thousands, apprehensive of death,
> whereupon God said to them, "Die,"
> then He revived them?
> Indeed God is gracious to mankind,
> but most people do not give thanks.
> (Q 2:243)[112]

A group of Jews presented the following exegesis of this verse to Caliph 'Umar ibn al Khattâb: the people who are mentioned here are Israelites who were struck by disease, and in that valley God showed Ezekiel their resurrection, first they were only bones, then flesh and skin appeared, and then the *spirit* entered them.[113] According to Mawdûdî, this verse refers to the Exodus of the children of Israel from Egypt,[114] which indeed should be understood as a death experience.

The Qur'anic exegesis and traditions give a lively description of the events to which these verses allude in connection with the vision of the dry bones (Ezek 37:1-4). According to some reports, a large number of the children of Israel—between three and ninety thousand—fled for their lives from a plague and sought refuge outside the city. But God let them die. As he passed by their bodies, Ezekiel called upon God to bring them back to life. God did so and thus showed his omnipotence to the children of Israel. Other reports add that Ezekiel called on God when the bodies were already torn to pieces and spread about by wild animals and birds and that they were reassembled in a miraculous way and were revived.[115]

Ezekiel had earlier already pronounced these comforting words:

> I [God] will pour out my Spirit upon you and bring you back
> to live on your own land. The exile will be ended; you will be
> redeemed from the house of bondage of Babylon, just like the
> oppression of Egypt came to an end in its time. And they shall
> say, This land that was desolate has become like the *garden* of
> Eden; and the waste and desolate and ruined cities are become
> fenced, and are inhabited. (Ezek 36:35)

111. KBS on Ezek 37:1.
112. Âya; Speyer, Die biblischen Erzählungen, 412-13.
113. Noegel and Wheeler, *The A to Z of Prophets in Islam and Judaism*, s.v., Ezekiel.
114. Mawdûdî, *Towards Understanding the Qur'an*, 54, n. 85.
115. Tabarî, Tafsir ii, 585-91. *EQ*, s.v., Ezekiel.

> The Lord will surely comfort Zion
>> and will look with compassion on all her ruins;
> he will make her deserts like Eden,
>> her wastelands like the garden of the Lord.
> (Isa 51:3; cf. Rev 2:7)

At the end of his Apocalypse, the seer of Patmos sees a river flowing through the middle of *the new Jerusalem*: "On each side of the river stood the tree of life, bearing twelve crops of fruit, yielding its fruit every month. And the leaves of the tree are for the *healing of the nations*" (Rev 22:2). That was inspired by Ezekiel's message: "Fruit trees of all kinds will grow on both banks of the river. Their leaves will not wither, nor will their fruit fail. Every month they will bear fruit, because the water from the *sanctuary* flows to them. Their fruit will serve for food and their leaves for *healing*" (Ezek 47:12; cf. Ps 1:3; Isa 44:4; Jer 17:8). Humankind is restored to what it was in the beginning and as it was intended and still is. "I will give you a new heart and put a new spirit in you; I will remove from you your heart of stone and give you a heart of flesh" (Ezek 36:26).

By addressing the prophet Ezekiel repeatedly as "son of man" (Ezek 12:1), God shows that he continues to care about human beings. Ezekiel is constantly addressed as the child of the Human Being. Whenever God appears to him in a human form that speaks to him, he does so as parent to child: "*Ben 'adam*, Son of the Human, stand up on your feet and I will speak to you" (Exod 2:1). "By addressing the prophet as Human Being, God shows that humanizing humanity is one of God's central concerns."[116] God wants "us people" to truly become humans, to become humanized. The goal of our lives is not to be or to become divine but to become genuinely, truly, *human*. Thus, the individual person does not become God but he or she becomes a flawless human being. True, genuine humanity is revealed to Ezekiel. It is apparent from Ezekiel's vision that actually, only *God is the "Fully Human One."*[117] The divine image in which "we humans" are created is intended to be completely realized in the lives of *all* people in all times and in all places.

CHAOS AND THE SPIRIT

"The Spirit of God was hovering over the waters" (Gen 1:2). God created the heavens and the earth, while his throne was on the water (Q 11:7)—"*hovered*

---

116. Wink, *The Human Being*, 31–32.
117. Wink, *The Human Being*, 29; capitalization is mine.

THE FIRST AND THE LAST THINGS: THE END OF VIOLENCE   257

above the water" would be a good translation.[118] The word "hover" occurs only a few times in the Bible. One such place is the fable told by Jotham. This youngest son of the judge Gideon, who had his eye on his father's position, told a parable of how the trees chose a leader. His father Gideon (cf. Judg 7:5–25; Q 2:249),[119] who began as an ordinary farmer, became a mighty army commander and eventually one of the great folk heroes of the Israelites. In some respects, he began to act like a king, but in the end he rejected any notion of kingship: "I will not rule over you, nor will my son rule over you," he declared when he was offered this. His answer testifies to the traditional Israelite understanding of God: "The Lord will rule over you" (Judg 8:23).[120]

After Gideon's death, his youngest son Jotham was the only one to escape the slaughter of his brothers by another of Gideon's sons, Abimelek. He then told the fable of how trees chose a leader. First, the valuable olive tree, fig tree, and vine were asked but declined. The olive tree answered: "Should I give up my oil, by which both gods and humans are honored, to *hold sway* over the trees?" (Judg 9:9). The verb used in the Hebrew text for "hold sway" is the same as that used for "hover" in Genesis 1:2. The fig tree (Judg 9:11) and the vine gave a similar response. The latter answered: "Should I give up my wine, which cheers both gods and humans, to *hold sway* over the trees?" (Judg 9:13). Apparently, the first three to be asked did not want to exalt themselves above the others and to *hold sway/hover* above them—a task that is reserved for God alone. To take on that role would mean that they would lose their own destiny. Finally, the thornbush answered, "If you really want to anoint me king over you, come and take refuge in my shade; but if not, then let fire come out of the thornbush and consume the cedars of Lebanon!" (Judg 9:15). The thornbush represents the deadly dominion that unjust rulers exercise time and again.

According to the creation story of the Qur'an, God wants human beings to be his representatives. The word the Qur'an uses for this is caliph, the shepherd and keeper of one's brother (Q 2:30). But Satan tempts man into wanting to be "king" instead: "Then Satan tempted him. / He said, 'O Adam! / Shall I show you the tree of immortality, / and an imperishable kingdom?'" (Q 20:120; cf. 7:20–22; 2:36). The devil later attempted in vain to tempt the "second Adam," Jesus, in the desert in a similar way. "The devil led him up to a high place and showed him in an instant all the kingdoms of the world. And he said to him, 'I will give you all their authority and splendor; it has

---

118. Speyer, *Biblische Erzählungen*, 22.
119. Cf. Speyer, *Die biblischen Erzählungen*, 368.
120. *Alle Bijbelse personen*, s.v., Gideon.

been given to me, and I can give it to anyone I want to'" (Luke 4:5, 6). When man gives way to that temptation, corruption and the shedding of blood on earth is the result—something that the angels warned God about when God announced his intention to create humankind (Q 2:30). Jotham told the above tale as a condemnation of Abimelek who had declared himself king. His kingdom lasted only three years (Judg 9:16-21, 50-55).[121]

The connection of the creation story with that of the Exodus of the children of Israel from Egypt shows, in contrast, what God's royal dominion entails and actually intends. The "song of Moses" relates how

> In a desert land [God] found [Israel],
>   in a barren and howling waste.
> He shielded him and cared for him;
>   he guarded him as the apple of his eye,
> like an eagle that stirs up its nest
>   and hovers over its young,
> that spreads its wings to catch them
>   and carries them aloft.
> (Deut 32:10-11; cf. Exod 19:4; Ps 17:8)

Here the word "hover" is used again, just as in the "counternarrative" of Jotham's fable. The care with which eagles care for their young in their attempts at flight is an image for God's loving care for his people: "The Lord your God, who is going before you, will fight for you, as he did for you in Egypt, before your very eyes, and in the wilderness. There you saw how the Lord your God carried you, as a father carries his son, all the way you went until you reached this place" (Deut 1:31; cf. 2:7; 8:1-6, 15-16; 29:4-5; 32:10-11).[122] Eagles carry their young on their back or on their wings to teach them to fly. "The eagle does not press himself on the young, but hovers, touching yet not touching. Yahweh acted similarly with Israel."[123] The long journey to "this place" in the Exodus from Egypt refers to the border of the promised land where the people of Israel arrived when Moses gave his long speech east of the river Jordan. Israel had been taken along this difficult road in the wilderness to learn to *surrender* themselves undivided to God and to seek security in him.[124] I deliberately put the word "surrender" above in italics because, in the Qur'an, surrender to God in complete trust indicates best what it means to be "muslim" and is the meaning of "islam" in the actual Qur'anic sense of the word.

---

121. *Alle Bijbelse personen, s.v.*, Jotam; Abimelek 3.
122. BW s.v., arend.
123. Lundbom, *Deuteronomy*, 880-881; with a reference to Rashi.
124. KBS on Exod 15:22.

God's Spirit hovers over the destructive powers of chaos, symbolized by "waters" (Gen 1:2). But God *broods* on another world than that of the waters of chaos, from which the beast-like rulers emerge time and again, beasts that represent unjust regimes. The creation by God means that he wants to and will make an ordered, just *cosmos* (world) from that terrifying *chaos* (cf. Q 13:2; 32:5; 10:31). That is the point of the creation story: the first things are connected with the last things. How can that be disputed (Q 10:34)? God completed the creation at the beginning the first time. *And he will restore it at the end*. He redresses everything and makes it good again: "Your Lord is God who created the heavens and the earth in six days. He then settled on his throne to rule the world by his Word" (Q 10:3). The Arabic word that is used for "word" (*amr*) is translated correctly by Paret in his German translation as Logos. Thomas O'Shaughnessy explains the intention by speaking of the "*Spirit of the Word of God*."[125]

God completes the creation the first time at the beginning and repeats it *at the end*: God began the creation and will then recreate it (Q 10:34). God's Spirit wants to make a *cosmos*: a world with a just order, a world where justice and love will dwell. "Daar woont Hij zelf, daar wordt zijn heil verkregen en leven tot in eeuwigheid" (There he himself lives; there his salvation and life forever are received).[126] That is God's plan of continuous creation (*creatio continua*).

"WHEN THE TRUMPET OF THE LORD SHALL SOUND"?

The idea has often reigned—and perhaps it should be said that this view is held by most believers—that the end, the last day, will dawn when the final judgment will be carried out "When the trumpet of the Lord shall sound."[127] Trumpets are, after all, often used to announce events associated with the end.

> Blow the trumpet in Zion;
>   sound the alarm on my holy hill.
> Let all who live in the land tremble,
>   For the day of the Lord is coming.
> It is *close at hand*.[128]
> (Joel 2:1)

125. Paret on Q 2:109.

126. Psalm 133 verse 3 (the Dutch rhymed version).

127. Cf. the popular hymn "When the Roll is Called Up Yonder" https://hymnary.org/text/when_the_trumpet_of_the_lord_shall_black.

128. KBS on Joel 2:1–11.

Darkness and *gloom* are two of the ways the day of the Lord is characterized (cf. Job 20:28; Sir 11:4; Joel 2:2; Amos 5:18-20; Zeph 1:15b) and are required elements of the appearance of God and an invading army.[129] A trumpet was also heard when the Torah was given.[130] The trumpet shall also be heard at the coming of the Son of Man (Matt 24:31): the last trumpet will sound (1 Cor 15:52). After all, when the command is given, when the voice of the archangel and the trumpet of the God resound, then the Lord himself will descend from heaven (1 Thess 4:16). When he was on Patmos, John was in the Spirit on the Lord's Day, when he heard a voice behind him like a trumpet (Rev 1:10; cf. 4:1). The day of the Lord is the day of Jesus' resurrection, which later became the "Christian" Sunday (cf. Matt 28; Mark 16:1; Luke 24:1; John 20:1; Acts 20:7; 1 Cor 16:2).[131] When the Son of Man will come on the clouds of heaven, then God will send his angels out with a loud trumpet call (Matt 24:31). The seer John sees seven angels standing before God to whom seven trumpets are given (Rev 8:2). These seven angels emerge from the heavenly temple of judgment sounding their trumpets to announce cosmic catastrophes (Rev 8:2—9:14) as well as *the end* (Rev 10:7; 11:15).[132] When the time has come for the seventh trumpet to be blown, then God's secret counsel (*musterion*)[133] will be fulfilled as revealed to his servants, the prophets (Rev 10:7; cf. Amos 3:7). That is the all-encompassing plan of God to bring about the definitive victory over evil.[134]

This message is confirmed in the Qur'an: "The day when *the trumpet will be blown*, / whoever is in the heavens *will be terrified* / and whoever is on the earth, / except whomever God may wish, / and all will come to Him in utter humility" (Q 27:87).[135] Isrâfîl will sound the trumpet on the last day. But it is now of crucial importance to understand that the end time is continually and repeatedly seen as *imminent*: the (last) day of the Lord is *near* (Isa 13:6). The word of the Lord comes to Ezekiel: "Son of man, prophesy and say: 'This is what the Sovereign Lord says:

---

129. KBS on Zeph 1:14-16; cf. Isa 2:6-21; 13:6; 26:20—27:1; Jer 30:5-7; Joel 1, 2; Amos 2:16; 5:18; 8:9-13; Obad 15.

130. Heb 12:19; cf. Exod 19:16-19; 20:18; Deut 4:11; 5:22.

131. KBS on Obad 11.

132. *BW*, s.v., bazuin.

133. Cf. Rom 16:25; 1 Cor 2:6-16; Eph 1:8-10; 3:3-12; 6:19; Col 1:26-28; 2:2, 3; 4:3. *BW*, s.v., bazuin.

134. KBS on Rev 10:5-7.

135. Cf. Q 6:73: Q 18:99; Q 20:102; Q 23:101; Q 27:87: Q 79:13; Q 37:19. Cf. Q 36:51; 37:19; 50:20; 69:13; 78:18; 79:13; 39:68.

> Wail and say,
> > "Alas for that day!"
> For the day is near,
> > the day of the Lord is *near*—
> a day of clouds,
> a time of doom for the nations.
> (Ezek 30:1–3)

"The great day of the Lord is *near—/ near* and *coming quickly*" (Zeph 1:14). "The day of the Lord is near / for all nations" (Obad 15). "Alas for that day! / For the day of the Lord is *near*; / it will come like destruction from the Almighty" (Joel 1:15; cf. 2:1; 3:14; Isa 13:6).

Nowhere in the Old Testament is the day of the Lord so emphatically presented as in the book of Joel: that day is *near* (Joel 2:1), "is dreadful. / Who can endure it?" (Joel 2:11); "The sun will be turned to darkness / and the moon to blood / before the coming of the great and dreadful day of the Lord" (Joel 2:31); "For the day of the Lord is near / in the valley of decision" (Joel 3:14), where the Lord will judge the nations (cf. Joel 3:12–14).

Precisely because the end is always *near*, the end cannot be seen as a *break* in history. The "doctrine of the last things" concerns precisely the opposite—the intention of history: namely, that the authority and dominion of God will be recognized by Israel and all peoples![136] Thus, "When the Trumpet of the Lord shall Sound" is not intended as something that will "perhaps" occur "some day." That, to put it bluntly, is like saying "when it snows in July"—thus never. But then one loses the mystery that is *revealed* here, and that is the real concern of apocalyptic.

God has made mercy incumbent upon himself, the Qur'an says (Q 6:12). "He will surely gather you on the Day of Resurrection, in which there is no doubt" (Q 6:12). God has sent the prophet Muhammad therefore only with the revelation as mercy for the nations (Q 21:107).

> When those who have faith in Our signs come to you, say,
> "Peace to you!
> Your Lord has made mercy incumbent upon himself:
> whoever of you commits an evil [deed]
> out of ignorance
> and then repents after that and reforms,
> then He is indeed all-forgiving, all-merciful."
> (Q 6:54)

---

136. *BW*, s.v., einde, 490.

> The day We shall roll up the sky,
> like the rolling of the scrolls for writings.
> *We will bring it back as We began the first creation*
> —a promise [binding] on Us.
> [That] indeed We will do.
> Certainly We wrote in the Psalms . . .:
> "Indeed My righteous servants shall inherit the earth."
> (Q 21:104–5)

Here the Qur'an confirms what Jesus said in one of the beatitudes in the Sermon on the Mount: "Blessed are the meek, for they shall inherit the earth" (Matt 5:5). And Jesus in turn confirmed what the Psalmist said: But the meek will inherit the earth and enjoy peace and prosperity (Ps 37:9, 11, 29, 34).

The fact that we must have a good understanding of the first things in order to understand the last things does not entail a law of eternal return. This is not a matter of *l' histoire se repète*, the history that is fated to repeat itself. Not at all. Going back to the first things is not a going back to how it once was in the beginning. The Bible and the Qur'an say nothing about that. But what both Scriptures do explicitly point to is the real problem since the beginning of time until its end. And the fulfillment of God's promises and the coming of the kingdom, of his dominion, is always near. That is why human beings are called *today* to listen to his voice (Ps 95:7; cf. 95:8–9; Luke 19:42–44): *now* is the time of decision.

Willem Barnard, theologian, poet, and writer, was once asked whether he still believed all of the Christian faith he had been brought up with. His answer was: "I don't know, but when I sing, then I do believe it." That is why, I think, answers to our questions need to be sought in song, perhaps preeminently in the psalms, the heart of the Tanakh. It is the Jewish book of prayer, thus also the prayer book of Jesus. Jesus felt his way through life via the psalms (Oepke Noordmans).[137] The psalms appear in this chapter various times. In Hebrew, the psalms are called "songs of praise."

I would like to look at this category of the psalms that are called "new songs." Psalm 149 is such a song. Now we will look at Psalm 33:

> Sing to [the Lord] a new song. (Ps 33:3)

It is striking that this designation "new song" arose in the time of the *exile*. John the seer was in exile on the island of Patmos. He also speaks of a *new song* being sung (Rev 5:9; cf. Ps 144:9; Isa 42:10).

---

137. Schuman, *Woord op Zondag*, 9.

The phrase "new song" has three meanings (Ps 40:3; 96:1; 98:1; 149:1; Js 42:10). (1) "New" is not opposed to old or aged but refers to a characteristic of making new, the renewal of the message. We are called to praise God who *again* turns his graceful face to human beings. (2) "New" indicates an eschatological dynamic. (3) Finally, "new" is the main theme of the new songs—the hope of the revelation, i.e., the *apocalypse*, of the universal kingship of God that includes two things: the life-threatening powers are robbed of their power, and the strength to live comes to all who accept God as their king. The taming and defeat of the powers of chaos is God's continuing sustained activity. All creatures must acknowledge this Creator and preserver of the world and live according to *his plan for history*:

> The Lord loves righteousness and justice;
>   the earth is full of his unfailing love.
> By the word of the Lord the heavens were made,
>   their starry host by the breath of his mouth.
> Let all the earth fear the Lord;
>   let all the people of the world revere him.
> For he spoke, and it came to be;
>   he commanded, and it stood firm.
> (Ps 33:5–6, 8–9)[138]

The righteous are those who treat God and people with justice.[139] They are called to praise God (Ps 33:1). The new song is a song of renewal, of revival. The Psalmist expects the imminent end of history and the beginning of new things, of a new age (Ps 40:4; 91:1–2; 98:1–3; 144:9; 149:1; Isa 42:9–10). The psalmist sees the coming of God's kingdom before him in the universe and in the history of humankind (Ps 33:4–7, 8–19): "Your kingdom come." The earth is full of the Lord's unfailing love (Ps 33:5b) and reflects his faithfulness that extends over the whole earth and to all peoples of the world. God's plan stands forever, and the purposes of his heart forever (Ps 33:11). Military power in itself does not represent authentic power: no king can win, no matter how strong or how powerful he is, no warrior can save himself, no warhorse can guarantee a victory; however strong it is, the warhorse cannot save. The eye of the Lord rests on those who fear him and trust in his love (Ps 33:16–18).[140]

---

138. Hossfeld and Zenger, *Die Psalmen*, 208–10.
139. KBS on Ps 31:19.
140. Terrien, *The Psalms*, vol. 1, 297–99.

Bibliography

Aalders, Wim. *De Apocalyptische Christus*. Heerenveen: Groen, 2001.
———. *De Septuagint: De brug tussen synagoge en kerk*. Heerenveen: Uitgeverij Groen, 1999.
Abels, Norbert. *Franz Werfel: Mit Selbstzeugnissen und Bilddokumenten*. Hamburg: Rowohlt, 1990.
Adonis. *Violence and Islam: Conversations with Houria Abdelouahed*. Translated by David Watson. Cambridge: Polity, 2016.
Akbar, M. J. *The Shade of Swords: Jihad and the Conflict between Islam & Christianity*. London: Routledge, 2002.
Alagha, Joseph. "Kunst en Hizbullahs mobilisatie." In *Islam in verandering: Vroomheid en vertier onder moslims binnen en buiten Nederland*, edited by Joas Wagemakers and Martijn de Koning, 299–306. Almere: Parthenon, 2015.
Ali, Tariq. *The Clash of Fundamentalisms: Crusades, Jihads and Modernity*. London: Verso, 2002.
———. *Protocols of the Elders of Sodom and Other Essays*. London: Verso, 2009.
Alle Bijbelse personen: Geïllustreerd biografisch woordenboek. Amsterdam: Reader's Digest, 2006.
Almond, Philip C. *The Devil: A New Biography*. London: Taurus, 2014.
Al-Tabari. *The History of al-Tabari*. Vol. 1, *General Introduction and From the Creation tot the Flood*. Translated by Franz Rosenthal. New York: State University Press of New York, 1989.
Attema, D. S. *De Mohammedaansche opvattingen omtrent het tijdstip van den jongsten dag en zijn voortekenen*. Amsterdam: Noord-Hollandsche, 1942.
Attridge, Harold W. *The Epistle to the Hebrews: A Commentary on the Epistle to the Hebrews*. Minneapolis: Fortress, 1998.
Balthasar, Hans Urs von. *Herrlichkeit: Ein Theologische Ästhetik*. Vol. 3.2, *Theologie*: Part 1, Alter Bund. 2nd ed. Einsiedeln Johannes, 1989.
Bauer, Walter. *Wörterbuch zum Neuen Testament*. Berlin: Töpelmann, 1958.
Beale, G. K. *The Book of Revelation: Greek Text*. Grand Rapids: Eerdmans, 2013.
———. *The Use of Daniel in Jewish Apocalyptic Literature and in the Revelation of St. John*. Eugene: Wipf & Stock, 2010.
Behm, Johannes. *Das Neue Testament Deutsch: Die Offenbarung des Johannes*. Göttingen: Vandenhoeck Ruprecht, 1949.

Beker, J. Christiaan. *Paul the Apostle: The Triumph of God in Life and Thought*. Edinburgh: T. & T. Clark, 1989.
Belo, Fernando. *Lecture materialisme de l'evangelie de Marc*. Paris: Cerf, 1975.
Ben-Chorin, Schlomo. *Zur religiösen Lage in Palestina: Ein Beitrag zur religiösen Antropologie der Gegenwart*. Tel Aviv: Matara, 1940.
Bentounes, Cheikh. *L' Homme intérieur a la lumière du Coran*. Paris: Édition Albin Michel, 1998.
Beuken, W. A. M. *Jesaja: Part II*. Nijkerk: Callenbach, 1986.
Reicke, Bo, and Leonard Rost, eds. *Bijbels-historisch Woordenboek*. Vols. 1–6. Utrecht: Spectrum, 1969.
Blachère, Régis. *Le Coran: Traduction selon un essai de reclassement des sourates*. Paris: Maisonneuve, 1951.
Bladel, Kevin van. "The Alexander Legend in the Qur'an 18:83–102." In *The Qur'an in Its Historical Context*, edited by Gabriel Said Reynolds, 175–203. London: Routledge, 2008.
Bleckmann, Bruno. *Konstantin der Grosze*. Reinbek bei Hamburg: Rowohlt, 1996.
Block, Daniel I. *The Book of Ezekiel: Chapters 25–48*. Grand Rapids: Eerdmans, 1998.
Bonhoeffer, Dietrich. *Letters and Papers from Prison*. New York: Macmillan, 1972
Brock, Sebastian, with Robert Hoyland. *The Seventh Century in the West-Syrian Chronicles*. Liverpool: Liverpool University Press, 1993.
Brotton, Jerry. *This Orient Isle, Elizabethan England and the Islamic World*. Harmondsworth: Penguin, 2017.
Bobzin, Hartmut. "Von Luther zu Rückert: Der Koran in Deutschland. Ein weitere Weg von der Polemik zur poetischen Übersetzung." *Akademie Aktuell* 1 (2010) 14–17.
Boccaccini, Gabriele, and Giovanni Ibba, eds. *Enoch and the Mosaic Torah: The Evidence of Jubilees*. Grand Rapids: Eerdmans, 2009.
Boda, Mark J. *The Book Zechariah*. Grand Rapids: Eerdmans, 2016.
Boxall, Ian. "The Many Faces of Babylon the Great: Wirkungsgeschichte and Interpretation of Revelation 17." In *Studies in the Book of Revelation*, edited by Steve Moyise, 51–68. Edinburgh: T. & T. Clark, 2001.
Bowersock, G. W. *The Crucible of Islam*. Cambridge: Harvard University Press, 2017.
Brueggemann, Walter. *Genesis*. Interpretation A Bible Commentary for Teaching and Preaching. Atlanta: John Knox, 1983.
———. *A Commentary on Jeremiah: Exile and Homecoming*. Grand Rapids: Eerdmans, 1998.
———. *Divine Presence Amid Violence: Contextualizing the Book of Joshua*. Eugene: Cascade, 2009.
———. *Isaiah 1–39*. Louisville: Westminster John Knox, 1998.
———. *Israel's Praise: Doxology Against Idolatry and Ideology*. Philadelphia: Fortress, 1988.
———. *The Message of the Psalms: A Theological Commentary*. Minneapolis: Augsburg, 1984.
———. *Out of Babylon*. Nashville: Abingdon, 2010.
———. *The Psalms & the Life of Faith*. Minneapolis: Fortress, 1995.
———. *Reverberations of Faith: A Theological Handbook of Old Themes*. Louisville: John Knox, 2002.
———. *Theology of the Old Testament: Testimony, Dispute, Advocacy*. Minneapolis: Fortress, 1997.

Brueggemann, Walter, and William H. Bellinger. *Psalms*. New York: Cambridge University Press, 2014.
Buber, Martin. *Werke*. Vol. 3, *Schriften zum Chassidismus*. Munich: Schneider, 1963.
Budge, E. A. Wallis. *The Book of the Cave of Treasures: A History of the Patriarchs and the Kings from the Creation tot the Crucifixion of Christ*. London: The Religious Tract Society, 1927.
Buhl, Frants. *Das Leben Muhammeds*. Darmstadt: Wissenschaftliche Buchgesellschaft, 1961.
Buiten de Vesting: Een woord-voor woord vertaling van alle deuterocanonieke en vele apocriefe bijbelboeken. Translated by Pieter Oussoren and Renate Dekker. Middelburg: Skandalon, 2008.
Cahill, Thomas. *Heretics and Heroes: How Renaissance Artists and Reformation Priest Created Our World*. New York: Random House, 2013.
Cameron, Dan Averil, and Lawrence I. Conrad, eds. *The Byzantine and Early Islamic Near East*. Princeton: Darwin, 1992.
Cardini, Franco. *Europe and Islam*. Hoboken: Wiley-Blackwell, 2001.
Caspar, Robert. *Traité de théologie musulmane*. Vol. 1, *Histoire de la pensée religieuse musulmane*. Rome: PISAI, 1978.
Carey, Frances, ed. *The Apocalypse and the Shape of Things to Come*. London: British Museum Press, 1999.
Charles, R. H., ed. *The Apocrypha and Pseudepigrapha of the Old Testament*. Vol. 2, *Pseudepigrapha*. Berkeley: Apocryphile, 2004.
Colby, Frederik S. *Narrating Muhammad's Night Journey: Tracing the Development of the Ibn 'Abbâs Ascension Discourse*. Albany: State University of New York Press, 2008.
Collins, John J. *The Apocalyptic Imagination: An Introduction to Jewish Apocalyptic Literature*. Grand Rapids: Eerdmans, 1998.
———. *Between Athens and Jerusalem: Jewish Identity in the Hellenistic Diaspora*. Grand Rapids: Eerdmans, 1999.
———. *A Commentary on the Book of Daniel*. Minneapolis: Fortress, 1993.
Collins, John J., and Daniel C. Harlow. *The Eerdmans Dictionary of Early Judaism*. Grand Rapids: Eerdmans, 2010.
Cook, David. *Contemporary Muslim Apocalyptic Literature*. Syracuse: Syracuse University Press, 2005.
———. *Martyrdom in Islam*. Cambridge: Cambridge University Press, 2007.
———. *Studies in Muslim Apocalyptic*. Princeton: Darwin, 2002.
Crone, Patricia, and Michael Cook. *Hagarism: The Making of the Islamic World*. Cambridge: Cambridge University Press, 1977.
Cross, Frank Moore. *Canaanite Myth and Hebrew Epic: Essays in the History of the Religion of Israel*. Cambridge: Harvard University Press, 1997.
Crossan, John Dominic, and Jonathan L. Reed. *In Search of Paul: How Jesus's Apostle Opposed Rome's Empire with God's Kingdom*. New York: Harper Collins, 2005.
Crowley, Roger. *Constantinople: The Last Great Siege 1453*. London: Faber & Faber, 2005.
Cuypers, Michel. *The Banquet: A Reading of the Fifth Sura of the Qur'an*. Bogotá: Convivial, 2009.
———. *A Qur'ânic Apocalypse: A Reading of the Thirty-Three Last Sûrahs of the Qur'ân*. Atlanta: Lockwood, 2018.

Dammen McAuliffe, Jane. *The Cambridge Companion to the Qur'ân*. Cambridge: Cambridge University Press, 2006.
Daniélou, J. *Geschiedenis van de kerk*. Part 1, *Van de stichting van de kerk tot de vierde eeuw*. Hilversum-Antwerpen: Pauls Brand, 1963.
Dante Alighieri. *The Divine Comedy*. Vol. 1, Inferno. Translated by Courtney Langdon. https://oll.libertyfund.org/titles/alighieri-the-divine-comedy-vol-1-inferno-english-trans.
Davies, Philip R. *Scribes and Schools: The Canonization of the Hebrew Scriptures*. Louisville: John Knox, 1998.
de Hamel, Christopher. *The Book: A History of the Bible*. New York: Phaidon, 2001.
Dekker, Wim, ed. *Verborgene die bij ons zijt: Dagboek*. Zoetermeer: Boekencentrum, 2004.
Delaney, Carol. *Columbus and the Quest for Jerusalem: How Religion Drove the Voyages that Led to America*. New York: Free Press, 2011.
Deurloo, K. A. *Genesis*. Kampen: Kok, 1998.
———. *Jozua: Verklaring van een Bijbelgedeelte*. Kampen: Kok, 1981.
———. *Schepping: Van Paulus tot Genesis: Kleine Bijbelse theologie*. Kampen: Kok, 2008.
Dictionnaire du Coran. Sous la direction de Mohammad Ali Amir-Moezzi. Paris: Robert Laffont, 2007.
Dictionnaire encyclopédique du Judaïsme. Paris: Cerf, 1996.
Dobbs-Allsopp, F. W. *Lamentations*. Louisville: John Knox, 2012.
Donner, Fred. M. *Muhammad and the Believers: At the Origins of Islam*. Cambridge: Belknap, 2010.
Donzel, Emeri van, and Andrea Schmidt. *Gog and Magog in Early Eastern Christian and Islamic Sources: Sallam's Quest for Alexander's Wall*. Leiden: Brill, 2010.
Ebach, Jurgen. *Das Erbe der Gewalt: Ein biblische Realität und Wirkungsgesichte*. Gütersloh: Mohn, 1980.
Ehmann, Johannes. *Luther, Türken und Islam: Eine Untersuchung zum Türken- und Islambild Martin Luthers (1515–1546)*. Heidelberg: Gütersloher Verlagshaus, 2008.
Ehrman, Bart D. *The Triumph of Christianity: How a Forbidden Religion Swept the World*. London: One World, 2019.
Eliade, Mircea. *The Encyclopedia of Religion*. New York: Macmillan, 1987.
Elliot, Neil. *Liberating Paul: The Justice of God & The Politics of the Apostle*. Minneapolis: Fortress, 2006.
———. "Paul's Letters: God's Justice Against Empire." In *The New Testament: Introducing the Way of Discipleship*, edited by Wes Howard-Brook and Sharon H. Ringe, 122–147. New York: Orbis, 2002.
The Encyclopedia of Islam. New ed. Leiden: Brill, 1960–2005.
Encyclopaedia of the Qur'an. Edited by Jane Dammen McAuliffe. 6 vols. Leiden: Brill, 2001–6.
Erasmus. *Hoe paus Julius II bij de hemelpoort aanklopt, maar door Petrus niet wordt binnengelaten*. 2nd printing. Rotterdam: Ad. Donker, 2007.
Erop, A. H. van. *Gesta Francorum Gesta Dei? Motivering en rechtvaardiging van de eerste kruistochten door tijdgenoten en moslimse reactie*. Amsterdam: Rowohlt, 1982.
Evans, Craig, A. *The Routledge Encyclopedia of the Historical Jesus*. New York: Routledge, 2010.
Filiu, Jean-Pierre. *Apocalypse in Islam*. Berkeley: University of California Press, 2011.

Finkel, Caroline. *De droom van Osman: Geschiedenis van het Ottomaanse Rijk 1300–1923*. Amsterdam: Metts & Schilt, 2008.
Fischer, Georg, and Dominik Markt. *Das Buch Exodus*. Stuttgart: Katholisches Bibelwerk, 2009.
Fitzmyer, Joseph A. *First Corinthians: A New Translation with Introduction and Commentary*. South Haven: Yale University Press, 2008.
———. *The Semitic Background of the New Testament*. Vol. 2, *A Wandering Aramean. Collected Aramaic Essays*. Grand Rapids: Eerdmans, 1997.
Firestone, Reuven. *An Introduction to Islam for Jews*. Philadelphia: The Jewish Publication Society, 2008.
Fletcher, Richard. *The Cross and the Crescent: Christianity and Islam from Muhammad to the Reformation*. London: Penguin Viking, 2004.
Francisco, Adam S. *Martin Luther and Islam: A Study in Sixteenth-Century Polemics and Apologetics*. Leiden: Brill, 2007.
Freely, John. *The Grand Turk: Sultan Mehmet II—Conqueror of Constantinople, Master of an Empire and Lord of Two Seas*. London: Taurus, 2009.
Gaddis, Michael. *There Is No Crime for Those Who Have Christ: Religious Violence in the Christian Roman Empire*. Berkeley: University of California Press, 2005.
Geerts, Guido, and Ton den Boon, eds. *Groot woordenboek der Nederlandse taal*. 13th revised ed. Utrecht: Van Dale Lexicografie, 1999.
Gesche, Bonifatia, trans. *Die Esra-Apocalypse*. Göttingen: Vandenhoeck & Ruprecht, 2015.
Gibb, H. A. R., and J. H. Kramers, eds. *Shorter Encyclopaedia of Islam*. Leiden: Brill, 1961.
Gills, Anton. *Gateway of the Gods: The Rise and Fall of Babylon*. London: Quercus, 2008.
Gimaret, Daniel. *Les Noms divins en Islam: Exégese lexicographique et théologique*. Paris: Cerf, 2007.
Gittings John. *The Glorious Art of Peace. From the Iliad to Iraq*. Oxford: Oxford University Press, 2012.
Glassé, Cyril. *The Concise Encyclopaedia of Islam*. Rev. ed. London: Stavey International, 2001.
Gowan, Donald E. *Daniel*. Nashville: Abington, 2001.
———. *Eschatology in the Old Testament*. Edinburgh: T. & T. Clark, 2000.
Griffith, Lee. *The War on Terrorism and the Terror of God*. Grand Rapids: Eerdmans, 2002.
Grosheide, F. W. *Korte verklaring der Heilige schrift: II Korinthe*. Kampen: Kok, 1939.
Grosheide, F. W., et al., eds. *Christelijke Encyclopedie*. 2nd printing. Kampen: Kok, 1961.
Grote Winkler Prins. 8th printing. Amsterdam: Elsevier, 1982.
Gruber, Christine, and Frederick Colby, eds. *The Prophet's Ascension: Cross-Cultural Encounters with the Islamic Mi'râj Tales*. Bloomington: Indiana University Press, 2010.
Guillaume, Alfred. *The Life of Muhammad: A Translation of Ishâq's Sîrat Rasûl Allâh*. Lahore: Oxford University Press, 1967.
Haenchen, Ernst. *Die Apostelgeschichte*. Göttingen: Vandenhoeck & Ruprecht, 1965.
Hagemann, Ludwig. *Christentum Contra Islam: Eine Geschichte gescheiterter Beziehungen*. Darmstadt: Wissenschaftliche Buchgesellschaft, 1999.
———. *Martin Luther und der Islam*. Altberge: Christlich-islamisches Schrifttum, 1998.

Han, Jin Hee. *Daniel's Spiel: Apocalyptic Literacy in the Book of Daniel*. Lanham: University Press of America, 2008.

Harper, Raymond. *Als God met ons is: Jacob van Maerlant en de vijanden van het christelijk geloof*. Amsterdam: Prometheus, 1998.

Haykal, Muhammad. *Life of Muhammad*. Translated by Isma'il Razi A. Al-Faruqi. http://static1.squarespace.com/static/5afc64e23917eebabeb22f4f/5afc93baaf6849 0874282c92/5afc93d6af68490874283183/1526502358178/muhammadbyhaykal .pdf?format=original.

Heering, Gerrit Jan. *De zondeval van het christendom: Een studie over Christendom, staat en oorlog*. 4th printing. Utrecht: Bijleveld, 1953.

Hendrix, Scott H. *Martin Luther: Visionary Reformer*. New Haven: Yale University Press, 2015.

Herrin, Judith. *Byzantium: The Surprising Life of a Medieval Empire*. London: Penguin, 2007.

Hertog, G. C. den, and S. Schoon. *Messianisme en eindtijdverwachting bij joden en christenen*. Zoetermeer: Boekencentrum, 2006.

Heschel, Abraham I. *The Prophets*. Vols. 1–2. New York: Harper Colophon, 1962.

Hillenbrand, Carole. *The Crusades: Islamic Perspectives*. Edinburgh: Edinburgh University Press, 1999.

Hoekstra, Hidde. "Samenstelling en toelichting." *Rembrandt en de Bijbel: Het Oude Testament: Part 3, Aan der stromen van Babylon*. Utrecht: Spectrum, 1984.

Holland, Tom. *The Forge of Christendom: The End of Days and the Epic Rise of the West*. New York: Doubleday, 2008.

———. *In the Shadow of the Sword: The Battle for Global Empire and the End of the Ancient World*. London: Abacus, 2013.

———. *Millennium: The End of the World and the Forging of Christendom*. London: Abacus, 2009.

Homer. *The Iliad*. Translated by E. V. Rieu. Harmondsworth: Penguin, 1950.

Horsley, Richard A. *Revolt of the Scribes: Visionaries, and the Politics of Second Temple Judea*. Louisville: Westminster John Knox, 2007.

———. *Hearing the Whole Story: The Politics of Plot in Mark's Gospel*. Louisville: Westminster John Knox, 2001.

———. *The Prophet Jesus and the Renewal of Israel: Moving Beyond a Diversionary Debate*. Grand Rapids: Eerdmans, 2012.

———. *Revolt of the Scribes: Resistance and Apocalyptic Origins*. Minneapolis: Fortress, 2010.

Horsley, Richard A., with John S. Hanson. *Bandits, Prophets & Messiahs: Popular Movements in the Time of Jesus*. Harrisburg: Trinity, 1999.

Horsley, Richard A., and Neil Asher Silberman. *The Message and the Kingdom: How Jesus and Paul Ignited a Revolution and Transformed the Ancient World*. Minneapolis: Fortress, 1997.

Hossfeld, Frank Lothar, and Erich Zenger. *Die Psalmen: Psalm 1–50*. Würzburg: Echter, 1993.

———. *Psalmen 51–100*. Freiburg: Herder, 2000.

———. *Psalms 3: A Commentary on Psalms 101–150*. Minneapolis: Fortress, 2011.

Howard-Brook, Wes. *The Church before Christianity*. Maryknoll: Orbis, 2001.

---. "Claiming the Victory Won over Empire." In *The New Testament: Introducing the Way of Discipleship*, edited by Wes Howard-Brook and Sharon H. Ringe, 188–206. Maryknoll: Orbis, 2002.

---. *"Come Out, My People!": God's Call out of Empire in the Bible and Beyond.* Maryknoll: Orbis, 2010.

---. *Empire Baptized: How the Church Embraced What Jesus Rejected. 2nd–5th Centuries.* Maryknoll: Orbis, 2016.

Howard-Brook, Wes, and Anthony Gwyther. *"Come Out, My People!": Reading Revelation Then and Now.* Maryknoll: Orbis, 1999.

Howard-Brook, Wes, and Sharon H. Ringe. *The New Testament: Introducing the Way of Discipleship.* New York: Orbis, 2002.

Hoyland, Robert G. *In God's Path: The Arab Conquests and the Creation of an Islamic Empire.* Oxford: Oxford University Press, 2015.

---. *Seeing Islam As Others Saw It: A Survey and Evaluation of Christian, Jewish and Zoroastrian Writings on Early Islam.* 3rd printing. Princeton: Darwin, 2007.

Houtepen, A. W. J. *In God is geen geweld: Theologie als geloofsverantwoording in een natheïstische cultuur.* Vught: Radboudstichting, 1985.

Iersel, Bas van. *Marcus.* Reprint, 's-Hertogenbosch, Louvain: KBS/VBS, 2002.

Im Lichte des Halbmonds: Das Abendland und der Türkische Orient. Leipzig: Ed. Leipzig, 1993.

Izutsu, Toshihiko. *Ethico-Religious Concepts in the Qurʾān.* Montreal: McGill University Press, 1966.

Jaber, Asad, and J. J. G. Jansen. *De Koran.* Edited and translated by by J. H. Kramers. Amsterdam: Arbeiderspers, 1992.

Janowski, Bernd. *Konflikt Gespräche mit Gott: Eine Antropologie der Psalmen.* 4th printing. Neukirchener-Vluyn: Neukirchener Theologie Neukirchener Verlag Gesellschaft, 2013.

Jeffery, Arthur. *The Foreign Vocabulary of the Qur'an.* Baroda: Oriental Institute, 1938.

Jenni, Ernst, and Claus Westermann. *Theologischer Handwörterbuch zum Alten Testament.* Vol. 1. Munich: Chr Kaiser, 1984.

Jewett, Robert. *Romans: A Commentary.* Minneapolis: Fortress, 2007.

Johansen, B. *Muhammad Husayn Haykal: Europe und der Orient im Weltbild eines Ägyptischen Liberalen.* Beiruter Texte und Studien 5. Beirut: Orient-Institut, Steiner, 1967.

Jones, Ken Sundet. "The Apocalyptic Luther." https://wordandworld.luthersem.edu/content/pdfs/25-3_Apocalypse/25-3_Jones.pdf.

Josephus, Flavius. *The Wars of the Jews.* Translated by William Whiston. http://www.isdet.com/_PDF/Complete_Works_%20of_Josephus.pdf.

Kaegi, Walter Emil. *Heraclius: Emperor of Byzantium.* Cambridge: Cambridge University Press, 2003.

---. *Muslim Expansion and Byzantine Collapse in North Africa.* Cambridge: Cambridge University Press, 2015.

Kaegi, Walter Emil, Jr. "Initial Byzantine Reactions to the Arab Conquest." *Church History* 38 (1969) 139–49.

Kaufmann, Thomas. *Luther's Jews: A Journey into Anti-Semitism.* Oxford: Oxford University Press, 2017.

Keller, Catherine. *Apocalypse Now and Then: A Feminist Guide to the End of the World.* Minneapolis: Fortress, 2005.

Khalidi, Tarif. *The Qur'an: A New Translation*. London: Penguin, 2008.
Kittel, Gerard. *Theologisches Wörterbuch zum Neuen Testament*. Stuttgart: Kohlhammer, 1949–.
Der Kleine Pauly: Lexikon der Antike. Munich: Deutscher Taschenbuch, 1979.
Köhler, Ludwig. *Lexicon in Veteris Testamenti Libros*. Leiden: Brill, 1953.
Koldeweij, A. M., ed. *Maria van Hongarije: Koningin tussen keizers en kunstenaars 1505–1558*. Zwolle: Waanders, 1993.
Korpel, Marjo, and Johannes de Moor. *Adam, Eva en de duivel*. Vught: Skandalon, 2016.
Kraus, Hans-Joachim. *Klagelieder (Threni)*. Neukirchen: Neukirchener, 1960.
Kroon, K. H. *Openbaring Hoofdstuk 1–11: Verklaring van een Bijbelgedeelte*. Kampen: Kok, 1979.
Kuitert, Harry, M. *De mensvormigheid Gods: Een dogmatisch-hermeneutische studie over de anthropomorphismen van de Heilige Schrift*. Kampen: Kok, 1962.
Küng, Hans. *Grosze christliche Denker*. Munich: Piper, 1996.
Lawrence, D. H. *Apocalypse*. New York: Viking, 1980.
Lawson, Todd. *The Qur'an: Epic and Apocalypse*. London: One World Academic, 2017.
Leemhuis, Fred. *De Koran: Een weergave van de betekenis van de Arabische tekst in het Nederlands*. Houten: Het Wereldvenster, 1990.
Lewis, Bernard. *Het Midden-Oosten: 2000 jaar culturele en politieke geschiedenis*. Amsterdam: Forum, 2001.
Liedboek: Zingen en bidden in huis en kerk. Zoetermeer: BV Liedboek, 2013.
Lind, Millard C. *Yahweh is a Warrior: The Theology of Warfare in Ancient Israel*. Scottdale, PN: Herald, 1980.
Linden, Nico ter. *Het verhaal gaat door: De verhalen van Lucas en Johannes*. Vianen: Balans, 2003.
Lucas, Shirley. *The Concept of the Messiah in the Scriptures of Judaism and Christianity*. London: Bloomsbury, 2011.
Lundbom, Jack R. *Deuteronomy: A Commentary*. Grand Rapids: Eerdmans, 2013.
MacCulloch, Diarmaid. *A History of Christianity: The First Three Thousand Years*. London: Lane, 2009.
Marsch, Charles. *Licht in het duistere: Het leven van Dietrich Bonhoeffer*. Utrecht: Kok, 2015.
Marx, Michael. *The Qur'an in Context: Historical and Literary Investigations into the Qurânic Milieu*. Leiden: Brill, 2010.
Marzahn, Joachim, et al. *Babylon Wahrheit*. Munich: Hirmer, SMB Staatliche Museen zu Berlin, 2008.
Mawdûdî, Sayyid Abul A'lâ. *Towards Understanding the Qur'an: Abridged Version of Tafhîm al-Qurân*. Leicester: The Islamic Foundation, 2007.
McKelvey, R. J. "The Millennium and the Second Coming." In *Studies in the Book of Revelation*, edited by Steve Moyise, 85–100. Edinburgh: T. & T. Clark, 2001.
Mealy, J. Webb. *After the Thousand Years: Resurrection and Judgment in Revelation 20*. Sheffield: Sheffield Academic Press, 1992.
Meer, Frits van der. *Apocalypse: Visioenen uit het boek Openbaring in de kunst*. Antwerpen: Mercatorfonds, 1978.
Mendenhall, George E. *The Tenth Generation: The Origins of the Biblical Tradition*. 2nd printing. Baltimore: Johns Hopkins University Press, 1976.
Milgrom, Jacob, and Daniel I. Block. *Ezekiel's Hope: A Commentary on Ezekiel 38–48*. Eugene: Cascade, 2012.

Miller, Patrick D. *They Cried to the Lord: The Form and Theology of Biblical Prayer.* Minneapolis: Fortress, 1994.
Miskotte, K. H. *Bijbels ABC.* Baarn: Ten Have, 1992.
Mommsen, Katharina. *Goethe und der Islam.* Frankfurt: Inselverlag, 2001.
Moyise, Steve. "Does the Lion Lie Down with the Lamb?" In *Studies in the Book of Revelation,* edited by Steve Moyise, 181–94. Edinburgh: T. & T. Clark, 2001.
Moyise, Steve, ed. *Studies in the Book of Revelation.* Edinburgh: T. & T. Clark, 2001.
Müller, Man, ed. "Die religiöse Auseinandersetzung mit dem Islam im Abendland von Mittelalter bis zur Aufklärung." In *Im Lichte des Halbmonds: Das Abendland und der Türkische Orient,* 68–73. Leipzig: Ed. Leipzig, 1993.
Myers, Ched. *Binding the Strong Man: A Political Reading of Mark's Story of Jesus.* Maryknoll: Orbis, 2017.
———. *Who Will Roll Away the Stone? Discipleship Queries for First World Christians.* Maryknoll: Orbis, 1994.
Oussoren, Pieter, trans. *De Naardense Bijbel: De Volledige tekst van de Hebreeuwse Bijbel en het Nieuwe Testament.* Middelburg: Skandalon, 2004.
Naastepad, T. J. M. *Elia.* Kampen: Kok.
———. *Geen vrede met het bestaande: Uitleg van het boek Openbaring.* Baarn: Ten Have, 1999.
———. *Menswording: Uitleg van het evangelie van Markus.* Baarn: Ten Have, 2000.
Nasr, Seyyed Hossein, et al., eds. *The Study Quran: A New Translation and Commentary.* New York: HarperOne, 2015.
Neuwirth, Angelika. *Der Koran.* Vol. 1, *Frühmekkanische Suren.* Berlin: In Insel Verlag, 2011.
———. *Koranforschung: Ein Politische Philologie? Bibel, Koran und Islamenstehung im Spiegel spätantiker Textpolitik und moderner Philologie.* Berlin: De Gruyter, 2014.
———. *Die Koranische Verzauberung der Welt und ihre Entzauberung in der Geschichte.* Freiburg: Herder, 2017.
———. *Scripture, Poetry and the Making of a Community: Reading the Qur'an as a Literary Text.* London: Oxford University Press, 2014.
———. *Studie zur Komposition der Mekkanischen Suren.* Berlin: De Gruyter, 1981.
Neuwirth, Angelika, et al. *The Qur'ān in Context: Historical and Literary Investigations into Qur'ānic Milieu.* Leiden: Brill, 2010.
Noegel, Scott B., and Brannon M. Wheeler. *The A to Z of Prophets in Islam and Judaism.* Lanham: Scarecrow, 2010.
Nooteboom, Cees, *Een duister voorgevoel: Reizen naar Jheronimus Bosch.* Amsterdam: De Bezige Bij, 2016.
Norwich, John Julius. *Four Princes: Henry VIII, Francis I, Charles V, Suleiman the Magnificent and the Obsessions that Forged Modern Europe.* London: Murray, 2017.
Oberman, Heiko A. *Luther: Mensch zwischen Gott und Teufel.* Munich: Severin und Siedler, 1982
———. *Wortels van het antisemitisme.* Kampen: Kok, 1983.
O'Connor, Kathleen M. *Lamentation & the Tears of the World.* Maryknoll: Orbis, 2002.
O'Hear, Natasha, and Anthony O'Hear. *Picturing the Apocalypse: The Book of Revelation in the Arts over Two Millennia.* New York: Oxford University Press, 2017.
O'Shaughnessy, Thomas. *The Development of the Meaning of Spirit in the Koran.* Rome: Pontifical Institutum Orientalium Studiorum, 1953.

Ovid. *Metamorphoses*. Translated by Mary M. Innes. Harmondsworth: Penguin, 1955.
Paret, Rudi. *Der Koran: Kommentar und Konkordanz*. Stuttgart: Kohlhammer, 1971.
———. *Mohammed und der Koran*. 2nd ed. Stuttgart: Kohlhammer, 1966.
Paret, Rudi, trans. *Der Koran*. 6th ed. Stuttgart: Kohlhammer, 1993.
Penn, Michael Philip. *Envisioning Islam: Syriac Christians and the Early Muslim World*. Philadelphia: University of Pennsylvania Press, 2015.
———. *When Christians First Met Muslims: A Sourcebook of the Earliest Syriac Writings on Islam*. Oakland: University of California Press, 2015.
Peters, Frank E. *Islam en de joods-christelijke traditie: Een verkenning*. Amsterdam: Boom, 2005.
Philips, Jonathan. *The Fourth Crusade and the Sack of Constantinople*. London: Penguin, 2004.
Portier-Young, Anathea E. *Apocalypse Against Empire: Theologies of Resistance in Early Judaism*. Grand Rapids: Eerdmans, 2011.
Powers, David S. *Muhammad Is Not the Father of Any of Your Men: The Making of the Last Prophet*. Philadelphia: University of Pennsylvania Press, 2009.
Qutb, Sayyid. *In the Shade of the Qur'ân (Fî Zilâl al-Qur'ân)*. Vol. 6, *Sûrahs 16–20*. Translate and edited by il Salahi. Leicestershire: The Islamic Foundation, 2005.
Rahbar, Daud. *God of Justice: A Study in the Ethical Doctrine of the Qur'ân*. Leiden: Brill, 1960.
Rahman, Fazlur. *Major Themes of the Qurân*. Minneapolis: Bibliotheca Islamica, 1980.
Reinink, G .J. "Ps.—Methodius: A Concept of History in Response to the Rise of Islam." In *The Byzantine and Early Islamic Near East*, edited by Dan Averil Cameron and Lawrence I. Conrad, 149–87. Princeton: Darwin, 1992.
Renard, John. *Seven Doors to Islam: Spirituality and the Religious Life of Muslims*. Berkeley: University of California Press, 1996.
Reston, James, Jr. *Defenders of the Faith: Charles V, Suleyman the Magnificent, and the Battle for Europe 1520–1536*. New York: Penguin, 2009.
Reve, Gerard. *The Evenings: A Winter's Tale*. Translated by Sam Garret. London: Pushkin, 2017.
Reynolds, Gabriel Said. *The Qur'an in Its Historical Context*. London: Routledge, 2008.
Rijser, David. "De tweede ronde: De slag om Troje in de Renaissance," In *Troje: Stad, Homerus Turkije*, edited by Günay Uslu et al., 105–111. Amsterdam: Allard Pierson Museum, 2012.
Roes, André. *Charles Dickens: Het zo gelukkig en toch zo ongelukkig bestaan*. Soesterberg: Aspekt, 2012.
Rooze, Egbert. *Amalek: Over geweld in het Oude Testament*. Kampen: Kok, 1997.
———. *Marcus als tegenevangelie*. Antwerpen: Halewijn, 2012.
———. *Schepping is bevrijding: Verrassende ecologie in de Bijbel*. Antwerpen: Halewijn, 2009.
Rowland, Christopher. "Foreword." In *Studies in the Book of Revelation*, edited by Steve Moyise, ix–xvii. Edinburgh: T. & T. Clark, 2001.
Sacks, Rabbi Jonathan. *Not in God's Name: Confronting Religious Violence*. New York: Schocken, 2015.
Schäfer, Peter. *Die Ursprünge der jüdischen Mystik*. Berlin: Verlag der Weltreligionen om Insel, 2011.
Schama, Simon. *Belonging: The Story of the Jews 1992–1900*. London: The Bodley Head, 2017.

———. *The Story of the Jews: Finding the Words. 1000 BCE–1492 CE*. London: The Bodley Head, 2013.
Sharbert, J. *Numeri*. Würzburg: Echter, 1992.
Schillebeeckx, Edward. *Gerechtigheid en liefde, genade en bevrijding*. Bloemendaal: H. Nelissen BV, 1977.
Schimmel, Annemarie. *Mystical Dimensions of Islam*. Chapel Hill: University of North Carolina Press, 1975.
Schimmel, Annemarie, et al. *The Mystery of Numbers*. Oxford: Oxford University Press, 1994.
Schmitz, Bertram. *Der Koran Sure 2: "Die Kuh." Ein religionshistorischer Kommentar*. Stuttgart: Kohlhammer, 2009.
Schuman, N. A. *Woord op Zondag, met zeven psalmen op weg naar Pasen*. Hilversum: Uitgave NCRV, 2002.
Schwartz, Gary J. *Hieronymus. De wegen naar hemel en hel*. Hilversum: Fontaine, 2016.
Seyed-Gohrab, A. A., et al., eds. *Embodiments of Evil: Gog and Magog. Interdisciplinary Studies of the "Other" in Literature & Internet Texts*. Leiden: Leiden University Press, 2011.
Shatanawi, Mirjam. *Islam in beeld: Kunst en cultuur van moslims wereldwijd*. Amsterdam: Sun, 2009.
Spain, Suzanne Alexander. "Heraclius, Byzantine Imperial Ideology, and the David Plates." *Spectrum* 52 (1977) 217–37.
Speyer, Heinrich. *Die biblischen Erzählungen im Qoran*. Darmstadt: Wissenschaftliche Buchgesellschaft, 1962.
Shoemaker, Stephen, J. *The Death of a Prophet: The End of Muhammad's Life and the Beginning of Islam*. Philadelphia: University of Pennsylvania Press, 2012.
Stählin, Gustav. *Die Apostelgeschichte*. Göttingen: Van den Hoeck & Ruprecht, 1968.
Stephenson, Paul. *Constantine: Unconquered Emperor, Christian Victor*. London: Quercus, 2009.
Stiegemann, Christoph, et al. *Credo: Christianisierung Europas im Mittelalter*. Vol. 1, Essays. Petersberg: Imhof, 2013.
———. *Credo: Christianisierung Europas im Mittelalter*. Vol. 2, Katolog. Petersberg: Imhof, 2013.
Stillman, Norman A. *The Jews of Arab Lands: A History and Source Book*. Philadelphia: The Jewish Publication Society of America, 1979.
Stoker, Wessel. "God en Apocalyps." In *Apocalyps in kunst: Ondergang of loutering*, edited by Marcel Barnard and Wessel Stoker, 153–57. Zoetermeer: Meinema, 2014.
Strickland, Debra Higgs. *Saracens, Demons, Jews: Making Monsters in Medieval Art*. Princeton: Princeton University Press, 2003.
Strohm, Stefan. "Luthers Vorrede zum Propheten Daniel in seiner Deutschen Bibel." In *Die Geschichte der Daniel-Auslegung in Judentum, Christentum und Islam*, edited by Katharina Bracht et al., 219–44. Beihefte zur Zeitschrift für die alttestamentliche Wissenschaft. Berlin: De Gruyter, 2007.
Suermann, Harold. "Early Islam in the Light of Christian and Jewish Sources." In *The Qur'ān in Context: Historical and Literary Investigations into Qur'ānic Milieu*, edited by Angelika Neuwirth et al., 135–45. Leiden: Brill, 2010.
Suetonius. *The Twelve Caesars: Suetonius*. Translated by Robert Graves. London: Penguin Books, 2000.

Sutton, Matthew Avery. *American Apocalypse: A History of Modern Evangelicalism*. Cambridge: Harvard University Press, 2014.
Terrien, Samuel. *The Elusive Presence: Toward a New Biblical Theology*. Eugene: Wipf & Stock, 2000.
———. *The Psalms: Strophic Structure and Theological Commentary*. Vol. 2, Psalms 73–150. Grand Rapids: Eerdmans, 2003
Trofimov, Yaroslav. *The Siege of Mecca: The Forgotten Uprising*. New York: Lane, 2007.
Uslu, Günay. "Mehmet II en Troje." In *Troje: Stad, Homerus Turkije*, edited by Ulu Günay Uslu et al., Amsterdam: Allard Pierson Museum, 2012.
Uslu, Günay, et al., eds. *Troje: Stad, Homerus Turkije*. Amsterdam: Allard Pierson Museum, 2012.
Unal, A. *De Koran: Vertaling voorzien van uitgebreid commentaar*. Rotterdam: de Rijn, 2018.
Verhoef, Eduard. *De Koran: Heilig Boek van de Islam*. Vught: Skandalon, 2016.
Vermes, Geza. *The Complete Dead Sea Scrolls in English*. Rev. ed. London: Penguin, 2004.
Voolen, Edward van, et al. *De "Joodse" Rembrandt: De mythe ontrafeld*. Zwolle: Waanders, 2007.
Waetzoldt, Wilhelm. *Dürer und seine Zeit*. Vienna: Phaidon, 1935.
Wallmann, Johannes. "Luthers Stellung zur Judentum und Islam." *Luther Zeitschrift der Luther-Gesellschaft* 2 (1986) 49–60.
Wannenmacher, Julia Eva, ed. *Joachim of Fiore and the Influence of Inspiration: Essays in Memory of Marjorie E. Reeves (1905–2003)*. London: Routledge, 2013.
Watt, W. Montgomery. *Bell's Introduction to the Qur'ân*. Edinburgh: Edinburgh University Press, 1970.
———. "The Condemnation of the Jews of the Banû Qurayzah." *The Muslim World* 42 (1952) 160–71.
———. *Companion to the Qur'ân: Based on the Arberry Translation*. London: Allen & Unwin, 1967.
Whalen, Brett Edward. *Dominion of God: Christendom and Apocalypse in the Middle Ages*. Cambridge: Harvard University Press, 2009.
Wensinck, A. J. *Mohammed en de Joden in Medina*. Leiden: n.p., 1908.
———. "Mohammed und das Judentum," *Der Islam* 2 (1911) 286–91.
———. *The Muslim Creed: Its Genesis and Historical Development*. 2nd impression. London: Frank Cass & Co., 1965.
Westermann, Claus. *Genesis Kapitel 1–11*. Neukirchen-Vluyn: Neukirchener Verlag, 1976.
Wessels, Anton. *Islam in Stories*. Leuven: Peeters, 2002.
———. *A Modern Arabic Biography of Muhammad: A Critical Study of Muhammad Husayn Haykal's Hayât Muhammad*. Leiden: Brill, 1972.
———. *De Moslimse naaste*. Kampen: Kok, 1978.
———. *A Stranger is Calling: Jews, Christians, and Muslims as Fellow Travellers*. Eugene: Wipf & Stock, 2017.
———. *The Torah, the Gospel, and the Qur'an: Three Books, Two Cities, One Tale*. Grand Rapids: Eerdmans, 2013.
Wheeler, Brannon M. *Moses in the Qur'an and Islamic Exegesis*. London: Routledge, 2002.

Wieser, Veronika, et al., eds. *Abendländische Apokalyptik: Kompendium zur Genealogie der Endzeit*. Berlin: Akademie, 2013.

Wilder, Amos N. *Jesus' Parables and the War of Myths: Essays on Imagination in the Scripture*. Eugene: Wipf & Stock, 2014.

Wink, Walter. *The Human Being: Jesus and the Enigma of the Son of the Man*. Minneapolis: Fortress, 2001.

———. *The Powers That Be: Theology for a New Millennium*. New York: Random House, 1998.

Winziger, Franz. *Albrecht Dürer: In Selbstzeugnissen und Bilddokumenten*. Hamburg: Rowohlt, 1971.

Wirth, Gerhard. *Alexander der Grosze in Selbstzeugnissen und Bilddokumenten*. Reinbek bei Hamburg: Rowohlt Taschenbuch, 1973.

Wright, Christopher J. H. *The Message of Ezekiel: A New Heart and a New Spirit*. Downers Grove: IVP Academic, 2001.

Wullen, Moritz, and Gunther Schauerte, eds. *Babylon Mythos*. Berlin: Hirmer, 2008.

Yücesoy, Hayrettin. *Messianic Beliefs & Imperial Politics in Medieval Islam: The 'Abbâd Caliphate in the Early Ninth Century*. Columbia: University of South Carolina Press, 2009.

Zenger, Erich. *A God of Vengeance? Understanding the Psalms of Devine Wrath*. Louisville: Westminster John Knox, 1996.

———. *A God of Wrath: Understanding the Psalms of Divine Wrath*. Louisville: Westminster John Knox, 1996.

———. *Gottes Bogen in den Wolken: Untersuchungen zu Komposition und Theologie der priesterlichen Urgeschichte*. Stuttgart: Katholisches Bibelwerk, 1983.

———. *Psalmen: Auslegungen in zwei Bänden*. Vol. 1, *Mit meinem Gott überspringe ich Mauern. 2 Ich will die Morgenrotte wecken. 3 Dein Angesicht suche ich. 4 Ein Gott der Rache? Feindpsalmen verstehen*. Freiburg: Herder, 2011.

———. *Stuttgarter Psalter: Mit Einleitungen und Kurzkommentaren*. Stuttgart: Katholisches Bibelwerk, 2005.

Zimmerli, Walther. *Ezechiel*. Neukirchen-Vluyn: Neukirchener, 1965.

Index of Names and Subjects

Aaron, 46
Abbasids, Abbasid Empire, 84, 111
'Abd al Malik, 68, 73, 75, 76
'Abd al-salîb, 170
Abel, 157
Abimelek, 257, 258.
Abram, Abraham, 212
    see Lot
Abû Ayyûb al-Ansâri, 64
Abû Bakr, 63
Abû Bakr al-Baghdâdi, 6
Abû Sufyân, 32, 63
Abû Tâlib, 99
    see Bahîra, Bosra
acharith, 10
Achaea, Achaeans, 205, 206, 221
Achilles, 207
Acre, 97
'Âd, people of, 38
    see Hûd
Adonis, Syrian poet, 112, 222
Adrian VI, Pope, 89
Aegean Sea, 28
Aeneas, 110
Afghanistan, 134
Agag, 122
Ahaz, king of Judah, 126
Ajax, 83
Akiva, Rabbi, 32
Aleppo, 6
Alexander the Great, XII, 9, 11, 67, 69–72, 81, 83, 104, 110, 111, 123, 132–135, 138–140, 142, 143, 148, 153, 158, 194, 201, 206, 207, 210, 211, 251
Alexander Legend, 71
Alexandria, 9, 63, 70, 135, 139, 195, 202
Alhambra, 88
'Ali ibn Abû Tâlib, 73
Allah ma'a sabarien, 189
Allenby, Edmund, 36
All-merciful, 26, 86, 122, 141, 261
All-mighty, 141
    see the All-merciful
Almohads, 100
Alpha and Omega, 155
Alvarus, Paulus, 100
Amalek, Amalekites, 59, 122
Ambrose, 111
Ammon, 148 n. 77
Ammon, the son of Zeus, 134
Amr, 153, 259
Anabasis, 81
    see Xenophon
Anatolia, 110
Ancient of Days, 105, 154, 155, 158, 252
Angels
    see Gabriel, Jibrîl, Michael
Ansâr, 31, 1, 58 n. 122
Antakya, 202
    see Antioch
Antichrist, 3–5, 8, 63–65, 70–71, 75, 77, 82, 94, 100–102, 105, 111
    see Dajjâl
anti-Judaism, 15

Antioch, 201, 203, 204 n. 42, 218
Antiochus IV Epiphanes, 9, 110, 133, 136, 139, 140, 151, 153, 175, 176, 238, 246, 251
anti-Semitism, 15
Aphrodite, 206
Apocalypse, apocalyptic, XI, XII, 1, 2, 4–15, 17–19, 28, 55, 64–68, 70, 76–78, 79, 92, 94, 100, 102, 109, 111, 112, 125, 127–131, 140, 158, 160, 170, 175, 177, 178, 187, 193, 197, 198, 218, 219, 246, 249, 251, 256, 261, 263
  American, 4
  Little, 10
  Isaiah, 11
  Apocalypse of Pseudo-Methodius, 18, 54, 66–68, 70, 75
  Qur'anic, 123
  Synoptic, 18, 182, 183
Apocalypse of Vladimir, 4
Apocalypsis cum figuris, 1
  see Dürer, Albrecht
apocalyptic
  age, 102
  beast, 153
  discourse, 114 n. 35, 184, 186
  king, 120
  language, 151
  moments, three, 18, 174
  reading, 251
  times, XI, 4, 5, 8, 19, 175, 223
  war, 102
apokalyptein, 9, 197
Aqsa, al-, mosque, 5, 8
Aquila, 134
Aquinas, Thomas, 40 n, 75
Arab empire, 73, 74
Arabia, 7, 20, 33, 59, 62, 63, 67, 99, 124 n. 76, 138, 194, 212 n. 68, 216, 218
Arabia, Himyarite, 63
Arab Peninsula, 17
Arabia, Saudi, 7
Aramaic, 32, 113 138, 139, 146, 155, 242
Ararat, 44
Aratus, 195

Ard, 64 n.52
  see earth
ark, Noah's, 30, 44
  see Noah
Armageddon, 2, 4, 5, 158
Armenia, Armenians, 17, 21, 44 , 60, 66, 74, 164, 170, 208 n. 57
Arrian of Nicomedia, 81
Asia, Asian, 81, 83, 88, 104, 110, 153, 163, 206, 210
Asia Minor, 39, 104, 120, 135, 174, 194, 201, 202, 205, 207.
Asians
  see Trojans, Mehmed II
Assyria, Assyrians, 104, 119, 151
Athena, 206, 243
attributes of God, 243
  see *sifât*
Augsburg, Diet of, 89
Augustine, 40 n. 75, 111
Augustus, 110, 161 170, 195, 207, 251
avenge(r), 83, 226, 228
al-Aws, 31, 33, 334
ayât, 24, 185

Baal, 43 n. 92, 51, 68 n.72
Babylon, Babylonian, 1, 11, 49, 58, 59, 79, 104, 108, 109, 113–120, 123, 124, 129, 131, 134, 135, 137, 139, 141–145, 148–153, 183, 184, 224, 225, 229, 230–232, 248–252. 255
Babylonian captivity, 150
Babylonian exile, 18, 28, 108, 109, 115–119, 137, 142, 149, 229, 255
Bach, J.S, 104
Badr, 26, 27, 32, 33
Baghdad, 6, 84, 98, 111, 170
Bahîrâ, 99
Banû Hâshim, 27
Banû Isrâ'îl
  see children of Israel
Banû al-Nadîr, 31, 36
Banû Qurayza, 31–34
Banû Qaynuqa, 31, 32, 36
Barbarians, 139, 193, 219–221
bar enash, 113

INDEX OF NAMES AND SUBJECTS 281

Bar Kochba, 32, 55, 138
Bar Koziba, 32
Barnabas, 201–203, 221
    see Paul
Barnard, Willem, 181, 262
Basel, 96, 97
bashâra; bushrâ, 46, 52
bashîr, 52
Basileia tou theou, 28 n. 27
Bathsheba, 114
Battle of Badr, 26, 27, 32, 33, 60
battle, final, 6
Battle of Hattin, 170
Battle of Issus, 134
Battle of Kerbala, 73
Battle of Milvian Bridge, 161
Battle of Mohács, 85
Battle of Pavia, 88
Battle at Siffîn, 73
battle song, 242
Battle of the Trench, 33–34
    see *al-Khandaq*
Battle of Uhud, 32
Battle of Yarmouk, 63
bear, 59, 151, 152, 153, 155
    see leopard, lion, Medes
beast, 8, 67, 69, 101, 104, 124, 128, 151–153, 155, 156, 181, 229, 259
    see *dabba*
beast-like rulers, 259
Beirut, 189
Belgrade, 85
Belshazzar, 141, 144–147, 159
ben 'adam, 113, 256
Benedict XVI, Pope, 192
Benjamin, tribe of, 194, 213
    see Paul
Benjamin of Tudela, 132
Ben Sirach, 149
Bergman, Ingmar, 2
Bethlehem, 57, 176, 184
beth midrash, 150
Big Bang, 247
Blake, William, 2
Blessed, 29, 41, 79, 83, 87, 122, 159, 167, 212, 213, 232, 235, 241, 250, 262
blood, shedding of, 157, 184 n. 84, 258
    see *fasâd*
Boabdil, 88
Bonhoeffer, Dietrich, 1, 222
Bosh, Jeroen, 3, 58
Bosra, 99
bow, 11, 42, 120, 126, 186, 215, 229
    see Parthians
Buda, 81, 96
Bukhtnasar, 142
    see Nebuchadnezzar
Burckhardt, Jacob, 163
Burckhardt, Johannes, 239
burn, burning, 49,126 ,173,184, 207, 214, 245
burning bush, thornbush, 12, 43, 162, 198, 257
Bush, George W., 5, 18
Byzantines, XII, 7, 20, 27, 54, 56, 57, 61–63, 66, 70, 74, 115
Byzantine Empire, 57, 61, 64–67, 75, 76, 82, 64, 111
Byzantine Orthodox, 67
Byzantium, 6, 15, 17, 55, 56, 60, 61, 62, 70, 71, 74, 163, 164, 208

cabbalistic, 147
Caesarea, 111,172, 205
Caesarea Philippi, 171
Cain, 157
Cairo, 84
calendar
    lunar, 6, 13, 132, 138
    Christian,, 207, 238
    Islamic, 132
calf, golden, 46, 145
Caligula, 136, 176
caliph, caliphate, 6, 57, 58, 63, 64, 68 n. 69, 69, 71, 73, 74, 84, 87, 132, 136, 157, 165, 170, 255, 257
Calvin, John, 91
Canaan, Canaanite, 119
    invasion of, 212
    new, 115
canon of the Bible, 8, 9, 11, 247
capitals, four Christian, 81
    see Constantinople, Buda, Vienna, Rome
Carthage, 66, 89

282 INDEX OF NAMES AND SUBJECTS

Caspar, Robert, 190
   see White Fathers, Islamic theology
Chaldeans, Chaldees, 13, 131, 148, 149
chaos, waters of, , 64, 119, 151, 157, 180, 234, 249, 256, 259
   see *tohu wabohu*
Charlemagne, 208, 211
Charles V, 18, 85, 87–90, 92, 95, 96, 168, 169, 211, 216, 218
Chapajeva, Dina, 4
Chariots, 11, 79, 80, 113, 121, 144, 186, 212, 215, 224, 263
Chechnya, 112
children of Israel, 16, 52, 74, 122, 127, 145, 157, 245, 249, 255, 258
Chirac, Jacques, 5, 110
Chi-Rho, 163
Christopher, St., 1, 3
Church of the Holy Apostles in Constantinople, 81
Church of the Holy Sepulcher, 56, 58, 165
   see Church of Refuge
Church of the Holy Wisdom, 82
   see Hagia Sophia
Church of Refuge, 165
Cicero, 219
Cilicia, 195
Claudius, 70, 201, 251
Cleanthes, 195
Cleopatra, VII, 135
cloud, clouds, 113 n. 30, 119, 154, 155, 159, 160, 174, 179, 186, 188, 243, 260, 261
Clovis, 210, 211
Columbus, 88
column of fire, 154
   see cloud
confirm, confirmation, XII, 13, 16 , 38, 39, 45, 46, 52, 53, 79, 115, 260, 262
Conrad, Joseph, 4
Constantine, 17, 18, 25, 57, 58, 60, 72, 73, 81, 83, 84, 161–168, 174, 211
Constantine, XI, 82

Constantinople, 6, 17, 55, 56, 59, 60, 63, 64, 66, 70, 81, 82–86, 91, 96, 98, 99, 161, 163, 208,
   see Istanbul
Constitution of Medina, 31
Cook, David, 5–6
Copts, Coptic, 164
Cordoba, 100
corners of the world, four, 66, 116, 123, 125
cornutus, 135
Council of Chalcedon, 57
Counter-Gospel, 171, 185, 186
Cranach, Lucas, 2–3
creatio ex nihilo, 247
creatio continua, 259
creation (narrative), XII, 44, 95, 129 n. 86, 210, 223, 229, 246–253, 257, 249, 262
cross, 18, 60, 71, 76, 85, 169, 170, 182, 196
   life-giving, 75
   of light, 162, 166
   true, 56–58, 65, 70, 75, 164, 165, 167
crucified, crucifixion, 25, 161, 165, 170, 171, 173, 174, 182, 195, 196, 198, 209, 211
crusade, 100
cry, crying, 30, 92, 172, 174, 188, 200, 230, 232, 252
cry for justice, 237
Ctesiphon, 62
   see *Madâ'in Kisrâ*
Cyprus, 59, 74, 133, 201, 218
Cyril, Bishop of Jerusalem, 166, 167

dabba, 101
   see beast
Dâbiq, 6
dagger-wielders, 137,
   see sicarii, zealots
Dahhak, 142
Dajjâl, al-, 5, 101
   see Antichrist
Damascus, 40, 69, 74, 84, 196, 200, 206, 212 218.

INDEX OF NAMES AND SUBJECTS 283

Daniel, XII, 5, 9, 10, 18, 28, 66, 67, 69–71, 98, 100–106, 115, 121, 128, 130–159, 175–177, 187, 197, 238, 244, 252
Dâniyâl, 132
Dante, 168, 169
dâr al-'ahd, 21
dâr al-islâm, 21
dâr al-salâm, 21
dâr al-sulh, 21
Darius the Mede, 115
Darius III, 133, 134, 207
David, 58, 59, 70, 79
  the new, 57, 58, 95, 114, 147, 152, 173, 183, 215
David Plates, 57, 59, 60
day of resurrection, 159, 260, 261
Dead Sea, 20
Dead Sea Scrolls, 11
death of Jesus, 18, 175, 191
  see apocalyptic moments
Deborah, 226, 239, 240, 241
decipher the signs, 140
Dedan, 124
Delilah, 227
Delphi, Delphic, 110, 188
De pace fidei, 98
  see Nicholas of Cusa
De Profundis, 92
deportation, first, second, 114
  see Babylon
devil, 78, 90, 96, 103, 106. 123, 181, 257
Deucalion, 188
dhû intiqâm, 224
Dhû al-Kifl, 109
dhû al-Qarnayn, 123, 134
Diadochi, 135
diaspora, 9, 36, 51, 92, 132, 137–139, 150, 195, 196, 221
Dickens, Charles, 199
dîn, 35
disciples, 11, 13, 30, 31, 39, 40, 44, 158, 171, 172, 174, 176–178, 180–184, 196, 201, 203, 211, 221, see helpers, *ansâr*
Divine Comedy, 191
Doctrina Jacobi, , 82

Dome of the Rock, 8, 74, 75, 170
Domitian, 251
donkey, 69, 79, 212
Donner, Fred, 26
dream, 2, 8, 28, 36, 37, 66, 94, 130, 142–144, 146–149, 151, 154–156, 158, 159, 162, 164, 175, 206 n. 48, 207, 249
dreams, interpretation of, 146
  see *peshar*
Dum Diversas, "Doctrine of Discovery", 82 n. 19
Dürer, Albrecht, 1–3, 17

eagle, 152, 176, 258
Eastern Orthodox Church, 17, 82
Eastern Roman Empire, 6, 82, 219
Eber, 22
Edom, 99, 111, 124 n. 77, 225, 231, 232
Eeden, Frederik van, 236 n. 40
Egypt, Egyptians, 11, 13, 14, 27, 36, 60, 63, 70, 80, 84, 104, 107, 112, 122, 124, 125, 133–135, 137, 138, 141, 162, 209, 212, 215, 216, 224, 245, 251, 255
  see Copts
Egypt, sultanate of, 6
Ekklesia, 159
  see *qahal*, *umma*.
El Escorial, 90
Eli, 198
Eliab, 59
Elijah, 68
  see Ilyâs,
Elisha, 118 n. 54
  see al-Yasa'
emigrants
  see *muhajirûn*
Emmaus, 214
end of days, 128
end times, XI, XII, 5, 12, 44, 65, 66, 69, 94, 100, 102, 123, 260
Endechrist, 103
ends of the earth, 9, 11, 18, 21, 28, 43, 120, 124, 178, 204, 192–194, 212, 214, 215, 217, 220
Enea Silvio Piccolini, 82
Enoch, 109

Enoch I, 11, 151 n. 94
en toutôi nika (ἐν τούτῳ νίκα), 162
Enûma Eliš, 250
Ephesus, 204, 205
Ephraim, 11, 215, 244
Ephrem the Syrian, 75, 110
Epimanes, 136
    see Antiochus
Epiphanes, 136
    see Antiochus
Erasmus, 1, 208 1, 216
Eretz, 64 n. 52
Eris, 206
    see golden apple
eschatology, *eschaton*, eschatological, 10, 44, 50, 51, 55, 65, 66, 70–73, 76, 78, 110, 111, 119, 123, 131 156, 183, 223, 230, 236
    see protology, First Things
Ethiopia, 56, 62, 63, 70–72, 74, 110, 119 n. 56, 212 n. 68, 217
Eulogius, Bishop of Toledo, 100
Europe, European, 1–3, 6, 14, 15, 60, 78, 80, 81, 83–85, 87–89, 91, 92, 97, 101, 105, 153, 161, 163, 167, 168, 188, 194, 204, 206, 207, 212, 214, 216
European Christianity, European Christians, 15, 111, 208, 210
Eusebius, Bishop of Caesarea, 161–163
evangelical apocalyptic exegesis of the Bible, 4
Eve, 107
    see paradise
exile, exiles, 18, 28, 32, 47–49, 51, 65, 108, 109, 112, 113, 115–119, 124, 127, 137, 141, 142, 148, 149, 151, 183, 229, 249, 255, 262
    see *gâlât*
Exodus, 13, 27, 60, 122, 132, 162, 180, 213, 216, 255, 258
    see *hijra*
    from Babel, 13 n. 54
    from Egypt, 13, 27, 122, 125, 162, 180, 258
    grammar, 14
    in Jerusalem, 13
    from Macedonia, 132
    from Mecca, 13, 27, 60
    see *hijra*
    from Ur of the Chaldees, 13
    see Abraham
Exsurge Domine, papal bull, 90
Ezekiel, 10, 71, 102, 106, 107–129, 152, 155, 183, 197, 250, 252–256, 260
    see Hizkîl

Faisal, King, 7
Falwell, Jerry, 5
Fatih Mosque, 81
Feast of Lights, 137
    see Hanukkah
Ferdinand I, 87–89, 102
Fides, 173
fig tree, 11, 257
final attack, 78
final battle, 143, 158, 240
final days, 221
final coming of Christ, 94
final destruction of Jerusalem, 118
final discourse by Jesus, 175
final hour, 64
final judgment, 64, 155, 223, 259
final king, 69
final Psalm, 242
final sacrifice, 218
final victory, 59, 163
final word: forgiveness, 229
final world emperor, 72
fire, 12, 49, 118, 121, 123, 125, 126, 131, 154, 155, 172, 177 n. 66, 181, 182, 184, 198, 252, 257
    see column of fire,
First Things, 19
    see Last Things
flame, 12, 94, 177 n. 66, 198, 248 n. 77
four
    beasts, 104,128, 152, 153
    Christian capitals, 81
    see Constantinople, Buda, Vienna, Rome
    corners of the land, 116,
    corners of the earth, 123
Four Horsemen of the Apocalypse, 1, 5, 8

INDEX OF NAMES AND SUBJECTS   285

see Graham, Billy
kingdoms, 66, 69, 70, 152
   see Daniel
metals, 142
   see Nebuchadnezzar, Daniel
rulers, 142
   see Nimrod, Dahhak, Solomon,
     and Alexander
winds of heaven, 135, 151, 254
   see Ezekiel
young men, 149
   see Daniel
fourth beast, 67, 140, 155
   see Alexander, Daniel
fourth empire, 71
   see Alexander the Great
Francis I, 89
Franks, 98, 166, 169, 170, 210
Frederick the Wise, 2, 102
Fulfilment, 45, 100
   see confirmation
Fuller, Charles, 5

Gabriel, 27, 29, 42 n. 82, 43, 45, 60,
     117, 140, 187, 201, 252 n. 103,
     253
   see Jibrîl
gabber, 178
   see Gabriel
Gadara, 172
Gâlât, 59
   see exile.
Galatia, Galatians, 39, 205, 211, 218,
     221
Galilee, 18, 136, 171, 172, 178, 180,
     211
Garden of the Abode, 42
Garden of Eden, 43, 69, 217 n. 91,
     253–255
Garden of Gethsemane, 172, 183
garden of the Lord, 256
gardens of pleasure, 159
Gaul, 143, 219
   see France
Gazi, 80, 81
geber, 187
genocide, 5
Gentiles, apostle of the, 37, 194

   see Paul
Gerasenes, 172
Germany, 2, 86, 90, 99, 101, 104, 105,
     208
Ghassanids, 62
Ghazwa, 80
Gideon, 257
Giles Antonini, Giles of Viterbo, 95
Gimaret, Daniel, 243 n. 64, 244
glory, divine, 28, 43, 113, 114, 116–
     118, 125, 127, 128, 134, 145,
     154, 156, 158, 183, 186, 218,
     238, 242, 245, 253 n. 107
goat, 133–135
   see Alexander
goblets, silver, 145, 146
gold and silver, 145
   see Belshazzar
God of justice, 59, 220
God of retribution, 227
God of vengeance, 223, 224, 228, 244
Gog and Magog, 5, 18, 66, 70 n. 80,
     71, 94, 101, 105, 107–113,
     119–129, 223
   see symbol
invasion of Gog and Magog, 111,
     125, 127
gold, 28, 131, 142, 143, 152 n. 98
gold, crowns of, 121
golden apple, 206
   see Eris
Golden Apple, 81
   see Turkey
golden calf, 46, 145
Golden Legend, 57
Golgotha, 71, 75, 166
Goliath, 59
   see *Jalût*
good news, XII, 15, 46, 47, 50–53, 115,
     171, 173, 174, 185, 186, 194,
     197, 203, 208, 254
   see *bushrâ*, fake news
good tidings, bringer of, 179
   see *bashîr*
Gorgons, 20
Gospel, see *Injîl*
gospels, apocryphal, 117
Gospel, eternal, 173

Goths, 98, 111
Graffiti, 159
Graham, Billy, 5
Granada, 84, 88, 168
Graves, Robert, 207
Greece, Greeks, XII, 15, 43, 66, 68, 69, 71, 72, 81–83, 104, 175, 133, 134, 136, 143, 148, 151, 153, 173, 188, 194, 195, 202, 205–207, 214, 217–221
Greek language, XI, 9, 11, 18, 19, 25, 70, 122, 128, 137, 138, 139, 161, 162, 173, 177, 190, 193
    see Septuagint, *paideia*
    koine, 138
Gregory of Tours, 164
Groen van Prinsterer, 199
Groot, Hugo de, 147
Gudula, St., 168
Gug, 120
    see Gog
Gustav Adolph, 238, 242

Habîb al-Najjâr, 202
Habsburg, 84, 87, 88, 99
Hagar, 26 n. 56
Hagemann, 83 n. 23, 98
Hagia Sophia, 82
Hajj, 23
    see pilgrimage
Hâkim bi Amr Allâh, 165
Haman, servant of Pharaoh, 107 n. 1
Haman, the builder of a tower, 107 n. 1
Hamonah, 126
hanîfan muslimân, 24
hanîfiyya, 23
Hannah, 93 n. 80
Hannibal, 58
Hanukkah, 137
    see Feast of Lights
Hârith ibn 'Abd Kulâl, al-, 63
Hasmoneans, 137
Hathor, House of Horus, 134
Haykal, Muhammad Husain, 36
hearing, 199
    see seeing,
heathens, 73, 75, 178, 220

heaven, 1, 11 n. 51, 18, 28, 29, 43, 72, 79, 112, 115, 119, 123, 133 n. 17, 134, 135, 143, 144, 146, 147, 154–158, 166, 167, 180, 184, 185, 186, 196, 203, 241, 249, 260
    and earth, 235, 241, 247, 248, 256, 259
    gates of, 208
    voice from, 174, 230
heavenly
    hosts, 125 n. 79, 161
    interpreter, 140
    journey, 17, 39- 43, 45, 114, 199
    see Paul
    judgment, 155, 197
    light, 199
    vision, 118
heavens
    Lord of the, 263
    seven, 129 n. 86
Hebrew, 15, 19, 28 n. 27, 37, 52, 64 n. 52, 92, 138, 140, 147, 158 n. 121, 197, 194, 196, 200, 201, 212, 213, 226, 238, 242, 244, 246, 248, 257, 262
Hebrew Bible, 9, 12, 16, 59, 137, 139, 150, 151, 224
Heering, Gerrit Jan, 176
Helen, 206
    see Paris
Helena, mother of Constantine, 57, 164, 165
Hellenism, Hellenistic, 131, 134, 138, 148, 150, 151, 194, 207
Hellenistic emperors, 144
Hellenistic empire, 138, 148
Hellenistic period, 136, 139, 195
Hellespont, 205, 206
helpers
    see *ansâr*
Henry the Navigator, 82 n. 19
Hera, 206
Heraclius, Flavius, 20, 54–63, 65–67, 96
Hercules, 168, 169
Hermes, 202
Herod Agrippa II, 196, 197
Herod the Great, 161, 175, 176, 184

INDEX OF NAMES AND SUBJECTS   287

Herodotus, 83, 175, 176, 184
Hijab, 117, 141
Hijra, 6, 13, 27, 30, 31, 55, 60, 114, 213,
    see Exodus
Hilten, Johannes, 104, 105
Himyarite Arabia, 63
Hinnom, 126
Hiram, 218 n. 96
Hiroshima, 125
Hitler, Adolph, 112, 209
Hizkîl, 109
    see Ezekiel,
Hodgson, Marshall G.S., 79
Holiness, 12 n. 52, 113, 127, 128
Holocaust, 15
Holofernes, 239
holy apostles, 163
holy city, 36, 55, 75
holy community, 49
holy hill, 259
    see Zion.
Holy Land, 25, 64 n. 52, 67, 73, 97,
    164, 165
Holy Mosque, 86
holy mountain, 38, 218
holy nails, 164
Holy Name, 127
Holy One, 125, 244, 250, 253
holy people of the Most High, 156
Holy Roman Empire, 85, 87, 104, 168
Holy Spirit, 141, 205
holy valley (Tuwâ), 251
Holy War, 21, 57, 80, 140, 144, 210,
    237, 238
    see *gaza* , *jihâd*
Homer, 81, 83, 142 n. 62, 205–207,
    214
Horeb, 12, 44, 213
horizon, manifest, 42 n. 82, 141, 201
horn, little, 100
horned, 235, see *cornutes*
horns, 104, 105, 123, 132, 133 n. 17,
    134, 135, 153, 155, 156
horse, horses, 36, 57, 79, 80, 120, 121,
    123, 124, 126, 144, 164, 186,
    215, 216, 218, 225
Horsemen, the Four, 1, 5, 8
    see warhorses

Hosea, prophet, 228 , 230, 244
hospitality, 203, 214, 252
hour
    final, 64
    of judgment, 12
    last, 12, 101
    near, 15 n. 9
house
    of bondage, 13, 255
    of Horus, 154
    see Hathor
    of instruction, 16, 150
    see Jewish study house
    of peace, 21
    see *dâr al-salâm*
    of war, 21
    see *dâr al-harb*
hover, 82, 117, 258, 259
    see Spirit of God, Hagia Sophia
hovering over the waters, 248, 256, 257
Hûd, 39, 48, 144
    see people of 'Ad
Huldah, 239
Hulst, W.G. van de, 177
Hungary, Hungarians, 78, 80, 85, 86 n.
    39, 87, 88, 101
Huns, 98, 111
Husayn, the son of 'Alî, 73

Iberia, 24
Iberian peninsula, 84, 88, 168,
Iblîs, 123
    see devil, satan
'*ibrî*, 212 n.67
Iliad, 206 n. 47, 207
    see Homer
illiterate prophet, 37
    see *al-nabi al ummî*
Illyricum, 217, 218
ilm al-kalâm, 144
Indus River, 83, 133, 134
inheriting the earth, 30, 58, 262
in hoc signo vinces, 161, 162
Injîl, 4, 37, 38
injustice, XI, 80, 96, 108, 122, 144, 185,
    226, 237
insân al-kâmil, 157
Iranian Revolution, 6

Iron Cross, 209
'Îsâ ibn Maryam, 6, 62 n. 40
Isabella of Castile, 88–90
Isaac, binding of, 209 n. 60
Ishmael, Ishmaelite, Ishmaelites, 23, 39, 66, 68–71, 109
Islamic Era, 66
Islamic law, 21 n. 3, 97, 193
  see *shari'ah*
Islamic State, ISIS,, 6, 63 n. 43, 64, 222
Islamic theology, 97, 190
  see *ilm al-kalâm*.
Islam, pillars of, 23
Ismaïl I, Safawid Shah, 84
Israel, state of, 5–7, 20, 32, 37, 112
  see Children of Israel
Isrâfîl, 260
Istanbul, 81, 82, 87, 208
ius tallionis, 231

Jabal, 43
Jabal al-Nûr, 44
Jabalqa, 43
Jabarsa, 43
Jacob, star out of, 32
Jacobse, Muus, 186
Jael, 240, 241
Jahanna, 131
Jalût, 59, 198 n. 24
Japhet, 120, 212 n. 68
Jehoiachin, 150
Jehoiakim, 108
Jeremiah, 41
  see Paul and Muhammad
Jerusalem
  new, 2, 168
Jerusalem
  destruction of, 109, 144, 171, 231, 248, 249, 251
  recapture of, 60
Jesus Christ, 4, 13
  see 'Îsâ ibn Maryam
  Second Coming of, 6, 70, 75, 163
Jesus Sirach, 16, 149 n. 82, 150
Jethro, 12, 48, 144, 240,
  see Shu'aib
Jews, diaspora, 9
  see Babylon, Alexandria, Arabia

Jewish law, 34
Jewish study house, 44
  see house of instruction
Jibrîl, 27
  see Gabriel
jihâd, 21, 90
  great, 90
  small, 90
jihâd fi sabîl Allâh, 25
jizya, 67
Joachim of Fiore, 100, 111
John the Baptist, 18, 69, 94, 114, 115, 140
  see Yahyâ
John of Damascus, 69
Joram, king of Israel, 126
Jordan River, 18, 163, 174, 176, 258
Josel von Rosheim, 92
Joseph
  new, 141
Josephus, 110, 182
Josiah, King of Judah, 80, 108, 109, 126
Jotham, 257, 258
journey
  heavenly, 17, 39, 41–43, 199
  night, 42, 45
  see Muhammad
  to the other side, 178
  see Jesus, Paul
  of Paul to Europe, 192, 194, 204–206, 210, 212, 214, 217, 225
  see Tarshish, Spain
  visionary, 115
  see Ezekiel
Jovian, 72, 73.
Judaism, Rabbinic, 244
Judas, the apostle, 172, 180
Judas the Maccabee, 136, 137, 238
Judith, 239, 240, 241
Julian the Apostate, 72 , 75, 76, 166
Julius II, Pope, 208
Julius Caesar, 179, 251
justice, divine, 6, 15, 46, 59, 79, 108, 122, 127, 128, 131, 148, 150, 180, 187, 190, 226, 227, 229, 237, 241–244, 259, 263
Justin II, Byzantine emperor, 73, 74, 75

INDEX OF NAMES AND SUBJECTS

Ka'ba, 44
Kanîsat al- Qiyâma, 165
   see Church of the Resurrection
Kanîsat al-Qumâna, 165
   see Church of Refuge
Katharina von Bora, 2
Kaufmann, Thomas, 92, 95
Kaysar, 61, 62
Kebar River, 112
Keiserthum, 104
Kemal Ataturk, Mustafa, 84
Kennite tribe, 240
Ketton, Robert, 96
Khalidi, Tarif, 29
Khâlid ibn Walîd, 63
Khandaq al-, 33
   see Battle of the Trench
Kharâj, al-, 31
Khaybar, 32–34
Khosrow II, Shah, 63
   see *Kisrâ*
king, see *malik*
king
   of Judah, 28, 48, 49, 68 n. 7, 108, 109, 117, 126, 144, 150, 186, 216, 224, 231
   Messianic, 216
   righteousness, 216
kingdom
   of the Antichrist, 4
   of the Arabs, 69, 71, 74
   Byzantine, 64
   of a circumcised man, 66
   coming, 79, 262
   eternal, 105
   of Ethiopia, 70
   everlasting, 79
   four, 152
   see Daniel, beasts
   of God, XII, 144, 167, 232, 263
   of the Greeks, 66, 70
   of heaven, 29, 162, 163
   of Ishmael, 66
   Jewish, 137
   see Hasmonean
   Judah, 28, 48, 68n72, 108, 109
   of justice and peace, XI
   of the Merciful, 159

   Messianic, 11
   Northern, 113
   see Israel
   of the Romans, 71
   of the Sassanid Persians (East), 55, 66
   Syrian (Seleucid), 133, 136
   Universal, 263
Kisrâ, 62
   see Khosrow II
Kissinger, Henry, 7
Kirill, Patriarch, 4
Kuklos, 218
Kûshat, daughter of Pîl, king of the Ethiopians, 70, 71

labarum, 162
Lake of Gennesareth, 180
Lakhmids, 62
lamb, 114
lambs, wounded, 229
Lamentations, lamenter, laments, 187, 188, 190
lampstand, 145
Land of Promise, 13, 36, 185, 186, 249, 258
language of Canaan, 14, 15
Last Day, last days, 22, 24, 30, 47, 76, 103, 110, 132, 223, 259, 260
Last Judgment, 12, 29, 101
Last Sigh of the Moor, 88
Last Things, 10, 19, 222–263
   see First Things
last world emperor, 72
Lawrence, D.H., 2
laylat al-Qadr, 44
Lebanon, 61, 84, 214
   see Phoenicia
legalism, legalistic, 94, 193
Legion, 172, 173
legion(s), Roman, 171–173, 182, 186, 208
legion of the boar (swine), 173
Leo X, Pope, 89
leopard, 151, 153, 155
Levites, 46, 201
Lex Mahumet pseudoprophete, 97
lex talionis, 227 n. 18

290 INDEX OF NAMES AND SUBJECTS

Licinius. Emperor, 161, 163
lion, 49, 59, 115, 118 n. 51, 121,151–153, 155
Lloyd George, David, 36
Lord Almighty, 49 n. 118, 50, 87, 240, 261
   see mighty
Lot, 30, 183, 212 n. 66, 224
   see Lût
Lote/lotus Tree, 42, 43
Louis II, King, 85
Louis IX, King, 111
Luther, Martin, 2, 17, 112, 238, chapter III
LXX (Septuagint), 9, 10, 122, 139, 149
   see Septuagint
Lydia, 214

Maccabean, Maccabees, 9, 133, 136, 137, 139, 140, 177, 238, 146
Maccabean revolt, 138, 239
Maccabee, Judas, 137, 238
Macedonia, Macedonians, 70–72, 132, 133, 153, 204–208, 217, 218, 221
Macedonian man, 204, 206
   see Alexander
Madâ'in Kisrâ, 62
Madînat al-munâwara, 13
Madyan, 12, 39, 48
   see Midian
Magdala, 171
Magnificat, 93
Mahdi, 8, 190
Mahdiyya, 190
Mahmet, 96, 103
   see Muhammad
Mahometh Reich, 104
Majūj
   see Gog, Magog
malakût, 29
malik, 29
malkût jahweh, 28 n. 27
Mamluks, 84
Mammon, XII, 251 n. 99
Manasseh, King of Judah, 126
Marble Emperor, 82
   see Ottomans

Marduk, 112, 145, 250
Maronites, 61, 164
Mary, 6, 28, 48, 62 n. 40, 93, 114, 117, 140, 180, 187, 199
Mary Magdalene, 171
Masîh
   see Messiah
Masîh al-Dajjâl, al-, 101
   see Antichrist
masjid, 114
masjid al-Aqsâ, 41
masjid al-harâm, 41
maskilim, 140
Mattathias, 136
mausoleum of the Holy Apostles, 163
Mawdûdî, 255
Maxentius, 163
Mecca, 12, 13, 23, 27, 34, 41, 44, 48, 55, 56, 60, 62, 63, 84, 86, 114, 115
Medea, 153
Medes, 11
Medina, 6, 13, 22, 27, 31–34, 36, 41, 55, 60, 63, 71, 84, 115, 190, 193
   see Yathrib, *Madînat al-munâwara*
Mediterranean Sea, 215, 218, 220
Medusa, 207
Megiddo, 158 n. 121
Megilloth, 187
   see Five Scrolls, Lamentations
Mehmed II, 81–84, 104, 208 n. 57
Melanchthon, Philip, 85, 86, 104
Memling, 2
Menasse ben Israël, 147
Mendenhall, George E., 224
Menelaus, 206
Mene mene tekel ufarsin, 146
Merciful, the all-, 26, 42, 86, 122, 123, 159, 170, 188, 204, 228, 229, 243, 244, 246, 261
   see *rahmân, rhm*
mercy
   triumph of, 244
Messiah, 4, 13, 23, 28, 29, 32, 50, 65, 67, 74, 95, 112, 117, 147, 122, 123, 147, 155, 174, 176, 177, 180 n. 76, 190, 196, 198, 214, 215, 218
   see *Masîh*

Messiahship, 176
Michael, 1, 125 n. 79, 155, 252 n. 103
Michelangelo, 135
Middle East, XI, 5, 54, 55, 60, 64, 84,
    98, 110 n. 9, 111, 135, 138, 153,
    169, 189
midrash, 15, 150, 253 n. 107
Midian, 12, 144
might, mighty, 28, 48, 50, 79, 121, 156,
    166, 240, 245 n. 71, 247
mighty angel, 225
mighty army, 120, 257
mighty king, 135
    see Alexander
mighty men, 126
mighty One, 240
mihrab, 114
Milan, Edict of, 111
Millennium, 2, 105
Milvian Bridge, 161, 163
Mirrors for Princes, 216
Miskotte, K.H., 14
Moab, 119 n. 56, 119, 225
Moloch, XII, 126
Mongolians, Mongols, 70, 84, 111
Mongolian invasion, 70
Monophysitism, Monophysites, 60, 61
monotheism, monotheistic, 23, 29, 31
Monothelitism, 61
Moors, Moorish, 88, 90
Mosaic law, 162, 193
    see *nomos*
Moses, 12, 13, 18, 37, 39, 40 n. 75,
    43–48, 43 n. 88, 44 n. 95, 52,
    58, 113 n. 30, 113, 122, 134,
    135, 145, 151 n. 94, 157, 162,
    174, 177, 185, 198, 199, 201,
    201 n. 27, 213, 224–226, 226 n.
    12, 239, 240, 245, 251–253, 251
    n. 98, 258
    new, 13
    see Mûsâ
Mount Hira, 44
Mount Judi, 44
Mount Lebanon, 44
Mount of Olives, 44, 166, 182, 183
Mount Zion, 50, 119, 232
mountain of God, 12

    see Horeb, Sinai
Mu'âwiyya, Umayyad caliph, 63
muhajirûn, 31
    see emigrants
Muhammad, 6, chapter 1
    see Jeremiah and Paul
mulku al-haqqa lir Rahmâni, 159
muminûn, 157
    see believers
Müntzer, Thomas, 238
Muqawqis, 63
mursalûna, 203
    see messengers
Mûsâ, 45
    see Moses
Mustafa Kemal Ataturk, 80
mystery, 129, 143, 144 n. 68, 230, 261
    see numbers
Mu'ta, 56
mythical anti-divine power, 121
    see Gog, Magog
mythical Babylonian stories, 250
    see *Enûma Eliš*
mythical cities, 45
    see Jâbalqa, Jâbarsa
mythological country, 120
    see Gog, Magog
mythological, poetic narrative, 247
    see creation (narrative)
mythology, Greek, 207
myths, creation, 44

nabi al ummî, al-, 37
    see illiterate prophet
Napoleon, 112, 207 n. 52
Nasârâ, 31
Nasr, Seyyed Hossein, 19
Near East, Ancient, 23, 66, 76, 119,
    122, 134
Nebuchadnezzar, 145
Negus, 62
    see Ethiopia
neqamah, 224 n. 5
Nero, 129, 209
Nestorians, 17, 60, 98, 99, 164
new age, 158
new era, 12
new heart, 256

new language, 14, 15
    see language of Canaan
new law, 115
new prophet, 63
    see Muhammad
new reign of God, 11
new song, 239, 263
new spirit, 256
new temple, 115
new world, 10
Nicea, Council of, 161,
Nicholas V, Pope, 82 n. 19
    see *Dum Diversas*
Nicholas of Cusa, 83
Nikopolis, 163
    see Constantinople
Nimrod, 15, 142, 251
Nisibis, 67
    see Monophysytes
Nixon, Richard, 7
Noah, 30, 39, 44, 47, 48, 120, 144, 253
    see Nûh,
nomad, 69, 110, 212
nomos, 139, 192, 193
Non plus Ultra, 168
Noordmans, Oepke, 262
Nooteboom, Cees, 3
Nqm, 224, 226, 227
    see *dhr intiqâm*
Nubian Gate, 170,
nuclear apocalypse, 4
Nûh
    see Noah
numbers, 129 n. 86
    see six, seven,

Obama, Barack, 4
Oberman, Heiko, 78, 94, 102
Odysseus, 206
Odyssey, The, 206
Oikoumene, 148
olive tree, 257
oracle, mysterious, 206 n. 48
Oriental Christians, 60
orthodoxy, 26, 169
Osman I, 80, 81
Ottoman, 6, 58, 64, 78, 80–85, 87, 89,
    98, 101, 102, 105, 208 n.17

Ottoman Empire, 6, 102, 105
"overthrown" cities, 10, 30, 107
    see Sodom and Gomorrah
Ovid, 202
    see Philemon and Baucis

Paderborn, 208
pagans, paganism, 82, 86, 210, 214
paideia, 139, 148, 150, 151
Palestine, 17, 32, 33, 37, 56, 57, 62, 64,
    66, 67, 84, 100, 111, 119, 132,
    136, 138, 161, 171, 173, 212,
    221, 239
parable, language of, 11, 109, 114, 201,
    202, 203
paradise, 249, 257
Paris, son of the Trojan king, 206
    see Helen
Parnassus, 188
path
    of God, 16, 21, 35, 38, 67 n. 64,
        128, 150, 151, 174, 179
    see *jihâd fi sabîl Allâh*
    Jesus', 184
    livable, 180, 234
    of Paul, 210
    straight, 52, 94, 150
    see *sirat al mustaqîm*
    of suffering (Jesus), 177, 178, 188
Parthians, 120
    see bow
Parvîz, "the Victorious", 55
Patmos, 28, 126, 260, 262
    see John
Paul, apostle, 4, 9, 17, 18, 22, 25, 37–41
    47, 48, 50, 51, 95, 135, 161,
    186, 192–221
    see *rasûl*, Muhammad
Paul the Hebrew, 212
Pax Augusta, 170
Pax Islamica, 21
Pax Ottomanica, 101
Pax Romana, 170
Peace of Augsburg, 89
Peasants' Revolt (Germany), 238
Peloponnesians, 83
Pentecost, 46, 137, 166, 210
people of 'Âd, 59, 144

INDEX OF NAMES AND SUBJECTS   293

People of the Way
    see Christians
Persepolis, 207
Persia, Persians, XI, XII, 12, 15 , 17, 21,
    27, 43, 54–63, 65–69, 71, 81 83,
    84, 87, 99, 104, 115, 132–134,
    140, 142, 143, 147, 148, 151,
    153, 206, 207
peshar, 146
Peter, apostle, 25, 38, 46, 161, 176, 177,
    183, 185, 192, 208, 209, 210,
    211
Peter the Venerable, 96
Pharaoh, 13, 15 , 48, 60, 79, 80, 120,
    125, 141, 162, 224, 251
Pharisees, 38, 185
Philemon and Baucis, 202–203
Philippi, 213
    see Macedonia
Philip II, 90
Philistia, Philistines, 119, 225
Phoenicia, 214
    see Lebanon
picture story, 125
    see cartoon
Pîl, 71
    see Ethiopians
Pilate, 13, 161
pilgrimage, 23
pistis, 173
    see faith, *fides*
Pius II, Pope, 83, 99
plagues, 125, 230
plan, divine, 59, 102, 103, 127, 259
Plautus, 206
Plus Ultra, 168
    see *Non plus ultra*
Polybius, 136
Potiphar, 212
Pompey the Great, 202
prayer direction, 115
    see *qibla*
predictions, XI, 56, 74, 100, 101, 104,
    184
Procopius of Caesarea, 111
promised land, 249
propaganda, imperial, 89
Protocols of the Elders of Zion, 7

Proctology, 223, 253
psalms, 16, 24, 47, 58, 77, 86, 190, 226,
    234, 238, 241, 242, 262
    see *zubur*
royal, 28
    of vengeance, 223, 233, 237, 239
Psalter, 24, 28, 190, 234, 242
Ptolemies, 195
Punic War, Second, 58
purple, 146, 213, 214
    see Philippi, Lydia
Putin, Vladimir, 4

Qâdî al-Fâdil, 170
Qâf, 43
Qaran, 134
qawm Mûsâ, 46
qawm-i.sâlih, 45
qibla, 27, 115
    see prayer direction
qitâl, 26
Quo Vadis?, 205
Quraysh tribe, 27

rabbinic legend, 142
rabbis in the temple, 99
rahîm, 244
    see *rehem*
Rachel, 176
Rahmân, 159
Ramadan, 27, 44
rasûl, 39, 141, 179 n. 68, 203 n. 38
    see apostle, messenger
Rayhana, 34
Reagan, Ronald, 5, 18, 112
rebellion
    Jewish32, 138, 228, 233, 236
    Maccabean, 136
reconquista, 84, 88, 168
Red Sea, 107, 218, 224
Reed Sea, 180
Reformation, 29
    see Calvin, Luther, Melanchthon
Refutation of the Qur'an, 97
    see Riccoldo da Monte di Croce
Regensburg, 92
Rehem, 244
Reinink, G.J., 75

religion
    of Islam, 21
    see *dîn*
    Jewish, 153, 238
    no new, 63, 222
        see Muhammad, Bonhoeffer
    of the Turks, 18, 78, 86, 90, 97, 100, 103, 104
    see Luther
Rembrandt, 147
remnant, 47–52, 156, 215 n. 81, *shear-jashub*
retribution, 59, 125, 223, 224, 227, 229, 234, 236, 237
    God of, 227
reveal, revelation, revelatory, 1, 3, 9, 12, 16, 24, 25, 38, 41, 42, 47, 54, 56, 103, 107, 112, 113, 124, 128, 132, 137, 141, 143, 145, 150, 154, 158, 159, 167, 175, 184, 194, 197, 204, 212, 219, 250, 251, 252, 256, 260, 261
    see *apokalyptein*
Reve, Gerard, 235
Revelation of John, XI, 1, 4, 8, 10, 17, 101, 102, 105, 106, 128
revenge, 83, 84, 206, 227, 229, 231, 234
rhm, 244
    see merciful
Rhine, 83
Richard Lionheart, 100
Riccoldo da Monte di Croce, 97, 98
rich, 15, 42, 114, 213
    see Mammon
righteous, 24, 30, 47, 215
    see *salihîna*
    community, 30
    laws, 200,
    people, 45, 112
    see *qawm-i.sâlih*
    servant(s) 58, 197. 262
righteousness, 41, 128, 187, 193, 213, 220, 263
    king of, 216
    punitive, 244
riyâh bushran, al-, 179
roadmap, 150
    see Daniel

Rome
    second, 6 15, 50, 56, 62, 70–72, 78, 81, 83, 86, 102, 111, 123, 129, 137, 142 n. 62, 161–164, 170, 171, 174, 184, 202, 205, 208, 209, 212, 217, 219, 225, 230, 234
    see *Rûm*
    church of, 95, 192, 210
Romulus, 70
Rooze, Egbert, 171
rosary, 243
    see *subha*
rûh Allâh, 205
    see spirit of God
ruins
    of Ammon, 248 n. 27
    of Jerusalem, 164, 248
    Troy, 83, 207
Rûm, 56, 63
    see Constantinople
Rûmî, Jamal al-Din al, 205 n. 44
Russia, Russian, 4, 70, 212
    see Putin

Sabeans, 124 n. 76
    see South Arabia
Sadrach, Meshach, and Abednego, 131
sacrifice
    child, 126, 127
    see Moloch
Sa'd ibn Mu'âdh, 34
Saladin, 170
Saddam Hussein, 18
sail, sailors, 124, 169, 178, 179, 180, 182, 253
    see Noah, Jonah, Tarshish
Sakîna, 107 n. 2
    see Rest of God, *Shekinnah*
Saladin, 100, 165, 170
salât, 23
Salîh, 39
    see Thamûd
salvation, 30, 127, 152, 189, 200, 214, 219, 259
    to all who believe in Him, 72, 220
    history, 74, 216
    of the Jewish people, 50

INDEX OF NAMES AND SUBJECTS   295

after three days, 185
   of the remnant, 47, 51
Samaria, 49, 230
Samson, 152, 227
Samuel, 9, 145
   see Samwîl
Samwîl, 59
   see Samuel
sanctuary, 114–117, 166, 198, 202, 256
   see temple
Sanhedrin, 205
San Marco, 82
   see Venice
San Pedro in Vincoli, 135
Saracens, 57, 67, 82 n. 19, 94, 111
Sarah, Sarai
   see Abraham
sarcophagus, 163
   see Constantine, mausoleum of the
      Holy Apostles
Sartre, Jean-Paul, 235
Sassanids, 99
Satan, satanic, 5, 49, 78, 90, 96, 100, 101,
      103, 123, 157, 177, 107, 257
Saudi Arabia, 7
Saul/Paul, 195, 196, 199, 201, 221
Saul, King, 59, 122, 173, 194, 245, see
      Tâlût
savior, 240
   of the poor, 216
   Ethiopian king-, 74
sawm, 23
sayf-l-slâm, the sword of Islam, 63
Schillebeeckx, Edward, 130, 235
Scipio Africanus, 58, 89
   see Charles V
scroll, eating a, 113, 118
   see Ezekiel
   tears on your, 191
scrolls, 10, 80, 255, 262
   Five, 187
   see Megilloth
   of the Psalms, 16
Scrooge Ebenezer, 199
Scythians, 120
Sea of Galilee, 171, 172
Sea of Reeds, 224, 225
seal, 57

seals, seven, 127
seal, sixth, 1
Seba, Sheba, 216, 217
Sebêos, 66
second angel, 79
   see Revelation of John
second coming of Christ, , 75
seeing, 199
   see hearing
seeker of God, 23, 24
Seeligmann, J.L., 138
   weer, 131, 140, 256
   see Daniel, John, signs
seer on Patmos, 126, 260, 262
   see John
Seleucia, Seleucid, 135, 136, 175, 201
Seleucus I, Alexander, Nicator, 135
Selim I, 79, 84
Septuagint, 9, 16, 18, 122, 128, 138,
      139, 150, 155, 173 , 218
   see LXX
Seraiah, 224
Sermon on the Mount, 44, 58, 223, 262
seven, 129
   angels, 260
   bowls, 127
   crowns, 133
   days, 64
   dreams of Joseph, 141, 146
   heads, 133
   letters to the churches, 127
   millennia,, 68
   months, 126
   oceans, 129 n. 86
   seals, 127
   trumpets, 127, 260
   visions, 127
   years, 116, 142
seven-headed dragon, 1, 100
   see Joachim, Saladin
seventh
   angel, 28
   day, the, 113, 253
   day, Moses was called, 113 n. 30
   heaven, 43
   trumpet, the, 29, 260
seven thousand, 51
   see Eliya, Ilyâs

Seville, 169
Shahada, 23
Shah Ismaïl, I, 84
Sham, Syria, 36
shâri'a, 85, 150, 193
    see Islamic law
Shear-jashub, 48
    see remnant
sheep to be slaughtered, 209
Shekinnah, 107
    see *Sakîna*, Rest of God
Shem, 212
shepherd, 49, 152, 157, 229, 257
    good, 229
shield, 124, 126, 169, 186, 258
    Achilles's, 207
Shock and Awe doctrine, 125
ship, 168, 169, 178, 179, 180, 194, 217
    see Jonah, Yûnus, Tarshish,
ships of Tarshish, 218 n. 96
Shu'aib, 39
    see Jethro, Midian, Madyan
Shush in Iran, 132
Sibylline Oracles, 110
Sicarii, 137, 177
    see dagger-wielders
Sisera, 140
Sicily, 100, 218
Sidon, 226
Sifât, 243
    see attributes
sign, 114, 154
    Chi-Rho, 162, 163
    coming, 11
    of the cross, 85
    of the end, 11, 56, 65, 69, 100, 110, 111
    of Jonah, 185
    of mercy, 40
    see Muhammad
    of salvation, 72
    see Jesus
    of the Son of Man, 167
signs, 24, 20, 42, 43, 179, 183, 261
    of the approach of the "Last Hour, 101
    see cloud, Ezekiel, *in hoc signo vinces*

Silas, 214
    see Paul
silver plates, 59
    see Heraclius
Sinai, Desert of, 212
Sinai, Mount, 13, 44, 107, 113n30, 134, 145, 154
Sinjar, 54,
sirat al mustaqîm, 150
    see path, straight
six days the cloud covered Sinai, 113
six, days of creation, 129 n. 86, 154, 247
six, three times (666)
    see Hitler
sixth day, the, 253, 259
sixth head, the, 100
    see Joachim, Saladin
sixth seal, 1
slaughter, 114, 127, 133, 171, 209, 257
    see lamb
sleep, asleep, 68, 177, 178, 180, 198
Sodom and Gomorrah, 10, 30, 50, 107, 144, 150, 183, 224, 212 n. 66, 230 n. 25
Sodom and God's law (*nomos*), 139
Sölle, Dorothy, 234 n. 37, 242, 243
Solomon, 5, 44, 80, 126, 142, 214, 215
    see temple, first
solus Christus clausas portas vulvae virginalis aperuit, 117
Son
    of God, 171
    of Man, 113
    of the Most High God, 172
    of a star, , 32
    see Bar Kochba
Song of Deborah, 226, 240, 241
Song of Hannah, , 93 n. 80
Song of Judith, 239
Song of Mary, 93, see Magnficat
Song of Moses, 224, 225, 258
songs of praise, 262
    see Psalms
    of renewal, 263
    royal, 28
Song of the Sea, 225
Sophronius, 57, 58

soterial wood of the True Cross, 167
South Arabia, 99, 124 n. 76, 217
Spain, 91, 95, 100, 104, 168, 169, 178,
    192, 194, 217, 218, 219, 220
    see Paul, ends of the earth
Spinoza, 147
Spirit, 102, 107, 117, 118, 181, 183,
    248, 254, 259, 260
    Holy, 137, 141, 199, 205
    of Jesus, 205
    trustworthy, 141
spirit
    new, 256
    of the Psalms, 239
    of Rachel, 176
    "violent", 210
    see Paul
    of wisdom, 148
spirits, impure, unclean, 173
    see pigs
Star, *surah* of the, 42
stars, 11 n. 51, 119, 243, 263
Steinz, Peter, 188
Stephen, 195
stone, 143, 145, 146, 165, 170, 172,
    182, 184, 195, 202–204, 207,
    211, 224–226, 256
    see Stephen, Paul, temple
street theater, 113
    see Ezekiel
storm, 154
    out of the north, vision of, 119
    see Gog
    and Jesus, 177, 178, 180
    and Jonah, 179
stormy sea churned by the four winds,
    151
    see Daniel
subha, 243
    see rosary
Sudan, South, 198
Suffer, 40 n. 76, 48, 130, 161, 200, 206,
    232, 234, 236, 250, 252
    see Paul, Jesus, Muhammad
suffering
    Jewish, 95, 136
    of the Messiah, 214
    path of, 177

purified through, , 49
    of the Son of Man, 176
Sulaymân, 79
    see Solomon, prayer direction,
    qibla
Sülaymân "the Magnificent", 18
    see the great Turk symbol Sultan
    Suleiman, 79
Sultanic Qanuns, 87
sun
    in the Bible, 126, 196,
    in the Qur'an, 11 n. 51, 80, 261
    sets in the west, 217
Sunday, "Christian", 260
supersession of Judaism, 165
surah
    -t-al-Fâtiha (1), 150
    "The Fig" (5), 11 n. 51
    Jonah (10), 11 n. 51, 179 n. 67
    "Night Journey" (17), 41
    Qâf (50), 43
    of the Star (53), 42
    "The Rolling Up" (81), 11 n. 51
    "The Runners," (100), 123
Susa, 140
sword, 35, 67, 103, 124, 125, 137, 144,
    172, 173, 186, 205, 208–211,
    223, 229, 230, 233, 237, 238,
    240, 241, 242
    of God, 63
    see *sayf-l-slâm*, Khâlid ibn Walîd
    of Osman I, 80, 81
    of the prophet Muhammad, 84
    see Selim I
    of Romans, 78
symbol, symbolism, symbolic,
    symbolize, 11, 43, 60, 62, 72,
    84, 105, 113, 120–122, 145,
    151, 152, 156, 166, 169, 170,
    178, 210, 217
Synoptic Apocalypse, 11, 18, 182, 183
synoptic gospels, 9
Syria, Syrian, 3, 17, 27, 33, 36, 56,
    62–64, 67, 111, 133, 134, 136,
    158, 182, 194, 196, 202, 210,
    212, 214, 222
    al-Sham synagogue, 14, 92, 93,
    196, 213, 242

Syriac, 70–73
Syrian Orthodox, 17, 60, 110, 164
sin, sinner, 30, 40, 74, 102, 169, 224,
    228–230, 230 n, 25

Table Talk, 77
    see Luther
Tâlût, 59, 194
    see Saul
Talmud, Talmudic, 147
Targum, 139, 242
Tarshish, 124, 178, 194, 216, 217, 218
    see Spain
Tarsus, 132, 194, 201, 207
    see Asia Minor, Turkey, Paul
Thamûd, people of, 39, 48, 59, 144
Tawra, 13, 23, 37, see Torah
tears, 191
telos, 192, 193
temple
    first, 5, 74, 137, 184
    of Jerusalem, desecrated, , 142, 175
    see Antiochus
    destruction of the first, 74, 114,
        137, 187
    curtain of the, 174
    of Dagon, 227
    see Samson
    rebuilding, 75, 140, 150
    second, 137, 142, 150, 184
    see Herod
    third, 5, 8
Titus, 142, 171, 182, 251
Temple Mount, 8
Temple State, 13, 149
Tenach, 228
ten horns, 104, 133 n. 17, 153
Thamûd, people of, 39
    see Hûd
theology
    Christian, 77 (Luther)
    Islamic, 6, 97, 190, 244
    see *ilm al-kalâm*,
    Jewish, 243
    Paul's apocalyptic, 193 n. 5
thornbush, 12, 257
three
    apocalyptic moments, 174

days, 185
    ghosts, 199
    see Dickens, Charles
    horns, 105
    times a day to worship, 116
    times called, 198
    see Samuel
three and a half years, 103 n. 138
    see Daniel
three thousand, 210
    see Pentecost
triumph, triumphant, triumphal, 52,
    57, 66, 73, 89, 170, 208, 219,
    144,
throne
    of the cherubs, 115
    of God, 29, 45, 119, 154, 252, 253,
        256, 259
    on the water, 256
Tiber River, 162
Tiberias, 138
Tiberius, 161, 176, 195
Tischrede, 85
Titans, 240
Titian, 90
tohu wabohu, 10, 248, 249
Toonder, Marten, 251 n. 95
Topkapı Palace, 83
Torah, confirmation of the Torah by
    Jesus and Muhammad, 16, 38
    see Tawra
Tower of Babel, 107, 145
Training, 108, 148, 149, 219
    see *paideia*
Transfiguration, Mount of, 13, 18
trees, 7
    see, fig tree, Lote/lotus tree
    forbidden, 107
    of life, 256
    Jotham' fable of the, 257
tribulations, eschatological, 70 n. 80,
    76, 92, 105
Troas, 194
    see Troy
trophy
    of the cross, 166
    of victory, 166
Trojans, 83

see Asians, Mehmed
Troy, 81, 83, 194, 204–207, 210, 212
    see Troas
Trump, Donald, 4
trumpet, 28, 30, 128, 154, 159, 259, 260, 261
    seventh, , 29
twelve
    apostles of Jesus, 25
    crops of fruit, 256,
    disciples, 39
    legions of angels, 173
twelve-year- old Muhammad, 99
    see Bahîrâ
Tunis, 89
    see Charles V
Tunesia, 190
    see Mahdiya
Tustar, 132
Turkey, Turk, Turkish, 3, 6, 7, 17, 18, 28, 54, 58, 64, 70, 77, 78, 80, 81, 84–92, 94, 96–98, 100–106, 112 , 132, 135, 169
two horns, man of the, 123, 134
    see *dhû al-Qarnayn*
Tyre, 57, 226
Ṭuwâ, 12

Uhud, Battle of, 32
Ulai, River, 140
'Umar ibn al-Khattâb, 57, 58, 62, 63, 69 n. 69, 132, 255
Umm Haram, 63
ummî, al-nabi al-, 37
ummôt hâ-'ôlâm, 37
una religio in rituum varietate, 98
Uriah, 114
Ur of the Chaldees, 13
    see Abraham
Urbanus, 70
'Uthmân, 68, 73

Vatican, 234f.
vengeance, 53, 207, 223, 226–229, 236–238, 241
    God of, 223, 224, 228, 244
    Psalms of, 237
Venice, 82, 85

see San Marco
Vespasian, 251
Via Appia Antiqua, 208
via crucis, 18, 174, 211
victory, final, 59
Vienna, 18, 70, 78, 80, 81, 85–87, 102, 105
violence, 220, 223, 228, 234, 236, 237
Virgil, 110
vision, apocalyptic, 67, 100
    see Daniel
    of Constantine, 162, 164, 166
    of Ezekiel, 115, 121, 128,
    heavenly, 118
    of Moses, 162
    see burning bush
    of the new temple, 115, 116,
    nightly, 154, 155, 156
    of Paul, 186, 194, 196, 197, 201, 204, 206–208, 210, 212
    see Damascus, Troy
visionary experiences of Muhammad, 42, 43, 114, 201,
visionary journey, 114
visions
    of Daniel, 67, 100, 104, 121,128, 131, 133, 140–142, 149, 151, 164
    of Zechariah, 140
Voltaire, 163
Vondel, Joost van den, 14 n. 61, , 175

Wadi of Egypt, 216
Wahb ibn Munabhîb, Walid I, Caliph al-, 69
warhorses, 11, 215, 263
warners, 52, 141
    see good news/tidings
wars
    Alexander's, 81
    Arab civil, 74
    Byzantine-Arab, 74
    Byzantine Persian, 67
    Napoleonic, 112
    of Turkish conquest,, 80
Wartburg, 93
wastelands, 256,

waters, primal, 10, 44, 116, 154, 157, 168, 178, 180, 181, 188, 224, 248, 249, 253 n. 106, 257
waves, 177, 178, 180, 188, 249
way
   of the cross, 18, 171, 211
   see *via cruces*
   of God, in the, 145
   see fi sabîl Allâh,
   to life, 150
   for the Lord, 94
   to Spain, 217
   people of the, 196, 210
Wensinck, Arent Jan, 31 n. 40, 34, 243
Western Roman Empire,, 219
white, 252
White Fathers, 190
   see Caspar, Robert
Whore of Babylon, 1, 129
Wilder, Amos, 206 n. 48, 247
Willem van Ruysbroeck, 111
William of Tyre, , Archbishop, 57
winds, 118 n. 118, 143, 177 n. 66, 180–182, 218
   harbingers of God's mercy, 179
   four, 135, 151
   God's messengers, 177 n. 66, 178, 179
wisdom, 16, 41, 79, 105, 141, 148, 149, 234
Wittenberg, 2, 77, 85, 92
   see Luther
woe, 108, 178, 236,
womb, 102, 144, 246
   see *rehem, rahîm*, 44, 126, 143, 146, 167, 170, 182
woodcuts, 1, 2
   see Cranach, Dürer
wrath, God's, 102, 125
wrath, time of, 103, 244

Xenia, Greek term for hospitality, 203 n. 35

Xenophon, 81
   see *Anabasis*

YHWH, 228
Yahweh, 37, 126, 218, 224, 258
Yahyâ, 215
Yajûj, 108
   see Gog
Yâqut, 43
Yarmouk, 62, 63
Yasa', al-, 118 n. 54
   see Elisha
Yathrib
   31, 32, 71
   see Medina
Yazîd I, Umayyad, Caliph, 64, 73
Yazidis, 54
Yûnus
   see Jonah, Man of the Fish,

Zadok, 215
zakât, 23, 91n71
Zaphon, Mount, 43 n. 92, 119
Zayd ibn Hâritha, 56
Zealots, 137, 171, 177
   see Sicarii, dagger-wielders
Zechariah, prophet, 10, 11, 140, 215
Zechariah, father of John the Baptist
   114, 115, 140
   see Yahyâ
Zedekiah,, 224
Zenger, Erich, 226–228, 232,
Zerubbabel, 144, 150
Zeus, 43 n. 92, 134, 136, 175, 176, 188, 195, 202, 203, 206
Zion, 59, 119, 186, 256, 259
   Daughter of, 215
   Mount, 50, 116, 119, 232
   Christian, 5
zubur, 24
   see Psalms
zulm, 144
Zwingli, Ulrich, 78, 91

Index of Scripture Texts

OLD TESTAMENT

Genesis

1	246, 247, 250
1:2	151, 154, 247, 256, 257, 259
1:1–5	248
1:3	253
1:3–31	253
1:7	253
1:26	251
1:26–27	252
1:27	254
1:29	229
2:3	248
2:18	216 n. 87
2:16–17	107
3:8	107
4:1–16	157
4:23–24	227 n. 18
6–9	227
6:6–7	245
7:11	10, 249
8:4	44
8:15–18	47
9:6	250
9:8–17	47
10	217
10:2	120
10:4	107, 133
10:7	217
10:21–30	212
11:1–9	145
11:4, 9	109
11:26–27	212
12:1–3	216 n. 87
14:13	212
15:18	216
16:12	69
17:6	29
17:15–16	29
18:1–2	252
18:2	252
18:16, 22	252
18:17	150
18:20	230 n. 25
18:20–21	144
18:21	107
19:4–11	144
19:17	183
22	199
22:16	209
22:10–11	199
25:12–18	69
35:11	29
28:11–15	147
39:6	141
39:17	212
40:8	146, 149
40:15	212
40–42	141
41:12	149
41:16	146

Genesis (continued)

41:25, 28	146
41:38	141
41:42	146
43:32	212
50:20	53

Exodus

2:1	256
3	43, 58, 162
3:1–6	12
3:2–4	198
3:7	252
3:8	107
3:14	145, 251
13:20–22	154
13:21–22	154
14:4	125
14:19–24	154
14:28	224
15	110, 226
15:1–18	226, 239
15:3–5	224
15:9	154
15:10	107
15:12–16	226
15:18	225
15:21	225
16	154
16:10	154
16:13	123
19:4	258
19:16	154
19:16–19	260
19:20	107
20:11	203, 247
20:18	291
20:23	145
21:24	227
21:24–25	256
24:10	252
24:12	157
24:15–18	154
24:15–27	113
24:16	113 n. 30
24:16–17	154
24:18	213
31:1	44, 145, 213
31:17	247
32:8	245
32:9–10	245
32:14	245
32:15–16	157
32:22	224
32:25–35	46
32:31	141
33:22–23	252
33:18–23	44, 213
34:6–7	228
33:11, 18–23	40
34:5	154
34:6–7	227, 228
34:29–30, 35	134
40:34–38	154

Leviticus

1:1	201 n. 27
14:19–20	227 n. 18
16:2, 15	45
17:10–14	250
18:21	126
25:18	127

Numbers

9:15–23	154
10:11–12, 34	154
11:17	107
11:25	154
12:5	154
12:6–8	37
16:42	154
23:19	245
24:1	122
24:7	122
24:8	122
24:17	32
24:7, 20	122
24:17	142

Deuteronomy

1:31	258
2:7	258
4:1–2	154

4:27	51	**1 Samuel**	
5:15	252	3:1–10	198
5:22	154	5–9	198 n. 24
8:1–6, 15–16	258	7:14	198 n. 24
17:16	80, 216	8	198 n. 24
18:14, 18	52	10	23, 59
18:15, 18	37, 46	15:4–9	122
18:18	185	15:8	122 n. 69
19:21	227 n. 18	15:11	245
20:12–14	35	15:18–33	122
20:12	14, 35	15:29	245
21:23	196	15:35	245
25:18	122	16:6–7	59
29:4–5	258	17:13, 28–29	59
32:10–11	258	17:34–37	152
31:15	154	17:41–51	59
32:18	226 n. 12	17:54	147
32:26	245	24:13	237
32:35	237	25:25	198
34:10–12	37	30	122 n. 69
Joshua		**2 Samuel**	
2:1f.	64	4:10	173
6:17, 22–25	64	7:16	28
6:20	64	8:4	215
8:29	196 n. 18	12–16	79
10:26–27	196 n.18	12:7	114
		12:7	114
Judges		15:1	215
3:9–11	232	15:30–32	183
4	241	22:10	107
4:21–23	240	23:20	152
5	226		
5:1–31	239	**1 Kings**	
5:19	158 n. 121	1:33–34	215
5:24	241	1:5	215
7:5–25	257	3:5–15	79
8:23	257	5:1	216
9:9	257	5	6, 115
9:11	257	5:16–20	44
9:13	257	6:11	5
9:15	257	7:2–12	44
9:16–21, 50–55	258	8:48	27
14:5–6	152	8:10–11	154
16:27–28	227	8:11	154
		9	4–5, 79

1 Kings (continued)

8:44–45, 48	115
9:17–19	215
10:2	16
10:3–4	149
10:22	218
10:26, 28–29	215
10:28	215
11:1–14	79
18:27	68
18:46	254
19	40 n. 75
19:8	44, 213
19:9	113, 113
19:9, 13	44
19:10, 14	51
19:11	213
19:18	51
19:37	44
10:26, 28–29	215

2 Kings

3:15	254
3:27	126
5:26	118 n. 54
6:32	118 n. 54
9:27	158 n. 121
11:12	133 n. 17
16:3	126
19:37	44
21:6	126
21:7	118 n. 53
22:8	80
22:16–17	239
22, 23	108
23:2	80
23:10	126
23:11	80
23:29	158 n. 121
24:10–17	231 n. 28
24:13–15	109

1 Chronicles

1:1–2:2	217 n. 91
1:5	120
1:7	133
1:29–31	70
17:14	28
24:16	215
28:5	28

2 Chronicles

1:14–18	215
5:13–14	154
23:29–30	158 n. 121
33:7–15	118 n. 53
34–35	108 n. 4
35:22	158

Ezra

3:7	44
9:8, 13–14	49

Nehemiah

1:1–3	49
9:6	203
9:17	228

Job

9:32	245
20:28	260
26:12	151
29:3	38
36:29–30	154
36:26	154
37:15	154
39:5–8	69

Psalms

1:2	47
2	123
2:2	123
2:9	216
5:8	115
7:16	227
8:3	190
8:5	155
9:16–17	226
17:8	25
18:12–13	164
18:13–14	164

19:5	51	102:25	154
19:2–7	51	102:28	154
19:7–8	38	103:19	28
19:8–15	51	103:22	28
22:9	232	104:3	154, 253
23:14	n. 61	110:5–7	216
28:2	115	119:1	99
29:10	253	119:105	38, 150
33	262	119:115	236 n. 41
33:4–7, 8–19	263	119:145–160	200
33:3	262	119:158	236 n. 42
33:2	239	130	92
33:16–18	263	133	253 n. 126
34:21a	226		137:58, 229, 230
37:9, 11, 29, 34	58, 262	137:5, 6	116
37:11	58	137:8, 9	59
40:4	263	138:2	115
42:8	249	139:1–6	233
44:23	209	139	236
47:9	232	139:7–8, 11–12, 17	235
48:2	119	139:23–24	233
48:6–7	218 n. 96	139:19–22	233
56	191	139:24	235
68:31–32	70	144:3	235
68:31	71	144:9	239
72	214	145:11–13	28
72:2–4, 12–14	216	148:2	125 n. 79
72:8–11	216	149	237, 239, 241, 242, 262
72:9–11	216		
72:10	216	149:1	239, 263
72:17	216	149:5–9	238
74:13–14	151	149:7	226
76:1–9	186	149:7–9a	241
77:9	188	149:8–9	241
85	15 n. 62	150	242
89:9–10	151		
91:1–2	263	**Proverbs**	
93:1	237	6:23	38
94:1–2a	226	10:17a	150
96:1	263	15:32	150
97:1	232 n. 34	26:27	226
97:2–3	154	29:18a, 19	130
98:1	262		
99:8	227	**Ecclesiastes**	
91:1–2	263		
98:1–3	263	6:10	245 n. 71
99:8	228	10:8	226
101:1	58		

Isaiah

Ref	Page
1:9	51
1:10	139
1:21	187
2:3	116
2:2–3	221
2:2–4	221
2:3	116
2:4	186
2:6–21	228
2:7	216
2:10	10
3:9	144
4:1	49
4:5	154
4:6	119
5:29	152
6:3	145
6:5	40 n. 75
6:13	49
7:3	48
10:19–22	49
10:21–22	48
10:22–23	50
10:28–31	120
11:3	145
11:6–8	229
11:7	152
11:11–12	49
12:3	221
13:6	260, 261
13:20	119
14:9	134
14:12	119
14:13	119
14:14	119 n. 58
14:31	119
17:12–13	178
18:7	70
19:1	154
19:18	14
23:1	133
24–27	10
24:1	10
24:1	10
24:18	10
25:6–8	221
26:20–27:1	260
26:21	237
27:1	151
28:4	11 n. 51
29:6	177 n. 66
30:15–17	228
31:1–3	228
34:4	11 n. 51
34–35	10
35:9	229
37:4	50, 51
40:3	94
40:11	229
40:17	249
40:23	249
40:25	253
41:4	155
41:29	249
42:7	197
42:9–10	263
42:10	262
44:4	155, 256
44:6	155
44:7	253
45:1, 4	70
45:18	249
46:3	49
46:3–4	229
46:5	253 n. 104
48:20	230
50:8	209 n. 61
51:3	256
51:9–10	151
51:10	250
51:12	155
52:7	50
52:11	230
52:12	154
53:1	9, 46, 51
54:9–10	47
56:8	219
57:15	215 n. 81
60:3	221
60:21	58
62:11	11
63:4	237
65:2	51
66:18	221

INDEX OF SCRIPTURE TEXTS 307

66:18–20	219–220
66:19	218

Jeremiah

1:5	194
1:14	119. 120
1:14–15	120
2:10	133
2:19	144
2:23	126
3:14	49
3:18	120
4:6	120
4:23, 26	248
4:24	248 n.79
5:8	49
6:1, 22	120
6:6	248 n. 77
6:16	39
6:22–23	120
7:31	126
8:3	51
8:13	11 n. 51
8:16	248 n. 78
9:23–24	41
9:41, 48	120
10:10	248 n. 78
10:22	120
12:10	249 n. 80
13:20	120
16:19	221
17:8	120
18:8	245
18:10	245
19:5, 6	126
22:15–16	109
25:16	248 n. 78
26:13	245
31:25	39
31:28	16
32:29	184
46:24	120
49:2	248 n. 77
49:21	248 n. 78
50–52	230
50:3	120
50:3, 9–41, 48	120
50:15	230 n. 25
50:29	226 n.16
50:41	120
51:9	230 n. 25
51:6, 45	230
51:20–26	59
51:25	184
51:29	248 n. 78
51:46	120
51:50	116
51:59–64	11
51:61–64	225
52:6	109
52:13	184
52:6	109
52:13	184
52:15	109

Lamentations

1:1	187
1:20–22	231 n. 28
3:64	226 n. 16
3:64–66	231 n. 28
3:44	188

Ezekiel

1	112, 116
1:1	109
1:4	119
1:26	252
1:26–28	118, 250
2:1	113, 155, 197
2:1, 3	113
2:2	118
2:9	118
3:1	113
3:12, 14, 24	118
3:12, 24	254
4:4–6	113
5:5	217
5:7	126
5:24	254
7:2	116
7:12–14	126
8:1	117
8:2	121

Ezekiel (continued)

8:2–3	118
8:3	254
8:3–4	118
8–11	116
10:1	121
10:10–22	112
10:8, 19	117
11:1	183, 254
11:1, 5, 24	117
11:22–24	117
11:23	183
11:24b–25	118
12:1	256
14:1–3	117
16:20–21	127
18:23	246
20:1–3	117
23:3:7–8	237
23:40–42	126
24:2	118
24:15–27	113
24:25–27	114
25:12–14	231 n. 28
25:13	124 n. 77
26:12	225
27:6	133
29:4	124
30:1–3	261
33:11	246
33:21	113
33:25	250
33:30–32	117
33:33	118
34:7–10	152
34:17	134
34:25–28	229
34:28	152
36:22–23	127
36:26	256
36:35	255
37	109 n. 8
37:1	254
37:1–4	255
37:1–10	109
37:3–5	254
37:9–10	254
37:10	254
38:2	108
38:3–4	120
38:3–9	124
38:4	124
38:6	120
38:6, 15	119
38:8	158 n. 121
38:10–13	128
38:11	124
38:12	218
38:13	124
38:14–16	123, 125
38:15	120
38:16, 23	128
38:18–23	125
38:21	125
38:23	125
38–39	5, 94, 101, 106, 108, 124, 217 n. 91
38:2–39:15	119
39:2, 4, 17	158 n. 121
39:3	120
39:6, 7, 22, 28	128
39:9–10	126
39:12–14	126
40–48	116
40:3	121
43–46	115
43:1–4	116
43:5	254
44:1–2	117
44:2	107
47:12	256

Daniel

1–6	140, 151
1:1	31
1:3–4	149
1:4–5	149
1:5	149
1:15	141
1:6, 8–16	149
1:17	149
1:20	149
2:2	142
2:5–6	142

INDEX OF SCRIPTURE TEXTS

Reference	Page	Reference	Page
2:8–9	143	7:13	155
2:11–13	143	7:13–14	158
2:16	143	7:14	156
2:22	145	7:15	141
2:25–28	143	7:15–16	156
2:28	146	7:17	156
2:31–33	143	7:18	157
2:31–37	28	7:18, 21, 27	156
2:34	143, 158	7:21, 25	156
2:34–35	143	7:25	103
2:35	145	7:27	28, 156
2:37	156	7:28	141
2:38	152	8:1–14, 23–24	153
2:40	144	8:3–4	134
2:44	144	8:5	133, 134
2:45	159	8:8	135
3:19–24	131	8:10, 24	137
3:25	131	8:11	136
3:28	131	8:11–13	136
4:1	42	8:15	121
4:2, 34	156	8:15–16	140
4:13	152 n. 98	8:16	140
5:1	47	8:17	113
5:1–2	145	9:6	139
5:4	145	9:21	140
5:5–9	146	9:27	136
5:8	148	10:4–5	140
5:10	146	10:6, 18	121
5:11	141	10:13	125 n. 79
5:12	146	11:3–4	135
5:14	141	11:21–45	137
5:17	146	11:30	133
5:19	156	11:31	136
5:22–25	146	11:33	137
5:23	145	11:34	137
5:29	146	11:36	103
6:1	52	11:36–37	153
6:11	27, 116	12:3	137
6:26	156	12:6	140
7	105, 128, 148	12:11	136
7:2–14	104	12:12	159
7:4	152 n. 98		
7:4–6	153	**Hosea**	
7:7	67, 144	2:1	50
7:8–10	100	2:18	229
7:8, 25	153	5:14	152
7:10	159	9:10	11 n. 51
7:11	155		

Hosea (continued)

11:8–9	244
11:9	245
13:7–8	152
13:16	230
14:1	59
14:4	216

Joel

1:15	116, 261
2:1	259, 261
2:1–11	120 n. 64
2:2	260
2:3–5	121
2:7	121
2:11	121, 261
2:20	120 n. 64
2:31	261
3:4	226
3:12–14	261
4:14	261

Amos

2:16	
3:7	9, 150, 260
3:12	49. 152
4:11	49
5:1	49
5:15	49
5:18	116
5:18–20	260
5:18	116
9:8, 9	49

Obadiah

11–14	231
15	232, 261
21	232

Jonah

1:3	194, 216
1:5	179 n. 69
1:6	178
1:12	179
2:1	185

2:3	249
2:11	179
4:2	228 n. 19
4:6–10	179
4:11	179

Micah

2:12	51
4:1–3	221
4:7	50
5:9	216

Nahum

2:4–7,11	121 n. 66
3:2–3, 15–17	121 n. 66
3:12	11 n. 51

Habakkuk

2:4	247

Zephaniah

1:14	116, 261
1:15b	260
1:18	154 n. 104
2:4–12	
2:13	119
3:10	70
3:2	50, 215 n. 81
3:12–13	

Haggai

1:14	49
2:21–22	144

Zechariah

1:9	140
2:10	119
4:4	140
6:6, 8	119
8:20–23	
8:6	49
8:11	49
8:6, 11	49

8:20–23	221
9–14	11
9:1–11:3	11
9:9–10	215
9:10	11, 216
10:3	134
12:11	158 n. 121
12:12–14	190
14:1–5	215
14:4	183

DEUTEROCANONICAL BOOKS

Tobit

3:11	116 n. 43

Judith

9:9–11	240
13:18	241
16:1	239
16:5–9	240
16:2	240
16:2–12	240
16:13	239
16:13–17	240

1 Maccabees

1:1–10	133
1–6	137
1:41–42	136
1:44–61	136
1:54	136
1:59	136
2:60	152
3:37	201

2 Maccabees

3–9		137
2 5	5–15	136
6:26		136
6–7		136
7:22–28		247
7:27–28		247

15:27	238

Wisdom

10:17	154
11:26	246

Jesus Sirach

11:4	260
27:27	227
38:25–39:11	16
39:1, 2	146
50:27–29	16
51:23	150
51:23–26	16

NEW TESTAMENT

Matthew

2:16	175
3:3	94
5:1–2	44
5:5	58, 262
5:38	223
5:38–39	227 n. 18
5:17	45
8:20	181
11:28–30	17, 39
12:40	185
15:29	44
17:1	44
17:1–8	44 n 95
21:5	215
21:18–22	11 n. 51
21:42–44	159
22:41–46	58
23:4	38
24:1–52	11
24:2–44	183
24:3	11, 44
24:15	136, 183
24:21	103
24:30	167
24:31	123
24:32	158
24:32–33	11

Matthew (continued)

24:36	30, 132, 184
24:31	260
24:36	132, 184
26:30–46	183
24:36	30
24:38–39	72
26:52	223
26:53	173
26:64	158
27:56	171
27:61	171
28	260

Mark

1:11	18, 174
1:34	176
1:17, 21	37
3:12	176
3:28	155 n. 109
4:1	177
4:35–41	177, 178
4:38–41	180
5:1–10	172
5:1–20	172
5:11–13	173
5:11–20	173
6:3–4	180
6:45–52	178
8:11–12	185
8:27	176
8:27–29	176
8:30	176
8:33	177
9:7	174
9:2–9	44 n. 95
9:9	176, 177
8:31	176
9:7	18, 37
11:10	79
12:35–37	58
12:49–50	37
13	114 n. 35, 183
13:1–2	114, 184
13:1–37	11
13:3	44
13:7	185
13:10	185
13:14	136, 175, 183, 186
13:32	132, 184
13:26	186
14:26–27	183
14:62	154
15:37	18
15:37–38	175
16	171
16:6	165
16:9	171
16:15	185
16:1	260
16:16	165

Luke

1:19	140
1:19, 26	140
1:26	140
1:33	28
1:46–55	93
2	171
2:1	161
2:42–49	99
3:35	212
4:5–6	258
6:15	177 n. 65
9:58	181
9:28–36	44 n. 95
9:31	13
9:58	181
11:29	185
11:46	38
15:15–16	173
15:7, 10, 32	246
19:42–44	262
20:41–44	58
21:5–36	183
21:37	183
22:39	183
24:1	260
24:20–33	214
24:45	214

John

1:46	180

3:16	209 n. 60
4:22	116
4:44	180
6:42	180
6:69	176 n. 63
8:1	183
8:11	246
8:36	39
12:15	215 n. 82
12:38	46
16:14, 26	37
18:12	172
19:31	196 n. 18
20:1	260
20:11–18	171

Acts of the Apostles

1:7	30, 132, 158, 184
1:21–22	39
2:11	137
2:41	210
3:22–23	46, 18,5
3:22–24	46
4:36	201
4:37	201
7:37	46
7:58	195
8:3	196
8:27–28	70
9:1–2	196
9:1–22	196, 179
9:3–4	196
9:27	201
9:4	199
9:5	199
9:7	197
9:10–18	197
9:27	201
10:1	172
11:19	202 n. 31
11:25	202
11:26	201
11:27	201
11:28	201 n. 29
11:29–30	221
11:30	201
13–14	201
13:1	201
13:1–3	201, 202
13:4	135
13:9	195
14:5–20	203
14:8–13	202
14:11	203
14:26	202
14:27	214
15:10	39
15:32	201
15:36–28–28:31	204
15:36–18:22	204
16:6–8	205
16:9	206
16:10	208
16:11–40	214
16:26–27	214
17	212
17:3	214
17:18	195
17:28	195
18:3	195 n. 15
18:22	202
18:22–23	205
18:23–21:14	205
19:9, 23	196
19:21	217
20:7	260
21: 15–23	35, 205
22:1–21	196
22:3–21	39 n. 69
22:3	213 n. 75
22:4	196
22:4–5, 19	196 n. 19
22:6–16	197
22:8	199
22:9	197
22:14–15	197
22:30–23:11	205
22:20	195
23:11	217
23:17–33	172
24:1–26, 32	205
24:5	201 n. 29
24:14, 22	196
24:17	221
26:9–23	197

Acts of the Apostles (continued)

26:9–20	39 n. 69
26:13	197
26:13–14	196
26:15	199
26:15–18	196, 197
26:16–18a	197
27:1–28:16	205
27:1	172

Romans

1:1	39 n. 69
1:2	194
1:5	194
1:10–15	217
1:14	220, 221
1:16	220
1:17	220
8:31–39	210
8:35	209
8:35–36	211
8:38–39	211
9:4	116
9:20	245 n. 71
9:27	48, 50
9:29	51
10:4	192
10:14–21	47
10:14–15	50
10:16	47, 50, 51
10:18–21	50
10:21	51
11:1–10	50
11:4–5	51
11:11–24	50
11:13	194
11:25–32	50
11:32	246
11:29	245
12:19	217, 237
15:16	219
15:22–24	192
15:24	192, 217
15:26–27	221

1 Corinthians

1:31	41 n. 77
2:2	211
2:6–16	260 n. 133
9:	39
9:1	197
10:1–2	154
13:32	154 n. 104
15:5–17	40
15:9	40
15:9–11	39 n. 69
15:19	196 n. 19
15:52	260
16:1–2	221
16:2	260

2 Corinthians

2:10	40 n. 76
3:7	134
10:14–16	217
10:17	41 n. 77
11:21–22	213
11:21–27	211
11:23–33	208
12:2–10	40

Galatians

1:1, 11–19	39 n. 69
1:13	196
1:13–14	195
1:14	198
1:15–17	194
1:16	194
2:6–9	39 n. 69
2:7, 9	194
2:10	221
3:1	211
3:11	220
3:13	196
3:25–29	193
4:3, 9	211
5:1	39
6:14	41 n. 77, 211

Ephesians

1:11	211

2:2, 3	211
2:20	201
3:8	40

Philippians

2:17	219 n. 101
3:5–6	213
3:6	196 n. 19, 198

Colossians

1:12–14	197
1:23	186
1:24	40 n. 76
1:26–28	260 n. 133
2:2–3	260 n. 133
2:8	211
4:3	260 n. 133

1 Thessalonians

1:8	217
4:15	154 n. 104
4:16	128, 260
5:2–3	72

2 Thessalonians

2:3–4	103

1 Timothy

1:13	196 n. 19
1:15	40

Hebrews

1:7	177 n. 66
10:30	237
10:38	237
11:30	64, 237
12:18	154
12:19	260 n. 130
18:3	195

James

2:13	244

1 Peter

2:9	197

1 John

2:18, 22	101
4:3	101
4:9–10	209 n. 60

2 John

7	101

Revelation

1:7	158
1:8, 17	155
1:10	260
1:17	113
2:7	256
2:27	216
4:1	260
4:2–3	113
5:9	262
6:1–11	123
6:13	11 n. 52
7:1	123
8:2	260
8:2–9	14, 260
9:7, 9	121
9:9	215
9:20	101
10:6	203
11:15	28 n. 29, 29 and n. 30, 260
12:1	11
12:3	133 n. 17
12:7	13, 125 n. 79
12:16	32
13:1	129
13:2	153
13:5	100
13:11	129
13:18	8, 129
14:14	158
15:1	102
16:16	158 n. 121
17, 18	11
17:9	129

Revelation (continued)

18:2	79
18:4–6	230
18:8	230
18:21	225
19:15	216
19:17–18	108, 126
19:19	123
19:20	102, 155
20:8	108, 120
20:7–8	123
20:9	123
20:7–10	5, 101, 108
20:10	101
21:6	155
21:28	32
22:2	256
22:13	155

Index of Quranic Texts

1:6	150	3:26	157
2:8, 62, 126, 128	22	3:35	23
2:20	157	3:37	115
2:30	157, 184 n. 84, 258	3:38–39	215
2:35	7, 107	3:50	16, 45
2:50	107	3:52	31
2:51, 54, 92	145	3:52, 53	39
2:57	154	3:67	24
2:78	37	3:73	252
2:97	46, 47, 140, 199	3:76	23
2:98	252 n. 103	3:110	26
2:100	46, 52	3:113–114	47
2:101	25, 47	3:114	22
2:115	115	3:113–115	24
2:119	52	3:117	144
2:135	23	3:123	27
2:135	24	3:187	25, 47
2:142	115	3:199	47
2:190–193	86	4:38	22
2:213	52, 61	4:56	40
2:233	32	4:84	26
2:243	109, 255	4:95	25
2:246	198 n. 24	4:125	23
2:247–250	194	4:153	145
2:248	107 n. 2, 245	4:157, 171	23
2:249	257	4:163	179
2:249, 250	59	4:163	58
2:251	59	4:171	39, 199, 205 n. 46
2:286	42	4:174	38
3:3–4	38	5:3	22
3:13	27	5:15	38
3:14	22, 145	5:19	52
3:19	22	5:27–23	157

INDEX OF QURANIC TEXTS

5:32	157	8:56	46
5:37, 72	23	8:58	32
5:44	38	8:65	26
5:46	16, 38, 45	8:67	26
5:64	252	9:5	26
5:69	22	9:11	26
6:12	20, 40, 261	9:18, 29, 44, 99	22
6:37, 109–111, 158	185	9:24	80
6:48	30	9:30	23
6:54	40, 253, 261	9:34	145
6:73	159	9:54	252
6:79, 161	23	9:70	107, 144
6:86	139, 179	9:72	43, 253
7:8, 9	154	9:73	26
7:19	22, 107	9:90, 97	21
7:20–22	257	9:100, 118	31
7:54	154, 247, 253	9:129	154
7:57	179	10:2	52
7:59	39, 144	10:3	154, 247, 253, 259
7:60	66, 75–77, 109 48, 154	10:20	185
7:64	48	10:31	259
7:65–72	144	10:34	259
7:66	48	10:37	48
7:73–79	144	10:44	144
7:75	79	10:47	39
7:80–84	144	10:73	48
7:85–93	12, 144	10:63	30
7:86	27, 184	10:90	107
7:90	48	10:98	246
7:109, 110, 127	48	10:103	23
7:136	107, 224	11:2	52
7:145	107, 157	11:7	154, 247, 256
7:148, 152	145	11:27	48
7:157	37, 38	11:36–48	249
7:158	37, 39	11:44	44
7:159	46	11:71	253
7:160	154	11:84–95	12
7:171	154	11:91	204
7:175, 176	122 n. 68	11:101	144
7:176	38	11:103	30
7:185	29	11:25–49	30
7:187	159, 184	12:31	141
7:188	52	12:43–48	129 n. 86, 141
7:203	185	12:111	47
8:5–18	27	13:2	259
8:9	27, 60	13:2	253
8:26	27	13:7, 27	185
8:54	107	13:23	43, 253

INDEX OF QURANIC TEXTS   319

14:9	48	21:87–88	179
15:28	157	21:91	205 n. 46
15:79	224	21:92	61 n. 38
16:31	43, 253	21:92–93	61
16:33, 118	144	21:95–96	128
16:36	39	21:96	120
16:102	141	21:104–105	262
16:103	99	21:105	58
16:120	24	21:107	20, 261
16:120, 123	23	21:107	40
17:1	41, 114	21:109	184
17:4–8	74	22:31	22
17:11	157	22:42	48
17:44	129 n. 86	22:25–26	159
17:55	58	22:56–57	159
17:64	123	23:20	44
17:90–93	185	23:24	48
17:103	107	23:44	39
17:105	52	23:52–53	61
18:20	204	23:62	42
18:56	40	23:88	157, 253
18:80	41	23:116	29
18:83–94	134	25:25–26	159
18:93–99	123	25:48	179
18:94–97	120	25:56	52
19:11	115	25:59	154, 253
19:16	117	26:29	251
19:16–19	117	26:59	247
19:17	205 n. 46	26:66–67	107
19:46	204	26:191–196	141
19:54	39	26:192–195	199
19:61	43, 253	26:193	162, 141
19:97	52	26:193–194	140
20:10–14	251 n. 98	26:194	140
20:14	251	27:63	179
20:28	107	27:82	101
20:39	253	27:87	260
20:76	43, 253	28:6, 8	107 n. 1
20:78	107	28:19	204
20:88	145	28:38	107, 251
20:120	257	28:40	107
20:120–121	107	28:46	39
20:133	185	28:87	185
21:5	185	29:24	131
21:68–69	61, 131	29:39	107
21:85	109	29:46	24
21:87	179, 249	29:39	107 n. 1
21:87	179	29:40	144

29:50	185	42:51	141
30:2–4	56	42:52	38
30:9	144	43:55–56	107
30:46	180	43:76	144, 165
30:47	224	43:85	132, 156, 184
30:30	23	44:24	107
31:27	129 n. 86, 184	46:12	30, 46
31:34	132, 159	47:13	30
32:2–4, 23, 24	145	48:4	107
32:3	39	48:8	52
32:4	247, 253	48:10	252
32:5	259	48:26	107 n. 2
33:7	48	48:27	41
33:9–32	33	48:29	39
33:26–27	33	49:14	21
33:37	56	50:34	30
33:45	52	50:38	247
33:63	132, 159, 184	50:41–42	30
34:28	52	51:1–4	123
34:44	39	51:5–6	30
35:24	52	51:12	159
35:33	43, 253	51:40	107
36:12–26	202	51:41–46	48
36:13–19	204	52:48	253
36:20–25	204	52:48	253
36:51	128	53:1–18	42
36:83	175	53:1–12	42, 201
37:8	157	53:13–18	43, 201
37:97	131	53:1–12, 13–18	201
37:114	39	53:5, 7	141
17:123	319	53:25	155
37:139–148	179, 194	53:53–54	107
37:139	39, 179	53:57–58	184
37:147–148	246	54:9	48
38:21	114	54:14	253
38:32	80	54:18, 23	48
38:35	79	57:4	278, 247, 253
38:48	109	57:29	252
38:50	43, 253	58:22	22
38:69	157	65:2	22
38:71	157	61:6	16, 39, 45
40:5	39	61:12	43, 253
40:8	43, 253	61:14	39
40:24	107	62:2	185
40:36	107	64:8	38
41:9–12	247	64:9	30
41:47	132, 184	66:12	205 n. 46
42:11	253	67:1	156

INDEX OF QURANIC TEXTS

67:25–26	30	81:1–2	11 n. 51
67:26	132, 184	81:19	140
68:48	179, 249	81:23–24	42 n. 82, 201
69:6	107	85:4–5	131
71:1	48	87:75, 88	48
72:25	184	89:20	80
75:6	159	92:13	155
77:1–6	123	95:4	44
77:16	12	95	11 n. 51
79:17	251 n. 98	96:1–2	201
79:24	251	97	44
79:42	159	98:8	43, 253
79:44	132	100:1	123
79:42, 44	184	100:8	80
79:105	123		

www.ingramcontent.com/pod-product-compliance
Lightning Source LLC
Chambersburg PA
CBHW050616300426
44112CB00012B/1523